HENRY JAMES'S THWARTED LOVE

WENDY GRAHAM

Henry James's Thwarted Love

STANFORD UNIVERSITY PRESS

STANFORD, CALIFORNIA 1999

Stanford University Press
Stanford, California
© 1999 by the Board of Trustees of the
Leland Stanford Junior University

Printed in the United States of America

CIP data appear at the end of the book

Acknowledgments

I am indebted to my tough-minded and uncompromising family for giving me the fortitude to complete this book. Thanks go to my grandmother Nellie, who knew the right way to do just about everything and who rode the bus to and from concerts at Lincoln Center when she was in her eighties so that her grandchildren could afford fancy postgraduate educations, to my Nana, who awakened the family on "snow days," having driven 250 miles from Norwich, Connecticut, to shovel out our driveway in the years before her hip replacement surgery, to my great-aunts, Rita and Marie, whose precision in everyday matters and accomplishments in business bespoke their tour of duty in the W.A.C., to my heroines, Judith Graham Pool and family friend Molly Holford, who tried to save the world and succeeded at least in making it a better place for thousands, I owe my dreams.

In addition to debts of a personal nature, I have acquired many professional debts. The National Endowment for the Humanities supported my postdoctoral research, providing me with a stipend to its Summer Institute on Medicine and Western Civilization, where I had the good fortune to study with Steven Marcus and Sander Gilman, whose trailblazing scholarship and good counsel have served me well. I have several colleagues at Vassar who are owed special thanks: Deborah Dash Moore and Anne Constantinople, directors of the American Culture Program, who encouraged my interdisciplinary scholarship and teaching by pairing me with renowned women's historian Nancy Schrom Dye, archaeologist Anne Pike-Tay, and psychology professor Randy Cornelius (who shares my fascination with William James). I've learned a great deal from these wonderful colleagues. I'd like to thank Donna Heiland and Heesok Chang for their illuminating conversation over the years and for their guidance on subjects in which our fields overlap. Most of all, I'd like to thank Beverly Haviland, lately of Vassar College, who welcomed, as few would, another James specialist to campus in the years before either of us had tenure and whose generosity, wisdom, and advice have richly informed my thinking about James.

To fellow Jamesians I owe an inestimable debt, since I'm toiling in a field in which others have exhaustively and productively labored. Leland Person read the entire book in draft and provided crucial commentary, leading as much by the example of his own work as through criticism. Hugh Stevens helped me sharpen my understanding of homosexuality as a form of eroticized lawlessness and shared several chapters of *Henry James and Sexuality* with me before its publication. Eric Haralson has been unfailingly generous and supportive. With his deep knowledge of James's life, Eric has helped me test my hypotheses and offered many provocative theories of his own. David McWhirter and John Carlos Rowe read the book in manuscript. The suggestions of anonymous readers for Stanford University Press were also extremely helpful. I hope I have been able to do justice to their insightful recommendations for revision. Jonathan Arac is due special thanks. His unstinting support from my graduate-schooldays to the present has encouraged me to persevere regardless of setbacks. Whenever I meet up with people who were in graduate school with me, they invariably report that Jonathan has followed their careers, reading their work with the same assiduous interest with which he read mine. In my estimation, he's a peerless mentor.

I am grateful for the help and support I received from the staff at Stanford University Press. Mimi Kusch, a rigorous and insightful copy editor, rescued my book from lapses in sense and grammar. Kate Warne, the in-house editor, supervised the many stages of production and demystified the complex process of editing the manuscript and preparing it for publication. I owe a special debt to humanities editor, Helen Tartar, whose skillful management of the review process and encouragement relieved me of the terrible strain of placing my first book. I would also like to thank my research assistants: Nina Wiener, Maggie Bittel, Lisa Mackie, and Caroline Griswold, who kept Vassar's interlibrary loan office jumping. Some of the material in Chapter 1 appeared in *Genders*; I am grateful to New York University Press for permission to reprint this material. Chapter 5 appeared in *Modern Fiction Studies*, which has also kindly granted permission to reprint. I want to thank the American

Academy of Arts and Letters for permission to reproduce Abbott Handerson Thayer's beautiful 1881 crayon drawing on paper of Henry James.

Thanks are due to my parents, who encouraged a reverence for culture, in my father's case, happily diversified by a range of highbrow and lowbrow interests. I would like to thank Cecile Kidd for minding my young son with tenderness and skill while I was writing and teaching. To Fran Goldwyn, who saw the project through from its inception to its completion, I dedicate this book.

W. G.

Contents

Abbreviations

The abbreviations listed below are used throughout the text and notes.

JAMES, HENRY

AS	*The American Scene*. Bloomington: Indiana University Press, 1968.
Autobiography	*Autobiography: A Small Boy and Others, Notes of a Son and Brother, The Middle Years*. Princeton: Princeton University Press, 1983.
Boston	*The Bostonians*. London: The Bodley Head, 1967.
HJL	*Henry James Letters*. 4 vols. Ed. Leon Edel. Cambridge: Belknap Press of Harvard University Press, 1974–84.
LC1	*Henry James: Literary Criticism. Vol. 1: Essays on Literature; American Writers; English Writers*. New York: Library of America, 1984.
LC2	*Henry James: Literary Criticism. Vol. 2: French Writers; Other European Writers; The Prefaces to the New York Edition*. New York: Library of America, 1984.
Notebooks	*The Complete Notebooks of Henry James*. Ed. Leon Edel and Lyall Powers. New York: Oxford University Press, 1987.
NYE	*Novels and Tales of Henry James*. 26 vols. The New York Edition. New York: Charles Scribner's Sons, 1907–9.
PE	*The Painter's Eye*. Cambridge: Harvard University Press, 1956.
Princess	*The Princess Casamassima*. Vols. 5–6. The New York Edition. New York: Charles Scribner's Sons, 1922.

RH	*Roderick Hudson* (1909). New York: Harper & Row, 1960.
RH2	*Roderick Hudson* (1878). Harmondsworth: Penguin Books, 1981.
Spoils	*The Spoils of Poynton*. Harmondsworth: Penguin Books, 1980.
Tales	*The Tales of Henry James*. 3 vols. Ed. Maqbool Aziz. Oxford: Clarendon Press, 1973–84.
Wings	*The Wings of the Dove*. Vols. 19–20. The New York Edition. New York: Charles Scribner's Sons, 1909.

JAMES, HENRY SENIOR

HJSr	*Henry James, Senior: A Selection of His Writings*. Ed. Giles Gunn. Chicago: American Library Association, *1974*.

JAMES, WILLIAM

CWJ	*The Correspondence of William James*. 5 vols. Ed. Ignas Skrupskelis and Elizabeth Berkeley. Charlottesville: University of Virginia Press, 1992–97.
WWJ	*The Works of William James*. 19 vols. Ed. Frederick Burkhardt, Fredson Bowers, Ignas Skrupskelis. Cambridge: Harvard University Press, 1975–88. (The titles published under the rubric *The Works of William James* were not organized chronologically. For this reason, the editors at Harvard declined to number them. For the sake of convenience, I number the volumes in the order in which they appeared in the series. The bibliography provides complete citations for individual volumes of the standard edition cited in this book.)
LWJ	*The Letters of William James*. 2 vols. Ed. Henry James, III. Boston: Atlantic Monthly, 1920.

"Frustration's only life," said Doctor Hugh.

"Yes, it's what passes." Poor Dencombe was barely audible, but he had marked with the words the virtual end of his first and only chance.

— "THE MIDDLE YEARS," Novels and Tales of Henry James, 16:106

Introduction

This book is about Henry James and the broad spectrum of identities, activities, and representations that fall under the rubric of sexuality. James was deeply conflicted in his sexuality, and his writings neither wholly affirm a conscious sexual preference nor capitulate to heterosexual convention. In this study I avoid labeling James "celibate," "repressed," or "closeted." And although my questions about James's sexuality are informed by current debates in queer theory, I am not primarily interested in "outing" him. What I am after is a sense of James as a constituent subject, one who shared the culturewide panic over changing gender and professional roles, one who practiced sexual abstinence both to forestall nervous collapse and to conserve energy for work.

This study posits a seamless transition from the mental-hygiene ethos to the doctrine of cultural sublimation.[1] Charting Henry James's response to the various discourses that formed sexual identities and shaped social behaviors during his lifetime, I foreground James's indictment of the disciplinary impact of these discourses. In the thirty-year interval between his first novel and his last, James became deeply depressed about his lifelong celibacy. In 1875 James had stressed the "compensations"—what he conceived of as the Sturm und Drang—of thwarted desire. However, as the homosexual gradually emerged as a public figure in the 1890s, and particularly after Oscar Wilde's trial in 1895, James began to mourn the love he had "insanely missed" (*NYE* 17: 124). For the bulk of his career, Henry James struggled to forge an erotic economy of artistic production, seeking to relieve the strain caused by smothered passion in the sublimation provided by art. This book is an attempt to understand the historically specific conditions fostering this uneasy truce between society and one of its sexual dissidents.

In *Henry James's Thwarted Love*, I take an author-centered approach committed to historicizing Henry James by placing him and his works within the discursive frameworks that emerged and matured within his epoch: mental hygiene, energy conservation, sexology, psychiatry, and cultural anthropology. It is a hybrid study—part cultural history, part textual analysis, and part biography. My method is to read James's sexuality and its textual reverberations in a manner scrupulously attentive to the historically available terms at his disposal, the terms in and through which he could make sense of his own same-sex erotic longings. James's professed failure to measure up to normative standards of Victorian masculinity figures prominently in this study. My thematic concatenation of James's effeminacy, celibacy, and nervous distress seeks to reanimate the presumptions and anxieties that made identification with interdicted gender roles so problematic for the men and women of his time. By cataloguing the various models of gender identity and sexuality available to James, I hope to underscore rather than to obscure the absurdity and contingency of then-acceptable parameters of masculinity and femininity.

It is useful to ask why effeminacy became the overriding identity sign for male homosexuals in the nineteenth century. Since the perception of the homosexual as feminine remains so disturbing even today (so much so that its refutation has been the focus of much queer theory), it is important to understand what was at stake for Henry James in his mimicry of the feminine. I am not so much concerned with the historical specificity of James's models of womanliness or the furtive pleasure of fantasmatic femininity as I am with his conception of gender as performance. James's fascination with role reversal is most memorably inscribed in the figure of the buttery materfamilias whom Henry impersonated in his letters to William James and in his description of Robert Louis Stevenson as a "male Cleopatra" (*HJL* 3: 278). In writing these letters, James transgressed the safe borders of gender identity, and he did so, more than occasionally, with ease and pleasure. For men of James's day, effeminacy was not aberrant *or* affirmative, as is usually assumed, but aberrant *and* affirmative.

Unlike Wilde and Proust, James wrote most of his books before the theoretical elaboration of homosexuality had been formalized at the end of the century. Until Wilde was tried for acts of gross indecency in 1895, generally speaking the tropes that emphasized or textualized homosexuality were emerging rather than established cultural assumptions. This is why it is useful to locate and elaborate earlier typologies employed to account for gender and sexual variants—not to render the homosexual visible at the earliest opportunity but rather to understand how cultural anxieties about flagging reproductive energies factored into the eventual pathologization of homosexuality. The categorization of certain men as homosexuals has not always served to project culturally repugnant qualities onto homosexuals. In the nineteenth century, masturbation was considered the chief threat to the institution of the family and to the hegemony of the middle class, whose sons were said to be "wasting capital" and "depleting their store of nervous force" through this heinous vice, while same-sex practices were still considered culturally consistent with marriage and paternity.

Henry James's autobiographical works, *A Small Boy and Others* (1913) and *Notes of a Son and Brother* (1914), make for fascinating reading. They record the defining experiences of James's boyhood and early manhood from a small boy's naive perspective, but they were written when James was an adult who possessed a critical vocabulary for making sense of his youthful longings. In not identifying himself as "father, husband, soldier, mentor" but rather as "brother, lover, *cher maître*" (dear master), James treated identity constructs as fictions or roles. Disqualifying himself from the duties of war service and paternity by fashioning a sickly and unmanly self, James freed himself to lead a more pleasurable and productive life. At the same time, he allowed the culture he inhabited to interpret his effeminacy as a sign of degeneracy. He therefore never escaped the constraint enforced by compulsory heterosexuality or felt free to pursue sexual intimacy with the young men he adored.

James's life history exemplifies the two extremes reflected by the marginal figure: the static position of abjection on the one hand and the positive movement toward self-production and transformative struggle on the other.

The six chapters that comprise this book combine readings of *Roderick Hudson*, *The Bostonians*, *The Princess Casamassima*, and *The Wings of the Dove*, novels that represent different stages of James's literary career, with reconsiderations of biographical questions. Chapter 1, "Henry James's Thwarted Love," attempts to reconcile two competing trends in James criticism that alternately portray the novelist as an anchorite indifferent to passional concerns and as an unconscious homosexual with an active fantasy life. My aim is to place James's sexual persona in historical perspective so that his effeminacy, celibacy, and sublimation of eros can be understood as exemplary of nineteenth-century sexuality rather than as idiosyncratic. The chapter lays out the familial background to James's efforts to define himself in relation to the dominant cultural canons: mental hygiene and late-Victorian sexual respectability, focusing on Henry's relationship with his brother William and on Henry's access, through William, to the contemporary medical discourse on the nature of the homosexual. William's bullying of Henry when he was a child influenced the latter's deflection in favor of femininity as an adolescent; however, effeminacy was both a socially imposed punitive label and a socially available idiom through which Henry James could understand and protect himself.

Chapter 2, "William James on Energy and Entropy," recounts William James's prolonged vocational crisis and the nervous distress that eschewing a traditional career provoked in William and thus in Henry, since Henry both overestimated and identified with William's artistic bent. The chapter contrasts the James brothers' career expectations and anxieties, reckoning their debates over remunerative and healthful employment versus "lonely self-culture" as an example of their differing conceptions of masculinity (*CWJ* 1: 192). In the 1870s, William counseled Henry to accept a position of "literary drudgery" as a hedge against the nervous erethism to which he believed the artistic temperament was prey (*CWJ* 5: 52; 4: 455). Crucial here is William James's pathologization of the creative life; the sermon he delivered to Henry borrowed freely from medical textbooks and from popular scientific theories, which William relied upon to explain his own and later his countrymen's enervation. William James's prominence in the early chapters of this book reflects the role he played for Henry as an authority on nervous exhaustion, energy conservation, and racial degeneration (each linked thematically to anxieties about sexuality and reproduction).

Chapter 3, "Dissipation and Decoration in *Roderick Hudson*," elaborates on how the functionalist tack William adopted to rationalize and resolve his suicidal despondency insinuated itself first into Henry's imagination and then into his fiction. Through its principal characters, *Roderick Hudson* counterposes the divergent cultural trends of meliorism and pessimism (the Janus faces of William's outlook in the 1870s). Whereas Rowland Mallet's melioristic ethos looks backward to Calvinism and forward to scientific management, Roderick Hudson's malaise signifies the artist's impotent protest against the spirit of the machine age. Through Rowland's thwarted love for Roderick, the novel acknowledges the pallid compensations of homosocial chastity, putting into question the ethos of energy conservation for the highest aesthetic as well as for the meanest acquisitive aims. Thus James can be seen at the outset of his career struggling with the strategy of cultural sublimation.

Chapters 1 to 3 rely heavily on James family history and work together to review the early part of Henry James's career, although Chapter 3, with its textual emphasis, may be said to perform a dual function. Chapters 4 to 6 constitute a move from James's investment in his fictional world and its characters to his engagement with nineteenth-century medical, legal, and pedagogical strategies for containing dissident sexuality. Chapter 4, "Degeneration and Feminism in *The Bostonians*," connects James's pairing of nervous illness and lesbian-feminism in the novel with a paradigm shift in late-Victorian conceptions of sexuality. The chapter argues that James's recourse to unflattering stereotypes of feminists and hysterics establishes a legible protolesbian identity for Olive Chancellor but challenges the general perception that James's depiction of abject homosexuality tacitly capitulates to homophobia and misogyny. Instead, the chapter focuses on Olive Chancellor's internalization of the prohibition against same-sex love and on the pathos evoked in the wake of her self-censorship and deformation.

Chapter 5, "The Politics of Sexual Dissidence in *The Princess Casamassima*," reveals James in dialog with the increasingly specific discourse on homosexuality that was emerging before the climactic Wilde trial. By excavating the covert sexual politics that James explores through his novel's more overt thematic concern with political unrest, the chapter evidences the convergence of discourses on sex, class, and race, demonstrating how new categories of difference are pieced together from preexisting taxonomies. Although the chapter does not explicitly invoke the vocabulary of mental hygiene, the doctrine of moral hygiene clearly informed late-Victorian notions of the contagiousness of same-sex passion, which aided and abetted efforts to criminalize homosexuality. Whereas Chapters 4 and 5 highlight the more coercive disciplinary mechanisms on display in James's fictional world, Chapter 6 elaborates on high cultural forms of sexual regulation, which were noteworthy for their restraint and glamour.

Chapter 6, "Signing Plenitude from the Abyss in *The Wings of the Dove*," explores James's atomization of cultural institutions such as museums and other genteel instruments of social management. James recognized and approved the cultural cachet of his novel as a work of high art. He recommended it to the well-bred reader, listing its merits, and advertised it to the upwardly mobile reader as a status symbol and instruction manual, calling his story "one of those chances for *good taste*, possibly even for the play of the very best in the world" (*Wings* 19: vi). Over the course of the novel, James deviates from this confident promotional strategy, denouncing these self-same techniques of acculturation as a type of "violent conformity" forced upon private individuals in public life (60). With special emphasis on the regulation and suppression of sexual nonconformity, the novel confirms that James in his later years viewed sublimation as a form of self-discipline rather than as an elevated mode of expressing desire.

My book signals a new direction in James studies, since it parts company with the old-guard assessment of James as sexless and complements more recent appraisals of James, such as Eve Kosofsky Sedgwick's *The Epistemology of the Closet* and *Tendencies*, Kaja Silverman's *Male Subjectivity at the Margins*, and Joseph Litvak's *Caught in the Act*. Although these books ably address James's fantasies and anxieties, they fail to treat his personal renunciation of sexual activity or to place the evidence for his putative homosexuality in context. In this sense, my project is allied with recent efforts to situate James's works within the context of crossdisciplinary conversations about modernity and market culture, such as Ross Posnock's *The Trial of Curiosity* and Mark Seltzer's *Bodies and Machines*. In my effort to provide thick descriptions of Henry James's fictional and private worlds, I have not favored one critical perspective over another or privileged the role played by literary culture in the historical formation of gender and sexual identities. By definition, my project requires multiple lines of approach and different critical vocabularies, which necessarily complicate the process of achieving synthesis. Working dialectically across the borders of history, biography, and literary criticism, *Henry James's Thwarted Love* attempts to provide the richest account, up to the present, of the cultural conditions that produced Henry James.

ONE

Henry James's Thwarted Love

"I never pretended to love you. I don't understand the word, in the sense you attach to it. I don't understand the feeling, between men. To me, love means quite another thing. You give it a meaning of your own; you enjoy the profit of your invention; it's no more than just that you should pay the penalty."

— MAXIMUS AUSTIN IN "A LIGHT MAN," *The Tales of Henry James*, I: 372

Much has been written of late concerning "the feeling between men." A perusal of texts on homosexuality, perversion, and gender, from Sedgwick's *Epistemology of the Closet* to Jonathan Dollimore's *Sexual Dissidence* to Silverman's *Male Subjectivity at the Margins*, suggests the debate has moved well beyond the question "Did so-and-so have boyfriends?" Without losing sight of the contributions of recent theorists of sex and gender (specifically, a greater awareness of multiple, nonexclusive affective investments and subjectivities), I want to call attention to the uses of literary biography in gay-culture studies. Operating under the premise that sexual identity is temporally contingent, one can dismantle as well as construct past and present identity categories; one can emphasize their inherent contradictions. In this regard, Henry James's relationship with his brother William is instructive. Although William James characterized intimate contact with individuals of one's own sex as "repulsive" and defined homosexuality as a "pathological aberration," he nevertheless encouraged Henry's near-obsessive attachment to him well into his middle age (*WWJ* 9: 1054). Indeed, William's sexual panic informed Henry's struggle to come to grips with his own sexual identity, inasmuch as William not only served Henry as a virile ideal but also played the part of an authority on medical and psychiatric concerns.

William's counsel regarding Henry's physical complaints and his susceptibility to depression and overwork was partly responsible for Henry's monastic existence, since this way of life was thought to be the prudent course for a neuropath to adopt. It is quite significant that before the theoretical elaboration of homosexuality at the end of the nineteenth century, a typology already existed to account for gender and sexual variants: that of hereditary degeneration. Although Henry James was adversely affected by the emerging medical discourse on homosexuality, he appears to have been comfortable, up to a point, with the notion of gender inversion. My intent in this chapter is to provide a better understanding of James's participation in the construction of homosexuality at the fin de siècle, particularly the way in which his effeminacy anticipated the majority of late-nineteenth-century medical, psychiatric, and legal representations of male homosexuals as psychical hermaphrodites. James's life exemplifies nineteenth-century sexuality in that it mirrors the turmoil produced and the introspection encouraged by the new scrutiny of marginal identities, albeit among a rarefied group of intellectuals whose constructions of homosexuality have proven highly influential. Moreover, at a time when gays are rejecting the historic association of male homosexuality with effeminacy as retrograde, it is well worth considering the meaning and allure of this identity sign.

Dollimore remarks that "the perception of the homosexual as feminized remains strangely disturbing—the supreme symbol, in the eyes of those like Norman Mailer, of a range of deep failures including the demise of masculinity, the abdication of masculine power, the desire for self-destruction, and, beyond that, the loss of difference" (263). Richard Dellamora and Silverman have acknowledged this difficulty in their own work, rehabilitating the domain of the feminine so that the rhetorical wish to become or the fantasy of becoming a woman may be read as a subversive and empowering move. This strategy is constructive in that it addresses present concerns about negative cultural stereotypes but counterproductive in the sense that it submits historical ambivalences and anxieties to erasure. I highlight Dellamora and Silverman's discussion of the place of femininity in male homosex-

uality, because the charge of James's effeminacy has bedeviled James enthusiasts, whether or not they have been willing to acknowledge his homosexuality. As early as 1902 J. P. Mowbray insisted that no comprehensive account of
James's work could fail to take note of his effeminacy, and in 1907 H. G.
Dwight compared James's late style to the "finicking inquisitiveness . . . [of]
a village spinster in a 'department store'" (both cited in Gard, 331, 436). As
Jonathan Freedman points out, homosexuality is the "unspoken subject that
clearly underlies the language of effeteness and effeminacy that anti-Jacobites
persistently used to describe James's putative aestheticism, and for which the
term 'aesthete' has long served as a virtual synonym" (xvi).

Passionlessness

For as long as critics have been proclaiming, hinting at, ignoring, or denying the homoerotic elements in James's life and works, they have partici-
pated in a critic's compact, a set of rules and guidelines for representing and,
more to the point, for concealing sexuality. We might forget that this was
the state of James criticism until very recently, particularly with no less an
authority than Sedgwick reminding us of "biographically inobliterable" evidence of James's homosexual desire (*Epistemology*, 197).[1] However, I am not
interested in castigating homophobic scholars. It is far more important to
understand that these critics were reading from a script supplied by the author himself and that in their embarrassment (or ignorance), they readily
and, one might say, uncritically accepted James's own equivocations. In 1979
Richard Hall, lay scholar and editor of the *Advocate*, chided James specialists
for ignoring the question of homosexuality in James's life and works. Singling out Leon Edel, who "by avoiding a frank discussion of James's homosexual leanings . . . had failed to present a full and complex picture of the
man," Hall threw down the gauntlet before a generation of academics who
accepted Edel's theory that James had sublimated eros in the service of art:
"He was, I suspect, the old-fashioned masturbating Victorian gentleman
who led a narcissistic sexual life. It was the simplest solution to his problem,
and the rest of his libido was poured into the eight hours a day he sat at his
desk" (Hall, "Leon Edel," 51). It was Saul Rosenzweig, rather than Edel,
who first articulated this widely held view of James. In his influential 1943

essay, "The Ghost of Henry James," Rosenzweig framed the issue this way: "His various novels and tales written both before and after the departure from America acquired their notorious peculiarities—precious overqualification of style and restraint of sexual passion—from the repressed pattern of his life" (454). In "Henry James Among the Aesthetes," Richard Ellmann echoed this refrain in his rather hazy account of James's rejection of British aestheticism: "James declined to burn this way. There was no doctrine which could have roused in him more revulsion than this one. For reasons which I have said remain obscure, he appears to have transposed his passions into his characters' lives, and not expressed them in his own" (211). Ellmann admits that "James knew and wanted to portray homosexuals," but he doesn't venture beyond the proposition that James had "an inclination towards men" or "equivocations about sexuality" until the end of the essay, where he characterizes James's passionate correspondence with the sculptor Hendrik Anderson as "an affair, or an approximation of an affair" (211, 209, 218, 228). It seems most critics were content to see James, in Hall's words, as "the golden capon of world literature" ("Leon Edel," 49).

More recently, in "The Portrait of a Lack," William Veeder has depicted James as a neutered male with a female consciousness, indicating both the staying power of this formulation and the fact that a critic of a radically different stripe feels comfortable with these terms (95–121). Sedgwick contends that James expressed his passional impulses indirectly through "homosexual panic." In her fine reading of "The Beast in the Jungle," she notes: "To judge from the biographies of Barrie and James, each author seems to have made erotic choices that were complicated enough, shifting enough in the gender of their objects, and, at least for long periods, kept distant enough from *éclaircissement* or physical expression, to make each an emboldening figure for a literary discussion of male homosexual panic" (*Epistemology*, 195). Although Sedgwick's work has been widely influential, it has received some intelligent criticism. For example, Dellamora complains that Sedgwick virtually ignores self-aware male homosexuals in *Between Men* and focuses on homophobic, rather than homoerotic, tendencies in writers in her later work (9). Sedgwick's reinvention of James as a self-deceiving or sexually dormant homosexual, though a step forward, is not entirely satisfying, for in spite of herself, she seems to equate genital activity (endpleasure) with sexual identity. Without attempting to categorize James, I would argue that his sexual escapades probably emphasized forepleasure and belonged to the regions of the mind where fantasies evolve. Posnock has suggested that James's love letters to male friends were "themselves pleasurable forms of sexual activity and not simply substitutes" (297n14).

James's biographers and critics have made much of what they consider his passionlessness. In 1902 F. M. Colby acidly described James's erotic universe as "a land where the vices have no bodies and the passions no blood, where nobody sins because nobody has anything to sin with" (cited in Gard, 337). In 1925 Dr. Joseph Collins, a fashionable New York neurologist who had treated James for depression and heart disease over a two-month period in 1911, shared his impressions of James's personality with the public in a book called *The Doctor Looks at Biography*. Describing James as an amalgam of feminine and infantile personality traits, Collins concluded that "the great defect in the makeup of Henry James was in the amatory side of his nature" (92). Apparently James confided in Collins, avowing that he had remained celibate throughout his life (95). The capon theory was clearly James's own invention. The autobiographical *Notes of a Son and Brother* contains a much-discussed revelation of a "horrid even if an obscure hurt" James sustained while turning a water crank in an attempt to extinguish a fire, an injury that deprived eighteen-year-old Henry of his virility and health, or so James implied (415). This chronic debility has been variously interpreted as castration, impotence, or as an incapacitating spinal disorder (Eakin, 675–92). It has been argued, with good reason, that Henry unconsciously chose disability as a way out of the trials of masculinity that surrounded him in 1861 (courtship and the Civil War). He describes the injury as a token badge of honor: "This was at least a negative of combat, an organised, not a loose and empty one, something definitely and firmly parallel to action in the tented field" (*Autobiography*, 417). However, James's reminiscences suggest that he saw himself as a spiritless poltroon throughout his childhood, particularly in relation to his bullying, supercompetent elder brother, William; Henry favors the word *impotent* in *A Small Boy and Others* to such an extent that he seems to be proclaiming his psychic emasculation well before he reveals his alleged castration in the flesh in *Notes of a Son and Brother*.

Rosenzweig has suggested that James's "obscure hurt" should be read as his act of "filial submission" to a "highly individualistic father" and to a "gifted sibling rival," a suspension of masculine identification occasioned by guilt and inferiority complexes (453–54). But what kind of ego need was served by James's representation of himself as a clueless, hapless youth castrated on the brink of manhood? Donald Moss has stressed the coexistence of "aim-limited homoeroticisms" and "fiercely articulated interdictions against *serious* same-sex erotics," which remind the individual that "the only permissible way to love the forbidden object is via (dis)identification with it" (288).[2] The established paradigms of biological sex and gender also reproduce reflex models of deviance; as Judith Butler puts it, "Spectres of discontinuity and incoherence [are] themselves thinkable only in relation to existing norms" (*Gender Trouble*, 17). James's effemination was an unconscious response to his incestuous longings for his father and brother, a heterosexualization of same-sex desire, which William Simon and John Gagnon have explained: "Intrapsychic scripting becomes a historical necessity as a private world of wishes and desires that are experienced as originating in the deepest recesses of the self must be bound to social life: individual desires are linked to social meanings" (53). Significantly, the less-than-exemplary virility of his family members forced James to bolster their masculine qualities in his imagination and memoirs. As if reading from some master script of monolithic sexuality, Henry can be said to have reinvented his crippled father and his neurasthenic brother.

William James may have been a gilded youth, but Henry Senior was more of a gelding than a virile ideal; he had lost a leg when he was thirteen in a catastrophe similar to his son's (Lewis, 18; Habegger, *The Father*, 66–71). In addition to losing a limb that restricted his activities and rendered him a problematic role model, Henry Senior suffered a nervous breakdown in May 1844 when his boys were toddlers (51; 211–33). In his *Autobiography*, Henry, or Harry, as he was familiarly known, at one point imputed "resources of high control" to his father and at another portrayed his father as an incompetent duffer out of step with the competitive tenor of American life: "Comparatively late in life, after his death, I had occasion to visit . . . an American city in which he had had, since his own father's death, interests that were of importance to us all. On my asking the agent in charge when the owner had last taken personal cognisance of his property that gentlemen replied only half to my surprise that he had never in all his years of possession performed such an act" (106, 43). Idle, contemplative Henry Senior was no model for a youth doubting his capacity for earning his keep. Perhaps this is why, as psychologist Howard Feinstein suggests, James's fictional Mr. Herbert urges Paul De Grey not to follow in his father's footsteps: "In America, in any walk of life, idleness [is] indecent" (230). Veeder equates the business sphere with masculine endeavor in general: "In James's America, a male who is not in business is feminine in gender because he is signed by, is singled out for, nonexistence. 'Castration' marks not the anatomically female sex but a culturally effeminated group" (99). In a fascinating passage from *A Small Boy and Others*, Harry unconsciously simulates a penis hanging limply between his father's legs. The passage's chief peculiarity is that the male child serves the father, rather than the mother, as a prosthesis: "I somehow feel morally affiliated, tied as by knotted fibers, to the elements involved. One of these was assuredly that my father had again, characteristically, suffered me to dangle" (105). Henry Senior relied on his wife and children to fill a void, to compensate for his publishing failures and for the ambivalent public reception of his lectures. One contemporary reviewer of the elder James's *The Secret of Swedenborg*, William Dean Howells, joked that the author "had not only written about the secret of Swedenborg but that he had kept it" (cited in Rosenzweig, 437).

I would argue against Henry's characterization of Mrs. James as the only family member on whom "[the] father rested with the absolute whole of his weight" (*Autobiography*, 342). He lived vicariously through William, inducing his eldest son to sacrifice an artistic career in order to fulfill his notion of a higher calling by becoming a founder of American psychology. And though he encouraged Henry Junior's hero worship of him, he denied his second born affirmation as his namesake and heir apparent—that was to be William's role. Henry Senior never disguised his preference for William. In reading Henry's memoirs, one feels he was actively constructing a myth about his close relationship with his father. This is evident in Henry's constant emphasis on his father's interest in him in *A Small Boy and Others*: "It documents for me in so welcome and so definite a manner my father's cultivation of my company"; "as a happy example again of my parent's positive cultivation of my society, it would seem, and thought for my social education" (41, 53). Sometimes James drops the pretense, and his jealousy of William's intimacy with their father is painfully obvious: "He was to remember, as I perceived later on, many things that I didn't, impressions I sometimes wished, as with a retracing jealousy, or at least envy, that I might also have fallen direct heir to" (*Autobiography*, 41). Henry Senior not only encouraged this rivalry but he also helped to forge the "active" and "passive" roles of the rivals. William won favor through derring-do, Henry through angelic behavior. Mrs. James preferred Henry to William because he was quiet and obedient. Shortly before his death, Henry Senior struck this chord in a letter to Harry: "I can't help feeling that you are the one that has cost us the least trouble, and given us the most delight" (Lewis, 339). As William and Harry matured, their rivalry was transformed. Instead of competing with his brother for his father's love, Henry competed with his father for William's.

Though Henry Senior preserved some of the dignity of the paterfamilias, he was also clearly an emasculated figure in Henry's eyes. It is therefore equally plausible that Henry's femininity stemmed as much from his identification with his castrated father as from his (dis)identification with his masculine characteristics. Unconsciously, Henry Junior must have weighed the costs and benefits of psychic emasculation before making the sacrificial gesture when he was eighteen. Even after his repressed fear of and fascination with castration emerged from the shadows and assumed the quasi-definite form of a symptom, Henry remained ambivalent about his choice. Reflections on sacrifice fill his fictional works, as if by replaying his own act of renunciation he could determine whether it had been worthwhile. In *The Bostonians* (1886), Olive Chancellor quotes Goethe: "Thou shalt renounce, refrain, abstain!" (93). In *The Princess Casamassima* (1886), Hyacinth Robinson's ambition is to offer "an example even that might survive him—of pure youthful, almost juvenile, consecration" (5: 343). This refrain is heard in James's private correspondence as well. "Life's nothing," James wrote to a friend, "unless heroic and sacrificial" (cited in Trilling, 80).

It is difficult to know how keenly James felt the loss of the phallus. Yet characters who have undergone amputations or mutilations of various sorts appear repeatedly in his fictional and autobiographical writings. In "The Story of a Year" (1865), the hero jokes about looking like a lady when he returns from the Civil War (*Tales* 1: 22). An interesting metaphor of amputation occurs in *A Small Boy and Others*, in which James explains his youthful disinclination to accept cousin Albert's invitation to visit his inherited property in Beaverkill, "reached by a whole day's rough drive from the railroad, through every danger of flood and field, with prowling bears thrown in and probable loss of limb, of which there were sad examples, from swinging scythes and axes" (72). *The Spoils of Poynton* (1897) is one of the few works in James's canon in which the mutilated figures are female, male, even objects: "In the watches of the night she saw Poynton dishonored; she cared for it as a happy whole, she reasoned, and the parts of it now around her seemed to suffer like chopped limbs" (57). Mrs. Gereth's supersession by younger women in her son's affections is signified by images of mutilation or denudation throughout the novel. At first one is struck by James's sensitivity to the feminine midlife crisis, but this representation of female castration serves more than one purpose. James knew that his father had been disinherited by William of Albany, the family patriarch (Maher, 150). Mrs. Gereth's disinheritance and subsequent mutilation link her to James's father: "Nevertheless, in the sense of having passed the threshold of Poynton for the last time, the amputation, as she called it, had been performed. Her leg had come off—she had now begun to stump along with the lovely wooden substitute; she would stump for life" (51). *The Spoils of Poynton* permits us to see Henry Senior through his son's eyes as an effeminate figure.

The word *stump* has particular resonance. In "The Jolly Corner" (1908), Spencer Brydon's alter ego is missing fingers from his right hand, "which were reduced to stumps, as if accidentally shot away" (*NYE* 17: 476). In *The Princess Casamassima*, Paul Muniment takes Hyacinth Robinson to meet the anarchist Hoffendahl after Hyacinth mounts "the stump" and rails against the revolutionists' inactivity (5: 360). Hoffendahl too is modeled on James's father. He possesses the disinherited son's rage against the patriciate as well as Henry Senior's softer qualities, his inwardness and sublimity, which link him to Henry Senior's Swedenborgian theosophy. The anarchists of *The Princess Casamassima* are essentially parricides; the head of state they are conspiring to assassinate is a duke, a surrogate for Hyacinth's father. The connection between actual and fictional fathers is enhanced by a remarkable statement in the novel: "[Hyacinth] was in a state of inward exaltation, possessed by an intense desire to stand face to face with the sublime Hoffendahl, to hear his voice and touch his mutilated hand" (5: 355). Even the substitution of a hand for a leg has a precedent in Henry Senior's life. In his cryptoautobiographical sketch, entitled "Immortal Life: Illustrated in a Brief Autobiographic Sketch of the Late Stephen Dewhurst, Edited, with an Introduction by Henry James," Henry Senior represents Dewhurst as having lost an arm because of a gunshot wound (*HJSr*, 33–34). When Hyacinth volunteers to "put his head in a noose" in Hoffendahl's presence, he is patently reliving the psychic dilemma, that is, the identification with a castrated figure who yet preserves a degree of power over him, that led to Henry Junior's invention of the obscure hurt (6: 51).

Inversion

In "From the History of an Infantile Neurosis," Sigmund Freud indicates the contrary impulses influencing the patient's tentative resolution of castration anxiety: "In the end there were to be found in him two contrary currents side by side, of which one abominated the idea of castration, while the other was prepared to accept it and console itself with femininity as a compensation" (9: 323). In context, Freud argues that the Wolf-man's identification with his mother was confined to his fantasy of assuming her place in relation to his father in the primal scene, in which his own anus would serve as the functional equivalent of her vagina. In no respect is the patient effeminated or seen as a case of interior androgyny. Rather, what we have here is an example of "fantasmatic femininity," in which the male ego disports itself with a fantasy of alterity (Silverman, 353). As Henry Abelove has demonstrated, Freud explicitly rejected Karl Ulrichs's notion of "anima muliebris in corpore virili inclusa" ("a female soul trapped in a male body," appropriated by Richard von Krafft-Ebing as "psychical hermaphroditism") as well as Hirschfeld's proposition that homosexuals were "sexual intermediates" (what Ulrichs had called a "third sex" (Abelove, 389). In *Three Essays on the Theory of Sexuality*, Freud remarks: "The theory of bisexuality has been expressed in its crudest form by a spokesman of the male inverts: 'a feminine brain in a masculine body.' But we are ignorant of what characterizes a feminine brain. There is neither need nor justification for replacing the psychological problem by the anatomical one" (7: 54).

Freud's successors are chiefly responsible for characterizing homosexuality as a pathological form of gender inversion, and they waited until Freud's death in 1939 before doing so publicly (Abelove, 390). In taking this position, Freud's disciples were actually invoking a late-nineteenth-century theory, shared by homosexual advocates and sexologists alike: "Here the soul which is doomed to love a man, and is nevertheless imprisoned in a male body, strives to convert that body to feminine uses so entirely that the marks of sex, except in the determined organs of sex, shall be obliterated."[3] J. L. Casper, a specialist in forensic medicine, put it this way: "In the majority of persons who are subject to this vice, it is congenital; or at any rate the sexual inclination can be followed back into the years of childhood, like a kind of physical hermaphroditism" (cited in Symonds, *Problem in Modern Ethics*, 26). This theory is problematic for a number of reasons, first and foremost because it regards homosexual behaviors and roles as transhistorical categories, failing to acknowledge society's place in the construction of homosexual identities.

Freud was, in fact, an early defender of homosexual rights, both as a contributor to Hirschfeld's *Festschrift* and as a signatory of a public appeal for the decriminalization of homosexuality in Austria and Germany (Lewes, 31). Nevertheless, it is wise to remain circumspect about the metamessages of his concepts, since they have lent themselves to certain prejudicial misconstructions. In "Deconstructing Freud (2): Perversion Against the Oedipus Complex," Dollimore criticizes the normative aspects of psychoanalysis and its privileging of the heterosexual path of psychosexual development (196). In "Leonardo, Medusa, and the Wish to be a Woman," Dellamora attributes to Freud heterosexist and homophobic anxieties, which he contends prevent him from conceptualizing the erotic possibilities of the male fantasy of becoming a woman (136). Freud should probably not be faulted for steering clear of Ulrichs, Krafft-Ebing, and Hirschfeld's variations on the theme of homosexual difference when his aim was to affirm the humanity of homosexuals; he insisted that "psychoanalytic research is most decidedly opposed to any attempt at separating off homosexuals from the rest of mankind as a group of a special character" (7: 56n1). However, Dollimore and Dellamora are right to harp on Freud's use of the interrelated concepts of identification, introjection, and object choice.

The real problem with Freud is not his homophobia but his male chauvinism. Although he acknowledges Freud's stated denial of any attempt to disparage the feminine psyche, Kenneth Lewes believes that early psychoanalysis clearly revealed a masculine orientation and ethos, which saw women and effeminate men alike as inferior (237). Moreover, as Frank Sulloway has illustrated in *Freud: Biologist of the Mind*, Freud often struck a compromise between essentialist and nominalist positions. Sometimes Freud overstated the case for biological determinism, as in "The Passing of the Oedipus-Complex" and "Some Psychological Consequences of the Anatomical Distinction Between the Sexes," in which he could not seem to shake the supposition that "anatomy is destiny" (7: 320). Yet, if I have correctly characterized Henry James's obscure hurt, it appears that James overcame his narcissistic interest in his penis, accepted castration, and retained the homogenital parent (or his surrogate) as a love object. It also appears that "the small bearer of the penis" ignored his anatomical destiny and followed a "feminine" path to the resolution of the Oedipus complex, right down to his wish to bear a child (Freud, 7: 321). One persistent feature of James's incorporation of a feminine identity is the extent to which he associated artistic creativity with pregnancy. In an 1891 letter to William, Henry conflates the production of his new play with the birth of William and Alice James's third son: "The anecdote of Margaret Mary and her babe [is] most delightful. It seems trivial at such a time to trouble you with *my* deliveries, but by the time this reaches you, you and Alice will have got a little used to yours. However, you are to receive news of the coming into the world of *my* dramatic first born" (*HJL* 3: 317). Henry's sense of being married to William, of collaborating in the production of infants, is evident in an 1884 letter, in which Henry recommends that William name his second son after a character in *Roderick Hudson*. Henry writes, "If I had a child I would call him (very probably) Roland! 'Roland James' is very good" (3: 340). After William's death in 1910, Henry wrote of his undying attachment to his ideal elder brother: "My life, thank God, is impregnated with him" (4: 562).

Georges-Michel Sarotte has suggested that William James was implicated in "the atrophy of masculine feelings from which Henry James appeared to have suffered all his life" (198). Setting aside Sarotte's morbid characterization of this relationship, any reader of Henry's autobiography must concur that William contributed to Henry's effemination. While documenting his own foundering attempts to make a success of himself in his *Autobiography*, Henry marvels at his elder brother's talents: "One of these, and probably the promptest in order, was that of my brother's occupying a place in the world to which I couldn't at all aspire—to any approach to which in truth I seem to myself ever conscious of having forfeited a title" (7). Henry's memory is remarkably selective. For example, he does not dwell on William's nervous troubles, which were capped off by a full-blown nervous breakdown in 1870 or 1872. He does not mention that this paragon of virility used his nervous illness to avoid Civil War service and self-reliance in general. For the fact is that William did not support himself until 1874, when he turned thirty-two. And he lived mostly at home before his marriage at the ripe age of thirty-six. Henry persisted in idealizing William as a gifted genius and an invulnerable tough who rejected the advances of his milksop baby brother with the memorable phrase, "*I* play with boys who curse and swear" (*Autobiography*, 147).

Before he reached his precarious puberty, William exacerbated his younger brother's inferiority complex by abandoning Henry, who was a mere fifteen months his junior, in search of sport and masculine companionship in other quarters. William also feminized Henry throughout their lives, assigning him the moniker "angel" while referring to himself as the "demon" in his letters home (*CWJ* 4: 450). One almost gets a sense of two male siblings playing house well beyond their infant years. The roles of mother and father are surprisingly well defined. In 1873 William wrote his family from Italy: "At present Harry is my spouse. I have been here with him boarding in a hotel for 2½ weeks" (4: 454). Another time, flushed with a renewed sense of health and vitality, Henry wrote William: "I am as broad as I am long, as fat as a butter-tub and as red as a British *materfamilias*" (cited in Edel, 2: 343). When William married in July 1878, Henry wrote to convey his congratulations as well as his sense of desolation: "I have just heard from mother that you had decided to be married on the 10th ult: and as I was divorced from you by an untimely fate on this unique occasion, let me at least repair the injury by giving you, in the most earnest words my clumsy pen can shape, a tender bridal benediction" (*HJL* 2: 177).

Hall wonders whether James, in "writing about Daisy Miller and Isabel Archer and Catherine Sloper . . . [was] maintaining the core of female identity which William created for him and whose marriage now denied it? That the unconscious demands of his life required such an identity, which now moved from life to art?" (*An Obscure Hurt: Part I*, 30). Edel was the first to claim that Henry increasingly identified with his female protagonists after William's marriage (2: 392). Indeed it was this observation that inspired Hall to conceptualize the relation between James's sexual inactivity and his homosexuality as a repressed incestuous passion for his brother: "Henry James had maintained a difficult, emotional and probably incestuous relationship with his brother William, and it was this that accounted for his lifelong sexual inactivity. This fixation had pre-empted his homosexual feelings until very late in his life. He was not in love with other men; he was in love only with William" (*An Obscure Hurt: Part III*, 50). Feinstein enlarges on this theme in his biography of William James:

> Henry James's early stories can be read as the creation of a young artist who had become painfully aware of himself as a female consciousness masquerading in the body of a man. It is not surprising that the brothers' 'singular life' blurred sexual distinctions between them. And it should not come as a shock that in Henry's fictive world there is a strong homosexual strand linking him to his brother William. (233)

Feinstein's observation that Henry "had become painfully aware of himself as a female consciousness masquerading in the body of a man" reveals the antiquated outlook and bias built into his psychoanalytic perspective. It rules out diversity in masculine as well as in homosexual identifications and it denies any pleasure to be had from the fantasy of being a woman. By attributing a feminine psychological core to Henry James, Feinstein accords ontological status to a drag performance (233); that is to say, he confuses James's incorporation or mimicry of the feminine with an essential self. According to Butler, the notion of a psychological core is a generally accepted truth that enables a false stabilization of gender roles in the interests of heterosexual dominance and the regulation of reproduction (*Gender Trouble*, 136, 135). Although the norm stifles certain impulses, individuals comply with it because it satisfies their longing for coherence. In this regard, James's obscure hurt may represent his unconscious attempt to bring gender identity, sexual preference, and anatomy into pseudo-coherence by effecting an imaginary sex change. Krafft-Ebing's accounts of male homosexuals who experienced menstrual cramps and birth pangs and whose longing for "authenticity" was so strong that they contemplated emasculation, "I should not have shrunk from the castration-knife, could I have thus attained my desire"; "If I had been single, I should long ago have taken leave of testes, scrotum, and penis" (208, 205, 202, 209), suggest that gender identity, whether inverted or conformist, is a "personal/cultural history of received meanings subject to a set of imitative practices" as Butler contends (*Gender Trouble*,

138). Krafft-Ebing's would-be transsexuals challenge the notion that anatomical sex is the ground zero of gender identity. And they subvert patriarchy through their willingness to sacrifice the penis-phallus.

What I am arguing against is reading James's gender confusion as some
kind of eternal truth about unhappy and unfortunate males predisposed to homosexuality apart from its historical context. James's incorporation of a feminine identity was a socially mediated act; that is, it was influenced by James's
desire to avoid unwelcome duties (military service and supporting a family)
and his upbringing. It is also true that James's self-portraits (fictional, episto-
lary, and autobiographical) are consistent with sexologists' constructions of
homosexuality during his lifetime. Casper published in the 1850s and 1860s.
Ulrichs and Carl Westphal published in the 1860s. By the 1880s a mass of information about homosexuality had accumulated, and much of it was remarkably uniform in outlook, in that it labeled homosexuality as simple gender inversion. By the 1880s inversion had become a mainstream concept, familiar
not only to European specialists on sexual disorders but also to American asylum superintendents: "The hair on the face is sometimes thin, the voice almost always soft. The 'Urnings' have a mincing gait, and sometimes the hips
are broad like those of women" (Shrady, 70); "A dandified man is always
ridiculous, but when he adds to his foppery, effemination, he then becomes
contemptible" (Weir, "Viraginity and Effemination," 360); "These are the
conditions which have been prolific in producing the antisocial 'new woman'
and the disgusting effeminate male, both typical examples of the physiological degenerate" (Howard, "Effeminate Men and Masculine Women," 687).
Homosexuals also became topics of discussion in the lay press. The 1871 trial
of the transvestites Ernest Boulton and Frederick William Park (known as
Stella and Fanny to their intimate friends), who were arrested and charged
with "conspiring and inciting persons to commit an unnatural offense,"
caused a stir on both sides of the Atlantic (Pearsall, 461–62).

James's effeminacy may also be seen from the perspective of his Victorian
contemporaries, who were in a better position to assess the eccentricity of
James's persona than we are now. Violet Paget, the pseudonymous Vernon
Lee, had much to say on this issue. Although Lee dedicated her first novel,
Miss Brown, to James, she ridiculed him in the 1891 story, "Lady Tal," whose
protagonist, Jervase Marion, is patently styled on James: "There is something
in being a psychological novelist, and something in being a cosmopolitan

American, something in being an inmate of the world of Henry James and a kind of Henry James, of a lesser magnitude, yourself: one has the pleasure of understanding so much, one loses the pleasure of misunderstanding so much more" (11). Lee mischievously subtitled the collection in which "Lady Tal" appeared *Polite Stories*. Henry James found them anything but polite; he cut off any association with her after the book was published. In a letter to William, Henry reviled Lee for her "blackguardly" portrayal of him: "Receive from me (apropos of extraordinary women) a word of warning about Vernon Lee. . . . She has lately, as I am told (in a volume of tales called *Vanitas*, which I haven't read) directed a kind of satire of a flagrant and markedly 'saucy' kind at me (!!)—exactly the sort of thing she has repeatedly done to others (her books—fiction—are a tissue of personalities of the hideous *roman-á-clef* kind), and particularly impudent and blackguardly sort of thing to do to a friend" (*HJL* 3: 402). Edel provides the fullest account of James's relations with Lee and suggests that she was rankled by his failure to thank her promptly for her 1884 tribute, *Miss Brown* (3: 333). Although Edel thought Lee's satire malicious, her narrator's commentary always seems right on the mark: "Indeed, if Jervase Marion, ever since his earliest manhood, had given way to a tendency to withdraw from all personal concerns, from all emotion or action, it was mainly because he conceived that this shrinkingness of nature (which foolish persons, called egoism) was the necessary complement to his power of intellectual analysis" (53). Is this not a fair imitation of James's theory of aesthetic sublimation, worked out in tales such as "The Lesson of the Master" (1888), in which a young novelist, Paul Overt, concludes that "Nature had dedicated him to intellectual, not to personal passion" (*NYE* 15: 96)?

Lee's depiction of James is a lampoon rather than a caricature, because, without much exaggeration, it publicizes what James had determined to keep private, at least before his startling revelations of 1913 about his "obscure hurt." When the narrator of "Lady Tal" comments "Marion, heaven knows, didn't like women who went in for *grande passion*; in fact passion, which he had neither experienced nor described, was distinctly repulsive to him," we recognize the superficial quality of sexual anesthesia in both James's life and works that must have prompted this nasty quip (73). Lee views the absence of sexual passion in James's life with the curiosity and suspicion of a modern reader; yet what is most remarkable about her treatment of James is her association of his "withdrawal from personal concerns" with

closeted homosexuality: "Marion was silent. He felt a weak worm for dislik-
ing this big blond girl with the atrocious manners, who insisted on pro-
nouncing his name *Mary Anne*, with the unfailing relish of a joke" (70). This
girlish name not only feminizes Henry James but also posits a link between
James and the homosexual underworld of London.[4] In 1889, two years before "Lady Tal" was written, British newspapers carried the story of the
Cleveland Street scandal, which captured the public's imagination for
months before its central figure, Lord Euston, was sentenced to a one-year
imprisonment for patronizing the working-class male prostitutes, or "Mary-
Annes," who worked at the Cleveland Street brothel. Through her character Jervase Marion, Lee also suggests that the artistic community James inhabited was well aware of his attempt to conceal his homosexuality by playing the courtier to Constance Fenimore Woolson and others: "Why couldn't
he take a stroll in a garden with a handsome woman of thirty without the
company being informed that it was only on account of Lady Tal's novel.
That novel, that position of literary adviser, of a kind of male daily gov-
erness, would make him ridiculous" (75).

Although I may be reading "Lady Tal" with a heightened sensitivity to its
innuendos about sexual inversion, the story itself calls attention to this subject by mismatching the gendered qualities of its characters: "Jervase Marion
had immediately identified her as the owner of that rather masculine voice
with the falsetto tone; and apart from the voice, he would have identified her
as the lady who had bullied the poor young man in distress about his side-
board" (16). Lee also mentions the works of John Addington Symonds and
Edward Carpenter, two outspoken homosexual advocates, in her story. Although the economic motives underlying a woman's adoption of a masculine
pen name are obvious, in Lee's case there also seems to be a connection between her pseudonym and her sexuality. According to Ronald Pearsall, Lee
carried the torch for a number of women during her lifetime and actually
suffered a nervous breakdown after her friend Mary Robinson became engaged in 1887 (485). In *Miss Brown*, Lee depicts several passionate female at-
tachments: "Mary Leigh smiled. She was proud of her little sister; and she
was, in a sort of way, in love with Anne Brown" (2: 138). Though wary of
physical contact, Lee seems to have fantasized about sex between women in
her novel: "Anne stooped down and kissed her shyly on her wan cheek. But
a sort of shudder passed through her as her own lips touched that hot face,

and grazed the light hair, which seemed to give out some faint Eastern perfume. This woman was so unlike anything she had ever seen—so unlike her own simple self" (2: 190). James travestied the decadent movement in his story "The Author of Beltraffio," published shortly before *Miss Brown*. However, his own account of aesthetic amorality was rather subtle, even obscure, and James found *Miss Brown* distasteful and criticized Lee for having "impregnated all those people too much with the sexual, the basely erotic preoccupation" (*HJL* 3: 86). It is conceivable that Lee, having read the first installments of James's treatment of a lesbian attachment in *The Bostonians* by the time she received James's missive, found this criticism both obnoxious and hypocritical. James's rejection of *Miss Brown* was clearly on Lee's mind when she wrote "Lady Tal." The story transparently recasts the events leading up to the production of *Miss Brown*, for Lady Tal also dedicates her first novel to her mentor. Positioned as a marginal woman in the throes of sexual panic, it is small wonder that Lee's revenge took this form, a send-up of James as a closeted homosexual. But it is worth reminding ourselves that Lee's vision was as precocious as it was acute.

'Le Vice Suprême'

Although effeminacy in men was increasingly associated with sexual inversion in the late-Victorian period, it was not rigidly codified. Sexual inversion was primarily associated with sex acts rather than with sexual persona.[5] And although "excessive" or "unnatural" effeminacy in a man would certainly have excited suspicion, James probably felt he could cultivate the feminine side of his personality without inviting the opprobrium connected with overt homosexuality.[6] The point is that James had a lot more latitude in which to indulge his femininity and homoerotic fantasies than has been previously thought. Edel assumed that James was "greatly shocked to find his old Parisian friend [Joukowsky] in a veritable nest of homosexuals" (*HJL* 2: 289n1). Ellmann has suggested that James was only tolerant of closeted gays: "Pater's homosexuality was covert, Wilde's was patent. Pater could be summed up as 'faint, pale, embarrassed, exquisite,' but for Wilde James found other epithets to describe his mind, manners, and probable sexual proclivities ('unclean beast')" ("Henry James Among the Aesthetes," 218).

Of course James's hostility to Wilde informs this theory of James's homophobia: "I went last night to the Lorings where you told me you had flung down your *sortie de bal* in the dusky entry, where it looked like a bunch of hyacinths,—and found there the repulsive and fatuous Oscar Wilde, whom, I am happy to say, no one was looking at" (*HJL* 2: 372).

Critics have unduly emphasized James's disdain for Wilde and interpreted it as somehow emblematic of his attitude toward homosexuals. This interpretation is reductive in more than one sense, for it implies that James had no other motive for loathing Wilde (such as jealousy over his dramatic success or contempt for his self-promotion) than his dandified dress and manner. Fred Kaplan falls into this trap when he observes that, for James, Wilde was "abhorrent insofar as he dramatized a flamboyant caricature of unmanly effeminacy" (300). If this were truly the case, James should have despised Howard Sturgis, a nurturing and tender man whose hobbies included knitting and embroidering as well as novel writing (Posnock, 212). Although Kaplan has contributed to our knowledge of James's romantic friendships with homosexuals and bisexuals, among them Paul Joukowsky, Hugh Walpole, Jocelyn Persse, Jonathan Sturges, Morton Fullerton, and Hendrik Anderson, he underestimates the erotic (that is, masturbatory) potential of James's passionate correspondence, a nineteenth-century equivalent of "party lines" and "phone sex." Along these same lines, Edel, Ellmann, and Kaplan have naively interpreted James's insistence that immorality and perversity disgusted him. His feelings of disgust and shame, as well as his claims of moral and aesthetic ideals, may have been reaction formations against keen, if unconscious, interest in unsanctioned sources of erotic gratification. They may have also signified plain dissimulation.

The decadent literature that James devoured, from Gautier to D'Annunzio to Huysmans, not only served James as mild homoerotic pornography but also enabled him to devise for himself a sexual persona that was consistent with his determination to abstain from physical love. In "The Image of the Androgyne in the Nineteenth Century," A. J. L. Busst explains: "It must not be thought, however, that because it is the product of the mind, it is removed from sexuality or from lasciviousness. On the contrary. For the lechery which is associated with the pessimistic symbol of the androgyne is above all cerebral; indeed, cerebral lechery is the *vice suprême* which best characterizes the attitude of disillusionment and withdrawal from practical life

which conditions the symbol" (42). Busst continues: "This particular perversion, cerebral lechery, is by no means incompatible with total sexual abstinence" (43). James's choice of the name Hyacinth for the sexually ambiguous hero of *The Princess Casamassima* aligns him with the decadent writers who used this name to blur the gender boundaries between heroines and
heroes (Novalis's *Marchen* in 1798, J. K. Huysmans's *Là-Bas* in 1891, and
Walter Pater's "Apollo in Picardy" in 1893). Of all the James scholars, Posnock has the keenest appreciation for the sexual dimensions of James's
friendships, fantasies, and fictions. Describing James as an example of the
"rarest and most perfect" sublimation, in which curiosity took the place of
sexual activity, Posnock stresses "the near hallucinatory force of James's
power of sublimation to express desire" (47).

For if James genuinely found Aubrey Beardsley's illustrations sickening
and "extraordinarily base," why did he bother to read *The Last Letters of
Aubrey Beardsley* or to acknowledge the receipt of the book with a warm note
to André Raffalovich, the book's editor and the onetime author of a tract on
"urningism"? (*HJL* 4: 691–92). James was clearly aware of Raffalovich's past
indiscretions and promiscuity, for he once made light of the latter's conversion to Catholicism in a letter to Logan Pearsall Smith. James beseeched his
sexually active friends, Walpole and Fullerton, to give him fuller accounts of
their private lives. He told Walpole, "I could have done even with more detail—as when you say '*Such* parties!' I want so to hear exactly what parties
they are. When you refer to their 'immorality on stone floors,' and with
prayerbooks in their hands so long as the exigencies of the situation permit
of the manual retention of the sacred volumes, I do so want the picture developed and the proceedings authenticated" (4: 695). And James himself was
capable of sharing titillating gossip with a homoerotic undertone, as when in
a letter to Edmund Gosse, he provided him with the rough outline of a "fantastic tale" told by Maupassant concerning a ménage à trois between "two
Englishmen, each other, and their monkey!" (4: 630). In the same letter,
James warmed to Gosse's account of Algernon Swinburne and Richard Burton ensconced on a sofa in the still of the night discussing the customs of the
Sotadic zone, presumably. James's curiosity about sexual matters was seemingly insatiable. He did not turn a hair while reading Byron's account of his
incestuous passion for his half sister, Augusta Leigh, though his colleague
John Buchan reported that while he was positively sickened by it, "[James's]

only words for some special vileness were 'singular'—'most curious'—'nauseating, perhaps, but how quite inexpressibly significant'" (4: 536–37n1).

James's scoptophilia stands out in all these illustrations: he would rather observe than participate in sexual activity. However, Freud's theory of component instincts permits us to recognize the exhibitionist counterpart to James's voyeur (7: 81). In transgressing the safe boundaries of gender identity (in a letter to Fullerton, James complained that a snapshot made him "resemble her late Britannic majesty" and protested "je suis mieux que ca [I'm better than that!]"), James was courting exposure (*HJL* 4: 215). James's sensationalizing of his own prudery is yet another kind of drag performance, for he hides his lusts behind a spinster's irreproachable petticoats. More important, James eroticizes the little shocks he endures. D. A. Miller's brilliant analysis of Wilkie Collins's sensationalistic novel, *The Woman in White*, locates homosexual panic precisely at the moment when the male protagonist mirrors the hysterical woman's intensity. Collins, however, does not leave his hero in this precarious state; he allows Walter to move from "identification with the woman to a desire for her, heterosexual choice replacing homosexual surprise" (173). James makes no such maneuver. His feminized nervousness remains fixed on outlawed homoerotic desire.

James's terror of blackmail is instructive in this regard. To borrow from Sedgwick's fine reading of Proust, James's writings occasionally express the "viewpoint of the closet" (*Epistemology*, 223). Although I am not claiming that James was sexually active in the conventional sense, I do maintain that James's abstention from full genital contact did not deprive him of a homosexual identity. Symonds, in his memoirs, puts the matter bluntly: "Many a man who never stooped to any carnal deed has wallowed in the grossest sensuality of thought. Inside the sphere of their desires such men are agent and patient, double-sexed, immersed in epicene voluptuousness, for ever longing, for ever picturing delights, for ever unassuaged" (127). Considering James's monastic existence, what did he have to fear from blackmailers? According to F. B. Smith, in the 1870s "there developed in the British public a rabid detestation of male homosexuality. In this context Labouchère's amendment [1885], with its weak provisions about evidence, and exposure of 'consent' and 'procuring' to expansive judicial interpretation, became a terrible instrument" (165). In *A Problem in Modern Ethics* (1891), Symonds attributed the unexplained suicides of young men to the strain of the homosexual's secret life and the machinations of blackmailers: "The miserable persecuted wretch, placed between the alternative of paying money down or of becoming socially impossible, losing a valued position, seeing dishonour bursting upon himself and family, pays, and still the more he pays, the greedier becomes the vampire who sucks his life-blood" (72). When Sturges died in 1909, James had all his letters to him returned so that he could promptly burn them. In their correspondence to each other, Gosse and James avoided spelling out Symonds's name after he declared his homosexuality. Instead, they referred to him as "J. A. S." and his groundbreaking treatise on homosexuality as "the pamphlet." When Wilde was arrested in April 1895, he too, was designated by his initials in James's correspondence, even though at that time the entire continent was buzzing with his name. In some respects, James seems to have enjoyed his chimerical predicament. Though he took some obvious precautions against blackmailers, avoiding guilt through association, he also flirted with exposure. Shortly after Wilde's arrest he wrote Gosse: "These are days in which one's modesty is, in every direction, much exposed, and one should be thankful for every veil that one can hastily snatch up or that a friendly hand muffles one withal. It is strictly congruous with these remarks that I should mention that there go to you tomorrow . . . the fond outpourings of poor J. A. S." (*HJL* 4: 12). Why James should pick this moment to send Gosse Symonds's treatise on sexual inversion, which he had kept in his possession for two years, is a mystery, but the letter is communicative enough in other respects, in that it effectively links Symonds, Wilde, and James in "strictly congruous" male-male desire.

Gosse had sent James *A Problem in Modern Ethics* in January 1893. Symonds's privately printed pamphlet would soon appear as an anonymous contribution to the second volume of Havelock Ellis's *Studies in the Psychology of Sex* (1897), a work the courts labeled "lewd and obscene" when it was published. Edel is deliberately obtuse about this episode, commenting simply that James was "being coy about the entire subject" of homosexuality when he wrote:

It was very kind of you yesterday, to supply—or rather to remedy—the injury of fate by bringing me those marvellous outpourings. I had at the B[oard] of T[rade] a lurking suspicion that you *were* within, but my natural modesty—though strangely impaired since yesterday P.M.!—made me shy of too grossly insisting. I was evidently avenged upon the erring janitor—but don't give him the sack (as I believe you fellows say), for then *I* shall have to support him!—J[ohn] A[ddington] S[ymonds] is truly, I gather, a candid and consistent creature, and the exhibition is infinitely remarkable. It's, on the whole, I think, a queer place to plant the standard of duty, but he does it with extra-ordinary gallantry. If he has, or gathers, a band of the emulous, we may look for some capital sport. But I don't wonder that some of his friends and relations are haunted with a vague malaise. I think one ought to wish him more *humour*—it is really *the* saving salt. But the great reformers never had it—and he is the Gladstone of the affair. (3: 398)

James clearly regarded the pamphlet as a work of importance, interest, and daring. He apparently read it the moment he lay hands on it. To use a favorite expression of James's, his reading "gave him wings," as he flitted excitedly from one double entendre to the next throughout the letter. His wry line about supporting the janitor seems to be a reference to one type of homosexual who favored working-class lovers. Though Gosse's lover, Hamo Thornycroft, was upper class, both Symonds and Carpenter had long-term relationships with working-class men. In an 1893 letter to Carpenter, Symonds commented, "The blending of Social Strata in masculine love seems to me one of its most pronounced & socially hopeful, features. Where it appears, it abolishes class distinctions, and opens by a single operation the cataract-blinded eye to their futilities" (3: 808). James implicitly acknowledges this type of homosexual couple in *The Princess Casamassima*, in which Hyacinth Robinson, an illegitimate descendent of aristocrats, observes of his would-be lover, Paul Muniment: "He had the complexion of a ploughboy and the glance of a commander-in-chief, and might have been a distinguished young savant in the disguise of an artisan" (5: 114).

James's comment about having his natural modesty "strangely impaired since yesterday P.M." refers both to the document's disclosures and to Prime Minister Gladstone ("P.M."), whom he mentions later in the letter. James's remark that Symonds is the "Gladstone of the affair," in the sense that both men are great social reformers, is quite significant, for, as Dellamora has shown, "there were special connections between Liberalism and self-awareness on the part of men who enjoyed sexual and emotional relations with other men. For one, there was the subterranean tradition of [Bentham's] Utilitarian polemic on behalf of decriminalizing sexual activity between males" (196–97). Although James did not directly proclaim his homosexuality, he took a roundabout course to that end by identifying Symonds with the liberal prime minister, who was both tolerant of sexual difference and a proponent of Home Rule for Ireland. James was of Irish extraction, and his sister, Alice, was passionately interested in the Irish question. In this way, James was declaring his fealty to Symonds and men like him. Though James was not well acquainted with Symonds, he came to esteem him highly. When Symonds died of tuberculosis, James wrote to console Gosse:

> I am very glad of the emotion that led you to write to me immediately about the sudden—the so brutal and tragic extinction, as it comes to one, of poor forevermore silent J. A. S. I had never even (clearly) seen him— but somehow I too can't help feeling the news as a pang—and with a personal emotion. It always seemed as if I *might* know him—and of few men whom I didn't know has the image so much come home to me. Poor much-living, much-doing, passionately outgiving man! (*HJL* 3: 409)

James's interest in Symonds dates from an earlier period. According to a March 26, 1884 entry in James's *Notebooks*, Gosse's revelations about Symonds's marital difficulties inspired James to write "The Author of Beltraffio." Evidently Gosse had outlined for James the general facts of Symonds's life, emphasizing his tragic consumption, his conflicts with his priggish wife, who declared his writings "immoral, pagan, hyper-aesthetic," and, presumably, some details of his double sexual life, which Symonds was no longer at pains to disguise (25). Earlier in that same year, James wrote to congratulate Symonds, ostensibly on his beautiful writings on Italy: "I wanted to recognize this (to your knowledge); for it seemed to me that the victims of a common passion should sometimes exchange a look" (*HJL* 3: 30). Is this common passion for Italy an ardor for places or for people? In 1869 James wrote an enthusiastic description of Italian men and sent it to brother William: "In the narrow streets, the people are far too squalid and offensive to the nostrils, but with a good breadth of canals to set them off and a heavy stream of sunshine to light them up as they go pushing and paddling and screaming—

bare-chested, bare-legged, magnificently tanned and muscular—the men at least are a very effective lot" (1: 142).

James's letter to Symonds preceded Gosse's tattle by a few months, but I am convinced that James knew Symonds was a homosexual when he wrote the letter. As Ellmann points out in "Henry James Among the Aesthetes," "it has been said that James did not know till later that Symonds was a homosexual, but in the 1880s one never mentioned this, while in the 1890s one admitted to having known it all the time" (218). Moreover, Symonds's *A Problem in Greek Ethics: Being an Inquiry into the Phenomenon of Sexual Inversion* (1883), was by then making the rounds among his friends and associates.

Symonds is not the only figure who has been suggested as the prototype for Mark Ambient. In a forgotten literary critical chestnut, "Stevenson and Henry James: The Rare Friendship Between Two Famous Stylists," George Hellman contends that James based "The Author of Beltraffio" on a report that Fanny Stevenson had convinced her husband to destroy a novel he had written about a prostitute (340). Though it is unlikely that Stevenson shared this anecdote with James at their first meeting in 1879 (the second did not occur until 1885), it is possible that a mutual friend, Sidney Colvin, served as the conduit for the information. There is no point in contesting James's version of what led him to compose his story, except to say that James was cagey about his sources. In an 1885 letter to William, he denied that the story was "a living and scandalous portrait of J. A. Symonds and his wife," though his contemporaries believed otherwise (*HJL* 3: 71). It is noteworthy that James's physical description of Ambient resembles Stevenson, not Symonds: "There was a brush of the Bohemian in his fineness; you would easily have guessed his belonging to an artist guild. He was addicted to velvet jackets, to cigarettes, to loose shirt collars, to looking a little dishevelled. . . . There were other strange oppositions and contradictions in his slightly faded and fatigued countenance" (*NYE* 16: 7). Andrew Lang introduced James to Stevenson in 1879. After their meeting, James described Stevenson to T. S. Perry in a letter as a "pleasant fellow, but a shirt-collarless Bohemian and a great deal (in an inoffensive way) of a *poseur*" (Edel, 3: 124–25). It is quite possible that Stevenson's manner and dress, which clearly made an impression on James, informed his description of Ambient; the resemblance between them is pronounced. William Archer retained the following impression of Stevenson when he visited Skerryvore cottage in the mid-1880s: "He now sits at the foot of the table rolling a limp cigarette in his long, limp fingers, and talking eagerly all the while. . . . He has still the air and manner of a young man, for illness has neither tamed his mind nor aged his body. It has left its mark, however, in the pallor of his oval face. . . . He is dressed in a black velvet jacket, showing at the throat the loose rolling collar of a white flannel shirt" (cited in Calder, 198).

It is quite significant that Stevenson struck his contemporaries as sexually ambiguous. To Lang, Stevenson looked "more like a lass than a lad" (43). In an 1890 letter, James feminized Stevenson, comparing his absent friend to "a male Cleopatra or buccaneering Pompadour of the Deep—the wandering Wanton of the Pacific" (*HJL* 3: 278). Stevenson's biographers, Jenni Calder and J. C. Furnas, have noted that Stevenson's intimate circle included many men who expressed a romantic attachment to him, among them James's good friends Gosse and Colvin. According to Lang, who introduced James to Symonds and Gosse as well as to Stevenson, "Mr. Stevenson possessed, more than any man I have ever met, the power of making other men fall in love with him. I mean he excited a passionate admiration and affection, so much so that I verily believe some men were jealous of other men's place in his liking" (51–52). Though James is not classed with these men as a Stevenson devotee, he should be. James joined this homosocial coterie in his imagination when he celebrated Stevenson in an 1888 essay, in which he returned again and again to the idea that Stevenson had a "feeling about life that [led] him to regard women as so many superfluous girls in a boys game." "There is something almost impertinent in the way, as I have noticed, in which Mr. Stevenson achieves his best effects without the aid of the ladies, and *Dr. Jekyll* is a capital example of his heartless independence" (*LC1*, 1238, 1252). James clearly relished his perception that Stevenson had no use for women. Even when he described Stevenson as a prodigious gallant and a Don Juan, James came back to his original perception of him: "A striking feature of that nature should be an absence of care for things feminine. His books are for the most part books without women, and it is not women who fall most in love with them. But Mr. Stevenson does not need, as we may say, a petticoat to inflame him" (1233).

In "Robert Louis Stevenson and Henry James," Colvin hinted at a hidden dimension to James's personality, which Colvin had detected from his own privileged vantage point, the closet. Describing the temperaments and predilections of his two friends, Colvin observed: "Both—though in the case of Henry James it needed intimate knowledge to realize as much—were men of exceptionally intense feeling, of an emotional nature doubly and trebly as strong as the common run of mankind" (318). The double entendres of this provocative, if inconclusive, passage are reminiscent of James's confession, "it seemed to me that the victims of a common passion should sometimes exchange a look," for James and Colvin both sincerely loved Stevenson. When Stevenson retired to the South Seas for his health, James wrote: "Your place in my affection has not been usurped by another—for there is not the least little scrap of other to usurp it. If there was I should perversely try to care for him. But there isn't—I repeat, and I literally care for nothing but your return" (*HJL* 3: 239). Colvin, who was heartsick when Stevenson married and who cordially hated Stevenson's wife, went to pieces when he died. James expressed his friend's devastation in a letter to Gosse, but stopped short of illuminating him about the depth of Colvin's grief: "I saw poor Colvin today—he is overwhelmed, he is touching: But I can't write of this—we must talk of it!" (3: 495).

By 1920, when Gosse composed his memoir of James, the social climate was marginally more hospitable to displays of homoerotic feeling:

> No episode of the literary history of the time is more fascinating than the interchange of feeling between these two great artists. The death of Stevenson, nine years later than their first meeting, though long anticipated, fell upon Henry James with a shock he found at first scarcely endurable. For a long time afterwards he could not bring himself to mention the name of R. L. S. without a distressing agitation. (1: 681)

It may be inferred from these quotations that Stevenson's marriage and discreet homosociability served to disguise the romantic fervor of his interactions with men like James and Colvin. It seems that James created a composite character in "The Author of Beltraffio." Stevenson's attire and androgyny stamped him as a Bohemian and congenital invert, whereas Symonds's writings linked him to literary decadence and homosexuality. James must have been struck, at first glance, with Stevenson's sexual ambiguity. He must always have been on the lookout for men who felt as he did, with whom he might feel at ease, since he surrounded himself with homosexuals both open and closeted.

Stigmatization

Scholars read "The Author of Beltraffio" as an attack on the aesthetic movement and, implicitly, on the homosexuals who were its figureheads. In *Professions of Taste*, Freedman calls the story "a tale of Gothic horror in which a mother lets her child die rather than grow up with a homosexual father" (172). Freedman also highlights the notions of contagion and tainted inheritance implicit in the story: "The novelist's highly moralistic wife allows their child to die of diphtheria, convinced by proofs of his latest book that Ambient's immoralism would inevitably infect their son. In this story, then, aestheticism is (as it was, paradoxically, for both the advocates and the detractors of 'decadence') linked with corruption and disease, and leads inevitably to moral tragedy" (144). These aspects of the story are compatible with extraliterary representations of both homosexuals and aesthetes in late-Victorian culture. In 1889 the former chief of the police department for morals in Paris, where homosexual activity was protected under the Napoleonic Code, expressed his conviction of "the contagiousness of antiphysical passion" (cited in Symonds, *Problem in Modern Ethics*, 20).

Mrs. Ambient's suspicions were echoed in the work of the American alienist William Lee Howard, who claimed: "The invert and the pervert is to be found among the aesthetic class. . . . Ninety per cent of these abnormal individuals are engaged in artistic pursuits" ("Psychical Hermaphroditism," 113–14). Lucien Arreat described the unmanning "nervous erethism" and "infeverishing passions" of creative individuals in an 1893 essay, "Pathology of Artists," in which he concluded that "artists are the most feminine of men" (86). Finally, Allan M'Lane Hamilton credited the novelist Théophile Gautier, among others, with alerting medical professionals to the existence of lesbian sexuality: "Krafft-Ebing, Moll, Chaddock, and numerous continental and American writers have reviewed the erotic literature of past times, and have collected many personal observations, so that within a short decade a subject which had been boldly discussed by French romanticists, and afterward by timid psychiatrists, has been given a definite place in modern psychological medicine" (503–4). Mrs. Ambient's self-righteous conduct speaks volumes about the general hostility toward homosexuals at this time and goes some distance in explaining why it was difficult for James to come to Wilde's defense or to identify himself publicly with the burgeoning homosexual rights movement. In his *Notebooks*, James has no liking for or sympathy with Mrs. Ambient. He styles her a "narrow, cold, Calvinistic wife, a rigid moralist"; James favors Mark Ambient, whose "godless ideas" are said to belong to the literary career and not to enter into his "perfectly decent" life (25).

This contrast between works of imagination and actions must be taken into account. James's avoidance of full genital sexuality made his passion for other men possible. Scholars have taken at face value James's celibacy, his equivocations on sexual matters, and, in particular, his animosity toward certain homosexual men. But we should not underestimate the amount of subterfuge made necessary by Victorian notions of decency. Literary scholars need to consider what it cost someone of James's class and background, not to mention personality, to emerge from the closet. Once again, Symonds serves as a foil for James. Conscious of his predilections early on, Symonds nevertheless held himself aloof from the debauches of Harrow and sought to transcend "crude sensuality through aesthetic idealization of the erotic instincts" (*Memoirs of John Addington Symonds*, 96). Homophobia, self-loathing, and prudery were in equal measure responsible for Symonds's ability to master his "unwholesome" passion: "While I was at school, I remained free in fact and act from this contamination. During the first half year the 'beasts,' as they were playfully called, tried to seduce me. But it was soon decided that I was 'not game'" (95). In 1859 Symonds exposed the love affair between a school fellow and Harrow's headmaster, a man named Vaughan. Apparently Symonds's conscience was pricked, since he reflected that he felt "a deeply rooted sympathy" with the man he brought down; but at the time he felt a greater allegiance to the conventional pieties (112). Might not this unfortunate incident explain Symonds's courageous defense of homosexuals thirty years later?

This tension between moral training and romantic inclination, resulting in a sexual stalemate—celibacy—was fairly common in the nineteenth century. In 1883 J. C. Shaw and G. N. Ferris published "Perverted Sexual Instinct," one of the first articles to translate and summarize for an American audience European case studies of sexual inversion. Several case histories, those of respectable and talented men, addressed the patients' profound shame at their inability to suppress homosexual inclinations and their proportionate misery at being unable to indulge them. One individual "had often longed to have intercourse with young men, which, however, he never had had. On account of this affection for men, he considered himself a complete reprobate" and "damned for all eternity"; another "well-educated young man, twenty-four years of age, of excellent character, during an acute attack of melancholia confessed his perverted desires toward his own sex to his physician. When seen a few days later by Westphal, all traces of his melancholy had disappeared. Recognized his sexual desire as perverted, and wished to be cured of it"; a third "felt attracted by young, handsome, strong men; desired to please them, and show them the many little attentions usually shown to a young lady; had never given way to these desires, but still could not control his imagination" (190, 193, 201).

Beyond the physicians' characterization of homosexuals as self-loathing deviants, it is worth taking note of the forums in which such articles appeared: *The Journal of Nervous and Mental Disease, The American Journal of Insanity, The Alienist and Neurologist,* and so forth. We must remember that among the medical establishment associating homosexuality with insanity, neurasthenia, hysteria, and melancholy was quite common. Nineteenth-century scientists, physicians, sexologists, and psychiatrists divided homosexuals into two camps: the congenital invert, who had inherited his or her inclinations from a forebear, and the debauchee, who merely indulged his or her salacious whims. Congenital inversion was associated with two bugbears of the nineteenth century: moral insanity (Henry Maudsley's term) and racial degeneration (atavism, devolution). In "Perverted Sexual Instinct" (1884), George Shrady observed: "In the reported cases of congenital perversion, the abnormal instinct begins oftenest as early as the eighth or ninth year, but shows itself at first, perhaps, only in an inclination to adopt the manners and practices of girls and women. The victims show the somatic basis of their trouble in various ways. There is often an hereditary psychopathic or neuropathic taint" (70). Frank Lydston, physician and criminal anthropologist, warned that acquired perversion could be transmitted to the next generation: "Men and women who seek, from mere satiety, variations of the normal method of sexual gratification, stamp their nervous systems with a malign influence which in the next generation may present itself as true sexual perversion" (255). In "Viraginity and Effemination" (1893), criminal anthropologist James Weir argued that these conditions are "due directly to the influence of that strange law laid down by Darwin—the law of reversion to ancestral types. It is an effort of nature to return man to the old hermaphroditic form from which he was evolved" (359). Even Symonds believed that the laws of evolution and devolution were inescapable: "We cannot evade the conditions of atavism and heredity. Every family runs the risk of producing a boy or a girl whose life will be embittered by inverted sexuality" (*Problem in Modern Ethics*, 4).

Sexual aberrations figured prominently within the more extensive framework of the degeneracy theory, which covered functional and organic diseases, insanity, alcoholism, criminal propensities, nervous exhaustion, and alopecia. The James family was well acquainted with this doctrine. Mrs. James's letters to her children regarding their work habits and their potential for nervous exhaustion read like crib notes from S. Weir Mitchell's *Wear and Tear: Hints for the Overworked* (1871). William apparently got the message. In his correspondence to his family, he claimed to have dedicated himself to "economising [his] feeble energies" (*CWJ* 4: 137). Henry was also familiar with the concept of overwork: "I am delighted to hear [William] was reassured on the subject of poor B[ob]'s balance of intellect and rejoice in the latter's having got rid of his unhappy newspaper. I hope he won't (whatever he does) embark in an *irritating* profession" (*HJL* 2: 231). Feinstein's major contribution to our understanding of the Jameses was his insight into the role that nineteenth-century concepts of heredity played in the family's psychic economy. As Feinstein pointed out, three of the eleven children of William of Albany who reached maturity—Henry, William, and Jannett—had breakdowns. Their youngest brother, Howard, was an alcoholic. Feinstein concluded that "the incidence of affective disorder, alcoholism, and other forms of psychopathology in the first three generations of this family [was] high" (304–5).

In *A Small Boy and Others*, Henry joked about "tipsy" Albany uncles and family members who "without exception had at last taken a turn as far as possible from edifying" (29). This notion was echoed, more grimly, in *The Princess Casamassima*, in which a character reflects: "The family, as a family, had gone downhill to the very bottom" (5: 66). In James's immediate family, Henry Senior had a nervous breakdown in 1844, Alice in 1868, William in 1870, Robertson in 1881, and Henry Junior in 1910. Robertson was also an alcoholic and had himself committed to an asylum in 1881. Alice spent her entire adult life in bed suffering from psychosomatic ailments. In 1884 Garth

Wilkinson, the only James sibling to have escaped nervous illness, died a physical wreck at age thirty-nine because of a war injury. The novelist had lifelong attacks of gastritis, constipation, headaches, and back pain, as well as episodes of severe depression. Under the circumstances, Kate Croy's observation in *The Wings of the Dove* concerning the demise of her own kin might be read as a cryptoautobiographical statement: "Why should such a set of people have been put in motion, on such a scale and with such an air of being equipped for a profitable journey, only to break down without an accident, to stretch themselves in the wayside dust without a reason?" (19: 4).

The Jameses' fear of passing along a tainted heredity is evident in their family correspondence. When Robertson contemplated marrying his cousin in 1869, William wrote to discourage him:

> After all, what results from every marriage is a part of the next generation, and feeling as strongly as I do that the greater part of the whole evil of this wicked world is the result of infirm health, I account it a true crime against humanity for anyone to run the probable risk of generating unhealthy offspring. . . . I want to feel on my death bed when I look back that whatever evil I was born with I kept to myself, and did so much towards extinguishing it from the world. (*CWJ* 4: 389–90)

William eventually changed his mind. By the time he composed *Principles of Psychology* in 1890, he no longer gave credence to notions of neuropsychopathic heredity, atavism, or degeneracy (Sulloway, 291); however, in his youth, he was tormented by the implications of these doctrines. A character in *The Princess Casamassima* gives voice to William's fears and resolutions: "He would never marry at all—to this his mind was absolutely made up; he would never hand on to another the burden that had darkened the whole threshold of his manhood" (5: 80).

Sexual Neurasthenia

Although the fear of tainted heredity may explain why James remained single while many homosexuals he knew (Gosse, Symonds, Wilde, and Sargent) married and fathered children, it is not yet clear how this apprehension influenced his decision to remain celibate. Reasonable objections to rigid homosexual/heterosexual dichotomies notwithstanding, some Victorian men who did not fancy women married because their families, doctors, or their own sense of pragmatism recommended it as a means of bolstering moral restraint and staving off exposure. Symonds's memoirs offer compelling testimony to the sorrows attending marriages of expedience: "Being what I am, the great mistake—perhaps the great crime of my life, was my marriage" (184). People like Henry and William James, who recognized many of the somatic or characterological warning signs of hereditary degeneration in themselves or in family members, believed that their minds and bodies would slowly but surely betray them. Feinstein explains that "the scion of such 'tainted' stock was at best condemned to a lifelong program of wilful resistance to his defective nature" (311). Though William had moved well beyond nineteenth-century notions of degeneracy by the time he published *Varieties of Religious Experience* in 1902, the most famous portions of that work, devoted to "the Sick Soul," reveal a palpable terror of an insane diathesis. Thirty years had passed between William's alleged encounter with an epileptic idiot at a local asylum and his report of that incident in 1902, an account he attributed to a depressed French correspondent. The anecdote has lost none of the poignancy of a personal experience, perhaps because William himself spent time as a patient at McLean's Asylum in 1867 or thereabout (Townsend, 43):

> Simultaneously there arose in my mind the image of an epileptic patient whom I had seen in the asylum, a black-haired youth with greenish skin, entirely idiotic, who used to sit all day on one of the benches, or rather shelves against the wall, with his knees drawn up to his chin, and the coarse gray undershirt, which was his only garment, drawn over them inclosing his entire figure. He sat there like a sort of sculptured Egyptian cat or Peruvian mummy, moving nothing but his black eyes and looking absolutely non-human. This image and my fear entered into a species of combination with each other. *That shape am I*, I felt, potentially. Nothing that I possess can defend me against that fate, if the hour for it should strike for me as it struck for him. There was such a horror of him, and such a perception of my own merely momentary discrepancy from him, that it was as if something hitherto solid within my breast gave way entirely, and I became a mass of quivering fear. (*WWJ* 15: 134)

In *Disease and Representation*, Sander Gilman contends that William's "Sick Soul" resembles a case of "masturbatory insanity." Gilman also likens William's depiction of the alleged epileptic to a plate in Esquirol's famous 1838 work on mental illness, which contained full-length portraits (76). Certainly William's figure, clothed in a coarse gray undershirt and seated on a shelf with his knees drawn up against his chin, assumed an identical posture. Moreover, the greenish cast of the idiot's skin links William's figure to nineteenth-century representations of masturbators: the skin "acquires a yellowish, leaden hue" (Cohen, 47). Finally, epileptic insanity was frequently described as the most serious consequence of "self-abuse," as it was then called.[7] Since "the Sick Soul" was originally conceived as one segment of a longer presentation on religious despondency delivered under the auspices of the Gifford Lectures on Religion at the University of Edinburgh from 1901 to 1902, James undoubtedly wished to avoid an "overtly autobiographical" presentation, as Gilman suggests (76).

Throughout the 1860s, William struggled with his melancholy and hypochondria; he was incapacitated in turns by visual disturbances, digestive disorders, back pain, and general malaise. One may infer from William's letters that he contemplated suicide in 1867. At the same time, William prayed fervently for an ennobling practical calling that might rouse him from his lucubrations and raise him from his sickbed. Shame appears to have been the subtext of William's self-exhortations to a kind of deliberate sublimation: "Through a knowledge of the fact that that enjoyment on the whole depends on what individuals accomplish, lead a life so active, and so sustained by a clean-conscience as not to need to fret much"; "But I really don't think it so *all*-important what our occupation is, so long as we do it respectably and keep a clean bosom" (*CWJ* 4: 248, 247). William's reflections on moral hygiene should be read in light of nineteenth-century descriptions of sexual neurasthenia and masturbatory insanity. Samuel Tissot's 1758 text on onanism inaugurated a booming market for publications of this kind. William Acton's *The Functions and Disorders of the Reproductive Organs* was widely available after its publication in 1857, and his ideas were rapidly disseminated by boarding school administrators, priests, and doctors, as Ed Cohen explains: "As the topic of frequent sermons, lectures, advice sessions, and disciplinary actions, masturbation became a primary focus for the enactment of pedagogical authority over middle-class adolescent boys" (44). In William's case, the drive for self-control and clean living appears to have been internally generated, but it also stemmed from terrifying medical and popular reports on the consequences of self-abuse. William's malaise, inanition, indigestion, and lack of concentration are all symptoms of what was then termed sexual neurasthenia. As an invalid given to solitary contemplation and bed rest, he was a prime candidate for this "vice."

William's lamentations about his listlessness and want of purpose are quite illuminating: "But my habits of mind have been so bad that I feel as if the greater part of the past 10 years had worse than wasted, and now have so little surplus of physical vigor as to shrink from trying to retrieve them. Too late! too late!" (*CWJ* 4: 225). What hope did science hold out to this young medical student who had enfeebled himself by recklessly expending his vital store of nervous energy [seminal fluid]? Self-discipline (and failing that, mechanical measures sold by quacks such as rings with sharp teeth for preventing erections, masturbation drawers, manacles, and potions) was the obvious remedy: "Man is distinguished from the brute by his self-control. Let him bear this fact in mind and raise himself above the animals by a determined effort of the will. Pure thoughts, and chaste associations, vigorous physical exercise and a resolute effort to act a manly part will always be successful" (Dana, "Clinical Lecture," 245). By 1873 William had recovered from his depression and declared himself "restored to sanity" (*LWJ* 1: 169). Henry Senior wrote to Henry Junior, transcribing William's account of the reasons for his improved outlook. The two most significant were his acceptance of French philosopher Charles Renouvier's doctrine of the freedom of the will and his rejection of the notion that all mental disorder is produced by physical catalysts. In addition, William's 1874 reading of Maudsley's *Responsibility in Mental Disease* strengthened his one real hope, that through self-control and willpower he could halt his decline into madness: "But an opposite course of regeneration of the family by happy marriages, wise education, and a prudent conduct of life is possible; the downward tendency may be thus checked, even effaced in time" (Maudsley, 300–1).

Henry Junior was in America from April 1870 through May of 1873, and he observed William's breakdown firsthand. In October of 1873, William visited Henry in Rome. At this time, William very likely expounded his views on the means to health and sanity to his brother, whom he was in the habit of advising on such matters. In 1869 William, the budding physician, had counseled Henry on his constipation; in May of 1873, Henry's gastrointestinal problems had resurfaced. William evidently thought that Henry was a hypochondriac like himself. In 1869 William diagnosed Henry's back ailment as "dorsal insanity" (*CWJ* 1: 82). William would not have been Henry's only source of the doctrine of willpower and abstinence. In *Henry James and the "Woman Business,"* Alfred Habegger provides a somewhat distorted picture of the paterfamilias: "Evidently Henry James, Sr., had a dream of what used to be called free love" (31). It is true he once wrote a letter to the editor of the *Nation* condemning marriage as presently administered in society as a "hotbed of fraud, adultery, and cruelty, . . . the parent consequently of our existing lasciviousness and prostitution," but his hyperbole served different ends than those Habegger (and Henry Senior's contemporaries) attributed to him (366). Henry Senior meant to decry the hypocrisy and iniquity of socially sanctioned relations between the sexes. Although Henry Senior had the reputation of a nonconformist and sexual libertine, he certainly exposed his boys to the gospels of chastity and self-control, very likely because he regretted his own youthful indiscretions, which included inebriety, gambling, and licentiousness. In a letter to his son Robertson that he wrote during the Civil War, Henry Senior advised that he "avoid all impure intercourse with the other sex; I mean all intercourse with impure people. And in your intercourse with pure women study to do nothing and say nothing and feel nothing but what would elevate them in their own self respect" (Maher, 74). Of all the James boys, Bob showed the greatest inclination to follow in his father's footsteps. In the 1870s, Henry Senior sensed that Robertson, though superficially stable, married, and pious, was sorely tempted by drink and extramarital affairs: "It would kill me if one of my boys, especially you, turned out an unkind husband, or a base man" (Maher, 128).

Whether Henry received this advice directly from his father and brother or indirectly from advice books, advertisements, and school chums, he surely heard it. As Charles Rosenberg explains in "Sexuality, Class and Role in 19th-Century America," from the 1830s on self-control, the need to repress childhood and adolescent sexuality, became issues of paramount importance in America (137). In "Late-Victorian Sexual Respectability and the Social System," Peter Cominos argues that Victorian men were socialized to conform to a program of "strict and extreme continence" and "exaggerated asceticism" (220). Masturbation was decried as the cause of impotence, sexual neurasthenia, immorality, madness, and failure in professional and business pursuits. In "The Spermatic Economy and Proto-Sublimation," G. J. Barker-Benfield summarizes the content of Victorian advice books such as *The Student's Manual*, which warned against the enervating effects of masturbation owing to the loss of vital fluids and recommended tonics, stimulants, exercise, and cold showers as methods for controlling the base impulse to self abuse (175). This doctrine would have found fertile soil in Henry James, for he was profoundly troubled in his sexuality. Moreover, as Cominos has observed, the respectable sexual ideology pitted "the inferior sexual emotions" against their superiors—reason, duty, and success (246). If masturbatory insanity was the big stick enforcing compliance with codes of respectable behavior, success was a rather large carrot proffered for the same ends.

Nevertheless, I would argue that Henry's fears of psychological, physical, and moral disintegration carried greater weight in his renunciation of physical passion. Feinstein has characterized Henry and William's early relationship as a "psychological twinship" (230). In spite of their strongly individual natures, their divergent career paths, and their increasing alienation from each other over the years, they remained closely identified. In 1901 William spent the better part of five months at his brother's home, Lamb House, working on a draft of *Varieties of Religious Experience*, in which his account of "the Sick Soul" appeared for the first time. According to John Auchard, "in conversation, in draft, in composition, and in final published form, *Varieties of Religious Experience* was perhaps the work of his brother which Henry James knew on most intimate terms" (96–97). William's remarkable statement, "*that shape am I*, I felt, potentially. Nothing that I possess can defend me against that fate, if the hour for it should strike for me as it struck for him," had tremendous resonance for Henry. In 1908 this remark served Henry as the donnée for one of his greatest stories, "The Jolly Corner," in which Spencer Brydon returns to his childhood home and stalks the spirit of what might have been, which is none other than the repressed "*alter-ego* deep down somewhere within [him], as the full-blown flower is in the small tight bud" (*NYE* 17: 449). Brydon expects to discover in his alternate self merely a capacity for business and worldly concerns. He considers himself the dissolute twin: "I've not been edifying—I believe I'm thought in a hundred quarters to have been barely decent. I've followed strange paths and worshiped strange gods" (450). Spencer Brydon is effectively the second coming of Mark Ambient. In Brydon we have another aesthete, who in spite of his "surrender to sensations" leads a perfectly decent life, who is homosocial rather than homosexual (456). Significantly, Brydon is horrified to discover that he is the pair's better half, and so he denies fraternity with the figure that confronts him at the tale's end: "Such an identity fitted his at *no* point, made its alternative monstrous" (477). It is precisely because his alter ego represents exactly what Brydon should have come to had he lived a fuller life that he disowns it. Here we have Jekyll and Hyde all over again:

> The stranger, whoever he might be, evil, odious, blatant, vulgar, had advanced as for aggression, and he knew himself to give ground. Then harder pressed still, sick with the force of his shock, and falling back as under the hot breath and the roused passion of a life larger than his own, a rage of personality before which his own collapsed, he felt the whole vision turn to darkness and his very feet give way. His head went round; he was going; he had gone. (477)

To some degree James's response to Wilde ("unclean beast") may be read as a protest against the perception of "the merely momentary discrepancy" between them. It bears noting that the distinction between the homosexual and homosocial in "The Jolly Corner" hinges on the notion of diachronic existence. It is not the person but the time and place that determine the advent of the beast: "I just transferred him to the climate, that blighted him for once and for ever" (449). As we have seen, suppressing sexual impulses was considered the only means of keeping this beastly self at bay. Like "The Beast in the Jungle" (1903), "The Jolly Corner" is replete with Bengal tigers, great bears, and monstrous stealthy cats waiting to spring upon the unwary, just as Brydon's double pounces on him with "the hot breath and the roused passion of a life larger than his own." This trope, which links anomalous or hypersexuality with degeneracy, had currency in James's day. In *La Bête Humaine* of 1890, Zola described the atavistic blood lust of Jacques Lantier as a "wild beast inside him" (66). In *Vandover and the Brute*, written in 1895 but unpublished until 1914, Frank Norris revisited Spencer Brydon's confrontation with his monstrous alter ego:

> He had been lured into a mood where he was himself at his very best, where the other Vandover, the better Vandover, drew apart with eyes

turned askance, looking inward and downward into the depths of his own character, shuddering, terrified. Far down there in the darkest, lowest places he had seen the brute, squat, deformed, hideous. . . . For now at last it was huge, strong, insatiable, swollen and distorted out of all size, grown to be a monster, glutted yet still ravenous, some fearful bestial satyr, grovelling, perverse, horrible beyond words. (159)

In his memoirs, Symonds described his thwarted lust in similar terms: "Oftentimes the beast within roars angrily for that its hunger was not satiated" (127). And Vernon Lee employed this figure of speech in an 1884 diary entry in which she meditated on the critical hue and cry provoked by *Miss Brown*: "Am I not perhaps mistaking that call of the beast for the call of God; may there not, at the bottom of this seemingly scientific, philanthropic, idealising, decidedly noble-looking nature of mine, lie something base, dangerous, disgraceful that is cozening me?" (cited in Gunn, 105–6). In "The Mark of the Beast" (1913), Henry's friend, the author Rudyard Kipling, combined sexual anomalousness with traits of uncleanliness and atavism in his description of "the leper," as if to strain a point, for lepers were conventionally linked to sexually transmitted diseases: "He mewed hideously, and even through my riding-boots I could feel that his flesh was not the flesh of a clean man" (302).

For most of his life, James went out of his way to avoid this fate, sealing himself off from physical intimacy and consoling himself with pen-and-ink fantasies: "During the earlier London years there had hung over [James] a sort of canopy, a mixture of reserve and deprecation, faintly darkening the fullness of communion with his character; there always had seemed to be something indefinably non-conductive between him and those in whom he had most confidence" (Gosse, 2: 29). After twenty-five years of friendship, James still came across as "a fountain sealed" to his close friend Gosse, who suspected that "life stirred his intellect while leaving his senses untouched" (2: 34). It is noteworthy that Gosse himself employed the figure of the "wild beast" when he wrote of his secret passion for other men in 1890: "I have reached a quieter time—some beginnings of that Sophoclean period when the wild beast dies. He is not dead, but tamer; I understand him and the trick of his claws. . . . And the curious thing is that it is precisely to this volcanic force, ever on the verge of destructive ebullition, that one owes the most beautiful episodes of existence, exquisite in all respects" (Thwaite, 195). In "The Beast in the Jungle," James expressed his tragic sense of what he, like John Marcher, had "insanely missed" by failing to discover that the beast was a figure of love and beauty as well as destructive ebullition:

> The sight that had just met his eyes named to him, as in letters of quick flame, something he had utterly, insanely missed, and what he had missed made these things a train of fire, made them mark themselves in an anguish of inward throbs. He had seen *outside* of his life, not learned it within. . . . It hadn't come to him, the knowledge, on the wings of experience; it had brushed him, jostled him, upset him, with the disrespect of chance, the insolence of accident. Now that the illumination had begun, however, it blazed to the zenith, and what he presently stood there gazing at was the sounded void of his life. (*NYE* 17: 124–25)

Breakdown and Recovery

In 1899 James fell in love with the sculptor Hendrik Anderson, a man thirty years his junior who hoped the infatuated novelist would champion his work or, at the very least, introduce him to a rich American patron of the arts. James's letters to Anderson are a gold mine, for they provide irrefutable evidence of James's homoerotic inclinations. Flirting with Anderson, James even played the part of the big bad wolf: "What an arch-Brute you must, for a long time past, have thought me! But I am not really half the monster I appear"; "What a cold-blooded Brute my interminable silence must have made you think me!" (*HJL* 4: 187, 268). James was not able to sustain this pose for any length of time, primarily because Anderson remained out of reach both emotionally and physically: "Don't 'chuck' me this year, dearest boy, if you can possibly help it" (4: 269). Of all James's young men (Joukowsky, Persse, Walpole, Sturges, Fullerton), Anderson appeared the most capable of surmounting the barriers James had erected to physical intimacy, had the sculptor been so inclined. Sarotte has appropriated the truly momentous passage in their correspondence for the title of his book, *Like a Brother, Like a Lover*. After Hendrik's brother, Andreas, died, James wrote to console him: "I return to Rye April 1rst, and sooner or later to *have* you there and do for you, to put my arm round you and *make* you lean on me as on a brother and a lover, and keep you on and on, slowly comforted or at least relieved of the first bitterness of pain—this I try to imagine and as thinkable, attainable, not wholly out of the question" (4: 226).

During the early years of their acquaintance, while James presumably considered whether sexual intercourse was "thinkable, attainable, not wholly out of the question" for himself, he began to complain of gastrointestinal distress, a problem that had not plagued him so persistently for thirty years. In *Three Essays on the Theory of Sexuality*, Freud argued that many neurotic symptoms, which have their basis in sexual conflicts, surface in nonsexual somatic dysfunctions: "The retention of the faecal mass, which is thus carried out intentionally by the child to begin with, in order to serve, as it were, as a masturbatory stimulus upon the anal zone . . . is also one of the roots of the constipation which is so common among neuropaths" (7: 104). Although I am uneasy with the ramifications of diagnosing James's constipation as suppressed anal erotism, I do see the relevance of Freud's articulation of symptom formation. The language of hypochondria (both somatic and literary) figures prominently in Henry's correspondence with his brother. Throughout 1869 Henry regaled William with the most intimate details of his illness, describing a proctological examination, bowel movements, piles, enemas, and the like to his keen auditor. Heralding the end of Henry's "moving intestinal drama" (*CWJ* 1: 127), William's letters reached a pitch of urgency and euphoria difficult to write off as the "enthusiasm of a neophyte physician and the compassion of a fellow sufferer" (Feinstein, 229). Extolling the "wonderful effect" of electricity, William might have been singing the praises of "masochistic *jouissance*" (Bersani, "Sexuality and Aesthetics," 41) when he urged Henry to insert one pole of an electrical battery into his rectum and apply a "strong galvanic current" (*CWJ* 1: 113). Whether Henry's costiveness and diarrhea represented the conversion of homosexual fantasies focused on the anus as an erogenous zone into somatic symptoms, his wordplay connected with these symptoms is certainly suggestive. In a letter to Anderson he wrote: "So I've pulled through—and am out—and surprisingly soon—of a very deep dark hole. *In* my deep hole, how I thought yearningly, helplessly, dearest Boy, of *you* as your last letter gives you to me and as I take you, to my heart" (*HJL* 4: 227). Wooing Anderson, James pictures himself at the base of his own bowel, yearning for his absent friend—a clear, if unintentional, conflation of disease and desire. And this is not a unique instance. Critiquing a pair of cooly disposed lovers, a recent addition to Anderson's "great nude army," James advised: "So keep at *that*—at the flesh and the devil and the rest of it; make the creatures palpitate, and their flesh tingle and flush, and their internal economy proceed, and their bellies ache and their bladders fill—all in the mystery of your art" (4: 394). In this scheme, indigestion seems to be commensurate with sexual ecstasy.

In 1904 James had adopted the practice of chewing his food to a pulp in the interests of losing weight and conquering his gastritis and constipation. Later he blamed this "Fletcherizing" for half starving him to death and for sinking him into despondency (Holly, 68–73). Early in 1910, Henry James suffered a nervous breakdown with all the trimmings, which for him included a "marked increase of a strange and most persistent and depressing stomachic crisis" (*HJL* 4: 547). William and his wife arrived in April 1910 and helped Henry through the darkest stages of his depression. Henry's terror of solitude was so great that Mrs. William James, at her husband's urging, stayed on with Henry at Lamb House while William traveled to Paris in search of relief for his own ailment, angina. By August 1910, William was on his deathbed and Henry was well on his way to recovery (Kaplan, 525–31). Scholars attribute James's depression to many precipitating factors, among them wounded vanity (his New York Edition had not sold well), loneliness (he was isolated at Rye), and the loss of loved ones. It is my opinion that James's unrequited love for Anderson was the principal cause of his illness. Long resigned to the sacrifice of sexual intimacy in the name of aesthetic sublimation and its compensations, James broke down when the sustaining myths of his life were swept aside by the hot gust of passion he felt for Anderson. For what lurking beast of congenital degeneration and sexual perversion had emerged to settle him at the end? Like John Marcher and Spencer Brydon, he had grown old without ever having really lived. If the late stories may be taken as evidence, in his late sixties James faced the "sounded void of his life" and prepared to jump at any chance of love. But it was too late; he was too old; he was not wanted. And James could not bear to drain this bitter cup to the lees, to acknowledge the futility of having sacrificed his passion in order to enable art and defer the nervous crisis that had afflicted his family members. In a sense James's nervous breakdown saved him from the unbearable self-knowledge that John Marcher acquired, for it confirmed James's whole cautious plan of existence. The beast had jumped after all.

During the fall of 1910 and the winter of 1911, James had four therapeutic conversations with the distinguished American neurologist James Jackson Putnam, one of William's closest and oldest friends and an early convert to psychoanalysis. Though James was out of the darkest patch of his depression by this time, Putnam may have helped him find the courage to carry on. In his correspondence with William, Putnam conceded that Freud's "terribly searching psycho-genetic explanations correspond only to one pole of human life, and that there is another pole in which he takes no interest," the moral sphere (cited in Hale, 79). In a series of letters spanning 1909 to 1911, Putnam encouraged Freud to expand the charter of the analyst: "Our psychopathic patients need, I think, something more than simply to learn to know themselves. If there are reasons why they should adopt higher views of their obligations as based on the belief that this is a morally conceived universe, and that 'free-will' has a real meaning, then these reasons ought to be made known to them" (95). Putnam's determination to wrest the concept of sublimation from Freud's grasp and to appropriate the term for his own elevated purposes amused Freud, who never tired of tweaking the American moralist:

> What would you have us do when a woman complains about her thwarted life, when, with youth gone she notices that she has been deprived of the joy of loving for merely conventional reasons? She is quite right, and we stand helpless before her, for we cannot make her young again. But the recognition of our therapeutic limitations reinforces our determination to change other social factors so that men and women shall no longer be forced into hopeless situations. (91)

In this excerpt, Freud has unwittingly described James's predicament to a nicety. Yet Putnam's meliorism, his quest for a higher moral synthesis, may have served James better than the talking cure. In praising free will and duty, Putnam echoed the precepts of the late William James, serving as an amanuensis for the philosopher-brother who had once written: "So that it seems to me that a sympathy with men as such, and a desire to contribute to the weal of a species, wh., whatever may be said of it, contains *All* that we acknowledge as good, may very well form an external interest sufficient to keep one's moral pot boiling in a very lively manner to a good old age" (*CWJ* 4: 250). Henry was ripe to hear Putnam's morally uplifting message, reminding him as it did that he might count on his brother William's wisdom to the last: "He had an inexhaustible authority for me, and I feel abandoned and afraid, even as a lost child. But he is a possession, of real magnitude, and I shall find myself still living upon him to the end" (*HJL* 4: 562). Shortly after his sessions with Putnam, James recovered his ability to work, which he described as "an unspeakable aid and support and blessing" (4: 596). Surely the strangest passage in James's history owes something to Putnam's ethic. Following the outbreak of World War I, Henry threw himself into the Allied effort with an energy and conviction that surprised his friends and acquaintances. He visited hospitals and refugee camps, supported the American Volunteer Ambulance Corps, and even wrote articles for war charities (Rosenzweig, 450–52). In short, this formerly exclusive aesthete contributed to the "weal of the species" in a highly practical and public manner. James's formal adoption of British nationality, conceived as a rebuke to the American government's isolationist policy, was also altruistic. Striking a pose worthy of Wilde, James compared his defection to that of "Martin Luther at Wittenburg" (*HJL* 4: 771).

James's history supports the conclusions of contemporary theorists such as Carole-Anne Tyler who question the liberatory potential of gender inversion (in Fuss, 51–58). James never really escaped the circuit of compulsory (dis)identification with the object of desire. He allowed the culture he inhabited to interpret his effeminacy for him as one of the stigmata of degeneracy. Yet James willingly sacrificed the penis-phallus. What benefit did he accrue from this gesture? It may be said that in this way James overthrew the regime of genital supremacy and was thus free to lead a polymorphously perverse imaginative existence. Tragically, James aborted his personal struggle with flesh and the devil just as it was getting underway, but his autobiography, correspondence, and fiction preserve a record of passion in "letters of quick flame."

William James on Energy and Entropy

Henry James's novel *Roderick Hudson* (1875) reanimates the James family squabbles of the late 1850s and early 1860s, when William struggled to convince his discouraging father that an art career would do him no harm: "I could not *fully* make out from yr. talk there what were *exactly* the causes of your disappointment at my late resolve, what your view of the nature of art was, that the idea of my devoting myself to it should be so repugnant to you" (*CWJ* 4: 39–40). Although *Roderick Hudson* fulfills Henry Senior's admonition concerning the spiritual dangers of the aesthetic life, the novel's presentation of the agonistic relation between art and morality is more censorious and utilitarian than anything Henry Senior espoused: "The Artist is merely the aboriginal ditcher refined into the painter, poet, or sculptor. Art is not the gush of God's life into every form of spontaneous speech and act" (*HJSr*, 84). Instead the novel paraphrases William's hygienic proscriptions and his warnings to his brother Henry not to pursue a taxing creative life in the early 1870s, and it anticipates the discourses published late in William's career, "The Gospel of Relaxation" and "The Energies of Men," for which William is justly considered a patron of scientific management. Commiserating with Thomas Ward over the difficulty of choosing a profession in 1866, William brought the mental-hygiene ethos to bear on the problem of self-actualization: "I am conscious of a desire I never had before so strongly or so permanently, of narrowing and deepening the channel of my intellectual activity, of economising my feeble energies & consequently treating with more *respect* the few things I shall devote them to" (*CWJ* 4: 137). Before turning to a discussion of Henry's novel, I mean first to establish the ambivalent authority of Henry James Senior over his sons in their choice of professions and to elaborate the key concepts of William's thought that were transformed and recast by the novelist.

Henry Senior's urgency that William elect a scientific career was partly informed by his philosophical distaste for the artist as society constructed him: "It is melancholy to see the crawling thing which society christens Art, and feeds into fawning sycophancy. It has no other conception of Art than as polished labor, labor stripped of its jacket and apron, and put into parlor costume" (*HJSr*, 84). Ralph Barton Perry was undoubtedly right in his claim that "James's disparagement of art expressed his sense of the overwhelming importance of religion. This, I take it, underlay his reiterated opinion that art was too 'narrowing'—literature, or any other art is so much less than life!" (1: 134). Certainly William understood his father to derogate the spiritual vacuity and egotism of his chosen vocation, for these were the terms in which he rebutted his father's views; unfortunately, Henry Senior's part in the exchange must be surmised from his son's responses because many of his letters are lost. "I do not see why a man's spiritual culture should not go on independently of his esthetic activity, why the power which an artist feels in himself should tempt him to forget what he is, any more than the power felt by a Cuvier or Fourier would tempt them to do the same" (*CWJ* 4: 40). William's rejoinder was ingenious, shifting the burden of proof to his father to reveal how the scientific calling ministered more efficiently to man's spiritual needs.

No satisfactory explanation of Henry Senior's preference has ever been set down: "I had always counted upon a scientific career for Willy, and I hope the day may even yet come when my calculations may be realized in this regard" (Perry, 1: 191). It seems fatuous to suggest that he saw himself encouraging his seventeen-year-old son's predilection for a field in which he had demonstrated a rare capacity; however, William had declared his interest in science on more than one occasion.[1] Descanting on the social arrangements that made it impossible to pursue anything but a practical and remunerative profession in America, William indicated that in a better organized society, astronomy and natural history would be the arts he would study.

> If I followed my taste and did what was most agreeable to me, I'll tell you what I would do. I would get a microscope and go out into the country, into the dear old woods and fields and ponds—there I would try to make as many discoveries as possible,—and I'll be kicked if I would not be more useful than if I laid out railroads by rules which others had made and which I had learned from them. (*CWJ* 4: 14)

William's letter to Edgar Beach Van Winkle is imbued with the spirit of utopian socialism. Although he does not mention Fourier by name, James's vision of a society in which all material needs are met, in which individuals pursue specialized tasks according to their enthusiasms and aptitudes, and in which "the duty of everyone [is] to do as much good as possible" is styled on phalanstery, a mode of life dear to Henry Senior's notion of human progress. Indeed William not only understood his father's partiality for science but he had, until quite later on, sympathized with its most idealistic elements.

Henry Senior had the highest regard for the sciences, which were at that time, with the radical brio a Fourierist brought to social questions, debunking the myths cherished by the pettifogging clerics: "My sole hope for humanity is that men will go on more and more to such a complete obedience of their natural instincts, that all our futile old rulers, civil and religious, will grow so bewildered as to abandon their thrones and leave the coast clear to scientific men" (Perry, 1: 192). Henry Senior was not the dull-witted enthusiast that his biographer, Habegger, made him out to be; he undoubtedly recognized that the emergence of the physical sciences threatened to overthrow Christian cosmogony.[2] Well before Darwin's *The Origin of the Species* was published, the geologist Charles Lyell had refuted the mosaic chronology, which depicted the earth as no more than a few thousand years old, and dispelled scientific credence in the Noachian flood.[3] In 1830 Louis Agassiz, who was to figure prominently in William's education, unveiled his glacial theory, an alternative to the biblical version of worldwide devastation.

Habegger confused Henry Senior's search for a moral plan for the universe with intellectually backward theories such as creationism.

In *Becoming William James*, Feinstein argues that William was caving in to paternal pressure (which he claims consisted of verbal and implicit suicide threats) when he suddenly abandoned his artistic endeavors after six months in William Morris Hunt's Newport studios and opted for a scientific career in 1861 (141). Of all the accounts of Henry Senior's intervention written by biographers who covered this period in detail—Perry, Gay Wilson Allen, and Daniel Bjork—Feinstein's is the most lurid and compelling. If Feinstein overstates the enmity between his principals, he makes up for it in his ability to intuitively feel his way into William's experience and to articulate his impotent rage and despair. Steeling himself against William's plea that his "life would be embittered" were he kept from art, Henry Senior clearly put the screws on William to choose another vocation (*CWJ* 4: 40):

> Willy especially felt, we thought, a little too much attraction to painting—as I suppose, from the contiguity to Mr. Hunt; let us break that up, we said, at all events. I hoped that his career would be a scientific one, as I thought and still think that the true bent of his genius was towards the acquisition of knowledge: and to give up this hope without a struggle, and allow him to tumble down into a mere painter, was impossible. (Perry 1: 192)

So much is made of Henry Senior's deprecation of painting, however, that the nuances of his viewpoint have been lost. The phrase "a mere painter" underlines Perry's observation that Henry Senior disdained any life plan that would prove too narrow. Henry Senior furiously resisted William's neurasthenic outlook and his pragmatic impulse to avoid personal and professional challenges, a tendency that emerged sometime in 1859 when he began to complain of ill health and that intensified in the following years. Throughout his twenties, William used his illness to shirk responsibilities, from the home front to the battlefield: "The prospective burden of a wife and family being taken off my shoulders simultaneously with the placing of this 'mild yoke' upon the small of my back, relieves me from imminent *material* anxiety" (*CWJ* 4: 302). William's defection from the art field remains a rich source for conjecture. Perhaps his daily congress with John La Farge, ten years his senior and destined for greatness, took the glint out of his eye:

William did not want to be second-rate. "There is nothing on earth more deplorable than a bad artist" (Perry, 1: 193).

Feinstein interprets William's inflammatory eye disease, from which he suffered in around 1865, as a delayed hysterical response to paternal coercion (108). Therefore, it bears noting that Henry Senior expressed similar objections to a scientific career once William's positivist bent manifested itself: "Now here it seems to me is exactly where you are as yet intellectually: in this scientific or puerile stage of progress," which could not transcend its fixation on observable phenomena and was, in consequence, "stupefied by the giant superstition we call Nature" (*CWJ* 4: 204–5). Such passages tend to confirm the view, pace Feinstein, that Henry Senior scorned a purely scientific career. He had thwarted William's artistic leaning in the interests of furthering his genius, and he was also not content to see William become a mere technician of science: "If I were able by assiduous pottering to define a few physiological facts however humble I shd. feel I had not lived entirely in vain" (4: 302). Writing to inform Henry of his brother's improved outlook in 1873, Henry Senior commended William for "shaking off his respect for men of mere science as such" and for becoming "even more universal and impartial in his mental judgments than I have known him before" (*LWJ* 1: 170). Pronouncements of this type incense biographer Bjork, whose contempt for Henry Senior disfigures his otherwise impressive portrait of William's youth, an account that is particularly valuable as a corrective to Feinstein's willful obtuseness on the question of William's scientific proclivities. Bjork maintains that William manifested no impatience with scientific study, no urgency to return to art school. Unfortunately, Bjork goes to the other extreme, dismissing Henry Senior's advocacy as a factor in his son's decision to enter the Lawrence Scientific School[4]:

> Visiting the James household must have required new intellectual diplomacy. The elder James must have seemed a relic of the transcendental past—a quaint, metaphysically obscure fellow, far out of step with the times, and not to be taken too seriously. Indeed, William was now clearly on a life course which would almost surely take him far from his father's expectations, both in terms of career and fundamental beliefs. (51–52)

Feinstein and Bjork cannot both be right, and acceding to the latter's view means reducing the chief influence in William's life to someone heckling a celebrity from the bleachers. Yet this is not how William characterized his relationship with his father: "Yours is still for me the central figure. All my intellectual life I derive from you; and though we have often seemed at odds in the expression thereof, I'm sure there's a harmony somewhere, and that our strivings will combine" (*LWJ* 1: 219). I am of Erik Erikson's mind that William's identity crisis stemmed from his not having sufficiently separated from his father and that his rage arose from his need to establish himself as a separate entity, but also I do not want to lose sight of William's affection for and devotion to Henry Senior (150–55). His father's paternal authority was both benevolent and exacting, and it is this mixture that made William's path in the 1860s so tortuous: "Having such a Father with us how can we be other than in some measure worthy of him though not perhaps as eminently so as the distance leads his fond heart to imagine" (*CWJ* 4: 37). I do not mean to diminish the vehemence of the ongoing struggle and philosophic debate that took place between William and Henry Senior but to shift the emphasis from the type of pursuit (aesthetic or practical) to the issues of identity, separation, and individuation.

Doubtless, in the early stage of his long and drawn-out vocational crisis, William held his father responsible for tearing him away from his first love—art. Sketching a prospectus of his academic life over the next few years in 1861, William baited his parents with a forecast of the unhappy results ensuing from their mandate: "Thus: 1 year Study Chemistry, then spend one term at home, then 1 year with Wyman [Anatomy], then a medical education, then 5 or 6 years with Agassiz, then probably death, death, death with inflation and plethora of knowledge. This you had better seriously consider" (4: 52). By 1869 William had completed his medical education and fallen into a funk about his prospects, but this time philosophy was the siren luring him away from a practical profession. Culling a suggestive phrase from William's 1880 address, "Great Men and Their Environment," Feinstein dramatizes William's abandonment of art as a type of self-murder (117). Substituting an intrapsychic context for William's paean to human adaptability or "the power of individual initiative," Feinstein discounts the evidence that William eventually became reconciled to his fortune in spite of a momentary wistfulness:

> Little by little, the habits, the knowledges, of the other career, which once lay so near, cease to be reckoned even among his possibilities. At first, he may sometimes doubt whether the self he murdered in that de-

cisive hour might not have been the better of the two; but with the years such questions themselves expire, and the old alternative *ego*, once so vivid, fades into something less substantial than a dream. (*WWJ* 6: 171)

It is not surprising that Feinstein's study trails off just where mine begins, because William expressed surprisingly little regret over the eclipse of his painting career once his scientific education was fully under way. He scarcely mentioned art to anyone other than Henry: "But I envy ye the world of art. Away from it, as we live, we sink into a flatter, blanker kind of consciousness, and indulge in an ostrichlike forgetfulness of all our richest potentialities— and they startle us now and then when by accident some rich human product, pictorial, literary, or architectural slaps us with its tail" (*CWJ* 1: 165). With the complete record before us, we can see that the novelist was largely responsible for the collective impression that William was some kind of artistic genius. Fifty years after William had closed the door to Hunt's Newport studio and enrolled at the Lawrence Scientific School, Henry Junior captured him for posterity in a favorite attitude: "As I catch W. J.'s image, from far back, at its most characteristic, he sits drawing and drawing, always drawing, especially under the lamplight of the Fourteenth Street back parlour; and not as with a plodding patience, which I think would less have affected me, but easily, freely and, as who should say, infallibly" (*Autobiography*, 118). For a number of reasons, William's artistry was far more important to Henry than to William. In this chapter I aim to clarify how William's forays into biophysics and scientific psychology mutually informed the functionalist cast of his later philosophy and, more important, provided his brother Henry with a critical framework for working out a response to William's pathologization of the creative life.[5] Whereas Chapter 1 focused on the familial and medical dogmas of prudence fostering Henry and William's sexual panic, this chapter will be concerned with the influence of the mental-hygiene ethos on William's choice of career.

Mental Hygiene

Feinstein has done the most to illuminate the conventional nineteenth-century wisdom on neurasthenia, as elaborated by American physicians

(S. Weir Mitchell and George Miller Beard) and British psychologists (Alexander Bain, Herbert Spencer, and Henry Maudsley), that informed William's career dilemma. But Feinstein's thesis, that William's suppression of purportedly morbid interests (painting in 1860 to 1861 and philosophy in 1870) caused his neurasthenia, while these same bouts of nervous depression "saved" him from unwelcome career commitments (medicine in 1867 and physiology in 1873), tends to obscure the continuity in William's vocational plans once he began his scientific education (321–22). It is clear enough reading William's correspondence that he tired of chemistry within eighteen months of declaring himself enamored of it, required a six-month hiatus from his studies before settling on comparative anatomy, became anxious about the financial prospects of a naturalist and decided on a medical degree by default, interrupted his medical instruction to join Agassiz on an expedition to the Amazon, gave up zoology, earned a medical degree he never intended to use, and fell into a job teaching comparative anatomy and physiology at Harvard—all the while hoping to be offered a chair in philosophy.

In spite of his reluctance to settle on any special branch of scientific inquiry, William was genuinely interested in medicine, physiology, and experimental psychology, chiefly because they held the promise of a cure for his nervous complaints. At the same time, his studies encouraged his hypochondria: "We have no space to discuss the sources of the English prejudice in favor of psychical determinism. Every reader of Mill's *Autobiography* will remember the striking passage in which he narrates the hypochondria which this doctrine produced in his youthful mind" (*WWJ* 17: 323). William's letters are riddled with the medical cant of his day that proscribed morbid introspection and overwork. Because of the increased professionalism of all disciplines from the exact sciences to the humanities, higher education was singled out as taxing the resources of intellectuals, for creating "forcing house[s] for thought" (17: 74–75).[6] Grumbling about the "increasing wear and tear" of university life, William defended his divagations in Europe and his frequent recourse to health resorts as necessary precautions (*CWJ* 4: 254). He believed that vitality could be stored like capital, affording bursts of productive activity. William's career vacillations, punctuated by intervals of acute nervous distress too numerous to itemize, also suggest that he was temperamentally and physically unsuited to the active life of a nineteenth-century scientist, which consisted of laboratory work, exploration, and specimen gathering. Recognizing his poor health as an obstacle to glory in the laboratory or field, William had not yet found the proper niche in science for his speculative genius. Protesting that he was not ashamed to discover that he was "one of the very lightest of featherweights," William nonetheless drew an invidious comparison between himself and men of sterner mettle:

> You must know, dear Father, what I mean, tho' I can't must[er] strength of brain enough now to express myself with precision.—The grit & energy of some men are called forth by the resistance of the world. But as for myself I seem to have no spirit whatever of that kind, no pride wh. makes me ashamed to say "I can't do that." But I have a mental pride and shame, wh., altho' they seem more egotistical than the other kind, are still the only things that can stir my blood. These lines seem to satisfy me, altho' to many they wd. appear the height of indolence & contemptibleness (*CWJ* 4: 107).[7]

Whereas Feinstein subsumes William's performance anxiety under a broader conception of his neuroses, I think it is of paramount importance. The pressure to live up to his family's idealization of his abilities fueled William's depression and uncertainty. With a father pushing science as a vocation and a brother pulling for art—and neither one prepared to admit that the bent of William's genius lay in another direction—William was faced with insuperable obstacles to success. Whatever path he chose, he would disappoint someone. On top of that, to be the best at something, anything, was the sine qua non of William's character: "But I feel somehow now as if I had no right to an opinion on any subject, no right to open my mouth before others until I knew some *one* thing as thoroughly as it can be known, no matter how insignificant it may be" (4: 137). This factor, rather than his abiding attraction to painting or even philosophy was what made his career dilemma so vexing. However, William was motivated as well as hindered by his bruised self-image. He brooked no compromise in a quest for perfection that would help him recover the pristine conception of himself as a young Apollo. It broke his heart to picture himself "driving my physicking trade like any other tenth rate man" (4: 141).[8] In spite of Bjork's opinion that William was "poised to participate in what has been called the professionalization of American culture, the penchant for career development and expertise that would increasingly characterize the nineteenth-century educational world" (19), William was also hamstrung by the genteel tradition, which, along with Henry Senior's appeals to a higher nature, took a dim view of many of the emerging professions and despised material prosperity as an end in itself: "But I fear there might be some anguish in looking back from the pinnacle of prosperity (*necessarily* reached, if not by eating dirt, at least by renouncing some divine ambrosia) over the life you might have led in the pure pursuit of truth" (*CWJ* 4: 86).

Shortly before resigning his appointment to the Massachusetts General Hospital in March 1867, William expressed his distaste for the "ambitious young men" of Harvard Medical School "toadying the physicians" to get into the hospital and spoke ruefully of his own capacity for "fawning & flattery" (4: 148). Eschewing the competitive atmosphere of the college, William fled to Germany in April, where he became strangely preoccupied with the Jews, whom he unwittingly confounded with his recent nemeses, the careerists of Harvard. In 1867 at the University of Berlin William attended physiology lectures, which were conducted by Hermann von Helmholtz's colleague Emil du Bois-Reymond and "2 ambitious young jews"—eleven in all per week (4: 233). Riddled with anxiety about his career prospects and dubious of his fitness for scientific endeavor, William turned his self-loathing against the Jews, whom he thought demonstrated a preternatural gift for obtaining their goals whatever obstacles were placed in their path. Tolerant, if contemptuous, of the Jew who knew his place, "a real jewish looking jew, with a long robe, a goat's beard, and two little ringlets before his ears, like those I saw at Teplitz, is quite a stylish animal, with an harmonious and pronounced expression of his own," William frankly despised those who "put on all sorts of christian graces, wear nothing but whiskers, and have an unnatural & revolting aspect" (4: 214). Unencumbered by the embarrassment that caused his literary executors to drop these passages from his published letters, William recounted the antisemitic calumnies of his day without demur: "Jews are more numerous here than any where in Germany and are said to own most of the wealth & edit most of the newspapers" (4: 215).[9] Energetic and pragmatic, in William's view, the modern Jew has sloughed off the phlegmatic disposition of his orthodox counterpart who kept company with William at the spa at Teplitz.

In 1868 when William abandoned his cherished plan of studying with Helmholtz after a six-day trial despite extensive preparation, it was not, as

Feinstein conjectures, because William longed for philosophy (315): "The fact is that I am about as little fitted by nature to be a worker in science of any sort as any one can be, and yet in virtue of that great law of the Universe already alluded to, '*miscent quadrata rotundis*,' &c my only ideal of life is a scientific life. I should feel as if all value had departed fm. my life if convinced of *absolute* scientific impotence" (*CWJ* 4: 346). The rigors of this discipline, from both a technical and physical standpoint, proved an impediment to even modest success, as William recognized virtually from the outset. Writing from Berlin in 1867, William briefed Ward on his failure to take full advantage of the university. "There is a bully physiological laboratory, the sight of wh., inaccessible as it is to me in my present condition, gave me a sharp pang" (4: 226). The same frustration colored his report to Henry Bowditch: "The physiolog. lab. with its endless array of machinery, frogs, dogs, &c. &c. almost 'bursts my gizzard' when I go by it, with vexation" (4: 233). This was no idle protest. Even if William had not been afflicted with lower back pain, compounded by visual and digestive disorders, insomnia, and depression, he would not have been much use in a physiology laboratory circa 1867. He had indifferent skills as a chemist and he was no mathematician, two essential prerequisites for this line of research: "If I had been *drilled* further in mathematics, physics, Chemistry, logic, & the History of metaphysics, and had established, even if only in my memory, a firm and thoroughly familiar *basis* of knowledge in all these sciences, (like the basis of Human Anatomy one gets in studying medicine,) . . . I might be steadily advancing" (4: 225).

It is clear from his correspondence that William was most attracted to biophysics, a branch of physiology founded by Carl Ludwig, Bois-Reymond, Helmholtz, and Ernst Brucke, which was physicomathematical and chemicophysical in orientation: "The physiologists of Germany, devoid for the most part of any systematic bias, have, by their studies on the senses and the brain, really inaugurated a new era in this science" (*WWJ* 17: 296). The pathbreaking work of the 1847 biophysics program, which was ascendant in Germany through the early 1870s, included the demonstration of the electrical nature of nerve impulses and the measurement of their conduction velocity, the electrical and chemical study of muscular contraction, the articulation of the law of energy conservation and its implications for animal and muscle heat as well as forays into psychology and sensory physiology.[10] In addition to his pioneering work in the physiology of vision and the mechanics of hearing, Helmholtz studied the relation between sensation and cognition, a subject that was to preoccupy William in such essays as "The Feeling of Effort" (1880), "What is an Emotion" (1884), "The Consciousness of Lost Limbs" (1887), and "The Physical Basis of Emotion" (1894), among others.

Though William could not hope to follow Helmholtz into the laboratory, he certainly kept pace intellectually with the advances proclaimed by the hard scientists. William understood the originality and importance of the effort to explain all vital phenomena in terms of physics and chemistry. In 1869 he allied himself with the materialist outlook in a letter to Ward: "I'm swamped in an empirical philosophy—I feel that we are Nature through and through, that we are *wholly* conditioned, that not a wiggle of our will happens save as the result of physical laws, and yet notwithstanding we are en rapport with reason.—How to conceive it?" (*CWJ* 4: 370–71). William's confidence in the empirical method of observation and experiment was also influenced by his reading of Bain, Spencer, and Maudsley, scientific psychologists who described volition as a neurophysiological phenomenon and reduced consciousness to a passive process that serves the development of environmentally appropriate habits to ensure the survival of the individual.[11] Though the automatists gave scant recognition to the concept of self-determination, they agreed nonetheless that abstinence, sound habits, and conscientious breeding practices could stall the degeneration process—hence William's predilection for practical tasks as a bromide against depression and worse.

Following the advice of the English psychologists and their American counterparts, William assumed that healthy-mindedness and personal happiness consisted of man's reconciliation with the laws of nature crudely conflated with the demands of the social and physical environment. This ethos placed him in a quandary, because it vetoed all his natural inclinations. In 1868, struggling with paralysis of will brought on by the uncertainty of his career prospects and his attraction to yet another impractical calling—that of philosopher—William first sounded the strains of melioristic pragmatism; he had begun to internalize the prescriptions of mental hygiene and transcribe them into a language all his own:

> I confess that, in the lonesome gloom wh. beset me for a couple of months last summer, the only feeling that kept me from giving up was that by waiting and living by hook or crook long enough I might make

my *nick*, however small a one in the raw stuff the race has got to shape, and so assert my reality. The stoic feeling of being a sentinel obeying orders without knowing the General's plans is a noble one. And so is the divine enthusiasm of moral culture (Channing &c) and I think that successively they may all help to ballast the same man. (*CWJ* 4: 250)

The optimistic tone of the preceding paragraph belies William's mood at this juncture, which was anything but stoic and more like deeply despondent: "I am poisoned with Utilitarian venom, and sometimes when I despair of ever doing anything, say: 'why not step out into the green darkness?'" (4: 347). Caught in a web of self-doubt reinforced by cultural mandates, William held fast to a program of moral, mental, and physical self-reclamation until 1870, when, inspired by his study of Renouvier, he veered from determinism to voluntarism. However, William's newly professed faith in the freedom of the will did not instantly rout his conviction in biological determinism. For several years more, William attempted to reconcile these contradictory doctrines.

According to Henry Senior's account, it was not until 1873 that William "[gave] up the notion that all mental disorder requires to have a physical basis," a conclusion that appreciably diminished William's anxiety about his neuropathic heredity (*LWJ* 1: 169–70). Nevertheless, William recommended Maudsley's 1874 treatise on insanity and eugenics, *Responsibility in Mental Disease*, to nervous bridegrooms and to medical professionals (*WWJ* 17: 276–79). It appears that it was not until 1875 that William explicitly challenged a fundamental precept of scientific psychology, the theory of passive, observant, but nondirective consciousness: "Bain, and Spencer are so desperately bent on covering up all tracks of the mind's originality" (17: 301). In an 1878 review of "Spencer's Definition of Mind," William elaborated on his reservations: "In other words, there belongs to mind, from its birth upward, a spontaneity, a vote. It is in the game, and not a mere looker-on; and its judgments of the *should-be*, its ideals, cannot be peeled off from the body of the *cogitandum* as if they were excrescences, or meant, at most, survival" (5: 21). If Henry Senior had a catchword, it was *spontaneous*, which, in his idiom, stood for the "divine selfhood" freed from the transient concerns of subsistence or social life to delight in its own nature and interrelatedness with God (*HJSr*, 83). What I am suggesting is that Renouvier's role in William's epistemological break with biophysics and Darwinian science has been somewhat overstated, by none other than William himself. Long before William read Renouvier, Henry Senior had posited the existence of a moral plan for the universe that no mere physical truth could verify and had espoused a vitalistic philosophy completely at odds with mechanistic materialism.

In 1875 William reviewed *The Unseen Universe; or, Physical Speculations on a Future State*, published anonymously by Balfour Stewart and Peter Guthrie Tait, two physicists and scientific popularizers who relied on Joseph Larmor's new "electromagnetic conception of nature rooted in and unified by ether" to postulate an alternative to heat death (the dissipation of mechanical energy): an invisible universe created out of the dust, ether, and energy cast off by the material world (Wynne, in Barnes, 169). As exponents of the Cambridge school possessing strongly marked theological interests, the physicists expressed a faith in suprasensual ether as an all-unifying medium, and they quarreled with positivistic science, which refused to recognize phenomena that did not submit to precise measurement (171). Extolling the "imagination" and inveighing against the "'cowardly security' of empirical sense-data," the Cambridge group supported the cultivation of "the neglected borderlands between the branches of knowledge" (172). In effect, they were scientific pluralists. The intersections embraced by the Cambridge intellectuals in the early 1880s brought William into direct personal contact with Henry Sidgwick, Edmund Gurney, Frederick Myers, and William Barrett, founders of the Society for Psychical Research (Perry, 1: 593–610). According to Brian Wynne, the society challenged "materialist cosmology," touting vibrations and crepuscular phenomena as evidence of "the unseen world"; at the same time, from their upper-class social and institutional vantage point, they derided spiritualism for pandering to the lower ranks of society and for pretending to be a science (176–79). Attending a "*soirée* of Gurney & Meyers's Psychical Society" in 1884, Henry complained of the "verdigreased human & social types congregated there" amid the dignitaries (*CWJ* 1: 373). The elite physicists of Victorian England were actively engaged in psychical research from 1870 onward, a circumstance that has significant implications for our understanding of William's scientific pursuits.

His 1875 response to *The Unseen Universe* is instructive, balanced as it is between scientific skepticism (William could not see what use the unseen universe had for second-hand energy) and qualified praise for the subjective method. He was particularly impatient with the authors' recourse to divine intervention, a tactic he classed with "those of the most primitive, 'unscientific,' and short-winded natural theologian" (*WWJ* 17: 292). Yet reversing himself in the space of a few paragraphs, William attempted to discipline scientific skeptics to accept the "betterness" of the other world on the basis of "teleologic trust" (17: 293). The religious demand was associated with personal well-being; the materialist outlook with an intellect "sicklied o'er and paralyzed by scientific pursuits," a schematization of Henry Senior and William's relative positions around 1870 (17: 294). William's equivocations signal the looming presence of Henry Senior, who had reproved his son in 1867 for the "purely *scientific* cast of [his] thought just at present, and the temporary blight exerted thence upon [his] metaphysic wit. Ontological problems seem very idle to the ordinary scientific imagination, because it is stupefied by the giant superstition we call Nature" (*CWJ* 4: 204). Lamenting his "rather hard non-receptivity of his [father's] doctrines" during his lifetime, William seemed blind to Henry Senior's profound influence on his thinking, perhaps because his own pursuits were secular, whereas "Father's cry was the single one that religion is real" (1: 344). William's review of *The Unseen Universe* concluded with a stunningly ambiguous endorsement of a book that failed to reconcile mechanistic reasoning about facts with teleological reasoning about ultimate causes:

> But the affirmation that this physical world has *also* a moral meaning and a moral plan is one that no argument drawn from purely physical truth can either establish or impugn. It is nevertheless an affirmation which either is or is not true, and which if true may, from the very nature of the case, be intended to command from us only that inward, free, or moral assent, or rather consent, in which the subjective method consists. (*WWJ* 17: 294)

This "inward, free, or moral assent" required or "intended" by a supernatural agent reprises the elder James's theory that evil exists to endow man with the "constitutional freedom" to embrace or revile God through his own actions (*HJSr*, 149). Henry Senior's passionate evocation of higher spiritual aims forced William to question his allegiance to scientific psychology, with its stark utilitarian view, and also to empirical science: "I am sure I have something better to tell you than you will be able to learn from all Germany—at least all scientific Germany. So urge me hard to your own profit" (*CWJ* 4: 208).[12] Yet at the same time William was frankly unreceptive to his father's theological discourses; he found them illogical and abstruse.[13] Although William was to spend a portion of his life in the service of his father's ideas, both as an editor of *The Literary Remains of the Late Henry James* (1885) and as an author of *"The Will to Believe" and Other Essays on Popular Philosophy* (1897) and *The Varieties of Religious Experience: A Study in Human Nature* (1902), he was a pragmatist who put his faith in his fellow man, who set his sights on furthering the weal of the species rather than on serving God: "If God is dead or at least irrelevant, ditto everything pertaining to the 'Beyond,' if happiness is our Good, ought we not to try to foment a passionate and bold will to attain that happiness among the multitudes?" (*CWJ* 4: 303).[14] William's attention to his father's ideas was a gesture of filial piety as well as an attempt to get within range of a good-news gospel. The most telling divergence between the humanistic philosophies of father and son was William's insistence on quotidian practical concerns, the banality, if I may be allowed, of William's moral aspirations, however tremendous in scope: "The idea, in short, of becoming an accomplice in a sort of 'Mankind its own God, or Providence,' scheme is a *practical* one. I don't mean, my dear Tom, by any means, to affirm that we must come to that, I only say it is *a* mode of envisaging life wh. is capable of affording moral support—and may at any rate help to bridge over the despair of skeptical intervals" (4: 250). William's "skeptical intervals" issued from teleological, not theological, doubts. Writing to Robertson in 1874, William commented:

> I had a crisis just before and about the time of your last visit here, which was more philosophical than theological perhaps, that is did not deal with my personal relations to God as yours seems to have done—but it was accompanied with anxiety and despair &c—I worked through it into the faith in free-will and into the final reign of the Good conditional on the co-operation of each of us in the sphere—small enough often—in which it is allowed him to be operative. (4: 489)

Unlike the elder James, who found solace in the writings of Emmanuel Swedenborg after the infamous Windsor "vastation" of 1843–44, William was emotionally impervious to the unscientific arguments of visionaries, and this explains why he subscribed to Renouvier's empiricism, which left room for subjective impressions rather than to his father's Christian metaphysics. William suspected that Henry Senior had his head in the clouds (even Henry's pious contemporaries scorned his revelations), but William admired his father's capacity to cheerfully endure, even relish, the chaos and uncertainty that paralyzed his son without blinking the reality of death and despair out of sight. That is not to say the elder James was cured once and for all of his neurasthenic proclivities; he continued to suffer from nervous exhaustion, brain fatigue, and other amorphous symptoms. However, Henry Senior had emerged from his depression undiminished and revitalized, whereas William lost some of his spark, the rich and varied texture of his intellect, when he relinquished art and philosophy to the discipline of the mind-cure professionals. It may seem an unpardonable exaggeration, but I agree with Feinstein's characterization of William's state of mind as he emerged from his vocational crisis in the 1870s:

> Instead of self-expression, the elder Henry's guiding principle, William scourged himself with the doctrine of habit. The patient, monotonous wearing away of channels in the nervous system held out the hope of success. Rather than the romantic heights of expressed divinity, vocation was turned into work and divine influx into mechanism, and the self was to be controlled by the straitjacket of science. (313–14)

In retrospect, William recognized that the pathologists had overstated the risk of insanity to men of nervous dispositions like him. Reviewing Dr. William Hirsch's *Genius and Degeneration* in 1895, William argued that cognitive "excesses and superfluities" were precisely what made life worthwhile: "Without love, poetry, art, religion, or any other ideal than pride in his non-neurotic constitution, he is the human counterpart of that 'temperance' hotel of which the traveler's handbook said: 'It possesses no other quality to recommend it'" (*WWJ* 17: 513). William had long upheld the importance of culture and religion; what was novel in his book review was that he castigated those who subscribed to a mental-hygiene ethos that reduced all human striving to the acquisition of fat, muscle, and blood. William's humor masked his genuine regret that he had followed their advice, that he permitted Maudsley and others to define what was noblest in his nature as a vice or a symptom of disease:

> The real lesson of the genius-books is that we should welcome sensibilities, impulses and obsessions if we have them, so long as by their means the field of our experience grows deeper and we contribute the better to the race's stores; that we should broaden our notion of health instead of narrowing it; that we should regard no single element of weakness as fatal—in short that we should *not be afraid of life*. (17: 513)

This stunning remark, made in 1895 and underscored by William himself, has powerful resonance for a reading of *Roderick Hudson*, in which Henry essentially interrogated William's life plan in 1873 and found it wanting in brilliance. Like Raphael Valentin in Balzac's *The Wild Ass's Skin*, William had adopted a program of austerity: "Glad almost to become a sort of automaton, he was abdicating life for the sake of living and plucking all the poetry of desire from his soul"; the comparison with a character who had "castrat[ed] his imagination" on the advice of doctors may seem far-fetched, but it is consonant with William's disparaging self-portrait (Balzac, 201)[15]:

> Partly sickness partly a morbid shrinking from the society of anyone who is alive intellectually are to blame however in my case. I, as I wrote, am long since dead and buried in that respect. I fill my belly for about 4 hours daily with husks—newspapers, novels & biographies, but thought is tabooed—and you can imagine that conversation with [Jeffries] Wyman should only intensify the sense of my degradation. (*CWJ* 4: 411)

It was several years before William grasped the toehold in stable reality that he had been seeking, and he did so, characteristically, with a divided mind. Complaining of "philosophical hypochondria" in 1872, William called his part-time teaching appointment to Harvard a "godsend," a welcome diversion from the morbid introspective studies that, in reality, most interested him (1: 167). Convinced by his reading of Maudsley that "philosophical activity *as a business* is not normal for most men, and not for me," William accepted a full-time appointment the following year in the biological sciences with the mood of a condemned felon or, better still, of a confirmed invalid

(*LWJ* 1: 170). The same refrain accompanies virtually all William's episto-lary reflections on his career choice—it is better from the point of view of mental hygiene: "On the whole this is the wiser, if the tamer decision—the fact is, I'm not a strong enough man to choose the other and nobler lot in life, but I can in a less penetrating way work out a philosophy in the midst of the other duties" (*CWJ* 1: 203). Yet as William approached the resolution to his career dilemma, old associations and fancies beckoned to him:

> I have been of late so sickened & skeptical of philosophic activity as to regret much that I did not stick to painting, and to envy those like you to whom the aesthetic relations of things were the real world. Surely they reveal a deeper part of the universal life than all the mechanical and logical abstractions do, and if I were you I wd. never repine that my life had got cast among them rather than elsewhere. (1: 173)

The regimen that was to have afforded William peace of mind and thus to have revitalized him instead placed unwonted burdens on his feeble nervous system, which could not withstand the "feverish sort of erethism in which the lecture or recitation hour le[ft him]" (1: 208). Abdicating the role of medical counselor and savant for that of the patient, William anticipated his brother's charge of malingering, denying that his ailments were "imagination & hum-bug"; William proposed a therapeutic holiday, provided Henry could vouch-safe from his own experience of "killing time" that the "experiment would be a safe one for a man in [William's] state to try" (1: 208–9). In October 1873 William took a year's leave from Harvard and joined Henry in Florence for a final spree amid the churches and art galleries. Though William remained abroad until March 1874, he apparently found his brother's companionship and the historic atmosphere less than beguiling. During this period, William proclaimed himself more sympathetic to American values and tastes, though his newfound preference for Yankee customs was hardly conveyed with en-thusiasm: "Strange to say, my very enjoyment of what here belongs to hoary eld, has done more to reconcile me to what belongs to the present hour, business, factories &c &c than anything I ever experienced" (4: 471).

William and Henry spent much of their few months together in Rome, the backdrop for *Roderick Hudson*. Henry had ample opportunity to study the changes in William since his scientific and spiritual reformation. To Henry,

William seemed slow to kindle to the aesthetic sensations they had formerly shared. In an 1874 letter to Howells, Henry parodied his "sternly scientific brother['s]" verdict on Rome: "Thank your stars at all events, that you are not living in a place whereof the delight demoralizes" (*HJL* 1: 425). William found Rome dirty, decadent, and repellent. *Roderick Hudson's* Mary Garland is a mischievous and carefully disguised portrait of William in Rome; she responds cooly and rationally to the masterpieces that Rowland Mallet parades before her in a semiconscious effort to awaken buried passions, both sexual and aesthetic. Confronted with multiform splendors, Mary insipidly asks, "How long will it take to see it all?" (*RH*, 219). Yet it would be a mistake to gloss over William's ambivalence. In so far as travel, culture, and speculative philosophy fired his imagination, William plainly schooled himself to accept a regimented, temperate existence as a means of evading the morbid depression that had plagued him intermittently for over a decade.

Writing to his sister, William spoke of the "fatal fascination" of Rome, of its power to disrupt the staid and settled course he'd set for himself: "Here all this dead civilization crowding in upon one's consciousness forces the mind open again even as the knife the unwilling oyster—and what my mind wants most now is practical tasks" (*CWJ* 4: 458–59). As a professor of comparative anatomy and physiology, William could expect fewer highs and, mercifully, fewer lows. But no sooner had he set foot on American soil than William experienced a wave of revulsion set off by the self-same "aridity of american life" that he had lately recommended to Henry as tonic: "I repent me of having interfered so then with your free mental inclination. I also loathe myself for my divided interest in things while I was in Italy. I was too weak for my circumstances. But now I am more satisfied than ever with my promised career at home if only I get strength enough to pursue it" (1: 226). Terrified of "cynical isolation," William elected the career of a public intellectual, but he continued to fret over his brother's resolve to pursue the selfish aims of the artist, a quest Emerson had dignified with the term 'self-culture': "My own spirits are very good, as I have got some things rather straitened out in my mind lately, and this external responsibility and college work agree with human nature better than lonely self culture" (4: 370; 1: 192).

William's mercurial attitudes are more easily understood in light of his personal dilemma. Having taken a leave of absence from his first real job, he must have been profoundly disconcerted by his brother's prolificacy and his assiduous adherence to a writing regimen, calling to mind Oliver Wendell Holmes, Jr.'s comment that he himself had forsaken philosophy for the law, William had forsaken his ideal for science, but "Harry never lets up on his high aims" (4: 290). Henry had embraced the principle that a man must channel his interests narrowly to be strong and had begun to be successful at his chosen vocation. Writing from the spa at Teplitz in 1868, William had drawn an envious comparison between himself and the James boys with independent incomes: "[Wilkie] and Bob are still the working ones of the family (Harry too though!) but I hope my day will yet come" (4: 256). Significantly, Henry's remunerative endeavors occurred to William as an afterthought. By 1873 William's letters home confirmed Henry's unstinting activity, but his acknowledgment was somewhat grudging, as when he referred to Henry "scratching away at the last pages of his Turgenieff article" or joining him at a café "with the flush of successful literary effort fading off his cheek" (4: 459, 471). Idle and bitter, William cast a pall over Henry's Roman spring with his dire prognosis of the fate that lay in store for Henry—overwork and brain drain—or so we surmise from William's transcription of his unheeded counsels: "I don't know whether he can ever be got to return home and take a position of literary drudgery editorial or other. I am sure that some kind of drudgery with a daily external responsibility that is *done* when tis done, and gives one no care till to morrow comes again is the healthiest thing for a man; and wd. suit his spirits better than pure literary production"; in spite of his reservations, William was forced to confess that Henry was well enough to "work hard, and that seems now to be the only thing he lives for" (4: 454–55). As a fellow traveler (Henry's back aches and constipation were a mainstay of their correspondence), Henry did not simply dismiss William's professional counsels; instead, he weighed the risks and benefits of a creative life against the course that William had elected.

Dynamics in Roderick Hudson

Although personalities figure prominently in my efforts to contextualize *Roderick Hudson*, I would now like to shift my focus to the confluence of cultural and scientific discourses that are evident in the novel's representation of the protagonist as a "nervous nineteenth-century Apollo" whose artistic gifts "fizzle" on him (*RH*, 195, 93, 157). Blurring the boundary between myth and science, the novel enlists the principles of the second law of thermodynamics, which recognizes a fundamental dissymmetry in nature: although the total amount of energy in a closed system (such as a motor, a body, or a universe) remains constant, its usefulness is eventually degraded. The application of popularized scientific notions in *Roderick Hudson* appeals to the supraliterary authority of science in one explicit sense: James's analogies explain the semiotics of the results and forecast Roderick's "fizzle." In place of character psychology, James imposes the rule of law: declination is inevitable and irreversible, and the body fatigues and fails: "As a form of Vital Energy he is convicted of being a Vertebrate, a Mammal, a Monodelphe, a Primate, and must eternally, by his body, be subject to the second law of thermodynamics. Escape there is impossible" (H. Adams, *Degradation of the Democratic Dogma*, 191).[16] Although the biologist's notion of degeneration, which stood for the decay or devolution of a person or society, was specifically associated with the dissipation of energy, it was conceived independently from the advances being made in theoretical physics at that time.

As Stephen Brush has illustrated in *The Temperature of History*, some of the concepts of thermodynamics were imported into the culture as leitmotivs. The demotic notion of "heat death" is an example of concept transposition. However, I am less interested in establishing *Roderick Hudson* as a literary analogue to a scientific genre than I am in exploring more substantial affinities between literature and science. Of course, my argument is initially dependent on the objective correlatives of dynamical theories presented as themes, tropes, and metaphors in *Roderick Hudson*; but the identity I hope to establish is more subtle, something more along the lines of the distinction Georges Cuvier made between the concepts of affinity and analogy that William James took the trouble to note circa 1860: "Affinity is founded upon identity of plan. Analogy upon the grafting of the features of one plan upon the body of the other" (Bjork, 27). *Roderick Hudson* vacillates between two contrary positions, each evolving out of contemporary theories of the enervating influences of modern life. One advises conservation and the channeling of energies in the face of moral, psychological, and physical decay occasioned by overexcitement, overindulgence, overwork, as when Rowland Mallet warns Roderick Hudson not to "play such dangerous games with your facility. If you've got facility, respect it, nurse it, adore it, save it up in an old stocking—don't speculate on it." The second advocates a romantic rebellion against the mundane, enervating quality of a life lived without passion (*RH*, 102).[17]

Readers of *The Wild Ass's Skin* will recognize Rowland's plea for parsimony as derivative, but so too is the notion that temperance, when taken to extremes, constitutes death in life. Employing the rhetoric of physics, that of his compatriot and contemporary the engineer Sadi Carnot, Balzac described Raphael Valentin's ascetic regime in the midst of luxury as "mechanical a life as a steam-engine" (201). Balzac drew his warrant for conflating man and machine from his study of pre-Darwinian evolutionary science and physics, which generalized the concept of force, taking growth, motion, and energy conservation as correlative instances of natural activity. At the same time, Balzac's work represented a departure from the Cartesian paradigm, in which the body was a mere machine and the soul was alone responsible for man's feelings and motivations. Balzac's research into the mechanism of the passions and the instincts, as manifested in the bestial poses and gestures of the orgy participants in *The Wild Ass's Skin*, has been likened to the "vitalistic materialism" of the great French physiologist, Xavier Bichat (Temkin, 322–23n3).

Freedman has elaborated on *Roderick Hudson*'s debt to James's reading of Pater's *The Renaissance* (1873), a text that does not instantly call to mind recent discoveries in the field of thermodynamics (133–66). Taking its epigram from Heraclitus, "all things are in motion and nothing at rest," the influential conclusion to the first edition of Pater's work actually commenced with a physics lesson, in which Pater outlined his understanding that a perpetual interplay of natural forces existed and that the laws governing physical life did not discriminate between organic and inorganic entities (174n150). Juxtaposed to this materialism was Pater's neo-Kantian assertion that "the whole scope of observation is dwarfed into the narrow chamber of the individual mind," imagining rich possibilities in the flight from what was acknowledged, even by Pater, to be reality (151). In this context, Pater's famous dictum, "To burn always with this hard, gem-like flame, to maintain this ecstasy, is success in life," may be read as an optimistic refutation of Carnot's entropy concept, a subjectivism that gave way before scientific verity at the end of the passage: "While all melts under our feet, we may well grasp at any exquisite passion, or any contribution to knowledge that seems by a lifted horizon to set the spirit free for a moment" (154). In *Roderick Hudson*, James modified Pater's maxim to something along the lines of "to 'burn out' with a hard gem-like flame," accepting without demur the inevitable dissipation of heat connected with the development of activity.[18]

Ceding primacy to the scientific elaboration of the theory begs the important question of what factors led to a widespread concern with energy conservation precisely at the moment when the Industrial Revolution, having gathered steam, obliterated older methods of manufacture and transport. Behind the objective, disinterested science of nineteenth-century studies of fatigue, neurasthenia, and declining birth rates lurked a productivist demand that people function as efficiently and reproduce as reliably as their machines: "She has induced him by some mysterious art to take up a profession that he abhors and for which he is about as fit as I am to drive a locomotive" (*RH*, 37). *Roderick Hudson* discovers and deplores the raw economic will to power informing this demand, which is why the "little experiment" that propels James's text is not, strictly speaking, an import from the domain of mechanics, though it is logically continuous with it (292). However, James's inquiry into what Henry Adams called "the eternal mystery of Force," through its contemporary phases and manifestations, is itself complicated by the cultural allure of the twin creeds—production and conservation—especially in their aesthetic modality (*Education of Henry Adams*, 427). Admittedly James was no closet physicist like his friend Adams, who stocked *The Education of Henry Adams* with paeans to the dynamo and elegies to civilization such as "Vis Inertiae," whose *The Degradation of the Democratic Dogma* was essentially a text of applied physics. But James was far more cognizant of the emerging sciences than has been allowed by scholars who seem to doubt that a figure of unparalleled imagination might also have had an insatiable curiosity about matters allegedly outside his ken:[19]

> The pen that now was tracing the history of the passionate and erratic Roderick among the artists of Rome was driven by the nerves and the temperament of an individual impervious on the whole to the great scientific strains of his century. He had not only read but had met Darwin in 1869; the new science, however, the challenge of evolution and the debates about determinism, was to take on particular meaning for Henry later only in its literary manifestations, in the *naturalisme* of Zola. (Edel, 2: 169)

Edel was mistaken. At the very least, James found these heavily freighted cultural metaphors useful tools. *Roderick Hudson*'s scientific leitmotivs serve as an apt metalinguistic vehicle for the personal history inscribed within the novel: the tale of an artistic free spirit transformed into a practical man of science, a foreseeable twist of fate that had dismayed William himself in 1858: "Poets may be laughed at for being useless, impractical people. But suppose the author of the 'psalm of Life,' had attempted to invent steam engines, (for which I suppose he has no genius) in the hope of being useful, how much time would he have wasted and how much would we have lost!" (*CWJ* 4: 13). As George Steiner has argued in his small gem of an essay, "The Great *Ennui*," literary decadence and romanticism palpitate with a nostalgic yearning for the heady emotions stirred by the French Revolution and the Napoleonic wars, quelled in the aftermath to make way for a relatively peaceful interlude of industrial progress and bloodless revolution. According to Steiner, for each nineteenth-century text professing "proud meliorism," there can be found a counterstatement of "corrosive *ennui*," of energies eroded by boredom and routinization (9–11). *Roderick Hudson* contraposes these divergent humors through its principals: Rowland's melioristic ethos looks backward to Calvinism and forward to scientific management, while Roderick's malaise embodies the impotent protest of the decadent artist in the machine age: "*L'art pour l'art*—[is] a snake biting its own tail. 'Rather no purpose at all than a moral purpose!'" (Nietzsche, *Twilight of the Idols*, 92). As Friedrich Nietzsche suggested, this defeatist posture tacitly acknowledged the subordination of art to normative values as a fait accompli; more broadly, it foregrounded the neurasthenic disposition of modern men like William James, "pruned of all [their] manliest drives and virtues" and lapsing into a "physiological regression" or torpor (139).

Between 1860 and 1900, over one hundred studies of nervous exhaustion, overwork, diseases of the will, and fatigue were published in the United States alone (Rabinbach, 20). In *L'Ennui* (1903), Emile Tardieu attributed the extreme subjectivism, morbid sensualism, and apathy of the decadents to fatigue rather than to the deadening effects of a rebarbative environment (42). Confidently stripping the poetic aura from the concept of ennui, Tardieu claimed to have uncovered the physiological foundations of this degenerative condition. Analogously, *Roderick Hudson* traces the regression from boredom to lethargy to invalidism, hinting at some inborn systemic perversity: "The poor fellow isn't *made* right" (*RH*, 194). In the course of the novel, Rowland is forced to revise his assessment of the "essential salubrity of genius": "If what I've seen is salubrity give me raging disease" (151, 193). This plaint derives from popular and medicophilosophic conceptions of genius as a stigma of degeneracy, signalized by intense sensibility of temperament and disproportionate talents and glaring weaknesses: "Genius was priceless, beneficent, divine, but it was also at its hours capricious, sinister, cruel; and natures ridden by it, accordingly, were alternately very enviable and very helpless" (152). In "On the Morbid Heredity and Predisposition to Insanity of the Man of Genius," Warren Babcock commented: "Undoubtedly, the preponderance of great natural gifts of mind, which in themselves insure great renown, entails a corresponding deficiency in other parts of the mental and physical economy, and though in many respects the man of genius may well be the subject of envy, he may in other regards, as consistently be the object of pity" (750). In the preface to his novel, James acknowledged that the accelerated "rate at which he falls to pieces" placed Roderick well beyond the reach of understanding and sympathy (*RH*, 14). Yet James made no effort to compensate for this apparent miscalculation in his revisions, because Roderick's deterioration facilitated the comparison with young William, the dejected artist manqué.

Roderick's morbid inertia is evidently a type of abulia, the volitional impairment that incapacitated William throughout the 1860s. Although he maintains both his reason and his ambition, the sculptor is inexplicably incapable of completing any of his cherished designs: "Do you suppose I'm trying *not* to work? Do you suppose I stand rotting here for the fun of it? Don't you suppose I would try to work for myself before I tried for you?" (283).[20] Cycling out of the manic phase of what may be some type of manic-depressive illness, Roderick sinks into an affectless stupor: "He was not alert"; "he expressed little of the irritation and ennui he must have constantly felt" (230, 285). Indifferent to the claims of filial piety and lacking even a "feeling heart," Roderick's disordered emotional life is the source of his psychosomatic enfeeblement (151): "The cause is then a relative insensibility, a general impairment of sensibility; what is attacked is the emotional life, the possibility of being moved" (Ribot, 40). Concentrating his passion on Christina Light to the exclusion of all other claims on his attention, Roderick is mistaken for a hedonist when, in fact, he is not in command of his faculties. Exhorted by Rowland, "if you've the energy to desire you've also the energy to reason and to judge," Roderick is beyond the reach of crude voluntarism: "The will, it seems to me, is an abyss of abysses and a riddle of riddles" (*RH*, 318, 102). Classifying melancholy as a disease of the will, J. E. D. Esquirol recorded his patients' sensation that an "abyss" divided them from the external world (206). Though William subscribed to Renouvier's doctrine of the freedom of the will as a means of countering morbid ideation, "the sustaining of a thought *because I choose* to when I might have other thoughts" (*LWJ* 1: 147), he knew from firsthand experience of the "abyss of horrors" (Cotkin, 179n27) that the appeal to personal volition stranded those "'all sicklied o'er' with the sense of weakness, of helpless failure, and of fear" to whom the "voluntary career" was but a "plaster hiding a sore it can never cure" (*WWJ* 11: 62).

Key elements of William's vocational crisis are reflected in Rowland's effort to manage Roderick's career and restore his powers of execution: "The power to choose *is* destiny. That's the way to look at it" (*RH*, 103). Apart from his naive conviction in the "essential good health of the sincere imagination" (50), Rowland is a fair mouthpiece for William, who insisted that diligence was the better part of talent: "To *do* anything with one's genius requires passion; to do much requires doggedness" (*WWJ* 17: 511–12). Rowland says to Roderick, "I believe in you if you're prepared to work and to wait and to struggle and to exercise a great many virtues" (*RH*, 41). And something of William's emphasis on orderly habits of mind, "by intense exercise in a variety of different subjects, getting the mind supple and delicate and firm" (*CWJ* 4: 225), comes across in Rowland's prosaic assessment of the vagaries of genius: "Are they all like that, all the men of genius? There are a great many artists here who hammer away at their trade with exemplary diligence; in fact I'm surprised at their success in reducing the matter to a virtuous *habit*; but I really don't think that one of them has his exquisite quality of talent" (*RH*, 195). I have underscored this term, a watchword of William's, because it is central to Henry's critique of his brother's pragmatic choices and hygienic counsels.[21] This same melioristic doctrine informs Rowland's position that sublimation is an elective course: "'By the wiser,' he sententiously added, 'I mean the stronger in reconsidered and confirmed purpose, in acquired willpower'" (102).

In "The Feeling of Effort" (1880), William sketched a descriptive psy-

chophysiology of volition heavily freighted with the language of moral up-
lift, such as the quaint classification of human motives as either "sensual" or
"moral" (*WWJ* 13: 119). Though William balked at the anthropomor-
phization of "will-muscle-force-sense," in so far as resistance was perceived
as externally rather than internally generated, he bundled dynamics and
strenuosity together in his definition of moral action: "Your will, it could be
said, *is* doing 'work' upon the system. 'Work' is defined in mechanics as
movement done against resistance, and your will meets with a resistance
which it has to overcome by moral effort" (13: 122). This synopsis favors the
mechanistic analogy at the outset, but it collapses into the secularized asceticism of mental hygiene. Retrospectively, Rowland Mallet's notion that
his strenuous self-discipline is "work" can be seen as an illustration of this
principle: "His moral energy had its sleeping and its waking hours, and . . .
in an attractive cause it would yet again be capable of rising with the dawn"
(*RH*, 300). "The Feeling of Effort" indicates the functionalist cast of William's thought in the decade in which *Roderick Hudson* was composed. Taken
together, the technical and fictional depictions of effort reveal a striking continuity between the new science of energetics and the Protestant work ethic.
However much William James may have consciously deplored American rapacity, his emphasis on individual productivity placed him in a paradoxical
position, that of the enterprising anticapitalist.

The transposition of science, philosophy, and aesthetics in *Roderick Hudson* attests to the acculturation of the dominant scientific paradigm of the late
nineteenth century. However, the mechanical conception of force was itself
an amalgam, drawing on long-standing philosophical suppositions regarding
the correspondence between will and energy, while serving as a vehicle for
cross-disciplinary endeavors such as Gustav Fechner's psychophysics. De-
nominating *Die Welt als Wille* the foundational text of the modern school of
energetics ("Schopenhauer held that all energy in nature, latent, or active, is
identical with Will"), Henry Adams remarked on the oddity of a philosophic
notion "gaining [a] foothold in science" (*Degradation of the Democratic Dogma*,
193). Historian Robert Young has effectively challenged the notion that science is autonomous and independent of political contrivance and economic
interests. Young argues "the emergence of functionalism, pragmatism, psycho-analysis and numerous other theorists and their schools can then be seen
as part of a continuous development. That development was the substitution

of one form of rationalization of the hierarchical relations among men, for another" (428). This is what Nietzsche had in mind when he scoffed at "the *barbarizing* effects of science: it easily loses itself in the service of 'practical interests'" (*Philosophy and Truth*, 9). Taking the Darwinists and psychologists to task for their common principle, "the smallest possible effort," Nietzsche reconsidered: "Notwithstanding [it may] be the right imperative for a hardy, labourious race of machinists and bridge-builders of the future, who have nothing but *rough* work to perform" (*Beyond Good and Evil*, 19).

The reciprocity among psychology, physiology, and physics at that time must be understood within the context of industrialization. The Lawrence Scientific School of Harvard University, founded in 1847 by botanist Asa Gray and mathematician Benjamin Peirce, was originally planned as an institution of higher learning, emphasizing postgraduate research and offering laboratory instruction to undergraduates in the hard sciences. After the textile manufacturer Abbott Lawrence donated fifty thousand dollars, the new school took its patron's name and established departments of engineering and applied science at his behest (Bjork, 37). The proliferation of factories, the garnering of steam power, and the invention of the dynamo forced the issue of humankind's compatibility with machines of manufacture, convenience, transport, and communication, affecting all areas of domestic and public life: "The first fact a man encounters in this modern world, after his mother's face, is the machine" (G. Lee, 6). A sociologist of science might say that the integration of organic and inorganic science, the pursuit of universal laws leading to the extrapolation of management techniques based on a presumed correlation between natural and mechanical energy systems, was driven by the demand that science serve the utilitarian aims of the burgeoning community of industrialists: "The nervous system of man is the centre of the nerve-force supplying all the organs of the body. Like the steam engine, its force is limited, although it cannot be mathematically measured—and, unlike the steam engine, varies in amount of force with the food, the state of health and external conditions, varies with age, nutrition, occupation, and numberless factors" (Beard, *American Nervousness*, 98–99).

The promulgation of universal laws governing the animate and inanimate promoted what Seltzer has called a "body-machine complex," the discursive and practical coordination of bodies and machines (*Bodies and Machines*, 3–4). As Seltzer has cogently argued, nineteenth-century theories of energy conservation and expenditure focused on the body, on the goal of achieving a balance among productivity, self-gratification, and self-control: "What is desired is an adjustment between conflicting practices, between the proper conservation of vital powers and the productive utilization of those powers" (41–42). Counterintuitively, the anxieties stirred by the advent of machine culture contributed to the reification of the human subject through the celebration of mechanical virtues: reliability, concentration, routinization, and productivity. These guidelines of "disciplinary individualism" appear in the private and public writings of William James (Seltzer, 83–84): "Society owes an immense debt to its nervous temperaments, its Shelleys, its J. S. Mills, and others. But who would not shrink from having the *type* grow strenuous and hectic like these?" Paraphrasing Maudsley, William continued, "The neurotic or overnervous type, which is often the type of genius too, may be the first step in the downward career" (*WWJ* 17: 277). In "The Gospel of Relaxation" (1899), William elaborated on the defects of the nervous temperament as viewed from the perspective of the industrial capitalist: "Your dull, unhurried worker gets over a great deal of ground, because he never goes backward or breaks down. Your intense, convulsive worker breaks down and has bad moods so often that you never know where he may be when you most need his help—he may be having one of his 'bad days'" (12: 124). Henry's repugnance for the social and human engineering slant of William's outlook imbues Rowland Mallet's conversation, which echoes the functionalist demand "If you've so much steam on, then, use it for something else!" (*RH*, 318). Mallet's conflation of artistic endeavor and factory work, his emphasis on purposive rather than pleasurable activity, is continuous with the outlook of the emerging managerial elites and, small wonder, when William James's "teleological instrument[ality]" supplied grist for the mill of scientific management (*WWJ* 5: 34).

Defending William's pragmatic mode of philosophic inquiry against the crude construction that many have placed upon it, that it was part and parcel of the American tendency to "judge all ideals by their practical efficiency, by their visible results, by their so-called 'cash values,'" Josiah Royce was forced to acknowledge that William James had become synonymous with the "efficiency doctrine" (34, 32). Although I cannot do justice to Frank Lentricchia's eloquent partisanship of Jamesian pluralism and antinomianism in this study, I am hard pressed to accept his claim that William James's rhetorical deployment of the idea of an inalienable property of selfhood turned "the cornerstone economic principle of capitalism to the advantage of a counterdiscourse and a vision of human sanctity central not only to pragmatism but also to the originating myth of American political history"(246).[22] From another perspective, this view is an example of possessive individualism, a libertarian perspective that reconciles the quest for personal freedom with the goals of laissez faire capitalism.[23] I am suspicious of William's recourse to such tropes as the "cash-value of experience," which imply a specious insularity from the marketplace (*WWJ* 2: 3). Moreover, the body of writing that Lentricchia considers, *Pragmatism* and a whiff of *Principles of Psychology*, is not fully representative; he omits any contemporaneous allusions to functionalist psychology or other variations on scientific rationalism, and he even neglects William's interest in spiritualism, which attests to William's unconventionality. Enthusing over the mugwump and pluralist, Lentricchia validates William's professed hostility to rationalists and imperialists (248); however, by segregating his philosophical and psychological texts, Lentricchia obscures the extent to which William's scientific rationalism and its technical applications (psychological testing, scientific management, and fatigue studies) lent authority to the industrial state by disseminating the "natural" foundations of class and political hierarchies. For example, although William resisted and challenged automatism in the mid-1870s, he continued to articulate a version of the body-machine complex throughout his life:

> Stating the thing broadly, the human individual thus lives usually far within his limits; he possesses powers of various sorts which he habitually fails to use. He energizes below his *maximum*, and he behaves below his *optimum*. In elementary faculty, in co-ordination, in power of *inhibition* and control, in every conceivable way, his life is contracted like the field of vision of an hysterical subject—but with less excuse, for the poor hysteric is diseased, while in the rest of us it is only an inveterate *habit*— the habit of inferiority to our full self—that is bad. (*WWJ* 11: 151)

This reconciliation of man and machine suggests a vision of human progress, consistent with that of Spencer, which embraced the disciplines of the factory system as tokens of the increased complexity of social life and the enhanced cooperation among humans routinized and perfected in the course of evolution (Trachtenberg, 45). Strategically, William's "The Energies of

Men" and "The Powers of Men," both published in 1907, were allied with Frederick Winslow Taylor's goal of bringing "workers' animal energies into line with the mechanical energies of the machines they service" (Banta, 96). Taylor first publicized his system in his 1903 lecture, "Shop Management." *The Principles of Scientific Management* appeared in 1911. Taylor's promotion of the "morality of efficiency" (98) harmonized with William's endorsement of "methodical ascetic discipline" (*WWJ* 11: 136). Borrowing a term from physiology to elaborate the "dynamogenic" effect of a class of moral ideas that have the power to unlock untapped reservoirs of vitality, William illustrated a seamless progression from mental hygiene and biophysics to Taylorism and psychical efficiency (11: 133). Redefining genius as "the power of achievement" in 1917, the librarian of the Pierce-Arrow corporation expressed his confidence in the "psychical efficiency of genius" in terms strikingly reminiscent of William and Taylor's encomiums to the "*better men*," whose energies never flag (11: 151; Banta, 96): "Many men are perfectly prodigal of their energies. The genius is not. All great men of the world have had their mental machinery well-equipped with energy, and the larger part of such machinery operating automatically" (McChesney, 178).

Rowland Mallet's sanguine view of the artist's "beautiful faculty of production" looks forward to psychical efficiency, which exults in the natural immunity of certain individuals from the ravages of industrial wear and tear (151). Coining the term *efficiency-equilibrium* to explain the mechanism of this immunity in "The Powers of Men," William James hypothesized that the metabolism might compensate for accelerated levels of activity: "His more active rate of energizing does not wreck him; for the organism adapts itself, and as the rate of waste augments, augments correspondingly the rate of repair" (*WWJ* 11: 148). Initially persuaded that Roderick had "established the happiest *modus vivendi* betwixt work and play" during their residence in Rome, Rowland is awestruck rather than alarmed, as he should be, by the intensity of Roderick's rate of production (*RH*, 80). Rowland mistakes the artist's hectic air and frenetic activity for "a fund of nervous force outlasting and outwearying the endurance of sturdier temperaments" (34). Harried by a "demon of unrest," Roderick actually lacks the curbs (self-restraint, willpower) that would arrest the unchecked expenditure of his personal resources: "He has developed faster even than you prophesied" (32, 195). Hudson's career evidences the "intersection of bodily and cultural forms and practices, what amounts to a cultural logistics" of neurasthenia, to use Seltzer's phrase (*Bodies and Machines*, 88). Introduced by Mallet to the disciplines of the marketplace, disguised as the old-fashioned work ethic, "achievement's only effort passionate enough," Hudson is driven to risk his capital (his stock of energy) in one spasmodic bid for fame: "Well, then, haven't I got up steam enough?" (*RH*, 71). Enlarging upon Mallet's axiom in the idiom of techno-economic dynamism, Hudson attests to his unwitting investment in indus-trial capitalism. When he crashes, his cry epitomizes the despair of the "so-cially informed body" (Bourdieu, *Outline of a Theory of Practice*, 124): "I'm bankrupt, bankrupt!" (*RH*, 272).

The precipitateness of Roderick's rise is an early warning of the trouble ahead: "You've gone up like a rocket in your profession, they tell me; are you going to come down like the stick?" (176). Balzac established the precedent for Henry's interpolation of biomechanical analogies within the framework of the novel: "She seemed quite intrigued to learn that the human will was a material force similar to steam-power" (124); however, James's deployment of statistical figures of speech to gauge the artist's "remunerative rate of pro-duction" was informed by more recent developments, such as the reorienta-tion of the social sciences toward performance and management studies (*RH*, 156). The intratextual debate between free will and determinism ef-fortlessly accommodates statistical or systematic understandings of individ-uals as anonymous producers and products of machine culture: "If you've pressing business to attend to don't wait to settle the name and work out the pedigree of the agent you dispatch on it: tumble to work somehow and see what it looks like afterwards" (158). Commandeering the laws of physics, Rowland's exhortation transcribes the principle of inertia: bodies at rest tend to remain so, while those in motion press on in a straight line. Declaring his "prejudice against tumbling, anywhere," Roderick resists a mechanical defi-nition of "motive power," holding out for vision and engagement (158). In 1878 the artist vehemently repudiated Rowland's advice: "'Set to work and produce abortions!' cried Roderick with ire. 'Preach that to others. Produc-tion with me must be either pleasure or nothing'" (*RH2*, 165).

Revisions undertaken in 1907 indicate that James had become more con-versant with scientific models, which are expertly grafted onto the text. An-ticipating that Roderick will more or less "sublimely fail," James evokes a chemist's definition of sublimation when he conceives of death as a distillation, a passage from a solid form to a vaporous state: "I shall disappear, dissolve, be carried off in a something as pretty, let us hope, as the drifted spray of a fountain" (*RH*, 157). Analogies of this sort sophisticate the textual contrast of capitalistic and humanistic conceptions of aesthetic practice, because applied science is a powerful engine of the transformation of culture. Moreover, the interfaces between literary and mechanical narratives of entropy ("the end of my work shall be the end of my life") underscore the parallel development of functional psychology, scientific management, energy conservation, and literature (157). In *Hermes: Literature, Science, Philosophy*, Michel Serres elaborates the interplay among "technologies, protocols, and theorems concerning heat" and other cultural narratives (39). Singling out the *Rougon-Macquart* cycle for its author's scientific pretensions, Serres remarks on the persistence of the steam engine as a symbol of the two energies, sex and death, that impel the devolution of hereditary flaws and crimes throughout a family of the Second Empire: "The genetic grill, imposed by decision of the author himself, clarifies the reading of the novels much more than the critical tradition grants. Properly generalized, it leads to a thermodynamic grill, more powerful and more efficient still, especially when it is completed by theories concerning processes of transformations, be they chemical or general" (39–40).

In "Le Roman expérimental" (1880), Zola forthrightly declared, "If the experimental method has been capable of extension from chemistry and physics to physiology and medicine, then it can be carried from physiology to the naturalist novel" (in Becker, 169). Stressing crossdisciplinary theoretical and methodological correspondences between the discrete branches of the sciences, Zola claimed that naturalism was a type of scientific psychology investigating the genetic determinations and environmental influences shaping the social and private life of man. He envisioned this work as a complement to biophysiology, which had made some small progress in articulating the laws governing sensory phenomena. Zola's reflections echoed William James's 1867 observation, "It seems to me that perhaps the time has come for Psychology to begin to be a science—some measurements have allready been made in the region lying between the physical changes in the nerves and the appearance of consciousness—(in the shape of sense perceptions) and more may come of it" (*CWJ* 4: 226).

Henry James may have had Zola's *Thérèse Racquin* (1867) or *La Fortune des*

Rougon (1871) in mind when he conceived his protagonist as a "desperate experiment," but the textual convergences of significance are isomorphic, not tropological (*RH*, 157). Following Serres, I am prepared to argue that *Roderick Hudson*, with its conception of energy reservoirs, expansion, compression, and entropy enters the domain of "the descriptive powers of thermodynamics," for the literary narrative functions as a kind of "trivial motor" (xxxvi, xxix). Although *Roderick Hudson* draws on other notions of the properties of energy such as philosophical, mythological, and rudimentary mechanical—"what if the watch should run down?,"—the steam engine serves as the novel's prototype for the conversion of heat into work (103, 93, 156). Emblem of full mechanization, dream of perpetual motion, the steam engine raises and dashes the brightest hopes of the captains of industry and the managerial elites, for energy dissipates and entropy increases: "The machine's running down" (194). Mallet fails to comprehend that the hot and cold reservoirs of Hudson's personality, "power and weakness," "good and bad," like the boiler and condenser of the steam engine, produce circulation because they are organized into hotter and colder areas: "At last, springing up, 'I want to strike out hard!' he exclaimed; 'I want to do something violent and indecent and impossible—to let off steam!'" (194, 153, 62). Once Mallet's goal of an equilibrium or average temperature is attained, no work can be performed: "The second law of thermodynamics accounts for the impossibility of perpetual motion of the second type; energy dissipates and entropy increases. From this moment on, time is endowed with a direction. It is irreversible and drifts from order to disorder, or from difference to the dissolution or dissemination of a homogeneous mixture from which no energy, no force, and no motion can arise" (Serres, 71–71).

Some such notion of devolution, irreversibility, and disorder has been a commonplace since the time of Heraclitus. Formally articulated by Carnot in 1824, historically the second law of thermodynamics actually preceded the first law, which was discovered in the 1840s when scientists began to think of energy as an elementary entity in nature (Gr. Meyers, in Brantlinger, 311). William James's hopeful accounts of energy conservation virtually ignore the second law. Investigating the phenomenon of second wind in "The Powers of Men," he proposed that certain individuals maintain a constant level of available energy just as some maintain a constant weight.[24] Deducing man's "energy-budget" from the physiologist's "nutritive equilibrium," William mishandled the template by which he gauged the long-term effects of exertion (*WWJ* 11: 148). Nutritional requirements alter with the passage of time, and the chemical energy latent in food is not wholly converted into useful energy; we burn calories in the process of metabolization. Possibly William had in mind Julius von Mayer's theory that body heat and muscular force are derived from the oxidation of food. The chemical energy latent in food is conserved by the body. His "'efficiency-equilibrium' (neither gaining nor losing *power* once the equilibrium is reached)" contravened the second law of thermodynamics by arresting time in its tracks and skirting the issue of the declination of physical capacities (11: 148): "It is a universal character of all known natural forces that their capacity for work is exhausted in the degree in which they actually perform work" (Helmholtz, 359). William James's formulation of an optimal, invariable balance between rest and work, which returns the individual each morning to his original condition, was a transparent appeal to the first law: "The total quantity of all the forces capable of work in the whole universe remains eternal and unchanged throughout all their changes" (360).

From the mechanical standpoint, William's article elided crucial phases in the relations among energy, force, power, work, and, most important, bodies and machines. Energy equals the capacity for doing work, it is power expended, and it can be measured in terms of work, the product of force applied to an object and its resultant motion. Because of the resistance of the air and the friction entailed in the mechanical process, some energy is converted into the form of heat. Nature places a restriction on the amount of work that can be obtained from thermal, chemical, and electrical engines (man included) because heat flows spontaneously only from hotter to colder bodies. "The Powers of Men" draped the banner of scientific inquiry over the techniques of scientific management. Having overcome the inhibitions of his previous neurasthenic existence through the prudent cultivation and husbanding of his energy reserves, William James urged a similar course on Americans bogged down by "formidable neurasthenic and psychasthenic conditions, with life grown into one tissue of impossibilities, that so many medical books describe" (*WWJ* 11: 150). In fact, William's public estimation of the untapped reserves of energy available to every individual belied personal experience. Writing to inform Henry of yet another "nervous smash-up" in October 1901, William commented, "It shows how little margin I have, as yet, to take liberties with, for the only cause to which I can ascribe it is over-excitement and activity incidental to the return. I had been leading such an ultra-protected and especially simplified life for the past two years, that the first touch of complex conditions seems to have bowled me over" (*CWJ* 3: 181). Situating "The Gospel of Relaxation" and "The Energies of Men" within the "the discourse of heroism," George Cotkin praises James's enlightened rejection of the dogma of energy conservation in favor of "letting-go" every once in a while (112). Cotkin does not see the continuity, which historian Roger Cooter has underlined, between conservative social agendas and functionalism transmitted as the political economy of bodily functions:

> Certainly it does not require a condescending view of ordinary people as passive vessels hoodwinked by clever propagandists to explain the popular acceptance of the proto-functionalist physiology that increasingly reconciled people to an alienating, inegalitarian, and dehumanizing social system. We can see that, being no less caught up in the disorienting forces of change than was the bourgeoisie, working people had little resistance to being socialized by the knowledge that linked them to the emergent social system through their own biology. (in Barnes, 86)

In an age of unrestricted expansion, capitalists were sometimes called upon to answer the charge that rapid industrialization and feverish competition sapped the energies of factory hands and businessmen alike, who have "been aptly likened to a steam engine running constantly under a forced draught" (Edson, "Do We Live too Fast?", 282). The body-machine complex pervades discussions of this subject across genres and on both sides of the question. Defending the cause of labor in "The Brain and Nerve Destroying Policy of Railways," C. H. Hughes peppered his plea for a shorter workday with allusions to overtaxed "brain and body machinery" (689). Turning his attention to the plight of businessmen, Hughes strained the same analogy: "These men have a healthy look, but so does a steam boiler or magazine, on the outside, to the ordinary observer till it explodes and then you see nothing but the wreck of the thing that was" ("Brain Bankruptcy," 465). However remote from the author's intentions, it seems obvious that Hughes's conflation of man and machine, the failure to posit distinctively human forms of suffering and exploitation, militates against any transformative critique of industrialism. Analogously, the premium set on the efficiency and productivity of the biomechanical entity known as man enmeshed William James in the strategy of the "big" national institutions and business organizations he clearly despised: "Imperialism and the idol of a national destiny, based on martial excitement and mere 'bigness,' keep revealing their corrupting inwardness more and more unmistakably" (*WWJ* 17: 154). Throughout works such as *Pragmatism* and "The Moral Philosopher and the Moral Life," certain types of highly abstract thought, most typically Hegelianism, are linked to absolutist and imperialist forms of tyranny. But in the practical matter of work, James took little notice of the burdens borne by people.

Sounding more like a social engineer than a philosopher, William reckoned in "The Powers of Men" that poor mental hygiene and neurasthenia were compromising the national economy: "In rough terms, we may say that a man who energizes below his normal maximum fails by just so much to profit by his chance at life; and that a nation filled with such men is inferior to a nation run at a higher pressure" (11: 149). Insistent that the fault lay with individuals rather than with their work conditions, William focused on the practical problem of "how can men be trained up to their most useful pitch of energy?" (11: 149). At the end of his essay, he proposed a new direction for the science of energetics, providing "a topography of the limits of human power, similar to the chart which oculists use in the field of human vision" (11: 161). In fact, such an apparatus already existed; pioneer-inventor Angelo Mosso's ergograph was capable of measuring various forms of muscular fatigue. Trained as a physiologist, Mosso presents an instructive contrast to William James. In his magnum opus, *Fatigue*, written in 1903, Mosso narrated a gruesome tale of harried, half-naked men slaving under the discipline of "gigantic automata," with whose inexorable motion the workers must keep pace or be ground to a powder, because time is money (171). Confirming Marx's thesis that so-called labor-saving machines have not diminished human fatigue "but simply the price of commodities" and have destroyed the wholesome social life of the artisan, Mosso deplored the fact that science had vouchsafed a "monopoly for machinery" at the expense of labor (173, 174). Consulting anthropometric tables prepared by, among others, James's Harvard crony Bowditch, Mosso compiled a poverty/misery index to gauge the effects of industrialization on the working poor: physical degeneration and impaired vitality (158).

As a man of science, Mosso was impressed by the "boundless wealth of force" tapped by scientific endeavor, but he prophesied that all this activity would come to a grinding halt when mechanical efficiency outstripped man's capacity to keep pace: "The law of exhaustion sets an insuperable barrier to greed of gain" (168). Unlike William James, Mosso never made a fetish of energy, reducing the factory operative to an automaton or a cog in the great wheel of industry. Mosso's humanistic science sheds an unflattering light on William's collocation of man and machine and his reflex employment of mechanical tropes, which suggests a rapprochement with modern industrial capitalism. Although William decried the "wholesale loss of opportunity under our *regime* of so-called equality and industrialism," he recognized no natural antipathy between the goals of machine and human culture (*WWJ* 6: 156–57). What did make his flesh creep was the crackbrained evolutionary hypothesis that "steam, electricity, and mechanical inventions '[were] superseding the necessity for the stalwart frames and heavy sinews which were in such prime demand a few years since'" (*WWJ* 17: 276). Prosaically extolling muscular strength and recreational exercise as remedies for nervous tension, William never considered the fate of displaced laborers. In "The Gospel of Relaxation," he recalled and embellished this futuristic vision of a race of huge-brained toothless weaklings talking philosophy while machines chewed their food for them and performed all physical tasks (12: 120–21). In the space of twenty-five years, *tedium vitae* had become a catch phrase of mental science, which does not excuse, though it might explain, William's indifference to the underlying environmental causes, his taking a culturally formulated problem for an a priori fact.

In "The Gospel of Relaxation," William harped on the "bottled-lightning quality in us Americans," an absence of repose conventionally attributed to climate, modernity, and "the hard work, the railroad speed, the rapid success, and all the other things we know so well by heart" (*WWJ* 12: 123).[25] Countering that such "wanton and unnecessary tricks of the inner attitude and outer manner" were merely "*bad habits*" caught from the social atmosphere, he derailed a critique of American over-pressure by invoking the "psychology of imitation" (12: 124, 123, 126). According to William, American nervousness was bred from bad example, what Hugo Münsterberg called "defective training," rather than from onerous living conditions: "We must change ourselves from a race that admires jerk and snap for their own sakes" (12: 125). Though William was certainly skeptical of modern industrial behaviorism, as George Fredrickson, James Gilbert, Martha Banta, and Frank Lentricchia have stressed, his melioristic prescription for hygienic reeducation was logically continuous with it. William's efforts to revitalize his countrymen have been variously characterized as partaking of the "discourse of heroism" (Cotkin, 112; Lutz, 94), as "functionalism" (Gilbert, 182; Posnock, 114), and as an incandescent appeal to the "strenuous mood," civic courage holding its own against the forces of imperialism and tyranny (Fredrickson, 235). All these portrayals share the outlook that William James's chronic indisposition set the stage for his philosophy of energetics. As Kim Townsend has suggested in *Manhood at Harvard*, neurasthenia was the cornerstone of William James's education, career, and mode of thought (78).

Moral Courage

It is terribly important that invalidism kept William James out of the Civil War, the definitive trial of manhood in his generation. It was hardly coincidental that his neurasthenia and disillusionment with painting coincided with the outbreak of the Civil War on April 12, 1861. Late in life, he became preoccupied with defining the *"moral equivalent of war*, analogous, as one might say, to the mechanical equivalent of heat," as a means of shoring up a masculine identity that had known only private strife and of unleashing repressed energy: "The martial type of character can be bred without war. Strenuous honour and disinterestedness abound elsewhere. Priests and medical men are in a fashion educated to it, and we should all feel some degree of it imperative if we were conscious of our work as an obligatory service to the state" (*WWJ* 11: 169, 172). Goaded by Theodore Roosevelt's disparaging remarks about effete anti-imperialists who deplored U.S. military intervention in the Philippines, William lambasted the party that "gushes over war as the ideal condition of human society, for the manly strenuousness which it involves, and treats peace as a condition of blubberlike and swollen ignobility, fit only for huckstering weaklings, dwelling in gray twilight and heedless of the higher life" (17: 163). Roosevelt had been a student of

William's at Harvard. William may have taken offense that Roosevelt had appropriated the concept of the strenuous life to use as the title of his own bellicose oration. Acknowledging war as "the gory cradle of mankind, the grim-featured nurse that alone could train our savage progenitors into some semblance of social virtue," William sought some milder "dynamogenic" stimulus for modern youth, something akin to Outward Bound or the Peace Corps (11: 72; 11: 133). In the deepest recesses of his consciousness, William James regarded his battle with depression as his "inner Civil War," to borrow Fredrickson's phrase, as a lonely trial of masculinity in which he was constantly found wanting (156–61).

Significantly, William's 1897 memorial address for colonel Robert Gould Shaw, the commander of the Fifty-Fourth Massachusetts Regiment under whom Wilkie James was serving when he was gravely wounded during the assault on Fort Wagner, became the platform for an alternative construction of valor. Extolling "the lonely kind of courage" Shaw had exemplified when he was enlisted to command the first Negro regiment, William deprecated the garden-variety courage of the bellicose in favor of the spirit of individualism (*WWJ* 11: 72). Eulogizing the Scottish-American philosopher "Thomas Davidson: Individualist" in 1903 as an "example of the ranges of combination of scholarship with manhood that are possible," he edged nearer toward a pleasing self-definition (17: 89). From Davidson, William took the measure of his radical pragmatist, bobbing contentedly in the sea of flux: "Individualist *à outrance*, Davidson felt that every hour was an unique entity, to whose claims one should lie open" (17: 92). William's adherence to this open-ended philosophy notwithstanding, Davidson tweaked him "for the musty and mouldy and generally ignoble academicism of [his] character" long habituated to the disciplines of college life (17: 90). Wholly out of sympathy with the functionalist cast of William's *Psychology*, Davidson reprehended the doctrine of habit in a manner worthy of Henry David Thoreau: "When he found himself in danger of settling into even a good one, he made a point of interrupting it. Habits and methods make a prisoner of a man, destroy his readiness, keep him from answering the call of the fresh moment" (17: 91–92). As it happens, William James was not the model for *Pragmatism's* "happy-go-lucky-anarchistic sort of creature"; the characterization was optative, not self-descriptive (1: 124).

Davidson personified this openness to the stream of experience, and his example suggests that possessive individualism was hardly compatible with realpolitik. Allergic to "socialisms and administrative panaceas," Davidson fostered idealism rather than practical measures such as trade unionism among the wage earners he lectured on the Lower East Side: "The real thing to aim at is liberation of the inner interests. Give a man possession of a *soul*, and he will work out his own happiness under any set of conditions" (17: 92). As if paraphrasing Henry Senior's notion of "the supremacy of man's associated life over his individual one" in the eyes of God (*HJSr*, 115), Davidson envisioned a fellowship of higher and lower men as a preliminary step toward a "republic of immortal spirits" (*WWJ* 17: 92). I prefer Henry Senior's homely declaration that "to a right-minded man, a crowded Cambridge horse-car 'was the nearest approach to Heaven upon earth'" (*LWJ* 1: 115n1). In William's tribute, Davidson's egalitarianism comes across as a patrician virtue. Poised to lead his army of Jewish wage earners on a crusade for self-culture, Davidson stooped to serve his brothers after the fashion of the magnanimous young colonel buried amid the "darkeys" of the Fifty-Fourth Massachusetts Regiment at Fort Wagner (*CWJ* 4: 84):

> Leveller upwards of men as Davidson was, upon the intellectual and moral level, he seemed wholly without that sort of religion which makes so many of our contemporary anarchists think that they ought to dip, at least, into some manual occupation, in order to share the common burden of humanity. I never saw T. D. work with his hands in any way. He accepted material services of all kinds without apology as if he were a patrician, evidently feeling that if he played his own more intellectual part rightly, society could make no further claim on him. (*WWJ* 17: 94)

Minimizing the inconsistencies in Davidson's program and mode of living, William portrayed Glenmore, Davidson's Summer School of the Culture Sciences, as a phalanstery where caste privileges for intellectuals were not only tolerated but endemic: "Spontaneously and flexibly organized social settlements or communities, with individual leaders as their centers, seemed to have been his ideal" (17: 94). William was not remotely disconcerted by the contradictions of "T. D., democrat," because he conceived of democracy somewhat differently than we do today, not as a collective sovereignty but as the opportunity for self-cultivation and social mobility, which would earn the masses the right to engage in participatory democracy. Davidson's program facilitated an unlikely reconciliation of institutional and individual destinies, unlikely in the sense that Davidson thought academic life "subdued individuality" and "made for philistinism" (17: 90). Immunized against "corporate selfishness," competition, and corruption, or so William alleged, colleges were democracy's fertile breeding ground for men of genius and goodness such as Davidson himself: "The sense for human superiority ought, then, to be considered our line, as boring subways is the engineer's line and the surgeon's is appendicitis" (17: 108). Scratch the surface of William James's platitudinous conception of the role of public intellectuals, "we are to be the yeast-cake for democracy's dough," and a contradictory and problematic image of an elite group of men promoting egalitarianism through exclusive institutions of higher learning emerges (17: 110).

Part of Davidson's appeal was undoubtedly his resemblance to the paterfamilias: "He led his own life absolutely, in whatever company he found himself, and the intense individualism which he taught by word and deed, is the lesson of which our generation is perhaps most in need" (17: 86–87). He faced a harrowing death from a bladder malady with the same equanimity that Henry Senior had shown when he died, convinced that he had entered spiritual life, "easily &, as it were, deliberately" from self-starvation and the aftereffects of an illness (*CWJ* 1: 338). Just as Henry Senior's theosophy sustained him and healed his sick soul, Davidson's philosophy brought him through "the paroxysms of motiveless nervous dread which used to beset him in the night-watches. Yet these never subdued his stalwartness, nor made him a 'sick-soul' in the theological sense of that appellation" (*WWJ* 17: 87). William James's account of Davidson's stoicism during his terminal illness generalized and inflected the character of that response until it resembled a virile rejection of philosophical pessimism. Davidson's fortitude was brought to bear on the very type and pattern of melancholy "panic fear" that William had endured in his late twenties (15: 134). This rhetorical maneuver also touches on William's abhorrence of Hamletian philosophic pessimism, which Cotkin has styled the ontological soul sickness of a Victorian youth entering manhood without a definite moral agenda (58–59). Cotkin concludes that William found solace in the power of belief, in mimetic healthy-mindedness, but I am not convinced. Writing to Davidson in 1880, William remarked: "I am tired of the position of a dried-up cynic and doubter. The believer is the true full man" (*CWJ* 5: 140). William's meta-physical anguish persisted over the years, fueled by self-deflating reflections on career choices or poor health and evidenced by his wife's coddling and his own report of nervous "smash-ups."

William cracked under the strain of fitting himself to nineteenth-century norms of masculine conduct, never mind the ideals. I believe that William's inveterate statements of antipathy to lonely self-culture—"no philosophy, however wide its sweep or deep its dive, will ever be a substitute for the tini-est experience of life"—were a mnemonic device for tripping the wires and rechanneling the inwardly directed energies outward toward the stream of life rather than ringing affirmations (*WWJ* 17: 489). Pragmatism was the philosophic equivalent of whistling in the dark, an uplifting philosophy born of despair, self-loathing, and a longing for virile engagement with life: "At such moments of energetic living we feel as if there were something diseased and contemptible, yea vile, in theoretic grubbing and brooding" (5: 62–63). Posnock has written insightfully about the "self-canceling" movement of William James's late philosophies, pragmatism and pluralism, noting that his tendency to repress or sublimate ambivalences arose from his youthful ter-ror of sustained introspection (115). The only quarrel I have with Posnock's deft handling of this subject is the emphasis he places on William's myopic strategy for self-actualization. Writing to his family in 1867, William joked about the "golden mean between an inane optimism & a stupid pessimism wh. has always distinguished me" (*CWJ* 4: 182). William's self-effacing pos-ture suggests that there was nothing stunted, at least, about his "self-in-sight," in spite of his surrender to the "administered world" of mental hy-gienics, functionalism, and teleological instrumentality (Posnock, 115, 110). There is a risk in taking William's hostility to philosophic pessimism too se-riously, as Posnock does, and in interpreting it as an example of the bromidic oversimplifications to which the neurasthenic intellectual is prey. Declining to participate in a commemorative celebration organized by Karl Hillebrand for Arthur Schopenhauer, that enemy of melioristic pragmatism who "would undo whatever of simple kindliness and hope keeps its life sweet," William blundered into a confession: "But if there be any kernal of truth in Schopen-hauer's system (and it seems to me there is a deep one) it ought to be cele-brated in silence and in secret, by the inner lives of those to whom it speaks: taking some things seriously is incompatible with 'celebrating' them!"

(Perry, 1: 723–24). What we have to come to terms with is not so much a "taboo on dialectical understanding" as an unlikely interdependence between pluralistic thinking and a recourse to administrative mediations (Posnock, 115). William James was less of a radical pragmatist contentedly bobbing about in a sea of flux and rather more like a monadic subject adrift and casting about for an anchor in a loose and tumultuous universe.

THREE

Dissipation and Decoration in 'Roderick Hudson'

One of the signal events of Henry James's career was his suppression of
Watch and Ward (1870) in favor of *Roderick Hudson* (1875), which he then
designated his first novel. However much this gesture may have reflected an
aesthetic judgment on James's part, it underscored the importance of the latter work as James's declaration of his intent to become a writer. *Roderick
Hudson* was, in part, a response to Henry Senior's attempts to dissuade his
sons from pursuing careers in the arts. As discussed in the last chapter,
Henry Senior claimed that the aesthetic life promoted irresponsibility, egoism, self-centeredness, and moral decay. He presented his budding aesthetes,
William and Henry, with the autobiography of the late Benjamin Robert
Haydon in the hope that Haydon's saga, ending in penury, bombast, and suicide, would warn the boys off this spiritually unremunerative profession.
Certainly Haydon's memoirs impressed Henry Junior, whose eponymous
hero Roderick Hudson took his own life after having scaled artistic heights
at the expense of his sanity and civility. However, as Lionel Trilling has

pointed out, the elder James was "brilliantly contradictory on the moral status of art," and his imprimatur can also be claimed for an exalted view of the artistic vocation (78).

In *Roderick Hudson*, Henry Junior staged a debate with his father over the respective merits of Christian and classical aesthetics. Whereas Henry Senior invoked Carlyle, whom he thought embodied a felicitous marriage of Calvinism and German spiritualism, his son seemed more inclined toward a Nietzchean cross-fertilization of the Apollonian and Dionysian spirit. The novelist characterizes Roderick, before his demise, as a "godlike" figure endowed with the same spirit of ecstasy and elation that Nietzsche attributed to the artist in *The Birth of Tragedy* (1872): "No longer the *artist*, he has himself become a *work of art*" (24).[1] Even after his suicide, Roderick is magically preserved and retains his status as an object of desire: "He was the most beautiful of men!" (*RH*, 332). Although Roderick's decadent lifestyle and tragic abuse of his talent are decried in the novel, most often by his patron, sidekick, and adorer, Rowland Mallet, the world this bright young man leaves behind him is dull as pitch: "Rowland understood how up to the brim, for two years, his personal world had been filled. It looked to him at present as void and blank and sinister as a theatre bankrupt and closed" (333). The image of the bankrupt theater is significant, since it reminds the reader, in light of Roderick's death, of the paltry achievements of the morally responsible, diligent characters such as the lawyer Striker and the capitalist Leavenworth, whose unflagging enthusiasm for American business practices is representative of the new technoeconomic dynamism. Even the middling watercolorist Singleton, who is often mistaken for the hero of the tale, is little more than an artist-machine: "You remind me of a watch that never runs down. If one listens hard one hears you always at it. Tic-tic-tic, tic-tic-tic" (308). Dubious of the advantages accruing to the national culture from the democratization of finance and industry, the novelist selectively allied himself with his father's published legacy when he rhetorically abused the panjandrums of capitalism in the novel: "I never felt proud of my country for what many seem to consider her prime distinction, namely, her ability to foster the rapid accumulation of private wealth" (*HJSr*, 106).

Though *Roderick Hudson* is often read as a cautionary tale about the artist who indulges his passions at the expense of his genius, most recently by Adeline Tintner in *Henry James and the Lust of the Eyes* (123), the novelist's concrete notions of the nature and effect of Roderick's overdraft of his resources are never acknowledged: "You can number them by the thousand—the people of two or three successes; the poor fellows whose candle burnt out in the night. . . . Who shall say that I am not one of these? Who shall assure me that my credit is for an unlimited sum?" (*RH*, 157). This same concern with the ephemeral nature of artistic genius informed James's 1873 review of the watercolorist Bonington who, like Roderick, died young, produced charming works full of "the brightness and vigor of youth," but who "lacked the germs of a materially larger performance" (*PE*, 73). The prologue to "The Madonna of the Future" (1873), a tale of irresolute genius, takes up the phenomenon of artists and writers who had "relapsed into fatal mediocrity" after "one spasmodic bid for fame" (*Tales*, 2: 202). And James's 1873 story, "The Sweetheart of M. Briseux," opens in a gallery furnished with "miniature works by painters whose maturity was not to be powerful" (2: 233). James also compares his story's protagonist, Harold Staines, another "incipient great man" like Roderick Hudson, to a "decorous young Apollo," but Staines is more of a handsome prig than a tragic figure possessed of artistic genius (2: 239).

It is significant that Henry James should harp so insistently on this theme in the 1873–74 period when, as Hall has argued, James had opted for a life of celibacy after a crushing, if obscure, romantic episode. Hall speculates that James felt in some way rejected or betrayed by William during their Italian holiday and that this blow to his affectional impulses prevented Henry from pursuing other love relationships ("Leon Edel," 50). With the benefit of hindsight, Hall's thesis can be seen to make overly fine distinctions between incestuous feelings and homosexuality, which may be mutually constitutive (as is the case with incest emotion and heterosexuality) rather than mutually exclusive. Although *Roderick Hudson* revolves around an intense fraternal bond, it departs from Hall's paradigm of rejecting older, and heartsick younger, brother figures. Improvising a dashing, brilliant, and callow youth for a hero, Henry James invested his unemployed libido in a very different sort of person from his idealized elder brother; put another way, he split off the qualities he had formerly attributed to William in order to see him as glamorous and commensurately endowed Roderick.

As it happens, Roderick's patron, the stodgy Rowland Mallet, has much in common with William, specifically his inability to fix on any remunerative occupation, though Rowland is not merely a caricature of William. The most interesting thing about James's fratricidal or giant-killing impulse, in light of Hall's thesis, is his novel's castigation of Mallet's hypocrisy about professional, monetary, and amatory matters. William had sublimated his desires in concession to societal dictates long before Henry had. It is no coincidence that the years 1873 and 1874 also marked a turning point in the life of William, who had finally settled on a career as an educator at Harvard when he was thirty-one years old. Ceding artistic endeavors to his younger brother, William gave Henry both an impetus for and a rationale with which to defend his commitment to literature. Recasting his father's injunction against an art career in the latest rhetoric as communicated to him by William, that of mental hygiene rather than theosophy, Henry assimilated William's voice and experience even as he used this received wisdom to different ends. Turning the old man's logic on its head, Henry defied his father's prescription to live and love all you can and consciously chose a celibate lifestyle as a counterweight to his profligate imagination. By focusing on the novelist's conception of the erotic economy of artistic production as it is worked out in *Roderick Hudson*, my reading challenges the prevailing notion that James favored the conscientious Rowland Mallet over his feckless protégé; however, I have no interest in furthering a dualistic juxtaposition of the novel's central figures. Rather, what concerns me is James's self-negating gesture, that is, his inability to sustain a vision of artistic activity inspired by ungoverned desire in *Roderick Hudson* and his reluctance to subject Roderick to the discipline of cultural sublimation that he chose for himself:

> Roderick, bearing the lamp and glowing in its radiant circle, seemed the beautiful image of a genius which combined sincerity with power. Gloriani, with his head on one side, pulling his long moustache like a genial Mephistopheles and looking keenly from half-closed eyes at the lighted marble [statue], represented art with a mixed motive, skill unleavened by faith, the mere base maximum of cleverness. (*RH*, 92)

When William arrived in Florence in October 1873, he brought with him a wealth of notions that were to furnish Henry with many of the themes in *Roderick Hudson*. In this chapter I will elaborate on the ideas put forth in the previous chapter, William's invocation of the principles of energy conservation, the debate between determinism and free will, and his anxiety over the nature of genius (whether it is a form of degeneracy or a token of the godhead), this time from Henry's perspective. As an artist, homosexual, and neurasthenic, Henry would have been hard pressed either to emulate or to ignore his brother's costly resolution to his nervous crisis of 1870 to 1872. Alternately brooding and rejoicing over his endowment, William had manifested, in his own estimation, the characteristic defects of the melancholic and monomaniac: interest in fads, sleeplessness, moroseness, mental exhaustion, and inanition. What is significant about this grouping, considered alongside then-popular literature on mental pathology such as Esquirol's *Des Maladies mentales*, is the association of these degenerative tendencies with the artistic temperament: "There are certain professions, which more particularly predispose to this malady, because they exalt the imagination and the passions, and expose those who practice them, to errors of regimen of every kind: such are musicians, poets, actors, and merchants who are engaged in hazardous speculations" (Esquirol, 212). In "Genius and Degeneration," Weir commented: "It is only the genius of aestheticism, the genius of the emotions, that is generally accompanied by unmistakable signs of degeneration" (131). And Cesare Lombroso coined the term *artistic mattoids* to distinguish among gifted hopheads, madmen, and men of real genius (209). Evidently William subjected Henry to a disquisition on biophysical and psychological verities of this kind in an effort to dissuade him from pursuing a career in the arts: "This is your dilemma: The congeniality of europe on the one hand + the difficulty of making an entire living out of original writing, and its abnormality as a matter of mental hygiene" (*CWJ* 1: 230).

If Henry cribbed his psychology and physiology from William, he did so with the intention of refuting the doctrines that Dr. James espoused. To paraphrase Posnock, whose invidious comparison of the brothers James nevertheless evinces an important truth about the fraternal relation: Henry embraced William's thought while refusing its defensive gestures (51). To be more precise, Henry was far from deaf to these arguments; he almost certainly chose a celibate lifestyle in response to William's cautions, but he also looked for ways to circumvent the logic of mental hygiene and to follow his ideal vocation. From the first, the method that Henry chose, a kind of voluntary sublimation patterned after William's self-management, was tinged with bitterness and uncertainty. For Henry experienced William's withdrawal from the sphere of art in favor of science as a personal rejection, as an interruption of the intimacy, if not harmony, between them that had characterized their youth. As late as 1873, William still evoked this sentimental mode, warmly addressing Henry as "my in many respects twin bro" in a letter (*CWJ* 1: 193). Feeling shut out and shortchanged by William's reformation, Henry reasoned that sublimation was a peculiarly insidious means of self-preservation, since it entailed the hoarding of affect, denying love to one's nearest relations. Providing Henry with a trenchant and cynical model of aesthetic sublimation, Balzac's *The Wild Ass's Skin* recommended itself as a compelling intertext for *Roderick Hudson*:

> The things that men call disappointments—loves, ambitions, setbacks, sadness are for me ideas that I convert into reveries; instead of feeling them I express and translate them; instead of letting them consume my life I dramatize and develop them; they divert me as though they were works of fiction which I can read thanks to an inner vision. Never having overtaxed my organs, I continue to enjoy robust health. (53)

The speaker, a thin-lipped antiquities dealer who seals Raphael Valentin's fate by giving him Solomon's talisman, is described as a cross between one of "those Hebraic heads which serve as types to artists when they wish to portray the prophet Moses" and "Gerald Dow's *Money-Changer*" (44). A millionaire and centenarian, the dealer has achieved these milestones by sublimating all desire and volition into thought: "In short, I have invested my life, not in the heart, so easily broken, nor in the senses which are so readily blunted, but in the brain which does not wear out and outlasts everything. No kind of excess has galled either my soul or my body" (52). Through this portrait, Balzac explicitly associated parsimony, asceticism, and longevity with the Jews, a connection that had currency in James's day. Matthew Arnold characterized Hebraism as a "motive power" in *Culture and Anarchy*, a model of sublimation progenitive of Puritan "self-conquest" (132). Arnold, of course, recognized the continuity between Hebrew and Christian ethics and exploited the British public's hatred of the Jews as a hortatory technique, urging a compromise between moral or civic rectitude and the disinterested spontaneity of the Hellenic spirit. Scratch the surface of James's analysis in *Roderick Hudson* of the costs and benefits of aesthetic sublimation, and antisemitic calumnies regarding the Jew's rapacity and indifference to cultural achievements, existing on a deeper stratum of the work, come into focus. Like Arnold, James did not have it in for Jews personally. His invocation of stereotypes is opportunistic, a means of highlighting the intercalation of apparently discrete facets of cultural sublimation, from mercenary motives ennobled by the work ethic to consumerism elevated by aestheticism, to loneliness transfigured by Christian chastity. For James, the stereotypical figure of the Jew mediates issues of gender, sexuality, and economy.

Homo Economicus

What sets Rowland Mallet apart from Balzac's jaded connoisseur is the squeamishness Mallet constantly evinces and his strenuously proper conduct. A combination of primness and inquisitiveness, Rowland denies fraternity with the idle pleasure seekers whom he superficially resembles: "It often seemed to Mallet that he wholly lacked the prime requisite of an expert *flâneur*—the simple, sensuous, confident relish of pleasure" (*RH*, 29). Yet something approximating the cool philosophy of passive, intellectual diversion informs Rowland Mallet's engagement with the reckless and intemperate sculptor. Rowland sponsors Roderick so that he may live through, as well as for, this luminous youth: "Oftenest, perhaps, he wished he had been a vigorous young man of genius without a penny" (30). Rowland's attachment to Roderick, of whom he becomes "abjectly fond," is a thinly veiled romantic relationship of the *senex-puer* variety: "Roderick was so much younger than he himself had ever been. Surely youth and genius hand in hand were the most beautiful sight in the world" (194, 73). There is something arch and knowing in Cecilia's suggestion that her bachelor cousin might like to look at a "remarkably pretty boy" (30).[2] One might argue that a companionable ogling of Hudson cements the bond between Mallet and the watercolorist Singleton, whose characterization is pure camp: "The visitor stood as a privileged pilgrim, with folded hands, blushing, smiling and looking up as if Roderick had been himself a statue on a pedestal. He began to murmur something about his pleasure, his admiration; the desire to say something very appreciative gave him almost an air of distress" (84). If sculpture is "work for men!" and painting not, then Singleton's delicate productions must be read through the lens of the novel's homosocial code (225). With his penchant for "sitting on very small-camp stools and eating the tiniest luncheons," Singleton embodies a principle of economy and industry that carries homoerotic inflections (84). By transcending the need to physically satisfy his appetites rather than repressing his desire altogether, Singleton has achieved a species of that "rarest and most perfect" sublimation, which Posnock has identified with Henry James's private life (47): "Sleeping on straw and eating black bread and beans, but feasting on local colour, making violent love to opportunity and laying up a treasure of reminiscences[, h]e took a devout satisfaction in his hard-earned results and his successful economy" (RH, 104).

Though Rowland apparently tolerates his untoward attraction to Roderick, as does Singleton, who makes no bones about it, Rowland's connoisseurship is closer to repressive substitution than it is to transcendent sublimation. After a lifetime of self-deception and inhibition, Rowland cannot correctly name the object of his desire, mistaking his possessiveness of Roderick for conventional jealousy. The reader, however, is not fooled by Rowland's professed devotion to Roderick's fiancée, the virginal Mary Garland, the pride of West Nazareth, Massachusetts. For if Rowland is seriously attracted to Mary, why does he want so terribly to see her married to Roderick? In this context, the excitement produced by homosocial intimacy gets vented through heterosocial channels. Explaining his reasons for proposing to Mary, Roderick puts the issue of any charm she might hold for him entirely to rest: "But you came and put me into such a ridiculous good-humour that I felt an extraordinary desire to spill over to some woman, and I suppose I took the nearest" (69). In this passage Roderick neatly illustrates Sedgwick's redeployment of Gayle Rubin's explanation of how patriarchy reinforces the bonds between men through traffic in women, who are treated as undifferentiated objects of exchange or property (Sedgwick, *Between Men*, 25–26). Chilly and impersonal in his defense of Mary Garland, Rowland is equally unconvincing in the role of languishing lover: "'I don't know what I wouldn't do,' he said, 'rather than that Miss Garland should be disappointed.' He heard himself grotesquely use this term—which might have applied to a shopgirl" (RH, 232).

The self-alienation revealed by the jarring discord that Rowland apprehends in his own remark confirms the relevance of Sedgwick's thesis, illuminating the marriage market as an arena in which men engage in homosocial competition, exchange, and bonding. To the extent that Rowland identifies the economic sphere with the affairs of powerful patriarchs, such as his imperious father, he opts out of rough commercial intercourse and retreats to the more coddling and feminine atmosphere of the salon. Given his sexual ambivalence, it may seem strange that Rowland chooses to inhabit a milieu populated by self-identified aesthetes, but Rowland's cohorts share his predicament and respect his privacy; moreover, in 1875 the homoerotic content of aestheticism was only just being noised abroad. It is quite significant that Rowland's heterosocial functions are a source of embarrassment to him, provoking guilt and self-recrimination but no remedial course of action. In keeping with the best traditions of the return-of-the-repressed, Mallet obsessively invokes the rhetoric of banking and finance to convey his sense of having "defrauded" Mary Garland and Mrs. Hudson of "a promised security" by transforming a restless law clerk into a restive sculptor (288). Although the acquisition and maintenance of women has never been one of Mallet's objectives, he recognizes that his patronage of Hudson has made the lad unfit for these selfsame obligations: "But I keep thinking of those two praying, trusting neighbours of yours, and I feel like a bad bungler when I don't feel like a swindler" (195). The pecuniary relationship between the two men is a variation on what Sedgwick has called "queer tutelage" (*Tendencies*, 91). As the practical substitute and emotional shunt for thwarted sexual desire, Mallet's economic collaboration with Hudson is tinged with illicit passion. Small wonder that Mallet insists that he is disinterested throughout the affair. In *Roderick Hudson*, avarice is both a primal and intractable instinct striving for recognition alongside repressed homoerotic impulses and a socially countenanced substitute formation. This cathexis opens up the framework within which the intricate network of personal motives and socioeconomic forces is reduced to a spurious irresoluble dualism. By unearthing vestigial traces of guilt and sex disgust in connection with Mallet's enterprise, I want to suggest how sublimation fails to relieve Mallet of the strain of intolerable emotion by allowing him both to invest his libidinal energy elsewhere and to preserve the dignity of a bourgeois and the sangfroid of the aesthete.

Rowland has imperfectly assimilated Calvinism's contribution to the rise of capitalism, an ethos that elevated the vice formerly known as avarice into a civic virtue entrusted with the lofty responsibility of taming the unbridled lusts of the citizenry and organizing their diverted energies to constructive ends (Hirschman, 130). Because his passions and worldly interests are insufficiently differentiated, for Rowland the field of commercial endeavor is fraught with temptations that have been sublimated by the culture at large. For Rowland, acquisitiveness and self-interest bear the residual taint of centuries-old disapprobation and have not been sublimed into purposive activity or inspired calling. Mallet has never learned the religion of doing; Calvinism has taught him only the principle of self-denial. Moreover, as James Eli Adams has suggested in his provocative book *Dandies and Desert Saints*, the effort to legitimize an existence devoted to disinterested spectatorship, mitigated by the discipline of asceticism, puts a man of Rowland's stamp at odds with bourgeois decorum (192–94). The "obloquy of idleness" that attaches to the flaneur, however little he may relish the part of sensualist, places Rowland in the camp of Adams's dandiacal gentlemen who maintain their caste by preserving the illusion of leisure-class indifference to economic concerns, falling below the standard of active manliness in the process (*RH*, 64, 29). Consequently Rowland's morbid conscientiousness and melancholy signal a higher order of social fragmentation and anomie than is readily apparent. He cannot think outside the prison of the American idiom, in which all forms of striving can be reduced to cash value. Even as he consciously rejects the modes of being that threaten to dehumanize or emasculate him, his blind adherence to the ideal of disinterestedness reveals that he has only mystified his relation to capitalism, not escaped it.

James's prose calls attention to the imbrication of ethical and financial notions informing Rowland's assorted scruples. Thus romantic self-interest is transcribed as an affront to the law of absolute financial probity: "Life owed him, he thought, a compensation and he should be restless and resentful til he should find it. He knew—or seemed to know—where he should find it; but he hardly told himself, thinking of it under mental protest, as a man in want of money may think of funds that he holds in trust" (205). Like the architect of a pyramid scheme that cheats orphans and widows, Rowland uneasily contemplates the role he played in the alienation of Roderick's "interest" and the decrement in his productivity: "She showed even in her face and step, meanwhile, the tension of the watcher and the time-keeper: poor Roderick's muddled sum was a mystifying page to a girl who had supposed genius to be to one's spiritual economy what a large balance at the bank is to one's domestic" (304, 288). James has put his readers in Rowland's head at this point. The allusions to double-entry bookkeeping and timekeeping bespeak a familiarity with the office and factory that Miss Garland lacks. Indeed, the commercial overtones of the passage are accented in the later edition. In the 1878 edition, Mary was a simple New England girl who regards Roderick's demise with the concern of a person "watching at a sick-bed" (*RH2*, 300). Rowland Mallet worked in his father's counting house before serving in the Civil War, where he earned a pittance and was treated like a drudge (*RH*, 29). More to the point, Mallet's compulsive analogizing highlights an identity that has been refracted into a dualism over the course of several centuries, culminating in the hegemony of the bourgeoisie. The imbrication of moral and financial terms in Rowland's head is always already before a given in the logic of American capitalism. Rowland's sublimation of mercenary impulses into moral idealism is a further development of this logic and not, as he supposes, its negation. The virtues of honesty, frugality, and diligence pragmatically advance the accretion of wealth and lend a spirit of righteousness to the enterprise (Weber, 52–53). Though Rowland steadfastly maintains a distance from the means of production and from commercial institutions, he still thinks like a capitalist.

Whereas Roderick is "the very copy of his poor father," the same cannot be said of Rowland, who defied Jonas Mallet's precepts and repudiated his shrewd commercial facility (*RH*, 59). Educated according to a principle of austerity that would have given a monastic order pause, Rowland learned thrift but not industry, as his father intended. Malletian connoisseurship is a *refinement* of rank consumerism. Choosing and discriminating as if in a climate of scarcity, Mallet checks his acquisitive impulses in order to lose himself in a flood of impressions. Shopping—"just looking"—becomes an end in itself. Rowland regards his alleged indifference to the possibilities engendered by an inherited fortune as slightly perverse, both with regard to his entrepreneurial Dutch forebears and to the bustling American scene: "But I have the misfortune to be rather an idle man, and in Europe both the burden and the obloquy of idleness are less heavy than here" (64).[3] Though Rowland is given to mild self-derision, as this passage makes clear, he has no intention of entering a profession, driving a trade, investing, or marrying to quiet his critics, Mary Garland and Barnaby Striker, who see him as frivolous: "'I suppose you're a very brilliant young man,' he went on, 'very enlightened, very cultivated, quite up to the mark in the fine arts and all that sort of thing. I'm a plain practical old boy, content to follow an honourable profession in a free country'" (57). The episode anticipates an 1881 Du Maurier lampoon of aestheticism as a threadbare screen for homosexual couplings, *Maudle on the Choice of a Profession* (Freedman, illustrations), with Mallet assuring a bewildered Mrs. Hudson of her handsome son's "distinctly remarkable powers" while Striker, who appraises Hudson's merits "of the light ornamental," casts a critical eye on the proceedings: "He paused a moment, stroking his beard, with his head inclined and one eye half closed, looking at Rowland. The look was grotesque, but it was significant, and it puzzled Rowland more than it amused him" (*RH*, 57, 53, 57).

A booster and braggart, Striker holds up the Protestant work ethic as the crowning achievement of the American way of life and of his own way of life: "I had to grease my wheels myself, and such as I am, I'm a self-made man, every inch of me!" (57). The generational conflict, with Striker standing in for the elder Mallet, is a pretext for airing the caste tensions attendant upon tradesmen and professionals being assimilated into the ranks of gentlemen. It is certain that Striker's descendants will have better manners and greater erudition, but less ambition, than their father, whose catchwords and flag waving will mortify them. Still, the apple does not fall far from the tree. For all his common sense, Striker cannot see that Rowland's urbanity simply exempts him from the dull round of toil that is the lot of the average American; it does not place him outside the relations of production and consumption altogether, as Rowland himself fancies: "If I'm not a producer I shall at any rate be an observer" (65). As Striker might say, a pig in a silk hat is still a pig. Though dynamic parents and indolent children are a predictable result of freshly garnered wealth and permeable barriers to social advancement, these are differences of degree, not kind. The discipline of frugality, the respect for wealth and power, is often deeply ingrained in the next generation: "Mr. Mallet, whenever he looked at his son, felt extreme compunction at having made a fortune. He remembered that the fruit had not dropped ripe from the tree into his own mouth, and he determined it should be no fault of his if the boy were corrupted by luxury" (27). Although a certain amount of fun is had at Striker's expense, his homily on the rewards of honest toil and the vice of idleness, "the crop we gather depends on the seed we sow. He may be the biggest genius of the age: his potatoes won't come up without his hoeing them," turns out to be a folksy version of Rowland's credo, "I don't propose to do anything. He must do for himself. I simply offer him the chance. He's to study, to strive, to work—very hard, I hope" (58, 54).

In a world in which productivity validates every state of being from health to wealth, Rowland is a speculator who ventures little of his capital while earning a tidy interest on his principal. He is a shareholder rather than a captain of industry. He is a consumer, not a laborer. Though Rowland confuses the issue of his economic relation to Roderick by treating him as a friend, a talent, a trial, Rowland nevertheless appropriates Roderick's capacity and work like a true capitalist: "I was bored to feel my hands always so empty. When it first occurred to me I might start our young friend on the path of glory I felt as if I had an unimpeachable inspiration" (49). Rowland's phrase is a felicitous linking of his self-serving, capital idea with aesthetic practice. Analogously, Rowland's conception of the "reflected usefulness" of financing Roderick's career obscures the remunerative aims of this investment by simulating labor (49). Roderick is Rowland's raw material, his engine, and his tool. Like another Jacobean "half of a genius" who envisioned a masterpiece while lacking the "hand of Raphael" to render it (*Tales* 2: 229), Rowland styles himself "a man of genius half-finished" and bemoans the absence of an expressive faculty (*RH*, 25). For this reason, Rowland's kowtowing before Roderick's genius is disingenuous, since he conceives of the younger man as an amanuensis or, more accurately, a prosthesis. Quite unintentionally, Rowland traffics in human commodities. He speaks of negotiating the shoals of Hudson's character—a predilection for wine, women, and gaming—as if he had hopes of bringing a precious cargo safely to port: "[Roderick] was strong, he was first-rate; I felt perfectly secure, and paid myself the most fulsome compliments. We had passed at a bound into the open sea and left danger behind" (194). Moreover, Rowland revels in the lionization of Roderick just as his contemporary, P. T. Barnum, impresario and humbug, might have done: "He said to himself that if he had staked his reputation on bringing out a young lion he ought now to pass for a famous connoisseur" (81).

In this sense, Rowland resembles the millionaire Leavenworth, the architect of a huge fortune, whose patronage of "indigenous talent" is a form of conspicuous consumption (134). The former proprietor of borax mines in the Middle West, Leavenworth is a familiar mixture of puritanical and commercial zeal. Sublimation is sound fiscal policy, proving the infinite convertibility of repressed impulses, buried substances like borax, into activities productive of wealth. No provenance could be more fitting for a man whose aesthetic criteria are founded on the virtues of a white powder, the principal ingredient of laundry detergent: "My dear young friend, never trifle with your lofty mission. Spotless marble seems to me false to itself when it represents anything less than Conscious Temperance—'the golden mean' in all things" (198). If John Ruskin were forced to write pamphlets for the Salvation Army, they might read like Leavenworth's perorations on the evils of tippling: "I remember at Florence an intoxicated figure by Michael Angelo which seemed to me a deplorable aberration of a great mind. I myself touch liquor in no shape whatever" (197). Leavenworth's preoccupation with clean living belies a deep-seated fear of sensuality and contagion, lately deepened by his wife's death and, more important, by the sale of his mining interests. The liquidity of Leavenworth's assets disrupts the felicitous marriage of ethics and avarice known as the Protestant work ethic. On the one hand, Leavenworth's free-spending ways indicate the quandary in which ready cash places him, as if he were trying to convert filthy money into golden bibelots. On the other hand, he enthusiastically celebrates the "convertibility" of American investments, "money right there in convertible securities—not tied up in fever-stricken lands and worm-eaten villas" (199).

Jews and Gent(i)lemen

What is fascinating about this formulation is Leavenworth's projection of unwholesome and decadent financial practices onto foreigners, specifically Jews. Though Leavenworth is not Catholic, he shares the superstition, derived from canon law, that it is wrong for a Christian to take interest on money. Only Jews sully themselves in that way. Yet as Marc Shell has observed in his account of verbal usury in Shakespeare's *The Merchant of Venice*, the kind of linguistic troping, punning, and symbolization in which Mallet and Leavenworth engage is an analogue to the practice of money lending, the generation of supplemental and unnatural meanings (49). Leavenworth's conversation implicates him, at every turn, in stereotypical Jewish behavior, from his disdain for wealth tied up in property, which Central and Eastern European Jews were forbidden to own, lease, or farm, to his tasteless acquisitiveness, to his spurious fidelity. Though Roderick assumes the widower came to him "under the influence of his bereavement" to order a tombstone, he soon infers from Leavenworth's unctuous address to Miss Blanchard that "a monument of his inconsolability might appear mistimed" (*RH*, 134). Sanctimoniously intoning platitudes that betray the secularization of his value system, "are we not told that the office of art is second only to that of religion," Leavenworth acquires "high-class statuary" with all the pomp and philistinism of a nouveau riche (134, 135).[4] In "The Dread of the Jew" (1899), a sympathetic editorialist felt obliged to admit: "Many Jews may be fond of pomp of a vulgar kind, and may affect what we confess personally to finding very disagreeable forms of Asiatic luxury; but these are externals" (338). Leavenworth's grand aesthetic vision of "Intellectual Refinement" in pure white marble is a counterfeit: "His conception is sitting on an india-rubber cushion with a pen in her ear and the lists of the stock-exchange in her hand" (*RH*, 136). James reaches into the grab bag of cultural clichés for this reproof, highlighting Leavenworth's resemblance to the stereotypical Jew: "His conversation rings upon the key-note of the dollar; his literature is the quotations of the market" (Morais, 269). With his narrowing preoccupations, religion and business, Leavenworth calls to mind Arnold's indictment of the Hebraising strain in Protestantism for its rigid conformity to moral law and its mercenary aspect (157).

Jewish caricatures keep turning up like bad pennies in *Roderick Hudson*, as indivisible signifiers of acquisitiveness as against higher moral or aesthetic goals. Exasperated by Leavenworth's instructions as to the proper "cerebral development" of the temporal lobes of his statue, Roderick snaps, "A sculptor isn't a tailor, and I didn't measure you for a pair of trousers" (*RH*, 200). This association of Jews with the garment trades is long-standing. Similarly, when Roderick smashes a bust of Barnaby Striker, he proudly announces, "I've driven the money-changers out of the temple!" (43). One of many "memorials of [his] wanderings," "Intellectual Refinement" is meant to grace a retreat that Leavenworth is building, where he hopes to "recover a certain degree of tone" (135). An example of syllepsis, the image of the worn-out wandering capitalist has paradigmatic significance, instantiating Leavenworth's resemblance to the Wandering Jew, the man who admonished Christ to "Walk faster!" as he paused to rest on his way to Calvary and was told, "I go, but you will walk until I come again" (Goldstein, 534–36).

By the late nineteenth century, the Wandering Jew had come to figure in psychiatric literature, most notably in the work of Jean Martin Charcot, the preeminent alienist in France, as a pathological type afflicted with a morbid and implacable need to travel, which found ultimate expression in untrammeled immigration (541). Nineteenth-century tracts warning of the menace migrant Jews posed to the Christian world emphasized their financial acumen almost as frequently as their alleged propensity to nervous ailments. Noting the high incidence of madness among Italian Jews, recorded in the census of 1874 to 1888, Andrea Verga reckoned that this statistical variation occurred throughout Europe, owing to "the feverish anxiety with which this strong and intelligent Semitic race pursue their interests" (cited in Mosso, 327). Leavenworth's deceptively smug depiction of the United States as a racially pure environment ("clean comfortable *white* humanity") betrays a fear of contamination and is reminiscent of appeals to end open-door immigration policies (*RH*, 199): "We shall have a similar experience with the Polish Jew, whose dwarf stature, peculiar mentality, and ruthless concentration on *self-interest are being engrafted upon the stock of the nation*" (Grant, 14). I have underscored Madison Grant's phrase to call attention to the compulsory distancing Americans of this period affected in relation to their monetary practices, which was no less an affectation than the utilitarian virtues that Ben Franklin perfected in the eighteenth century were.

The reputation for a "ruthless concentration on self-interest" binds Jews and Americans rather than classing them off from each other.[5] The author of "The Dread of the Jew" casually observed that "even the richest men in the world to-day are not Jews, but Americans" (339). At this time the pursuit of wealth was not only perceived as an ethical dilemma but also as a health crisis endemic to the harried pace of American industrial society: "American nervousness, like American invention or agriculture, is at once peculiar and pre-eminent" (Beard, *American Nervousness*, 13). In "Do We Live Too Fast?" Cyrus Edson fretted over the American propensity to work body and soul to the breaking point: "The American pursues the Almighty Dollar with an energy, a zeal, a persistence, that is amazing" (282). Mitchell despaired of wooing businessmen away from their exacting vocations: "The sermon of which these words are the text has been preached many times in many ways to congregations for whom the Dollar Devil had always a more winning eloquence" (7). Leavenworth's confidence in the superiority of American social institutions, as opposed to the "tyranny of class distinctions" elsewhere, is inextricably linked to this cynical counterdiscourse of overwork and brain bankruptcy (*RH*, 198). American social mobility imposed strains of a special order, competitive striving and constant friction: "A factor in producing American nervousness is, beyond dispute, the liberty allowed, and the stimulus given, to Americans to rise out of the position in which they were born, whatever that may be, and to aspire to the highest possibilities of fortune and glory" (Beard, *American Nervousness*, 122).

Even the time and money expended on recreational pursuits is calculated with an eye to "profit." There is no mistaking the primacy of business interests in American society, which are so ingrained as to be self-actuating principles of conduct. Commiserating with Robertson over the latter's "fatigue from overwork" in 1880, William declared, "I don't suppose I cd. live at all without a vacation and I think our business customs wh. don't provide for them are literally infamous." Describing in the same breath an upcoming vacation in Europe as a "hygienic investment of capital which I shall draw on for two or three years to come," William unwittingly derailed his critique of business practices by confounding his domestic and energy budgets (*CWJ* 5: 91). To return to the novel, Leavenworth is not one of the "millionnaires of nerve-force—those who never know what it is to be tired out, or feel that their energies are expended" (Beard, *American Nervousness*, 9). His travels are evidently therapeutic; he seeks a respite from mourning and from enervating business cares in that vaunted Mecca of relaxation, Europe: "I've sustained a considerable loss" (*RH*, 134). Writing in 1882, E. L. Godkin, a James family friend and the editor of the *Nation*, proselytized for the travel industry: "For a weary business man there is nothing like Europe, and Europe means change of scene, and surroundings that will interest and excite. It is in the fact that Europe is not to be had on this continent that most of the American difficulty about vacation lies" (417). Although its subject is the health benefits of leisurely recreation, Godkin's editorial is rife with contradictory messages, such as its emphasis on convenience. This obligatory sublimation of authentic interests, this internal self-correction (what Freud would call a defense mechanism), is never entirely successful in discharging accumulated anxiety or excitement. Similarly, projecting all distasteful qualities of American consumer society onto the acquisitive Jew does not excise the qualities of covetousness and greed from popular consciousness; rather, this projection brings the marginal Jew forward as consumer society's token, rendering him both objectionable and ubiquitous—and requiring his suppression.

The difficulty of dislodging the Jew from his hiding place within the cultural figuration of the capitalist is that the identity between Jew and Christian must be denied at all costs; the geographical and social segregation of the Jew is a blatant example of this imperative. In *Roderick Hudson*, Rowland Mallet is drawn to the "dusky swarming purlieus of the Ghetto" during his frequent peregrinations along the Trastevere (*RH*, 183). Perhaps he goes to study the recently enfranchised Italian citizens of Jewish descent, who gained their majority in 1870? In virtually every case, James highlighted the negative typology associated with the Jew in his later edition. Thus the incommunicable "charm" Mallet experiences in the Jewish quarter in 1878 takes on a "sinister" cast in 1907 (*RH2*, 191; *RH*, 183). In 1904 James returned to New York after an absence of twenty years and found the "Hebrew in possession" (*AS*, 132). During James's absence, Jews comprised the second largest class of immigrants to America, surpassed only by the Italians (Wilkins, 583–95). In *The American Scene*, James is hard pressed to find a language vigorous enough to convey his alarm at the "immitigable," "innumerable," "bustling," "swarming" Jewry that he encounters on the Lower East Side (131). His descriptions of the ghetto are deceptively upbeat. Apart from their tone and texture, these passages tally with nativist diatribes, lamenting the superior reproductive capacities of the immigrants and their threat to the self-proclaimed native stock.[6] Jews in particular are singled out for their low infant-mortality rates, longevity, and special immunity from disease: "The advanced age of so many of the figures, the ubiquity of the children, carried out in fact this analogy; they were all there for race, and not, as it were, for reason." He continues, "It could only be the gathered past of Israel mechanically pushing through" (*AS*, 132). James's reflex conflation of the "mythical Jew" with the modern ghetto Jew is a hallmark of racial stereotyping (Sarna, in Gerber, 58).

My point is not to gauge James's reactions to the new Jerusalem as more or less xenophobic than those of the next fellow but to uncover the buried historical contexts that variously gave rise to sympathetic and anxious appraisals of the ghetto dweller. Returning to *Roderick Hudson* and its Roman backdrop, something can be made of the fact that the Jews of the papal city were, within recent memory, legally encumbered with the most onerous social and professional disadvantages in Europe, prompting the author of "Our Israelitish Brethren" (1870) to remark, "Rome [is] a fragment of the Past preserved, like an Elgin marble, for the inspection of the moderns" (Parton, 389). Well into the 1860s, Roman Jews were forbidden to attend college, law school, medical school, and science academies. They were also forbidden to attend art school, work as artists, or even "enter a public gallery for practice in art" (389). As a reader of the *Atlantic Monthly* and an avid tourist, James must have been aware of the legal instruments and papal contrivances that remanded Jews to the geographical and social quarantine of the ghetto, though the practice of closing the gates at dusk had been discontinued. In *Roderick Hudson*, James deploys ethnocentric commonplaces about the rapacity of Jews and their indifference to culture to advance his case against civilized sexual morality and its authorized canons of behavior.

The textual conflation of capitalists and Jews severely reproves the smug and hidebound Calvinism of the era, anticipating Nietzsche's scornful judgment on an "anti-Semite": "What? you have chosen virtue and the heaving bosom, yet at the same time look with envy on the advantages enjoyed by those who live for the day?—But with virtue one *renounces* 'advantage'" (*Twilight of the Idols*, 34). There are no Jewish characters in the novel, only descriptions of typical gestures and attitudes; however, James's manipulation of the cultural hermeneutic that enables the Jew to be seen in relation to the social totality is far from crude. In part James establishes the relation between Jew and Christian through contiguity. He encourages us to read Leavenworth as a psychic Jew by introducing him on the heels of a startling conversion—the transfiguration of the Catholic Christina Light into the "Jewess" Salome (*RH*, 133). Leavenworth's boast that he could find Christina a husband, "a specimen of clean comfortable *white* humanity" with a quarter million in disposable income, smacks of pandering (199). His speculations regarding the fortune that an "American Christian maiden" on the auction block might fetch suggest an unsavory alliance between Leavenworth and the Jews, who lend Mrs. Light money because of her daughter's beauty: "I've raised money on that girl's face! I've taken her to the Jews and bidden her put off her veil and let down her hair, show her teeth, her shoulders, her arms, all sorts of things, and asked if the mother of that young lady wasn't safe" (198, 170). The contrivance of an unnatural mother, this striptease both mimics and updates Salome's dance of the seven veils, which in

this instance, is aimed at salvaging economic, rather than religious and domestic, privilege. Mrs. Light's usurpation of male prerogatives, her propri-
etary stance, is itself strongly marked by racial typecasting, since gender relations among Jews are allegedly altered by the ritual circumcision of males.

In the popular and scientific conception, the modern Jew is no Herod;
rather, he has outgrown the taste for "Asiatic luxury," relying on his reputed
sensuality to promote costly self-indulgence in others: "Rowland had never
been in the East, but if he had attempted to make a sketch of an old slave-
merchant calling attention to the 'points' of a Circassian beauty he would
have depicted such a smile as Mrs. Light's" (126). Significantly, Leavenworth's interest in Christina is economic, not personal. At no time does he
express a desire for this incomparable beauty. The Borax king behaves as if
he possessed a racial memory that warned him off this type of woman. Although I am attuned to the textual emphasis on Christina's resemblance to a
variety of lethal women, from Homer's Circe to Keats's *belle dame sans merci*
and Lamia to Heine's Salome, I believe the accent on the daughter of Judea
is paramount (Praz, 189–271). Richard Strauss's "Orient-und Judenoper,"
Salome, with a libretto by Wilde, premiered in London in 1905, the year
Wilde's play was finally performed (Gilman, *Disease and Representation*, 157).
The ethnographic content of the novel's stylized scenarios of decapitation/
castration (Roderick's friends envision his head on a charger) symbolizes cultural anxieties raised by the image of the feminized male (*RH*, 133). Gilman
has written eloquently about the "indelibility of circumcision" as a sign of
impaired masculinity (*Freud, Race, and Gender*, 49). Analyzing Strauss's musical allusions to the conversational and oratorical style of the Jews in *Salome*,
Gilman notes that they are identified with the "thin, whining sound" of the
oboe and that the highest note in a quintet falls on the German word for *cir-
cumcised*, a witticism that also signals the librettist's homosexuality: "The
high-pitched note used by Strauss pointed toward that association as well as
the link between the Jews' discourse and that of the homosexual, the feminized male" (*Disease and Representation*, 170, 173).[7] Indeed, Strauss's musical
pun signals culturewide associations between homosexuality and Jewish
identity for late Victorians.

This textual codification of the homosexual through the vocal organs is
also at play in *Roderick Hudson*, which engenders Roderick through sound as
well as sight: "It was a soft and not altogether masculine organ, and pitched

on this occasion in a somewhat plaintive and pettish key" (*RH*, 33). Perhaps because he is master of the gaze, Rowland remains untroubled by Roderick's femininity, the beauty of the "fair and slender stripling" (34). But since aural sensation is passive and the human voice intrusive, Mallet reacts with irritation to Roderick's reedy, insinuating falsetto: "Rowland was a trifle annoyed. 'Be a man,' he was on the point of saying, 'and don't, for heaven's sake, talk in that confoundedly querulous voice!'" (108). Just as evolutionary science made a case for congenital circumcision, that is, the absence of the prepuce, a birth defect allegedly common among Jews, sexology argued for congenital homosexuality, which came with its own highly characteristic physiological markers: "This man's voice and manner of speaking are decidedly feminine; all the little mannerisms and affectations of a society woman being faithfully reproduced" (Weir, "Viraginity and Effemination," 360). Though Roderick lends himself to heteroerotic as well as homoerotic construction, this trait marks him as essentially different from the dominant males of the tribe: "Your voice, at any rate, *caro mio*, condemns you; I always wondered at it; it's not the voice of the conqueror!" (*RH*, 175). In the late nineteenth century, the high-pitched intonation of Jew and invert was thought to be a direct result of castration, a pervasive misunderstanding of both circumcision and homosexuality.

Castigated in polemics against race suicide and degeneracy, the Jew and the homosexual were an odd couple, linked by physical and psychical stigmata. Fearful of free intercourse within society and therefore cliquish, both were accused of antisocial tendencies: inbreeding and infecundity. However, whereas the prospect of recuperation through reeducation of the sexual appetite, marriage, fatherhood, or sublimation was held out to the homosexual, the disease of race was considered irremediable. The unassimilated Jew of the *payess* and *tefilin* was despised by the culture at large; the cosmopolitan Jew, vigorous, pragmatic, modern—and most feared in his incarnation as the banker-financier-capitalist, was abhorred. For James, the Jew was the pariah in extremis, which explains why he made no attempt to soften or undercut the stereotypes he employed. The Jew was the bogeyman who scared the homosexual back into the relative security of the closet. However, the rapprochement thereby achieved between society and its sexual dissidents was tenuous, because the social contract on which it rested could, in special cases, be revoked. For the Jew, sublimating distinct racial qualities did not guarantee assimilation. In so far as sublimation was essential to the survival of homosexuals in Victorian America and England, James was forced to conclude that the Jew, rather than the system, was at fault. Ghostly and insidious, the Jew is a noxious presence in *Roderick Hudson*, constituting a kind of cultural effluvium, like the bad air hanging over the coliseum, that is both a cause and a consequence of society's devolution.

According to James's contemporary Nietzsche, the Jew had become a sort of expert at sublimation, channeling his vital force and concentrating his energies in the interest of self-preservation: "Considered psychologically, the Jewish nation is a nation of the toughest vital energy which, placed in impossible circumstances, voluntarily, from the profoundest shrewdness in self-preservation, took the side of all *décadence* instincts" (*Twilight of the Idols*, 147). Herein lies the paradox of the Jew as a dark mirror of the Christian mind. The Jew represents the *ne plus ultra* of moral rectitude as described by Arnold, epitomizes the laws of energy conservation as propounded by Spencer, and embodies the logic of capitalism as exemplified by Franklin; for what Nietzsche meant by "*décadence* instincts" approximates Max Weber's conception of Franklin's utilitarian virtues. Although Nietzsche's idiosyncratic terminology echoes the barbed observations of *Beyond Good and Evil* and *The Genealogy of Morals* regarding the Jewish inversion of aristocratic values through the "slave revolt in morals," it is inextricably bound to the broader cultural perception of the Jew as fomenting vice, disease, anarchism, and financial panics (*Beyond Good and Evil*, 104; *Birth of Tragedy*, 167–68). Nietzsche's statement crystallizes the cultural antinomies emerging from the contradictory figurations of the Jew as weak, impotent, and diseased and as vigorous and predacious: "The Jews of the world having obtained control of cosmopolitan finance, act together in the interests of their race, and inflict grievous injuries upon nations" ("The Dread of the Jew," 338).[8] In *The American Scene*, James comments on the "unsurpassed strength of the race," a perception underscored by his synecdochical blurring of what he calls new and old Jerusalem (132). Like the Terebratula and the Pteraspis, species that have retained their chief characteristics from the beginning of the geological record to the present, for James, the Jewry of turn-of-the-century Manhattan embodied, physiognomically and otherwise, the concentrated force of the Israelites since the time of Herod. Spencer's revision of Darwin's law of natural selection, the survival of the fittest, is incorporated wholesale into this scheme of social evolution. James's interest in the extent of the "Hebrew conquest of New York" casually evokes an antisemitic climate in which the Jew serves as the scapegoat for the failing indigenous elites who cannot withstand the relentless competitive striving of the interloper (*AS*, 132).

Entropy, Conservation, Sublimation

Appearances notwithstanding, in *Roderick Hudson* James does not invoke for its own sake the infamous stereotype of the "parasitic" Jew, a "usurer and a bloodsucker" who saps the strength of the Christian at home and abroad as does Du Maurier in *Trilby* ("The Dread of the Jew," 338).[9] This stereotype is part of a complex network of cultural codes signaling the use, abuse, and appropriation of human vitality by a series of villains, from capitalists to sexual partners, who constitute the individual's public and domestic environments.[10] The projection of culpability for the fatigue, impotence, and idleness of the novel's principal onto these trumped-up villains is concisely illustrated by the novel's reinvention of Christina as a decidedly modern Salome who owes as much to James's lucubrations on the mystery of the eternal feminine as she does to the gospels. Miss Light's depredations are chiefly figured in terms of waste and entropy and of the life force she has drained from her unwary prey like a "vampire" (*RH*, 154). Although the grandiloquent artist Gloriani imagines that he might have "pumped every inch of her empty," it is Christina who succeeds in vanquishing her would-be masters through her frigidity and cruelty; she makes them no return for their extravagant passion (132).[11] Unlike a "poor Trasteverina," presumably a model of the Jewish quarter, Christina cannot actually be pumped dry; her stores are both inexhaustible and inaccessible. Although she makes an exception for Hudson and "offers to feed him with her beauty," this offer leads to a destructive oversatiation, which whelms his healthy appetites nearly at once, leading to languor and unproductivity, as when he declares, "I'm intoxicated with her beauty!" (133, 141). However, Rowland's construction of Roderick's demise makes light of the lack of fit between Roderick and his prosaic family and friends: "I'll lay you a wager that this is where the shoe pinches" (44). Roderick's craving for sensation is not a newly acquired taste, although it is inflamed by his Roman holiday: "Northampton Main Street—even for three days again—has become, I think, my principal *im*possibility"; "As [Mary's] lover I should mortally hate her. Do you really urge my marrying a woman who would bore me to death?" (123, 233).

Characterized by a puritanical distaste for pleasure in any form, Roderick's home turf would seem the worst possible location for a budding aesthete: "'If beauty's the wrong thing, as people think at Northampton', said Roderick, 'she's the incarnation of evil'" (77). Ever mindful of the utilitarian perspective of his neighbors, Roderick effortlessly recodifies their social mores—modesty, purity, and economy—as a misguided canon of taste. Pitched simultaneously in muted and amplified registers, the comment instantiates Christina's difference from the sober maidens of New England. Because Roderick's statement resembles a syllogism (consisting of a major premise, a minor premise, and a conclusion) without a middle term, it calls attention to the crucial elision, the unspoken calumny undergirding all suppositions regarding Miss Light: her illegitimacy. Though Christina must bear the brunt of her adulterous mother's sin, her personal conduct is blameless. She errs involuntarily, for superlative beauty is a double-edged endowment like genius—both a sign of the godhead or a hallmark of depravity and egotism. Christina is a femme fatale because she is immoderate, passionate, and volcanic; she's "a terrible explosive force" in a shell-shocked world that must marshal its stamina to withstand the strain of competitive striving (253). As Balzac recognized, when every outlay of emotion must be weighed against physical limits that cannot be safely trespassed, hedonism (as in Valentin's cry, "I want to live to excess!") is tantamount to suicide: "Perhaps evil is only a violent pleasure" (Balzac, 54).

Although Roderick's jilting of Mary Garland comes across as sentimental pap, Mallet's conviction that it would be better for Hudson "to marry than to burn" is of a piece with the novel's most provocative thesis. Rowland's morality, as he sees it, makes a virtue of necessity: the conservation of force for the highest aesthetic and philosophic aims. Deriding the "necessary turbulence of genius," Rowland attempts to harness and control Roderick's diffuse powers, a restriction the artist heartily resists: "That I believe, but what I resent is that the range of your vision should pretend to be the limit of my action. You can't feel for me nor judge for me, and there are certain things you know nothing about" (*RH*, 49, 320). Amoral and improvident, Roderick lives in the moment, while his stodgy counterpart plays by the rules and serves as the novel's conscience. Roderick is a *viveur* in Balzac's sense of the term. Like Raphael Valentin, he burns the candle at both ends: "I became a *viveur*, to use the picturesque word which the language of orgy has consecrated. I made it a point of honour to burn myself up as fast as possible, to outdo the merriest rakes in verve and vigor" (Balzac, 176). It is not that Roderick aims to destroy himself; rather, he is an extremist who cannot moderate his behavior, an idealist who cannot tolerate imperfection, least of all his own. Testing his powers in a crucible of fire, Roderick hopes to confirm that he is immortal: "When Phidias and Praxiteles had their statues of goddesses unveiled in the temples of the Aegean, don't you suppose there was something more than a cold-blooded, critical flutter? The thing that there was is the thing I want to bring back. I want to thrill you, with my cold marble, when you look. I want to produce the sacred terror; a Hera that will make you turn blue, an Aphrodite that will make you turn—well, faint" (*RH*, 88–89). Promethean in his craft, aspiration, and destiny, Roderick courts tragedy rather than abiding with an illusion of supremacy: "If I'm to fizzle out, the sooner I know it the better. Sometimes I half suspect it" (153).

Although Rowland's infatuated vision of his protégé ("the beautiful image of a genius which combined sincerity with power") buoys the artist in moments of self-doubt, Roderick is evidently aware of the banality of Rowland's conception of artistic endeavor: "You demand of us to be imaginative, and you deny us the things that feed the imagination. In labour we must be as passionate as the inspired sibyl; in life we must be as regular as the postman and as satisfactory as the cook" (92, 153).[12] Roderick's gibe is right on the money; Rowland fancies himself a connoisseur, but he thinks like an arts administrator. Recalling Leavenworth, Rowland sees the sculptor as a better class of servant in whom clockwork regularity is prized. Convinced that loose living will take a toll on Roderick's innate gifts, Rowland attempts to drive a wedge between the lovers: first by apprising Christina of Roderick's engagement and second by begging her for mercy. Seeing straight through his appeal, Christina curtly summarizes the protoscientific management ethos informing Rowland's intervention: "If I leave him alone he'll go on like a new clock, eh?" (189). The flaw in Rowland's formulation is that it applies the same law across the board without regard for the special sensibility of genius. For Rowland, Roderick's trouble is merely a mechanical difficulty that can be corrected through reengineering: "The talent's there, it's the application that has broken down" (195). Replace the conduit, hook up the battery, and start your engine. Certainly Roderick comes to grief as a result of his ill-advised passion. Rowland's conviction that his friend is better off without "the stimulus of strong emotion, of precarious passion" might be literally correct, but it is no remedy for what ails the artist (189). Deriding as "mere emotions" Roderick's life outside the studio, Rowland reduces Roderick to an automaton or "machine" (194). However, sculpture is not work in a purely mechanical sense; it entails a transmutation of feeling into material form: "'I've only one way of expressing my deepest feelings—it's this.' And he swung his tool" (152).

Contrary to Mallet's surmise, Roderick's ejaculation, "I'm intoxicated with her beauty!,'" is neither a cry of despair nor a herald of disaster (141). Having discovered "a breathing goddess" in the precincts of the Ludovisi gardens, Roderick has fresh hopes of reviving the lost art of the Greeks Phidias and Praxiteles, who had the "advantage of believing in their goddesses" (114, 89). Turning his back on what Pater called "the crabbed Protestantism, which had been the *ennui* of his youth," Roderick embraces the Hellenic ideal in theory, the sensuous motive in art (Pater, 120). Roderick's sense of indebtedness and relatedness to the ancient Greeks mirrors the antiquarian outlook described by Nietzsche in "On the Uses and Disadvantages of History for Life" (1874). Similarly, Roderick's belief in man's inherent nobility, the promise of greatness transmitted to a handful of descendants, corresponds to Nietzsche's outline of the monumental approach to history. Although Roderick's critical faculty is weak, he does manifest the impulse to break up the past and employ it in the service of new forms of life: "The other day when I was looking at Michael Angelo's Moses I was seized with a kind of exasperation, a reaction against all this mere passive enjoyment of grandeur" (*RH*, 70). Hudson is no ordinary neoclassicist, latecomer, or epigone. Rather, he is an untimely man, to use Nietzsche's terminology, one who, as a thoroughgoing Platonist caught in the age of mechanical reproduction, is out of harmony with the zeitgeist: "Your friend Stendhal writes on his book-covers (I never got further) that he has seen too early in life *la beauté parfaite*. I don't know how early he saw it; I saw it before I was born—in another state of being. I can't describe it positively; I can only say I don't find it anywhere now" (182).

Chastened by New England's stern moralism and nauseated by the tawdry pleasures of the beau monde, Roderick is a far cry from a modern epicurean. What he demands for the "freest development" of his imaginative faculty is the emotional tension generated by the contrast of bad and good together: "I confess I need a month's work to take out of my mouth the taste of so many lies" (153, 100). Roderick's immersion in the demimonde whets his appetite for productive endeavor and enlivens him to the highest ideals of his profession: "I feel as if nothing but the chisel and a sledge-hammer would satisfy me; as if in fact I could tear a figure straight out of the block even as Michael of old" (99). He evinces "an intellectual condition similar to that of a palate which has lost its relish," to borrow a phrase from another tale of aesthetic malaise, "Benvolio" of 1875 (*Tales* 3: 26). Roderick's resolution is strained to the breaking point by the continued pressure to rebound from the stimulating or stultifying ambience of his environment du jour. Acceding to Rowland's characterization of him as "a very sick man," Roderick temporarily subordinates his appetites to the functionalist imperative (*RH*, 209). But Rowland has no warrant for his mood of self-congratulation that attends Roderick's submission. The episodic pattern of Roderick's dissipations and subsequent reformations indicates that though he openly rebels against the canons that circumscribe his liberty, he is in no way free. Though Rowland and the Northampton quilting society mistake him for a full-blown sybarite, the sculptor pays his obeisance to the gorgon of decency, allowing Mrs. Light to superintend her daughter's portrait and letting Christina off with "the mere sacrifice of her head" (132). In taking the narrowest possible measure of his freedom (Mrs. Hudson hopes to see her son "tethered to the law like a browsing goat to a stake"), Roderick's family and counselors actually encourage his waywardness (45). If only there were some middle territory between Northampton and Sodom, James implies, Roderick need not go "utterly to the devil" to escape the mundane (272).

Though the novel's *belle dame sans merci* is the catalyst for Hudson's debacle, she is an "inexorable need" of genius as far as the prodigy is concerned, though Rowland thinks otherwise: "It's in fact another case of Ulysses and the Sirens; only Roderick refuses to be tied to the mast" (53, 194). This cameo of "bound" excitation approaches Rowland's ideal of sublimation, which always tends toward what Freud calls the "quiescent cathexis" rather than expression (11: 302). Roderick, however, is more uninhibited, more responsive to his sexual instincts and less troubled by reproductive imperatives or civilized morality; consequently, his excitation is free flowing and tends toward discharge (11: 303). Freud's theory of sublimation introduced an "economic" viewpoint into psychoanalysis, likening metapsychological processes to economies of force in terms any biophysicist would recognize as derivative (11: 275). In so far as psychic processes obey the teleological imperative of consuming excess energy, returning the individual to an unruffled state of alertness, Rowland's strategy for channeling libidinal energy into work or exalted aims may be seen as a natural safeguard against pain and overstimulation.[13]

Rowland's "mental protest" against transgressive desire reveals itself in a pattern of self-censorship and sacrifice, wherein the libidinal energy detached from this untoward interest flows into other channels: those of "moral passion" and "moral energy" (*RH*, 205, 151, 316). These reactively reinforced currents are continually in flux, recharged and fagged by contact with the electric current of feeling that Roderick excites in Rowland: "He felt just now more than ever that a fine moral agitation, adding a zest to life, is the inevitable portion of those who, themselves unendowed, yet share romantically the pursuits of the inspired" (151). Rowland's striving for perfection, his repression of sexual instincts, and his equation of stability with pleasure anticipate Freud's "pleasure principle," especially in so far as Rowland derives a queer excitement from the tension produced by his instinct's persistent demand for recognition and satisfaction (11: 305, 314–15). Why else would he abjectly endure the displeasure and upheaval that Roderick causes him? Furthermore, Freud's economic viewpoint sheds light on Mallet's unconscious conflation of love and money. Rowland intends to spare himself the unremunerative outlay of feeling qua energy. In a hermetically sealed psyche, one that invests libido in the ego and "pays none of it out in object-cathexis," there is no dissipation and no expenditure, and the level of energy available for psychic work (repression, displacement, and abreaction) remains constant (11: 323). Sublimation assists in the process of maintaining constancy by keeping excitation in check. However, much to Rowland's chagrin, this system, though perfect in theory, like Carnot's ideal frictionless motor, is impracticable in reality: "To extend this process of displacement indefinitely is, however, certainly not possible, any more than is the case with the transformation of heat into mechanical energy in our machines" (12: 40). Sexual satisfaction cannot be avoided indefinitely without consequence; energy cannot be conserved in perpetuity: "He recognized a sudden collapse of his moral energy; a current that had been flowing for two years with a breadth of its own seemed at last to submit to shrinkage and thinness" (*RH*, 316).

In this sense sublimation represents the triumph of the higher psychical functions over the more primary ones, the subordination of the instincts of self-gratification to the reality principle, but at a price—the diminution of enjoyment (Freud, 12: 267). The theory of cultural sublimation compensates the individual more generously, siphoning libido into acceptable outlets while preserving the intensity of the displaced aim, as in the artist's embodiment of a fantasy. Pater's study of the classicist Winckelmann offers a wonderful analogue to this notion of displacement, one that has the added merit of illustrating the pervasiveness of the law of dissipation of energy: "Other interests, practical or intellectual, those slighter talents and motives not supreme, which in most men are the waste part of nature, and drain away their vitality, he plucked out and cast from him. The protracted longing of his youth is not a vague, romantic longing: he knows what he longs for, what he wills. Within its severe limits his enthusiasm burns like lava" (119). But important differences exist between Pater's elaboration of this concept and Freud's. Overdetermined by natural laws, such as the ego's instinct of self-preservation and the second law of thermodynamics, Freud's theory of sublimation prioritizes the redirection of energy into prudential channels (those ministering to survival in nature or society). It follows that the reservoirs of psychic energy tapped for cultural activities are made available through the suppression of so-called primitive, infantile, or perverse forms of sexual excitation (12: 41).

In "'Civilized' Sexual Morality and Modern Nervous Illness," Freud comments that "an abstinent artist is hardly conceivable," yet in "Civilization and Its Discontents," he makes the suppression of the sexual instinct a condition of artistic practice and valorizes this course as "finer and higher," especially for homosexuals who in this manner are atoning for their proscribed desires (12: 48, 267). I will not attempt a substantive critique of Freud's theory, other than to suggest alternative explanations of the interrelation of sexuality and aesthetics, which do not posit these aims as mutually exclusive.[14] Extolling Winckelmann's "romantic, fervent friendships with young men" as evidence of a temperamental "affinity with Hellenism," Pater made homoerotism a virtual condition of aesthetic appreciation, a conclusion that scandalized clerical Oxford (122–23). In reality Pater was certainly nothing of the sybarite. His friendships were apparently platonic; he confined his ardor to the printed page exactly in the manner of one of Freud's repressed discontents. Yet judging from his writing and milieu, Pater was discreet rather than confused about his sexual inclinations. Deprived of coveted academic appointments because of the machinations of conservative Oxonians, who pegged him as an agnostic and homophile, Pater cultivated an impenetrable reserve, which James seized upon as the key to his character: "He is the mask without the face, and there isn't in his total superfices a tiny point of vantage for the newspaper to flap its wings on" (*HJL* 3: 492).[15]

In spite of this vaunted inscrutability, Pater appears an open book to James, who speaks of "faint, pale, embarrassed, exquisite Pater!" as though the author of *The Renaissance* had been caught in a compromising position by his acolyte (3: 492). James's attention throughout these passages to Pater's physical presence is striking; the word *superficies* connotes the violation of personal space and therefore the breach of a secret compact as well. James's letters are riddled with innuendos to the effect that Pater's exemplary discretion saved him from some kind of public exposure intricately bound up with the fact of his effeteness: "What is more delicate than the extinction of delicacy—and what note more in place than that of 'discretion'—in respect to the treatment of anything that might have happened to Pater—even the last thing that *could* happen?" (3: 483). Given the tenor of these remarks, the "last thing" does not signify death, but a sexual climax. Moreover, this witticism is exactly the sort that one of James's boyfriends, Walpole or Fullerton, might have come up with at his expense. James's depreciation of Pater is partly a function of professional jealousy. This crack is indicative of James and Pater's relative status among the British aesthetes, a homosexual coterie if ever there was one, who scarcely recognized James as a fellow traveler, in spite of his contributions to the *Yellow Book*. Though he conceded to Gosse that the late author of *The Renaissance* might take his place in the pantheon of letters, James spitefully trimmed Pater's wick, reducing the "hard, gemlike flame" to a glowing "phosphorescence, not a flame" (3: 492). It is both touching and significant that James's deprecation of Pater subtly bolsters his self-regard and affirms his sensuality, an ignis fatuus if ever there was one, if the biographers are to be relied on.

What prevented James from recognizing Pater as his precursor? How could James possibly overlook the affinity between Pater's goal of "a quickened, multiplied consciousness" and his own life plan (153)? Should we blame his misprision on the "anxiety of influence" (Bloom, 77) or on "homosexual panic" (Sedgwick, *Epistemology*, 186)? James must have hated the status of epigone conferred on him by Pater's priority, just as he resented being a "mere junior" for much of his life. Moreover, the Paterian amplification of the aesthetic credo seems to have embarrassed James. Pater was indiscreet enough to mention the curled darlings of Raphael, Leonardo, and Michelangelo, intimating that the Renaissance masters ogled their pages and male models in the manner of Greeks at the palaestra. Reading Pater, James was agitated by the magnified travesty, as opposed to the "alienated majesty," of his own persona: the balding, bulging, would-be lover of handsome youths (Emerson, cited in Bloom, 48). Would some younger fellow one day write off James with a disdainful flick of the wrist, just as James had deposed the erstwhile master of Brasenose, "who is far from being as beautiful as his own prose" (*HJL* 2: 212)? James's uneasiness with Pater's demeanor (being "delicate" becomes a liability once the bloom is off the bud) grievously diminished James's enthusiasm for the published exhortations to gather the splendor of experience, as it were, passively. Underlying James's hostility to Pater is a (dis)identification with epicenism and preciosity, a reaction to the increasing legibility of homosexuality through the efforts of the sexologists, journalists, and aesthetes themselves.[16] As it happens, these epistolary commemorations of Pater date from the 1890s, when James began to cultivate the "legend of the Master," engendering the self in more definitely masculine terms, a move that should not be confused with a conversion to heterosexuality (Edel, 3: 313). James undermines this impersonation of a normative gender identity by camping it up quite a bit. His instructions to Walpole regarding the appropriate form of address, "*très-cher Maître*," or "my very dear Master," are the late-Victorian equivalent of that modern paradox, the "leather queen" (*HJL* 4: 520).

By belatedly modifying his sexual persona, James was indirectly acknowledging the pallid compensations of homosocial chastity. This realignment favors the repressed aggressive impulses of the component instinct so long under the sway of the so-called "feminine" masochistic inclinations (Freud, 7: 71–71n2). Put another way, as sexual gratification cannot be deferred indefinitely, the displaced aim gradually reasserts itself. As I see it, *Roderick Hudson* prefigures the inevitable crisis in James's ability to hold up under the pressure of these sublimated sexual drives. I respectfully disagree with Freedman's view that Roderick's extremism, like that of Swinburne and Baudelaire, appalls the prudish novelist. James's posturing about the absence of moral sensibility in Swinburne, which Freedman contends makes James sound like an "urbane prig" (141), is overdone, even arch: "For we do not mean simply to say that the author does not understand morality—a charge to which he would be probably quite indifferent; but that he does not at all understand immorality" (*LC1*, 1283). Taken out of the context of our reflex conception of James, this epithet smacks of Oscar Wilde, not Miss Grundy. It is condescending, not sanctimonious. The particular turn James gives his fastidious criticisms of the earthier elements in *Les Fleurs du mal*, "we take it that he did not use the word flowers in a purely ironical sense," comes across as the fin de siècle equivalent of *shade*, the trick of dismissing competition as insufficiently refined (*LC2*, 155). In the 1870s, when James conceived these review-essays, he apparently felt at liberty to flaunt his effeminacy and sexual nonconformity. Superficial primness notwithstanding, the reviews are pitched to an audience of cognoscenti, men on whom no hint of eroticism is lost. Swinburne's "Chastelard" might have appealed to Christian Women's Temperance Association types as well as to aesthetes, but it is hard to imagine these ladies engrossed in *Les Fleurs du mal*. Speaking of Gautier's excessive praise for Baudelaire's "endowment" or linguistic facility, James cheekily opined, "It is the admiration of the writer who gushes for the writer who trickles" (156). I am suggesting here that James's finical criticisms and hysterical expletives ("nasty!") are continuous with the transgressive postures and affectations of aestheticism itself (155).

If anything, James felt he was too attracted to the tides of passion and therefore resigned himself to expressing them in his fiction alone. For the young James, cultural sublimation was manifestly more than an elective defense against illicit passion, a mechanism for shunting sexual excitation; it was also the promise of a potentially richer pleasure unconstrained by civilized sexual morality, which proved elusive for that very reason. To paraphrase Leo Bersani, whose brilliant article, "Sexuality and Aesthetics," lays out the terms in which sublimation may be reckoned an extension of desire and not a repressive substitute, James resists domesticating every carnal impulse that makes its way to the surface of the text (37): "At last, springing up, 'I want to strike out hard!' he exclaimed; 'I want to do something violent and indecent and impossible—to let off steam!'" (*RH*, 62). Though Mallet and Hudson superficially personify the antagonism between civilization and ungoverned sexuality in *Roderick Hudson*, on a deeper level they both exemplify the "shattering tension" attending sexual excitation, Rowland by seeking to evade this disturbing tension and Roderick by seeking to repeat or heighten it (Bersani, "Sexuality and Aesthetics," 33–34).

It is interesting to note, with regard to Bersani's reading of *L'Après-midi d'un faune*, that *Roderick Hudson* recapitulates the domestication of sexual instincts through Rowland's primary attraction to and secondary effort to suppress what is feral and faunlike in Roderick: "Looking at him as he lay stretched in the shade, Rowland vaguely likened him to some beautiful, supple, restless, bright-eyed animal, whose motions should have no deeper warrant than the tremulous delicacy of its structure and seem graceful to many persons even when they should be least convenient" (*RH*, 39). James's characterization of Roderick and some of the novel's picturesque details evoke Nathaniel Hawthorne's *The Marble Faun*, whose tragicomic hero, Donatello, is likened to "the very Faun of Praxiteles" (14). The pastoral undertones of Mallet's idyll, set to the music of babbling brooks and whispering pines, replicate the golden age of same-sex love. The scene presages the repression of this companionable tenderness by trailing off into unintelligibility; nevertheless, it is evident why creatures such as Roderick prove inconvenient. Rowland is overcome by a feeling of "prospective regret" while in the midst of his reverie; he has already begun to renounce his desire (*RH*, 39).

If sexuality is a "tautology for masochism," as Bersani argues in "Sexuality and Aesthetics," Roderick's métier is continuous with Bersani's stunning reformulation of the genealogy of artistic endeavor as "masochistic *jouissance*" (34, 41): "I want to thrill you with my cold marble, when you look. I want to produce the sacred terror; a Hera that will make you turn blue, an Aphrodite that will make you turn—well, faint" (*RH*, 88–89). Describing the visual impact of late-Assyrian bas-reliefs depicting scenes of carnage, Bersani and Ulysse Dutoit contend that the friction between the narrative violence of the sculptures and their formal elegance "immobilize[s] the viewer in the mimetic fascination of sadism" and in its complement, masochism (*Arts of Impoverishment*, 137). Analogously, Roderick intends for his "divine forms" to replicate the experience of being shattered into sexuality; his bravura manner belies a hidden identification with the viewer's frisson, the sublime thrill of aesthetically induced pain and fright: "I have been thinking lately of making a Cain, but I should never dream of making him ugly. He should be a very handsome fellow indeed, and he should lift up the murderous club with the beautiful movement of the fighters in the Greek friezes who are chopping at their enemies" (*RH*, 89, 88).

Hellenism

Critics of *Roderick Hudson* routinely dismiss the protagonist as a romantic or derelict or, in any case, as a complete failure; from this vantage point, the sculptor's professions seem empty boasts.[17] But Roderick's war cry against philistinism—"the Greeks never made anything ugly, and I'm a Hellenist; I'm not a Hebraist!"—is a scholarly annotation of sorts, highlighting his kinship with Victorian enthusiasts for classical models: Pater and Arnold (88). Arnold's contraposition of Hebraism and Hellenism in *Culture and Anarchy* informs Hudson's declaration, particularly his emphasis on the Greek striving for perfection: "Greek art and beauty rest on fidelity to nature,—the *best* nature,—and on a delicate discrimination of what this best nature is" (Arnold, 147–48). Hebraic conformity to the law dictates that Hudson's Cain should be as ugly as sin and that a marble Judas should serve as a salutary reminder of evil.[18] Hudson is most definitely no neoclassicist copying "the prize bores of Olympus" to win fame and fortune, for he is animated by "a kind of religious awe in the presence of a marble image newly created and expressing the human type in superhuman purity" (*RH*, 89, 88). The very quality that critics fix on as Hudson's insufficiency, his petulance or hubris, is exactly what inspires his peers with tremulous passion: "It's against the taste of the day, I know; we've really lost the faculty to understand beauty in the large ideal way. We stand like a race with shrunken muscles, staring helplessly at the weights our forefathers easily lifted. But I don't hesitate to proclaim it—I mean to lift them again! I mean to go in for big things; that's my notion of art. I mean to do things that will be simple and sublime" (88). Listening to Roderick "open-mouthed, as if Phoebus Apollo had been talking," Sam Singleton offers an alternate take on Roderick's prodigious egotism (87). Egotism is a manifestation of a will to power in which "art masters ecstasy": "In this condition one enriches everything out of one's own abundance: what one sees, what one desires, one sees swollen, pressing, strong, overladen with energy. The man in this condition transforms things until they mirror his power—until they are reflections of his perfection. This *compulsion* to transform into the perfect is—art" (Nietzsche, *Philosophy and Truth*, 16; *Twilight of the Idols*, 83). Nietzsche's philosophy is the closest we come to the ideals informing the unabashed hero worship resonant in *Roderick Hudson*, well before the novelist snatches defeat from the jaws of hope and glory: "'I confess,' Singleton pursued, 'I can't judge him rationally. He fascinates me; he's the sort of man one makes one's hero of'" (*RH*, 267).

I am not insisting on James's precocious acquaintance with the works of Nietzsche, even the contemporaneous texts, for James might have picked up similar notions of the artist's divinity from his father: "It is simply the man who in all these modes works from an ideal, works to produce or bring forth in tangible form some conception of use or beauty with which not his memory but his inmost soul is aglow" (*HJSr*, 138). With his evangelical bent, Henry Senior compares aesthetic activity to a sacrament, in which the artist consecrates the work of his hands by casting off the shackles of convention in pursuit of an ideal that will bring him closer to a spiritual reunion with God. By disavowing conventional pieties, preaching that the "true vigor of humanity" has never lain just in the direction of good but also in the "effectual reconciliation" of good and evil, the elder James facilitated his son's secular appropriation of his ideas: "Hence Art may be styled man's characteristic activity, as expressing the whole of his nature, or inviting the freest play of both its moral elements. It excludes from its field neither the saint nor the sinner, neither serpent nor dove, but perfectly authenticates the aspiration of both" (144–45).[19] Rebounding from excess to asceticism and back again, Roderick Hudson exemplifies the possibilities and pitfalls of this new type of man: "I believed he would do fine things, but I was sure he would intersperse them with a good many follies, and that his beautiful statues would spring up out of the midst of a dense plantation of wild oats" (*RH*, 97). Playing to his strengths, Hudson soars when freely pursuing his spontaneous attractions; skittish and irresolute, he scatters the "wild oats of his genius" to the winds (*HJSr*, 84).

Henry Senior's dismal forecast of the artist's fate in polite society was confirmed by the history of that "hapless artist," Haydon, whose autobiography and monumental canvases fascinated the brothers James in the mid-to-late

1850s (*Autobiography*, 177). Beyond the incidental resemblances between Haydon's life and the events of *Roderick Hudson* (for example, the hero's uncompromising disdain for the popular and remunerative art of portraiture, the grandiose conception of himself as salvaging his nation's cultural heritage, and his prodigality and suicide), Haydon's memorable first encounter with the Elgin Marbles, which struck him as a revelation of naturalistic technique destined to overturn the "false *beau-ideal*" of the academicians, set a precedent for Roderick's fervent Hellenism (Haydon, 1: 67). Modifying his protagonist's vocation to reinforce the connection between Hudson and his classical forebears, James mimicked Haydon's recourse to the sculptors Canova and Fuseli to support his unqualified admiration: "De Greeks were godes! de Greeks were godes!" (1: 68). Intent on recapturing the vanished glory of Greek art, Hudson is a reprise of Haydon, with one important difference: he initially appears capable of assimilating the past, of applying it to his own needs in an entirely original way, sui generis, as Henry Senior would say: "I've an indigestion of impressions; I must work them off before I go in for any more. I don't want to look at any more of other people's works for a month—not even at nature's own. I want to look, if you please, at Roderick Hudson's" (*RH*, 70).

Roderick's swaggering may appear to place him at the heart of a fancy-dress genre piece, but it is not a lightly considered dramatic effect. The "reaction against all this mere passive enjoyment of grandeur, and, above all, against this perpetual platitude of spirit under imposed admirations" steels the artist against the tyranny of past forms, helping him to avoid the creative paralysis of the museum curator or the historicist in Nietzsche's pejorative conception (70). A bold temperament is the mandate of the "architect of the future": "The stronger the innermost roots of a man's nature, the more readily will he be able to assimilate and appropriate the things of the past; and the most powerful and tremendous nature would be characterized by the fact that it would know no boundary at all at which the historical sense began to overwhelm it" (Nietzsche, *Untimely Meditations*, 94, 62–63). Nietzsche's "plastic power" or faculty of selective appropriation presupposes a fund of strength, an overweening sense of self, that insulates the individual from the traps of a historical sensibility: passivity, reflection, and imitation (62). Unfortunately, Roderick is only intermittently a "man of gigantic will," a "law unto himself" (*HJSr*, 102, 131). Hudson is the great man in embryonic form, an American Adam who has bitten off more than he can chew: "There's a career for a man, and I have twenty minds to embrace it on the spot—to be the typical, original, *ab*original American artist!" (*RH*, 40). Even so it would be shortsighted to disparage Hudson's aspiration because he fails to realize what is best and noblest in himself, or in Henry Senior's words, to "despise the shapeless embryo because it is not the full-formed man, and burn up the humble acorn because it is not yet the branching oak" (*HJSr*, 113).

Had James wanted to write a morality play or a novel of manners, he need not have gone to the trouble of outfitting Hudson with a full-blown aesthetic vision. Hellenism is the artist's necessary illusion; without it, the "genius" is "condemned to revolve as a star without atmosphere," soon to "wither and grow hard and unfruitful" (Nietzsche, *Untimely Meditations*, 97). However, the historical sense serves as both a boon and curse to the artist, as Nietzsche predicted. Roderick "spoil[s] on the tree" because he loses faith in his endowment the instant his inspiration wanes (*RH*, 196). From that point on, he mistrusts his instincts, loses his spontaneity, and grows faint of heart. Denigrating his accomplishments, measuring his creations against an impossible standard, Roderick falls into the mode of ironical self-consciousness from which vantage point no task is noble, no effort worthwhile: "I don't know what's the matter with me. Nothing comes; all of a sudden I hate things. My old things look ugly; everything looks asinine" (94). What I am suggesting is that Roderick's dissipations mask the impairment of his creative instinct; decadence is a consequence of, rather than a cause of, inanition. Although Roderick never compromises his ideal by reverting to "violence, to contortions, to romanticism, in self-defence" as Gloriani predicts, he allows himself simply to "fizzle out" when his illusions no longer sustain him, which mystifies and exasperates his friends: "I don't understand so much power—because it *is* power—going with so much weakness, such a brilliant gift being subject to such lapses" (90, 153, 194).

This incongruity in Roderick's makeup manifests a tragic duality closely resembling Nietzsche's elaboration of the psychology of Greek dramaturgy, which focuses attention on the dissolution and impermanence of forms while generating new illusions in the service of life. In tragedy, the Dionysian apprehension of chaos coexists with the Apollonian will to form, the dream of transcendent value. As latecomer, as modern, Roderick necessarily perceives these warring impulses as irreconcilable, as evidence of his own fragmentation, "I'm an ass unless I'm an angel" (158). The hero self-destructs in the course of events only to rise, in the minds of the novel's principals, from the ash heap of discarded ideals as the once-and-future symbol of a beautiful illusion: "It was as if violence, having wrought her ravage, had stolen away in shame. Roderick's face might have shamed her; it was indescribably, and all so innocently, fair" (332). In *The Birth of Tragedy*, "Apollo overcomes individual suffering by the glorious apotheosis of what is eternal in appearance: here beauty vanquishes the suffering that inheres in all existence" (102). Hudson too dreams of life eternal, projected in an unending chain of exquisite forms, from his plans for a statue of the youthful David looking like a "beautiful runner at the Olympic games" to his vision of a "ripping Christ" (*RH*, 87). His nostalgia for antique marbles is of a piece with his faith that one individual's striving for perfection will elevate the mass of humanity, a conviction that founders on the shoals of personal failure: "'Those things of mine were pretty devilish good,' he answered. 'But my idea was so much better—and that's what I mean!'" (182). Hudson's idea, "the perfection of form, you know, to symbolize the perfection of spirit," is integrally bound up with the life-affirming power of Apollo, the patron of the plastic arts, with whom he is closely associated through his peerless beauty and "his look as of a nervous nineteenth-century Apollo" (88, 195).

Apollonian mastery and enchantment, particularly of the visual sense, stand as the hallmarks of tranquil genius, but Roderick is notoriously nervous and high-strung, just like the Dionysian artist he so greatly resembles, whose emotional system responds to stimuli as did the fabled aeolian lyre. Frequently we discover the artist at his cups, "lying prone" and "miserably the worse for liquor" (196). As Dionysian man, the spiritual and mortal heir of a bibulous Virginia planter, Roderick comes by this predilection naturally enough (37). But James seems at pains to show that Hudson's talent issues from the same wellsprings as his hedonism, a nod to popular romantic stereotypes of undisciplined genius, which is something more than an attempt to shrink-wrap the novel in the tidy sheath of received opinion. Hudson's first delightful statuette is entitled *Thirst* (31). Bedecked with a "loosened fillet of wild flowers," the youth portrayed is a Dionysian figure and not a "little Water-Drinker," as Rowland naively supposes (31, 40). In important ways, all Roderick's works reflect the moment-to-moment experiences of their creator; he sculpts *Adam* and *Eve* when his powers are godlike, *Lady Conversing Affably with a Gentleman*, which should be subtitled *Conversation with a Courtesan*, after an extended debauch at a fashionable spa (which included gaming, drinking, and sexual excess), and *Lazzarone* after he has lost all motivation for any productive endeavor: "Lying dead drunk's not a transitory attitude. Nothing's more permanent, more sculpturesque, more monumental" (81, 92, 104, 197).

The ironic inversion of sense and substance carried out in the preceding sentences exemplifies a pattern of subversive rejoinder to the commonplace wisdom of Mallet and his cronies, which disrupts the staid and predictable surface of the text just as Hudson disrupts their lives. Mindful of this pattern, Roderick's ejaculation, "I'm intoxicated with her beauty!," becomes the rallying cry of the artist divested of petty motives, obligations, and scruples (141). It looks forward to Freud's observation that the "motive forces of artists are the same conflicts which drive other people into neurosis and have encouraged society to construct its institutions" (15: 53). But his declaration is closer in spirit to Nietzsche's assertion that intoxication is a precondition for aesthetic activity, that it produces a feeling of "plenitude and increased energy" akin to "Dionysiac rapture" (*Twilight of the Idols*, 82–83). Unleashing rather than harnessing the sublimated drives, this intoxication is a will to power that arrogantly resists the domestication of the instincts in the service of cultural production: "From out of this feeling one gives to things, one *compels* them to take, one rapes them—one calls this procedure *idealizing*" (83). The interconnections I am forging here signal a radical departure from the conventional understanding of James's personal conception of artistic production. The sublimation of eros, both a theme in James's works and a facet of his creative life, does not simply reroute libidinal energy into acceptable channels of activity. The correspondences among the aesthete, the classicist, and the homophile, whose amorous longings remain cerebral events but are no less passionate for that, are mediated by a "masochistic economy" of art, which is focused on prolonging sensation ("burning") rather than on achieving endpleasure.[20]

Nietzsche's aesthetic is rooted in the sublime, in the primal unity of pleasure and pain manifest in Dionysian revelry but cleaved from the time of the ascendancy of Apollo, who rejects all license: "For [even] now in every exuberant joy there is heard an undertone of terror" (*Birth of Tragedy*, 27). Although the two elements are interdependent, Nietzsche regards the transcendence of the Apollonian *principium individuationis*, as if through the communal clamor, ecstasy, and lawlessness of the Dionysian rite, as the highest achievement of art, for it allows the mystical unity of man to show forth (22): "Dionysian art tells us that we no longer have to be single; it undoes the privileges and remedies the lost solitariness of psychological individuality. And this means renouncing the superstition of difference and recognizing the superfluity of the self's value" (Bersani and Dutoit, 140–41). The shattering of the principium individuationis, which forms the centerpiece of Henry Senior's narrative of his nervous breakdown, obeys the conventions of the sublime as well. In a "lightning flash," Henry Senior found himself "inwardly shrivelled to a cinder" by his delusion that a fetid demon was squatting by his fireside (*HJSr*, 55, 67). Positing the subject's "vastation" (the destruction of his spurious self-sufficiency) as a precondition for his spiritual regeneration, Henry Senior subscribed to a communal imperative much the same as Nietzsche's: "Now the Artist is saturated with this sentiment of universal unity, this sentiment which binds all nature together in the unity of man" (143).

However lavishly they may praise the artist who facilitates this glorious communal transfiguration to which the ritual functions of art have been adapted, Nietzsche and Henry Senior hold the artist of no personal account: "The Artist has typified the perfect man, because in the sphere of work or production he has wrought only from ideas, or from within outwards. But he has not *been* the perfect man, because in the sphere of life he has exhibited precisely the same conflict between the ideal and the actual as other men exhibit" (143). I offer this distinction as an alternative to the overworked romantic paradigm inveterately trotted out to explain Hudson's catastrophe. Personifying the "hideous, mocking mystery" of creative genius and its mischances, Roderick's tragic dissolution serves as an allegory for the procreative lust of the world seen as an engine of death: "If I hadn't come to Rome I shouldn't have risen, and if I hadn't risen I shouldn't have fallen" (*RH*, 193, 280). The knowledge Hudson puts on with his power as an artist is mythopoetic, embracing the fact of death and forestalling its terrors by simulating the "fecundity of the world will," which commands that all that exists prepare to make way for the new: "Pity and terror notwithstanding, we realize our great good fortune in having life—not as individuals, but as part of the life force with whose procreative lust we have become one" (Nietzsche, *Birth of Tragedy*, 103).

Projecting works that "will be simple and sublime," the sculptor does not arbitrarily hit on a ready-to-hand cliché of romanticism, as has been frequently suggested (*RH*, 88). In fact, the correspondences between James and Nietzsche, who taught Greek philology at the University of Basel, might be traced to a shared legacy, Longinus's treatise *On the Sublime*. The classical rhetorician's dictum, "Sublimity is the echo of a great soul" (Longinus, cited in Abrams, 73), mutually informs James's hagiography of early Hudson and Nietzsche's stunning portrait of the inspired artist: "No longer the *artist*, he has himself become a *work of art*: the productive power of the whole universe is now manifest in his transport" (*Birth of Tragedy*, 24). Though such notions were to become staples of romantic criticism through Edmund Burke's influence, certain fundamental premises of *A Philosophical Enquiry into the Origin of Our Ideas of the Sublime and the Beautiful* originate with Burke, and to these James's text is indifferent or hostile. Where Burke disassociates the sublime and the beautiful (the former affording pleasure in the contemplation of horror, the latter an unmixed delight), the novel explicitly conflates them in the femme fatale. Where Burke presumes the antithesis of pain and pleasure, scripted as the opposition between aesthetic images capable of exciting terror or panic and those inspiring feelings of love or sympathy, the novel assumes their intrication: "Extremes meet! I can't get up for joy" (*RH*, 255). However, even Burke's agonistic conception of the relationship between beauty and sublimity facilitates a departure from aesthetic formalism, as Richard Kuhns has remarked: "The experience of art [is] thrown into the domain of feeling" (288).

In so far as theories of sublimity focus on the emotion of terror, on "the transport that results from the lightning revelation, the shattering image, or the stunning burst of passion," they are lineal forebears of masochistic *jouissance* (Abrams, 73–74). Through his art, Roderick attempts to organize the chaos within him, to effect a unifying mastery of what Freud would later call the "ego or death instincts" with the "sexual instincts" along the lines suggested by Nietzsche in "On the Uses and Disadvantages of History for Life" (Freud 11: 326). Planning statues of "all the Forces and Elements and Mysteries of Nature" (*RH*, 89), the sculptor approaches the Greek "conception of culture as a new and improved *physis* [nature]" by casting off the conventions and gimcrackery of high Victorianism and "thinking back to . . . [his] real needs" (Nietzsche, *Untimely Meditations*, 122–23). Predictably, this lofty aspiration of Hudson's is pooh-poohed by his contemporaries, who dismiss his effort to recover the aboriginal face of human desire and playfully cry out for smelling salts. Notwithstanding their posture of indifference, Hudson's auditors are personally in the throes of unrequited love and regale one another with tales of domestic violence: "I like to talk to a man whose ancestor has walled up his wife alive" (*RH*, 181). Roderick's prostration before Christina, "she's quite wiping her feet on me," is but a single link in a daisy chain of unhappy liaisons, from Rowland's entanglement with his protégé, "I'm too abjectly fond of the hapless youth; I can never give him up," to Mary's humiliating passion for Roderick: "Rowland looked at the question rather than asked it, since everything hung for him on her possible appetite for sacrifice, on his measure, so to call it, of what she would abjectly 'take.' Was she one of those who would *be* abject for some last scrap of the feast of their dream?" (179, 194, 287).[21]

For the denizens of the salon world, art exists as a decorative accessory to civilized sexual morality, not as the stripping bare of civilizing pretensions. For the master and clients of atelier Gloriani, a parodic version of the modern school, "a consummate work is a sort of hotch-potch of the pure and the impure, the graceful and the grotesque. Its prime duty is to amuse, to puzzle, to fascinate, to report on a real aesthetic adventure" (83). Roderick is an untimely man who has glimpsed and discovered for himself Nietzsche's precept that "culture can be something other than *a decoration of life*, that is to say at bottom no more than dissimulation and disguise" (*Untimely Meditations*, 123). These considerations bring us round again to Hudson's tussle with Leavenworth over the counterfeit conception of "Intellectual Refinement": "But your interest is somehow fatal to me. I object to your interest. I can't work for you" (*RH*, 200). Hudson is within his rights to charge the fashionable world with conspiring against him, for its notion of the office of art profanes the enterprise. Even Mallet foresees Hudson's ensuing debacle, declining to "officiate as chorus to the play" and chart the circle of his tragic metamorphosis (182).

Hudson is tragic because he lacks the stamina to press forward in the service of life when "everything else that lives cries No" to his efforts (Nietzsche, *Untimely Meditations*, 68). As a consequence of the "perfect separateness of his sensibility," the artist can neither draw upon the human resources of the collective nor serve the needs of his community: "He never saw himself as part of a whole; only as the clear-cut, sharp-edged, isolated individual, rejoicing or raging, as the case may be, but needing in any case absolutely to affirm himself" (*RH*, 276). But what species of affirmation is available to a man without roots in the present, whose tenuous commitment to quotidian reality is his passion for a modern girl resembling a "Medicean Venus," a "goddess on a cloud or a nymph on a Greek gem" (112, 196)? Christina's betrayal forces the issue, but Roderick is devastated by the frangible illusion of mastery over "her beauty—so fitful, so alive" rather than by any personal loss: "What befooled me was to think of it as my own property and possession—somehow bought and paid for. I had mastered it and made it mine; no one else had studied it as I had, no one else so understood it" (307).

Roderick eventually regresses to a "gravedigger of the present," a pessimist, in Nietzsche's sense of the term, "directed by the presentiment of coming disaster and therefore sluggishly indifferent to the wellbeing of others and to [his] own as well" (*Untimely Meditations*, 62, 100): "'Do me good?' cried Roderick. 'What do I want of *good*—what should I do with *good*?'" (*RH*, 319). Freedman deftly glosses the "Lotus-Eating" scenes in *Roderick Hudson*, tracing the devolution of the habits of idleness and contemplation to Mallet's pupil, who comes to resemble "a parodic version of the Baudelairean dandy" and who outdoes his mentor in self-indulgence (138–40). I fail to see why Freedman lets Rowland off so lightly, exculpating the parasitic quality of "detached but sympathetic contemplation" in order to demonize the "aetheticist voluptuary" who is only endeavoring to shock himself awake (141, 140). Stupefied by his impoverished existence, the aesthete treats beauty as a stimulant: "She makes me live again—though I admit there's a strange pain in the act of *coming* to life" (*RH*, 318). Sensuality is a symptom rather than a cause of the disaggregation of the will, as Nietzsche observes. "My *restored* reason says: when a people is perishing, degenerating physiologically, vice and luxury (that is to say the necessity for stronger and stronger and more and more frequent stimulants, such as every exhausted nature is acquainted with) *follow* therefrom" (*Twilight of the Idols*, 59).[22] Besotted and defeated, Roderick comes to exemplify "the spirit of vain paradox and of loose pessimism," but he has known a livelier mode of existence; he has not always been a lotus-eater like Rowland (*RH*, 290). With the "very taste of lotus in the air," Roderick briefly recovers his former sense of self: "For one hour of what I *have* been I'd give up—everything I'm not" (297).

Culminating in a nihilistic exclamation of loss and negation, Roderick mourns the impairment of his facility for aesthetic transformation, for mating beauty and desire: "Good-bye, adorable world!" (298).

Lacking in Freedman's reading is any sense of the terrific struggle between Roderick's life-affirming instincts (will) and the forces that drag him down (psychic paralysis): "Don't say that he was stupefied and senseless, that his perception was dulled or his aspiration dead. Say he trembled in every nerve with a sense of the beauty and sweetness of life; say he rebelled and protested and struggled; say he was buried alive, with his eyes open and his heart beating to madness" (297). Speaking of himself in the third person as though he were already dead, Roderick improvises an epitaph ripe with pathos and allusion. The lotus-eaters are not the only stalwarts of brave Ulysses who find their way into the text of *Roderick Hudson*, which may be likened to a voyage of the damned. An ill-starred Ulysses, Roderick is waylaid by every obstacle he encounters. He stops to eat the flowers, hearkens to the sirens, and comes to crash at the cave of Scylla and Charybdis: "But before he could answer the tempest was in possession and the rain, about them, like the sound of the deeps about a ship's sides" (328). Roderick speaks flippantly of his altered attachment to his mother and fiancée once he has known Circe's embrace: "They mean no more to me than a piano means to a pig" (232). As such callous remarks indicate, Roderick loses every vestige of civility and self-restraint in the course of his downward spiral, but a regard for social niceties has never been a hallmark of artistic genius—quite the reverse. According to Nietzsche, the "great discoverers in the realm of the sublime" are "Tantaluses of the will, plebeian parvenus, who knew themselves to be incapable of a noble *tempo* or of a *lento* in life and action—think of Balzac, for instance,—unrestrained workers, almost destroying themselves by work; antinomians and rebels in manners, ambitious and insatiable, without equilibrium and enjoyment" (Nietzsche, *Beyond Good and Evil*, 188–89).

Mourning and Melancholia

Nietzsche's conception of the artistic temperament in open rebellion against bourgeois morality is a hundred times truer to Hudson's character than the valuation of his nearest friend, whose aim is to bring the high-flying artist to heel. Roderick understands only too well that the authentic artist is a lawless renegade, the sworn enemy of the social polity: "Shoot them, the poor devils, drown them, exterminate them, if you will, in the interest of public morality" (*RH*, 153). If Hudson goes back on the rule of law, the canons of taste, under the sign of Hellenism, then Mallet is a "stiff-necked" Hebraist who introduces moral and manufactural controls into the cultural sphere (Arnold, 101): "It's no matter at all that you don't like your work," he opines. "You'll do the wisest thing you ever did if you muster the resolution *not* to chuck up a commission so definitely accepted. Make the effort necessary at least for finishing your job" (*RH*, 201). Like Leavenworth, on whose behalf he chastises the insolent sculptor, Rowland is a tourist rather than a native of Bohemia. Seen through the lens of Arnold's juxtaposition of Hellenism (spontaneity, sweetness, and light) and Hebraism (obedience, strictness of conscience), James's account of Mallet is more critical than is generally acknowledged. Mallet is not James's mouthpiece, but a cultural Philistine who sacrifices his potential for harmonious human development in his pursuit of moral perfection and of his business interests, such as they are (Arnold, 107, 161). Mallet's idea of felicity is a "network of prescriptions to enwrap his whole life, to govern every moment of it, every impulse, every action," whereas Roderick trips along with the "aerial ease, clearness, and radiancy" of a sleepwalker in the midst of a dream, blithely indifferent to all obstacles (131, 134).

Early in the novel, Rowland offers a definition of genius, culled from his reading, as "a kind of safe somnambulism" in which the "artist performs great feats in a lucky dream" (*RH*, 36). However, Rowland does not subscribe to his own felicitous conception. From the first, he drones on in praise of austerity, self-mastery, and duty, because hard-won achievement is the only thing to which "narrow mediocrities like himself" might aspire (132). Small wonder that Mallet makes a fetish of willpower, the one superior endowment he possesses. Brooding over his creative impotence, he envies "his friend's large easy power" with a bitterness approaching hatred (132). As Roderick teeters on the brink, Rowland muses on smoothing the descent into the "misty gulf": "He felt himself, in a word, a man cruelly defrauded and naturally bent on revenge" (206, 205). Mallet's revenge is consistent with the morality of *ressentiment*, which takes no positive action but poisons the wellsprings of noble self-affirmation by decrying egotism: "You think only of yourself and believe only in your own history" (322). Strenuosity and spontaneity are alternative names for the countervailing theories of aesthetic practice already glossed as sublimation and masochistic *jouissance*. Rowland's disparagement of the sensuous motive in art apparently leaves him with no outlet for repressed urges that cannot find employment in daily life. Malletian connoisseurship approaches the state of disinterested aesthetic contemplation ridiculed by Nietzsche in his critique of the neo-Kantian notions of Schopenhauer, who called beauty a "sedative of the will": "'What does it mean when a philosopher pays homage to the aesthetic ideal?' we receive our first clue: he craves release from torture" (*Birth of Tragedy*, 240). Similarly, Pater has observed that art may serve as a means of escape from the tyranny of the senses for the spectator but never for the artist, whose inspiration is wedded to the sensual realm (142–43).

The outward serenity of the ascetic or moralist is belied by his preoccupation with matters of conscience, a byword of Rowland's (*RH*, 103, 132, 150, 195). Lacking external objects for his vehement reprobation, the legacy of humankind's violent suppression of the instincts in deference to the requirements of sociality, the individual begins persecuting himself "like a wild beast hurling itself against the bars of its cage" (Nietzsche, *Birth of Tragedy*, 218). Nietzsche locates the origin of civil society in the debtor-creditor relationship, in the association of punishment with compensation. Philology validates this perception, finding common roots for the terms *guilt* (*schuld*) and *indebtedness* (*schulden*) (194). Nietzsche reveals the amoral foundations of ethics in the barbarous convention that a creditor is due his pound of flesh, the debtor's pain affording the creditor sadistic pleasure in lieu of material compensation (196). The contractual arrangements of *Roderick Hudson* are established on this premise that suffering has an exchange value. Roderick is "a nature all *unconsciously* grateful," the phrase a softened substitute for the complaint that he reneges on his debts (*RH*, 151). Roderick is likened to a "noble and incurable young spendthrift," and his insensibility to moral suasion is conflated with prodigality (234). He indifferently reports his misdeeds to Rowland, the "disagreeably lucid but quite trusty man of business," who eagerly assumes responsibility for his debts: "Don't you understand that I've taken you away from her, that I suffer for it in every corner of my mind, and that I must do what I can to give you back?" (234).

Nietzsche's formulation of the debtor-creditor relation, which Hayden White has crisply summarized as "the capitalization of pain," explains Rowland's investment in perpetuating a bad conscience (162). Guilt and abjection are the twin scourges of repressed homosexual object choice (Butler, *Gender Trouble*, 64); however, internalizing the prohibition against homosexuality, a prohibition that, according to Freud, stands at the gateway to culture, pays an unexpected dividend: the relatively unfettered indulgence of masochism. "Oh miserable, oh merciless youth! When you've hit your mark and made people care for you, you shouldn't twist your weapon about at that rate in their vitals" (*RH*, 183). In spite of this declaration, Rowland has not attained true object relatedness, and the extent to which he has sublimated his sadism into masochism and his masochism into self-reflexive "moral passion" confirms this fact (151). He has withdrawn his libidinal investment from the object and taken flight in the original reservoir of narcissistic or ego-libido: "The transformation of object-libido into narcissistic libido which thus takes place obviously implies an abandonment of sexual aims, a desexualization— a kind of sublimation, therefore" (11: 369). This pattern dovetails with Freud's account of ego formation in "Mourning and Melancholia," which hypothesizes that the introjection of a desired other's attributes determines the character of the ego. When the relationship has been ambivalent, love for the object splits into narcissistic identification and sadism directed at the substitute object: "The self-tormenting in melancholia, which is without doubt enjoyable, signifies, just like the corresponding phenomenon in obsessional neurosis, a satisfaction of trends of sadism and hate which relate to an object, and which have been turned round upon the subject's own self" (11: 260).

Shortly after James introduces Rowland, the reader discovers that he is prey to "frequent fits of melancholy" (*RH*, 29), a diagnosis that goes some distance toward explaining his dejection, inanition, feelings of worthlessness, guilt, and inability to love (Freud, 11: 254). Presenting a clinical picture of melancholy, Rowland's self-denying and self-abasing disposition mirrors his father's attitude toward him: "His father, a chip of the primal Puritan block, had been a man of an icy smile and a stony frown. He had always bestowed on his son, on principle, more frowns than smiles, and if the lad had not been turned to stone himself it was because nature had blessed him inwardly with a well of vivifying waters" (*RH*, 26). Rowland's strenuous moralism constitutes more than a calculated strategy for evading feelings, conserving energy, and accumulating capital; it is knitted to his psyche, at once constitutive and foreign. Malletian sublimation (denial, repugnance, and shame) veils but does not obliterate its origin in masochistic *jouissance*. For the alter ego comes into being through a "sublime alienation," a violent rejection of the self in favor of another, which must be tirelessly repeated lest the ego reemerge from banishment (Kristeva, 9).

Owing to the confusion between inside and outside and self and other, such a personality is not motivated by desire but based on exclusion (6). In keeping with "the mimetic logic of the advent of the ego," Rowland pursues rejecting and indifferent partners in order to sustain identification with the father and not because he longs for intimacy and has poor judgment (10): "It represented Mary Garland standing there with eyes in which the horror seemed slowly, slowly to expire, and hanging motionless hands which at last made no resistance when his own offered to take them" (*RH*, 207). Experiencing the love object as fragmentary and impassive, Rowland rehearses the maternal neglect that sealed his fate.[23] Described as "a woman heavily depressed," consumed with the wreck of her marriage during her son's infancy and childhood, Mrs. Mallet wore a "mask" of stern compliance by her husband's order (28). Rehabilitated in the "later time" as a "saint," presumably on account of her "spiritual torpor," the mother is another ego ideal influencing Rowland's ascetic bent, detachment, and emptiness (28). Framed in this manner, the tension between the protagonists assumes a different complexion. Mallet embodies the forces mobilized to contain Hudson's anarchic impulses, in keeping with Bersani's notion of the threat that unsublimated desire poses to the form of realistic fiction and, by extension, to the bourgeois social order (*Future for Astyanax*, 68).

Degeneration and Feminism in 'The Bostonians'

"I don't object to the *old* old maids; they were delightful; they had always plenty to do, and didn't wander about the world crying out for a vocation. It is the new old maid that you have invented from whom I pray to be delivered."

— BASIL RANSOM IN *The Bostonians*, 337

Focusing narrowly on literary texts and the social contexts that inspired them, in this chapter and the following, I will eschew biographical assays in favor of treating Henry James as a late-Victorian informant on issues relating to male homosexual social consciousness. James's anxious participation in the emerging discourse on homosexuality underscores the historically variable meaning, the unreliability, of sexual identity as an experiential category from which attitudes and behaviors may be confidently deduced. For Victorian males, effeminacy was the quintessential sign of homosexuality. How does one reconcile psychic transsexualism with the ardor for manliness driving homosexual object choice, if the reports of nineteenth-century sexologists and Westphal's correspondents are creditable? Can we presume that practicing Victorian male inverts supported, on principle, a woman-centered lifestyle? In fact, in the late nineteenth century, lesbians and homosexual men tended toward separate forms of assembly and activism, meeting in cafés and salons but seldom making common cause politically. As James's scathing depiction of lesbian-feminism in *The Bostonians* (1886) suggests, interactions between homosexual males and lesbians were often adversarial.

The Bostonians elaborates a "hermeneutic of suspicion" informed by culturally dominant theories of sexual and gender nonconformity (Sedgwick, "Paranoid Reading," 3–6). Excerpting medical treatises and featuring in its cast of characters a lady physician drawn from life, the novel documents a paradigm shift in late-Victorian conceptions of sexuality, which had become far more reliant on medical norms than on moral sanctions. *The Bostonians* appears to attack lesbian-feminism in the person of Olive Chancellor, whom James clearly satirizes: "It proved nothing of any importance, with regard to Miss Chancellor, to say that she was morbid; any sufficient account of her would lie very much to the rear of that. Why was she morbid, and why was her morbidness typical?" (*Boston*, 20). In *Henry James and the "Woman Business*," Habegger quotes this passage and complains, "Who is she supposed to be typical *of*—New England spinsters, suffragists, Bostonians? James never says, or indicates, and neither does the novel unfold this mystery, or rather twin mysteries—why she is morbid, why her morbidity is typical" (187). On the contrary, Olive Chancellor markedly resembles the congenital degenerates, moral perverts, and constitutional neurotics populating contemporary medical and literary journals:

> The female possessed of masculine ideas of independence, the viragint who would sit in the public highways and lift up her pseudo-virile voice, proclaiming her sole right to decide questions of war or religion, or the value of celibacy and the curse of woman's impurity, and that disgusting antisocial being, the female sexual pervert, are simply different degrees of the same class—degenerates. (Howard, "Effeminate Men," 687)

James appears to endorse this view in *The Bostonians* when he represents Olive Chancellor's nervous affliction as a consequence of her sexual repression and as a function of her gender, political outlook, class standing, and educational background. James was relying on an established taxonomy when he created an unmarried, sexually ambiguous, and feminist heroine for his tale of New England derangement. Demographically, Olive's gender, marital status, class, and hometown placed her in the high-risk group for nervous malady. Olive's homosexuality, political stridency, and oversophistication carried stigmata of a different variety. They marked her as the kind of person physicians and citizens expected to fall ill, when in reality the young mother of one or two small children was the more typical patient. In the person of Olive Chancellor, James framed the debate between extreme factions elaborating the causes of nervous disease and the merits of female suffrage. From the reader's point of view, the issues are not so tidily compartmentalized; the novelist's satire of feminism is derailed by the solicitude he elicits, intentionally or not, on Olive's behalf.

In *The Bostonians* James constructs a fictional world in which family values are under fire and the feminine appears to be the corrupting influence. In *The Speech and Manners of American Women* (1907), he disparages the suffragists' "proclamation of indifference" to the cultural institutions—etiquette, proper elocution, and matrimony—that make common cause with social and biological reproduction (cited in Wardley, 643). *The Bostonians* also gives the campaign for female suffrage short shrift, barely elucidating the political program of its fictional feminists.[1] James frequently lampoons Olive's radicalism in the novel: "She's a female Jacobin—she's a nihilist. Whatever is, is wrong, and all that sort of thing" (*Boston*, 15). At the same time James satirizes Basil Ransom's conservatism with equal gusto. From what vantage but that of patriarchal privilege does a man who cannot earn a living tell a successful lady orator that women are "for public, civic uses, absolutely—perfectly weak and second-rate," insinuating that he knows what women are good for: "But privately, personally, it's another affair. In the realm of family life and the domestic affections" (339)? By dramatizing the debate over suffrage in terms of women's abdication of private life and emergence into the public sector, as individuals and not as appendages to the family, James taps into what historian Ellen DuBois has identified as the most radical implication of the woman's movement, the threat that raised the hackles of the patriarchs: "The 1867 New York Constitutional Convention expressed this fear for the future of the family when it rejected suffrage because it was an innovation 'so revolutionary and sweeping, so openly at war with a distribution of duties and functions between the sexes as venerable and pervading as government itself, and involving transformations so radical in social and domestic life'" (68). Although feminists, such as Dr. Mary Putnam Jacobi, scoffed at the notion that "familial bonds were mere 'political contrivances' requiring the disfranchisement of women to sustain them," suffragists were apparently as committed to the ideals of bourgeois domesticity as were their opponents (68, 65).

This blindness to the "political contrivance" informing *natural* social arrangements prevented nineteenth-century women from elaborating the inequities, oppression, and constraints of private experience into a critique of domesticity; this was to follow much later. As Carroll Smith-Rosenberg, Ann Douglas, and Barbara Sicherman, among others, have shown, nineteenth-century investigations of the psychical problems underlying hysteria, neurasthenia, and so on emphasized the domestic setting in which patients developed their illnesses, received treatment, and, occasionally, recovered their health, but they did not question reproductive imperatives and social arrangements.[2] Describing hysteria as an authoritarian construct rather than as a disease, Michel Foucault has remarked, "The Mother, with her negative image of 'nervous woman,' constituted the most visible form of this hysterization" (*History*, 104). Many physicians and lay critics took the women's movement to task for alienating women from their wifely and maternal duties. Female dissatisfaction with domestic routines seemed to contribute to the high incidence of nervous collapse among the well-to-do, those who could afford to take to their beds:

> [In] so far as they avoid the conscientious discharge of those duties which devolve upon them by virtue of their high mission as wives and mothers, and seek, instead, to follow occupations and professions for which they cannot be best qualified by reason of their nature, physiological activities, and duties of their sex . . . , in just so far are they deviating from that great highway which leads to mental health and the highest interests of humanity." (Stearns, 195–96)

Physicians and laymen were aware, or at least sensed, that women used illness as an option to marriage and motherhood. As Foucault explains, the "thorough medicalization of [women's] bodies and sex, was carried out in name of the responsibility they owed to the health of their children, the solidity of the family institution, and the safeguarding of society" (*History*, 146–47). Oliver Wendell Holmes styled the nervous invalid into a monster of selfishness: "[She] is like a vampire, sucking slowly the blood of every healthy, helpful creature within reach of her demands" (cited in Mitchell,

32). The hysteric had become emblematic of a family system in crisis, with personal and economic resources flowing outside their proper channels.

James departs from the conventional terms of discussion when he represents the precipitating causes of female nervous disorder as a woman's desire for a meaningful existence independent of marriage and motherhood, an epiphany that may have had something to do with his sister's thwarted life. Recording his impressions of Alice James's posthumously published diary in 1894, Henry remarked: "But it also puts before me what I was tremendously conscious of in her lifetime—that the extraordinary intensity of her will and personality really would have made the equal, the reciprocal life of a 'well' person—in the usual world—almost impossible to her—so that her disastrous, her tragic health was in a manner the only solution for her of the practical problem of life—as it suppressed the element of equality, reciprocity, etc." (*HJL* 3: 481). Intermittently in adolescence and permanently thereafter, Alice was a chronic invalid, a neurasthenic who tested the ingenuity of a wide assortment of medical attendants and who made constant demands on those who loved her. After she moved to England, Henry described her as "a great anxiety and occupation" to him (3: 85). Without exaggerating the parallels between Alice James and Olive Chancellor, who is a functioning hysteric, not a bedridden case of nerves, it could be argued that Olive's "disastrous, tragic" life represents the imagined debut of Alice James in the normal world, particularly in view of their shared sexual nonconformity.[3]

Edel's contention that "the figure of Olive Chancellor of *The Bostonians* had appeared upon the novelist's very doorstep" in the person of Katharine Loring makes moot the question of which party to the affair James took as his model for Olive (3: 68). William's wife, Alice Howe Gibbens James, in her correspondence harped on the "*strangeness*" of Alice James's relationship with Miss Loring and thought of Katharine as an interloper: "She is painfully prominent in the family" (*CWJ* 5: 380, 344). After Henry Senior's death in December 1882, the family hoped that Alice James would continue to provide a home for her maternal aunt, Catherine Walsh. The "extraordinary tie between [Alice] and Katharine" initially obstructed this cherished scheme, which Henry, overcoming a palpable reluctance to speak plainly, urged on his sister while he was a resident in Garden Street, Cambridge (5: 360). The conversation reputedly cost him a few weeks in bed with a headache. Of all the family gossip reinforcing a hermeneutic of suspicion guided by theories of sexual and psychical difference, none is more resonant than Mrs. Alice's grudging assessment of her sister-in-law's freedom to arrange her affairs as she pleases: "I am finally sure of this: she is not made as other women—our ways of feeling are not hers so we have no right to decide" (5: 347).

Since the late nineteenth century, medicine has played a leading role in the social construction and scientific elaboration of sexual inversion (Sedgwick, *Epistemology*, 225). In *The Bostonians*, James appears to have lifted terminology directly out of well-known medical treatises. The clinical tone of the opening passages, the scrutiny paid to the female body as the index of a range of gender performances, from Olive's androgyne to Mrs. Luna's would-be vamp, "he probably wondered what body of doctrine *she* represented," underscores the paradigm shift in conceptions of sexuality mentioned previously: "The vague compassion which his cousin's figure excited in his mind, and which was yet accompanied with a sensible reluctance to know her better, obvious as it was that with such a face as that she must be remarkable" (*Boston*, 16, 20). James's recourse to contemporary stereotypes of spinsters and feminists, hinging as they do on the pathology of woman-centered lifestyles, provides all the material needed to bring the specter of a not-yet-articulated female homosexuality into relation with the extant male model: "He wanted to know since when it was more becoming to take up with a morbid old maid than with an honourable young man; and when Verena pronounced the sacred name of friendship he inquired what fanatical sophistry excluded him from a similar privilege" (388). Foucault has documented the disciplinary techniques of the "normalizing society," which enlist the cooperation of individuals in scrutinizing, cataloging, and investigating alterity, so perhaps we can see James's clinical analysis of the "pathology of lesbianism" as tactically allied with the state's interest in reproduction (*History*, 144). Citing the emergence in the late-Victorian period of "a 're-verse' discourse" through which homosexuals began to speak on their own behalf, often using the same vocabulary and categories with which their predilection had been "medically disqualified," Foucault creates a space for an affirmative, if conflicted, Victorian conception of homosexuality (101). In this chapter, I would like to interject Henry James into the breach.

The morbid old maid of *The Bostonians* is mentally ill, not just politely depressed; she is militant, not resigned; she is a lesbian, not a discarded virgin.

It bears noting that James does not censure Olive for her anomalous sexual preference. Given his audience, James could not openly proclaim Olive a lesbian. Instead he forged an unmistakable "lesbian type" and dealt with her emotional predicament (her unhappy entanglement with Verena Tarrant) without explicitly calling this relationship anything but a friendship: "It was a very peculiar thing, their friendship; it had elements which made it probably as complete as any (between women) that had ever existed" (*Boston*, 384). Nancy Sahli argues that tolerance for romantic friendships between women began to fray around 1875, when these friendships were no longer sanctioned as preparation for heterosexual courtship or as evidence of woman's affectionate nature (8). Describing the phenomenon known as "smashing" (girls courting one another) at women's colleges, Sahli documents the growing concern over student love affairs among the parents, teachers, administrators, and trustees of institutions such as Vassar; significantly, published reports of college life attribute the hothouse atmosphere and emotional strain to academic pressures alone (22). In *The Bostonians*, James comes closest to unveiling the public conception of the Boston marriage when, in conversation with Olive, Mrs. Burrage classifies Verena as "the very person in the world you want most to keep unmarried!" and intimates that it would be safer for Olive to form an alliance with the forbearing and cosmopolitan Burrages than to risk Verena's attracting a more possessive lover: "It was not agreeable to Olive to have the fact in question so clearly perceived, even by a person who expressed it with an air of intimating that there was nothing in the world *she* couldn't understand" (*Boston*, 307). This exchange captures the "viewpoint of the closet," Sedgwick's evocative formulation of the dodges associated with closeted homosexuality (*Epistemology*, 223), to a tee, as when Miss Chancellor chafes under Mrs. Burrage's innuendos and devises an impersonal response, "'it only proves how little such an association as ours is understood, and how superficial still'—Olive felt that her 'still' was really historical—'the interpretation of many of the elements in the activity of women, how much the public conscience with regard to them needs to be educated'" (*Boston*, 311).

The class and age disparities James introduces into this relationship when he pairs a Boston Brahman with a working-class waif typified male homosexual relationships at that time. Women tended to bond with their peers, although class-blind relationships in settlement houses and schoolgirl crushes on older women were fairly common. In *The Bostonians*, James conflates male and female homosexuality, up to a point, as a means of disguising and representing his own sexual orientation. Luce Irigaray has shown impatience with this erasure of female homosexuality, which is made to serve the vanity and fantasy demands of men: "The object choice of the homosexual woman is [understood to be] determined by a *masculine* desire and tropism" (cited in de Lauretis, 18). From another perspective, "sexual indifference," as applied to lesbians, who are undifferentiated from male homosexuals and disavowed by the culture at large (17), may serve as a poignant illustration of how society eliminates alternative sexual identifications by rendering them "culturally unthinkable and unviable from the start" (Butler, *Bodies That Matter*, 111). However, the "exclusionary matrix" that forecloses on Olive's same-sex desires and causes her to assume a position of abjection lacks sufficient force to reconstitute a lesbian as a heterosexual subject; Olive's dysfunctional mode of embodying femininity suggests that sex and gender are "citational practices" that can fail (3, 108): "And the emancipation of Olive Chancellor's sex (what sex was it, great heaven? he used profanely to ask himself) would be relegated to the land of vapours, of dead phrases" (*Boston*, 331). Thus when James speaks of Olive's morbidity or neuralgia, it is always within the context of her repudiation of lesbian possibility: "The specifically gay melancholia, a loss which cannot be recognized, and, hence, cannot be mourned" (Butler, *Bodies That Matter*, 113): "A smile of exceeding faintness played about her lips—it was just perceptible enough to light up the native gravity of her face. It might have been likened to a thin ray of moonlight resting on the wall of a prison" (*Boston*, 17–18). Although the association of sexual difference with psychotic dissolution may be read as an endorsement of normalizing prohibitions, I suggest that it be seen as a protest against their extremity: the "death threat" for violating sexual taboos that unhinges the gay-identified subject (Butler, *Bodies That Matter*, 98).

Because I experience Olive Chancellor as a figure of abject homosexuality whose martyrdom James makes out none too subtly as enabling Verena Tarrant's heterosexual identification, itself no promise of happiness, I am struck by Claire Kahane's altogether different interpretation of the novel's gender issues: "But the more hysterically charged issue of *The Bostonians* is the imperiled future of sexual desire and the difference on which it is based, which James saw as threatened by the women's movement" (288–89).

Though I do not believe that James makes common cause with Basil Ransom over the "imperiled future of heterosexual monogamy," I do think Kahane's deductions are instructive. It is through the textual device of ridicule that she recognizes a "blatant similarity" between the narrator and Basil Ransom and forges the novelist's discursive alignment with a hectoring patriarchy (290). But for an article on speech acts, Kahane's is curiously monologic. The over-the-top humor of *The Bostonians* is camp humor, the queer jargon of inauthenticity, which Gregory Woods has described as "the 'secret' that privileges the homosexual reader. What renders it effective is, precisely, the distance heterosexuals are determined to keep between themselves and the very idea of homosexuality. It is a distance leaving ample space for irony" (131). Raising and eliding the specter of homosexual stigmatization in his characterization of Matthias Pardon, a compact and youthful person with "pretty eyes" and a penchant for gossip who is given to unmanly exclamations such as "'goodness gracious!' and 'mercy on us!'—not much in use among the sex whose profanity is apt to be coarse" and blessed with a darling French sobriquet, *enfant de la balle*, James intended to siphon off some of the terror of exposure that Olive's characterization would have aroused in a select coterie of sympathetic readers (*Boston*, 128, 129). Mr. Pardon, a bowery aesthete, personifies the *"repudiation* of the depth model of identity" affected by Wilde (Dollimore, 42). He bears witness to the acuity of Susan Sontag's claim that "camp is a solvent of morality. It neutralizes moral indignation, sponsors playfulness" (290). Having provoked the voluble Mrs. Luna into an indiscretion, which she atones for by throwing a tantrum—"if you have the impertinence to publish a word about me, or to mention my name in print, I will come to your office and make such a scene!"—Pardon completely disarms her with his repartee, "Dearest lady, that would be a godsend!" (*Boston*, 421–22). In contrast, Olive Chancellor plays to the pathos of camp: "The excruciating is also one of the tonalities of Camp; it is the quality of excruciation in much of Henry James . . . that is responsible for the large element of Camp in his writings" (Sontag, 287). Of the two models, Pardon's impersonal style fits James like a glove, allowing him to avoid the "risks of fully identifying with extreme states of feeling" except on those special occasions when he felt up to making a scene (287). If James infrequently betrays his tenderness for Olive, it is because, like some nineteenth-century Edith Piaf, her self-consciousness and seriousness of purpose have left her ridiculously vulnerable to suffering: "Least of all was she a 'thing'; she was intensely, fear-fully, a person" (*Boston*, 101). Saucily commending Symonds's courage in circulating his treatise on sexual inversion as "a queer place to plant the standard of duty," James disavowed political activism for himself; camp was his preferred survival strategy (*HJL*, 3: 398).

Lady Doctors

"[Dr. Prance] says she's the only woman in Boston that hasn't got a doctor. She was determined she wouldn't be a patient, and it seemed as if the only way not to be one was to be a doctor."

(MISS BIRDSEYE IN *The Bostonians*, 217)

Intrepid in professional matters, controversial, and self-consciously leading the vanguard of feminist concerns in medicine, Jacobi plays a large part in this chapter. Dr. Jacobi's work will help me forge connections between this chapter and Chapters 1 and 2, in which I have compared and contrasted James's sexuality and the representations of sexuality in his fiction with the views of the dominant culture. As a prominent woman physician character-izing hysterics, nervous invalids, and moral perverts in her writings, Jacobi covers much the same ground as Henry James does in *The Bostonians*. First cousin of James Jackson Putnam, who was a close friend and colleague of William James and niece of Miss Elizabeth Peabody, Dr. Jacobi may have served as the model for "(Mary J. Prance)," who shared her unusual pen-chant for clinical medicine (*Boston*, 34).[4] Dr. Prance is overheard "sharpen-ing instruments (it was Miss Birdseye's mild belief that she dissected), in a little physiological laboratory which she had set up in her back room, the room which, if she hadn't been a doctor, might have been her 'chamber,' and perhaps was, even with the dissecting, Miss Birdseye didn't know!" (48).[5] Though it is unlikely that James read Jacobi's work, she is significant to this study because she was working out her own conflicted identification with the New Woman in the same New England atmosphere in which James located his hysterical lesbian suffragist.

Just as the disease neurasthenia obscured the social construction of hyste-ria, medicine interpolated cultural axioms of woman's nature while pretending to deal only with observable facts. Jacobi shows us how difficult it is to draw aside this curtain of received notions. Her views are both critical of the commonplace explanations for feminine nervous weakness and incapacity for mental work or careers and broadly representative. Jacobi rehearses the conventional arguments in her thoughtful rebuttals to them, but she also ends up endorsing many of them in spite of herself. She vacillates between resenting the medical profession's demotion of biological woman to second-class status and resenting her female patients' abdication of domestic responsibility. In one article, Jacobi describes her patient as an excessively pampered, self-absorbed weakling who would benefit greatly from "enforced stoicism" or "wholesome neglect"; Jacobi seems to think that corporal punishment might restore hysterics to their senses quicker than medical attention: "To knock the nonsense out of them, to direct attention from self, to substitute a cosmic horizon for that of their own feelings, who does not know the importance of this for thousands of hysterical women? and equally the impossibility of attaining it?" ("Modern Female Invalidism,", 175).

Throughout her career, Jacobi subscribed to the mental-hygiene ethos: mental health for women is ensured by marriage and child rearing but endangered by any other life course. We can guess where this leaves women who are unable or unwilling to marry, though Jacobi does have sympathy for spinsters. In "Modern Female Invalidism," Jacobi attributes the shattered nervous systems of young women in part to "enforced celibacy due to bad social arrangements" (175). Though she is more attuned to the social causalities of nervous invalidism than are her colleagues, at bottom she holds with the most conservative of them, agreeing that the female economy of life is overdetermined by reproductive capacity. Women deprived of heterosexual intercourse and affection may suffer in the fashion Jacobi suggests or they may find other means to fulfill themselves, though Jacobi would not be among the first to endorse Boston marriage, which never enters her mind as a possibility.

Jacobi is preoccupied with the havoc that unwed women—unfit wives and mothers—create in society and the family, which explains why she concentrates on two of the many symptoms of hysteria peculiar to women: the perversion of coupling and maternal instincts. Jacobi maintains that hysterics are frequently sterile and, more often than not, avoid marriage out of sheer perversity, even when their reproductive systems are in good working order.

Jacobi is chary in her observations about the sexual disposition of hysterics. She reserves comment for a footnote: "The classical notion that the sexual impulses are particularly strong in hysterics is certainly erroneous. Both physically and morally, these are often either singularly deficient or singularly perverted, the latter trait constituting one of the first links with insanity" (*Essays on Hysteria*, 18). This statement substitutes some newly stigmatized behaviors (homosexuality, androgyny, and celibacy) for a traditionally stigmatized sexual behavior (promiscuity). Though Jacobi aims to put to rest the myth of oversexed hysterics, she very clearly posits a link between hysteria and sexual deviancy. For Jacobi, homosexuality and other forms of degeneracy are as symptomatic of madness as the hysteric's epileptoid seizure.

Jacobi associates the inherited predisposition to mental illness with congenital physiological dysfunctions such as infertility. Indeed, the implied relationship between degeneration and hysteria is a commonplace in the medical literature of the period. Influenced by B. A. Morel, nineteenth-century physicians saw sterility as a sign of individual degeneration and as a harbinger of familial and, finally, racial extinction: "If those who have not reached a certain point of this degeneration can still reproduce the great family of man, it is under the invariable condition of an hereditary transmissibility damaging to the generations which follow. The most afflicted of these degenerate beings are known to be impotent" (cited in Wing, 219). The high incidence of congenital as well as psychosomatic uterine dysfunction among women of childbearing age convinced Jacobi that the American better classes were threatened with extinction. Jacobi's fears were not irrational when considered in light of late-nineteenth-century trends, especially common in the New England region: the growing disinclination of young ladies for marriage and childrearing, the growing preference among women for higher education and careers, and the increasing use of birth control and even abortion by well-to-do families. This cultural background informs the medical response to falling birth rates. Though Jacobi was herself an educated, professional woman, she would agree with the assessment of her colleague, Dr. Cyrus Edson: "The primary duty of the majority of women is to bear children. This is not less the fact because a large percentage of educated American women tacitly deny it and silently agree with the utterances of the small number who openly claim women were created for 'something nobler than slavery to children'" ("American Life," 444). Jacobi's work possesses a moral urgency, a preoccupation with themes of sexual, gynecological, and obstetrical health that cannot be fully explained by the frequency of uterine disease and amenorrhea in cases of hysteria. Jacobi believed that the elimination of hysteria would signal a return to normal patterns of marriage and procreation and would literally ensure the preservation of the race.

Jacobi's "Shall Women Practice Medicine?" provides an effective illustration of her competing professional and personal loyalties. In this essay, she dismisses every conceivable objection to female doctors. Jacobi eloquently sketches the context in which innovations in feminine enterprise are received and rejected, noting: "In this as in everything that women do, the question of capacity is often outranked by the question of taste. . . . These ask not, 'Is she capable?' but, 'Is this fearfully capable person nice?' Will she upset our ideal of womanhood, and maidenhood, and the social relations of the sexes? Can a woman physician be lovable; can she marry; can she have children; will she take care of them? If she cannot, what is she?" (54). Jacobi is attuned to gender bias of every sort, except, perhaps, her own. She is aware of how prevailing cultural ideas of women's place and function restrict their avenues of self-expression and labor. Though she herself prefers that mothers take up medicine, she denies the assertion of conservatives that single women entering the profession in any way endanger existing social arrangements: "Thousands of women, from manifold causes quite extraneous to medicine, remain celibates all their lives; yet no one reproaches them for refusing the duties of wife and mother" (54). However, buried within this statement is the germ of an idea that bore strange fruit over the course of Jacobi's career, that is, the notion that mental work for women is somehow allied with their impaired reproductive capacities. This theory applies to hysterics and to normal women who evince no other signs of degeneration than their avoidance of motherhood.

Interesting in this regard is Jacobi's article "Modern Female Invalidism," in which she expresses her own ambivalence about higher education for women, the issue dividing mental health professionals and proponents of female suffrage. On the one hand, Jacobi rebukes her peers for maligning college women, as if "these constituted the mass of nervous invalids." And she reports that the "least ill-health is found among women who have been most highly educated" (175).[6] On the other hand, she is deeply, and characteristically I might add, troubled by her perception that these cultivated women are avoiding marriage and maternity. She posits a relationship between the mental development of women and their reproductive imperfections, which borrows from the reactionary physicians' critique of high-pressure education:

> But until now, women have not held a normal position as complete human beings; their mental activity, though often considerable, has been spontaneous, untrained, unsubjected to systematic educational drill. I think the flagging of reproductive activities, due to temporary impairment of race vitality, has facilitated this extraordinary new departure in the *régime* of the race, whereby the sex whose brain has been hitherto neglected, is to-day educated, stimulated, often unnaturally forced. (175)

Jacobi is not consistently optimistic about the prospects of female scholars in the paragraph quoted, as the phrase "unnaturally forced" indicates. She seems to regard the education of women as a fashionable innovation, like the corset, that improves the outward woman considerably while damaging her constitution and impairing her faculties. Jacobi's thesis, that the "flagging of reproductive activities" is responsible for recent cultural trends encouraging women to seek higher education in this period, is extremely troubling. She alleges that this "temporary impairment of race vitality" has afforded a generation of women an unprecedented opportunity to improve their minds, since they have had fewer babies to worry about. It is difficult to say whether Jacobi views diminished reproductive capacities as a cause or a consequence of emerging educational patterns or whether she sees them as an evolutionary development in their own right. However, it seems clear to her that maternal instincts are losing ground to the unnatural ambition for a life lived wholly outside the home. It must be remembered that Jacobi previously identified hysterics with congenital sterility and a perverse indifference to the fundamental interests of family. In 1895 she attributed these same qualities to average women in the population at large. With Henry Adams, Jacobi cried out at the end of the century: "Of all the movements of inertia, maternity and reproduction are the most typical, and women's property of moving in a constant line forever is ultimate, uniting history in its only unbroken and unbreakable sequence. Whatever else stops, the woman must go on reproducing" (*Education of Henry Adams*, 441).

As a physician operating in New England in the late nineteenth century, Jacobi attempted to live up to an ideal of healthy femininity that blended marriage, motherhood, and career. With ten brothers and sisters in her immediate family but only two children to her credit (one of whom, a boy, died when he was eight), Jacobi may have concluded that "systematic educational drill" and the trials of a career had sapped her own reproductive vigor. Though she painstakingly evaluates all the medical theories calling into question female strength, intelligence and endurance, she is not the uncomplicated feminist that Regina Morantz-Sanchez and Carroll Smith-Rosenberg have styled her (262, 55). In too many respects, Jacobi's outlook on nervous invalidism supports the dominant male culture's effort to squash feminist innovations in lifestyle and education by conflating female self-determination and the risk of disease or adverse consequences for society.

Case Studies

There is no mention of George Miller Beard in Henry James's published correspondence; however, William James consulted Dr. Beard, the preeminent nerve specialist of his day, from 1879 to 1883, both for medical advice and to discuss their shared interest in spiritualism. Writing to his wife, whom William tweaked for some perceived slight when Dr. Beard visited the household during his absence, William remarked: "I don't wonder you winced at Beard. But with all his faults he is emphatically no fool; & I feel a certain sort of liking for him because he knows the secrets of my prison house" (*CWJ* 5: 390). Other members of the James family endured the Mitchell rest cure and Beard's galvanic treatments administered by less noteworthy physicians. Though I am not claiming that James actually read the *Boston Medical and Surgical Journal* I do not see why it would be any less interesting to him than to Mrs. Alice, who quoted passages of Mitchell's *Lectures on the Diseases of the Nervous System Especially in Women* to her husband (5: 406). My point is that nervous diseases were so pervasive at that time that Henry could easily have read about them in the *Nation*, the *Forum*, *Scribners*, the *Atlantic Monthly*, and the *North American Review*. Beard, Jacobi, and Mitchell all published in these journals. Mitchell also wrote novels, such as *Doctor and Patient*, that outlined his professional experience.

If James did read any of the major treatises on nervous disease, he might have looked at the most famous, Beard's *American Nervousness*. It was Beard who first coined the term *neurasthenia*, christening it the "American disease." Though I see great continuity between James's portrait of a nerve case and those of his medical contemporaries, I think James may have paraphrased Beard in a key passage of *The Bostonians*. In *American Nervousness*, Beard details the physiognomic peculiarities indicating a nervous diathesis:

> The fine organization is distinguished from the coarse by fine, soft hair, delicate skin, nicely chiselled features, small bones, tapering extremities, and frequently by a muscular system comparatively small and feeble. It is frequently associated with superior intellect, and with a strong and active emotional nature. . . . It is the organization of the civilized, refined, and educated, rather than of the barbarous and low-born and untrained—of women more than of men. (26)

James's heroine Olive Chancellor strongly resembles Beard's representative nervous invalid:

> She was not so plain on further acquaintance as she had seemed to him at first; even the young Mississippian had culture enough to see that she was refined. Her white skin had a singular look of being drawn tightly across her face; but her features, though sharp and irregular, were delicate in a fashion that suggested good breeding. Their line was perverse, but it was not poor. . . . With all this, there was something very modern and highly developed in her aspect; she had the advantages as well as the drawbacks of a nervous organization. (*Boston*, 27)

The connection between the passages goes further than physiognomy and appearance. Both James and Beard recognized that there are "advantages" as well as "drawbacks" to a nervous disposition. In this light, the neurasthenic is invested with "superior intelligence," a "civilized, refined, and educated" organization. Of all the American physicians whose works I have consulted, Beard is the only one who wholeheartedly applauds the intellectual activity of women: "A well-trained intellect is itself medicine and hygiene, enabling its possessor to guard successfully against the appeals of passion and the storms of emotion. . . . The nervous female patients of our time do not come from the most intellectual of the sex" (*American Nervousness*, 337–38). Beard deviates sharply from his counterparts on this topic. Since Beard's status within the medical community is of peripheral interest here, I will not try to explain how his contemporaries managed to ignore his views on the benefits of education for women. Beyond Beard's reputation and comprehensiveness, James undoubtedly would have been drawn to his celebration of cultivated feminine intellects.

James captures the most minute details, the behavioral peculiarities and tics of the neurasthenic type, in his characterization of Olive. Dr. Beard informs us that nervous invalids are usually hysterically unsociable. This form of morbid fear is "often accompanied with the turning away of the eyes and hanging down of the head, but not necessarily so, and usually so only in the severer cases" (*Practical Treatise*, 34). James repeatedly documents this odd behavior in *The Bostonians*: "Olive made no answer; her head remained averted, she bored the carpet with her conscious eyes" (73). Olive Chancellor's nervous tics and morbid anxieties take a variety of forms. James calls attention to the clinical character of his heroine's anxieties every chance he gets: "She saw all this through the blur of her shyness, the conscious, anxious silence to which she was so much of the time condemned. It may therefore be imagined how sharp her vision would have been could she only have taken the situation more simply; for she was intelligent enough not to have needed to be morbid, even for purposes of self-defence" (158).

The connection among oversophistication, education, and ill health is also evident in Miss Chancellor's case, particularly when James contrasts her with the vivacious ingenue, Verena Tarrant. Verena is bursting with health and vitality. Whereas Verena seems a child of sunny and healthful climates, Olive is a "daughter of Winter," frigid and unwomanly: "The curious tint of her eyes was a living colour; when she turned it upon you, you thought vaguely of the glitter of green ice. She had absolutely no figure, and presented a certain appearance of feeling cold" (27). These intimations of asexuality, Olive's lack of warmth and feminine attributes, are consistent with nineteenth-century medical accounts that identify organic infertility with the conscious disinclination for marriage and motherhood. As Jacobi observes, "the reproductive imperfection in question may show itself at first by no more tangible symptoms than moral incapacity for love or marriage, or fantastic perversity of sentiment in regard to these fundamental interests, this incapacity frequently involving or determining social situations that re-act most disastrously upon the health of the 'highly strung' individual" ("Modern Female Invalidism," 175). This passage helps us to understand James's depiction of Olive Chancellor as a "signal old maid": "There are women who are unmarried by accident, and others who are unmarried by option; but Olive Chancellor was unmarried by every implication of her being. She was a spinster as Shelley was a lyric poet, or as the month of August is sultry. She was so essentially a celibate that Ransom found himself thinking of her as old" (*Boston*, 27).

Though nineteenth-century physicians tended to treat their patients' physical maladies while ignoring the social ills underlying their complaints, they correctly noted the unfortunate interaction among patient, family, and community. In *The Bostonians*, the isolation of the "incurably lonely" nervous invalid exacerbates morbid tendencies and positively inclines her for death: "Olive perceived that the great effort must now be made. Great efforts were nothing new to her—it was a great effort to live at all" (384, 117). Dr. Beard held that for these patients "abstaining from dying demands a degree of force just as the mere keeping in an erect position . . . is only possible to those who have a certain quantity of nerve strength. Abstaining from dying, like abstaining from falling, is in one respect a negation only, but neither is possible without an expenditure of force" (*Practical Treatise*, 25). Beard's characterization of the dejected and worn-out neurasthenic is sympathetic. He pleads with his colleagues to overcome their antipathy to nerve patients, to recognize that mental and psychosomatic illnesses are every bit as painful as other maladies. The antipathy in question partly arises because of the in-tractability of nervous disorders and the patients' resistance to getting well. This antipathy is still more frequently occasioned by the physician's invol-untary repugnance to the type of woman who falls ill with this disease. Ran-som shows a similar disinclination to become intimate with cousin Olive, even before she insults him: "At this period, I say, it was very easy for him to remark to himself that nothing would induce him to make love to such a type as that" (*Boston*, 26). Classifying her as an "unflirtable," a contemporary term for dowdy college women (Sahli, 19), Basil dismisses Olive as a sexual object: "It was inconceivable to him, though he had just seen the little prophetess kiss her, that she should ever become anyone's 'dear'" (*Boston*, 101). This incessant probing of Olive's sexuality keeps the question of lesbianism open, even though homosexuality is repudiated by the character herself.

In "The New England Invalid," Robert Edes's summary of the social relations of nervous invalids enhances our understanding of their marginality: "If one were willing to use the vernacular in a form which might be offensive to those to whom it applied, he would be likely to speak of that class here called 'constitutional neurotics' as 'cranks' or 'crooked sticks', persons whose inherent peculiarities of nervous organization are such as prevent them from acting or living in harmony and comfort with a community of a more average and less peculiar character" (55–56). In Olive Chancellor's case, her inability to live in harmony with a community of a "more average and less peculiar character" takes a decidedly political turn: "It was the usual things of life that filled her with silent rage; which was natural enough, inasmuch as, to her vision almost everything that was usual was iniquitous" (*Boston*, 21). Taken together, Jacobi and Edes's observations go a long way toward explaining the alienation of the nervous invalid, a creature emotionally and constitutionally set apart. Or, as James depicts her, at odds with the world: "Of all the things in the world contention was most sweet to her (though why it is hard to imagine, for it always cost her tears, headaches, a day or two in bed, acute emotion)" (23). Shut up in a bedroom or out of the boardroom, the nervous invalid is denied affirmation by the mainstream community and culture. Flat out on her back or screeching from the rooftops, the nerve patient exacts attention, if not respect, from those around her.

Olive unconsciously uses her periodic prostrations and fits of shuddering to control Verena: "When [Verena] felt her trembling that way before luncheon it made her quite sick to realize how much her friend was wrapped up in her—how terribly she would suffer from the least deviation" (291). Such episodes not only mimic neurasthenic seizures and prostrations, they also indicate the psychological motivation for this behavior. It is only natural that ordinary middle-class women would prefer this method of quiet-but-effective self-empowerment to rioting or joining the short-skirts league, but it is noteworthy that Olive, an outspoken feminist, uses this technique. In his characterization of Olive Chancellor, James draws on public and private instances of female unrest, consciously stating parallels that are only implicit in popular and medical indictments of neurasthenics who use their health to express dissatisfaction with their status at home and in the world.

In this sense, the allegations of medical personnel regarding the connection between mental illness and social rebellion are right on the mark. Suffragism and neurasthenia are equally potent, though very different, responses to the restrictions that the dominant male culture placed on women in the nineteenth century. In either case, the woman refuses to cooperate, physically or emotionally, with her husband, father, senator, or president. When she falls ill, however, she rebels against herself as well as against her tormentors. The nervous invalid is not merely in greater pain than other mortals, she is further from her goal of self-determination. Lay critics of the woman's movement objected to granting suffrage to women precisely on the grounds that they were nervous, excitable, and impulsive. We hear an echo of this sentiment in Basil Ransom's notion that "the whole generation is womanized; the masculine tone is passing out of the world; it's a feminine, a nervous, hysterical, chattering, canting age, an age of hollow phrases and false delicacy" (334). Elizabeth Cady Stanton tried to combat this superstition, arguing that "women have not become 'nervous,' 'excitable,' or 'impulsive,' but more calm, dignified, and sedate in assuming their new duties" (437). In his effort to capture the most typical features of the "woman question" in the United States, James was careful to leave this Gordian knot tangled: women are not qualified for full status as citizens because they are emotionally unfit; women are nervous wrecks because they are denied self-governance and franchise. James made Olive's private life problematic so that her personal anguish would reflect and effect her public struggle for franchise.

Lesbians and Others

"Whom do you mean by 'us'—your whole delightful sex?
I don't understand *you*, Miss Olive."

(BASIL RANSOM IN *The Bostonians*, 102)

Nineteenth-century psychiatry was a fledgling discipline when James wrote *The Bostonians*. Though subliminal states of consciousness were imperfectly understood before 1894, the concepts of repression and conversion were bandied about in professional circles during the 1880s. Even after American psychiatrists read Freud's writings on defense mechanisms and hysterical phe-

nomena, they were reluctant to consider, or talk about, the role of sexual feelings in the development of neuroses: "Modern canons of taste forbid any but
the most distant allusions to what is going on among us in many ways, and he
is considered immodest or even indecent who seeks to draw the veil" (Edson,
"American Life," 441). Edes, one of the first Americans to embrace Freud's
work, blamed "the modern habit or manners of repression, of keeping the
feelings concealed, a habit which increases with civilization and fashion, with
higher social position" for the high incidence of neurasthenia in the United
States (56). Curiously, he never paused to consider of what these incapacitating feelings might consist. Psychiatrists, who were just beginning to contem-
plate the influence of family and environment on the hysterical diathesis in
the mid-1890s, challenged religious and educational institutions on the
grounds that these promoted morbid introspection, but they did not question
the sanctity and healthfulness of normal domestic arrangements. Lay students of human nature also recognized a morbid conscience as an early symptom of neurasthenia. Columnists warned their readers against habitual self-
scrutiny, a vestige of the days of religious diaries that no longer suited the
spiritual requirements of the anxious and depressed denizen of the city.

Physicians and journalists alike looked to New England for the type of
woman burdened by morbid conscience, just as they had noted rampant nervous distress in the maids and matrons of the northeastern corridor (Putnam, 73–99). They spoke of "New England self-consciousness and morbid
conscientiousness" (Wells, 818). Physicians, laymen, and even psychiatrists
commonly regarded repression as an indigenous feature of the New England personality, a culturally sanctioned but dubious method of coping with
emotions. Edes, who put the trouble down to cultural baggage, queried,
"Would it not be better if our customs and 'good form' permitted a patient
to scream, as she so often says she wants to, instead of restraining her feelings for propriety's sake, and developing a neuralgia or paralysis or an attack
of 'nervous prostration'?" (56). Edes understood that inhibition contributed
to the onset of nervous disorders, but that was as far as he progressed with
Freud and Breuer's theories. Like many others of his time, he showed a
marked reluctance to address sexual inhibition.

In 1887 the eminent psychiatrist Edward Cowles published a paper entitled "Insistent and Fixed Ideas" in the premier issue of the *American Journal
of Psychology*. The subject of the paper is a young suicidal woman who fancies

that she has committed homicide and who develops a host of compulsive behaviors to ward off future evil, ranging from obsessive dressing and undress-
ing to shooting herself and taking poison. The young woman possesses a
monomania, an obsession with a childhood friend whom she admires greatly
and whom she once, so she believes, tried to murder. In the subsequent
stages of her illness (from which she suffers over a fifteen-year period), the
patient continues to fantasize about the harm she might do her "friend," in-
vents a laborious method of "binding herself over" by oaths and impreca-
tions to do certain things lest she injure her, and eventually falls into the
habit of substituting vicarious "sufferers" for the cruel injuries she wishes on
her young friend. The patient's problems are magnified when, in the natural
course of events, some of her scapegoats actually come to grief. Cowles deals
mainly with the patient's morbid ideation, the process that turned a fairly
normal girl of a jealous and conscience-smitten disposition into a psychotic.

Cowles was struck by the fact that he could clearly distinguish the stages
of morbid ideation, thereby monitoring the evolution of the disease, but this
discovery did not allow him to advance much beyond elaborating on the
psychical processes attendant upon a case of obsessional neurosis. In other
words, he understood the fixation perfectly and the unconscious motivation
but little. Cowles's analysis is hampered by his lack of interest in the patient's
family life and early childhood experiences. He only remarks that the patient
was an exceptionally bright, truthful, and conscientious student and suggests
that her overactive conscience, early in evidence, lay the psychical foundations for the fixations and compulsive behaviors manifested during her adolescence. In reporting on the adolescent stages of illness, Cowles notes that
the schoolgirl who excited his subject's animosity was "beautiful in person,
lovely in character, and destined to exercise an extraordinary influence upon
the afterlife of the patient M. The latter was the intellectual superior, but became jealous, she says, of the attention C. received, although she admired
and loved her very much" (239–40). Cowles concludes that the patient was
psychically ill-equipped to cope with the trials of ordinary jealousy, particularly when jealousy turned to hatred; her peculiar cast of mind was responsible for the development of morbid symptoms. In brief, Cowles believes that
his patient became ill out of fear of the suffering she would herself endure if
her wishes came true; she feared that her own unforgiving conscience would
exact some terrible retribution.

A contemporary interpretation of this patient's unconscious motivations would not stop, as Cowles's did, at her self-loathing and murderous impulses but would draw certain inferences from her compromise ideas, which illustrate the constraints imposed on her desire. Cowles was not in a position to question whether the patient's conscious hatred of the other girl was driven by a repressed attraction of a distinctly sexual nature: "All her former admiration of her friend's character and beauty revived, but with it of course came the feelings of antagonizing jealousy, and these opposing feelings went on together. Her friend was lovely, fortunate and happy; she felt herself to be the contrary, and managed to evolve the notion that her friend was somehow to blame for her own sufferings" (246). The envy and resentment the patient feels toward her charming "rival" conceals the jealousy that seems to have this girl as its love object. The patient blows hot and cold over her friend, suggesting that the loathing she feels for her is more complicated than it appears. The intolerable idea of homosexual attraction (which is unbearable because of social mores and attitudes) cannot emerge unchanged in consciousness, as Cowles precociously grasps when he says the patient "managed to evolve the notion that her friend was somehow to blame for her sufferings." This notion constitutes a compromise formation, a self-reproach transformed by repression, which explains why the patient's ritual vowing and swearing to ward off harm is charged with redistributed affect. Cowles does not consider the possible role of sexual feeling in his case study, though he informs us that her fixations commenced at the onset of puberty. Despite these omissions, Cowles has provided us with insight into the late-nineteenth-century understanding of a compulsive personality disorder, insights that aid us in evaluating James's clinical evaluation of Olive Chancellor and explain why James decided that psychic dissolution was the penalty for sexual alterity.

The same complication of motives, the same morbid ideation, are in evidence in Miss Chancellor's fictive case history: "Such is the penalty of being of a fastidious, exclusive, uncompromising nature; of seeing things not simply and sharply, but in perverse relations, in intertwisted strands" (*Boston*, 149). Olive also possesses a conscience-smitten disposition: "It was in this poor young lady's nature to be anxious, to have scruple within scruple and to forecast the consequences of things" (30). This type of disposition is not only a sign of Boston rectitude, it is a symptom of guilt and repression. Olive is tyrannized by a series of delusions, and she also adopts an elaborate scheme for evading the tyranny of her fixed ideas without directly confronting them. To this end, she is driven to mortify her refined sensibilities, to deprive herself of enjoyments, and to put herself constantly in jeopardy: "It's part of our life to go anywhere—to carry our work where it seems most needed. We have taught ourselves to stifle repulsion, distaste" (253). Olive's relationship with Verena, a gilded lily of a girl, serves her purpose of self-mortification: "I have never understood how Olive can reconcile herself to Verena's really low style of dress. I suppose it's only because her clothes are so fearfully made. You look as if you didn't believe me—but I assure you that cut is revolutionary; and that's a salve to Olive's conscience" (260).

Olive Chancellor, a card-carrying feminist, breathes fire and brimstone over the oppression of women while she herself lives in a Back Bay townhouse and has veal chops for dinner. The contrast between Olive's grievances as a feminist and her acceptance of class hierarchies is a major focus of characterization: "The Chancellors belonged to the *bourgeoisie*—the oldest and the best. They might care for such a position or not (as it happened, they were very proud of it), but there they were, and it made Mrs Farrinder seem provincial (there was something provincial, after all, in the way she did her hair too) not to understand" (42). Olive has some limited experience of how the poor live, but her social work is infrequently alluded to and is discounted by the narrator, who delights in reminding the reader that ascetic, self-sacrificing Miss Chancellor is an awful snob about furnishings. Olive has inherited class standards, both aesthetic and sanitary, that prevent her from crossing the lines she needs to cross to join with the downtrodden of her sex in poverty. She is relentlessly bourgeois: "Olive of course held that home-culture was perfectly compatible with the widest emancipation" (96). James places Olive in circumstances in which her cultivated tastes will inevitably clash with the tawdry reality of the low-rent lifestyles of her close friends, Miss Birdseye and Verena Tarrant. Olive has only the vaguest notions of the problems besetting the poor girls she attempts to befriend, and even to imitate: "She took them more tragically than they took themselves; they couldn't make out what she wanted them to do" (43). James ridicules Olive's striving for women's equality, because she starts her campaign on an unequal footing with her chosen comrades. Olive seems to think that only the poorest creatures need to be liberated from the tyranny of men; she confines her notion of sisterhood to women of the lowest classes: "I want to know every-thing that lies beneath and out of sight, don't you know? I want to enter into the lives of women who are lonely, who are piteous. I want to be near them—to help them" (44).

Olive's feminism is rooted in fantastic notions of female victimization. Rather than focusing on the political agenda of her day, Olive meditates on an irrational and transhistorical summary of woman's grievances: tears, tor-ture, and crucifixion. "The unhappiness of women! The voice of their silent suffering was always in her ears, the ocean of tears that they had shed from the beginning of time seemed to pour through her own eyes" (45). James suggests that he finds less emotional versions of feminism, such as Dr. Prance and Mrs. Farrinder's, more acceptable: "[Verena and Olive] insisted so much, for instance, on the historic unhappiness of women; but Mrs. Far-rinder didn't appear to care anything for that, or indeed to know much about history at all. She seemed to begin just today, and she demanded their rights for them whether they were unhappy or not" (168). Though James clearly disapproves of Olive's ideology and methods, he is at pains to show how es-sential this vision of female exploitation is to her character, how it justifies and confirms her. Olive's emphasis on suffering dooms her political enter-prise to failure, but it is absolutely necessary to her private vision of herself as a tragic victim. Olive's political outlook is actually overdetermined by her subliminal repudiation of homosexuality. Notwithstanding Verena's youth-ful charms, she is a prime target for Olive's affection because she is both poor and virginal. Olive's passion thrives because she disguises it as a demo-cratic overture, consistent with her aim of reaching out to the downtrodden of her sex: "With her bright, vulgar clothes, her salient appearance, she might have been a rope-dancer or a fortune-teller; and this had the immense merit, for Olive, that it appeared to make her belong to the 'people'; threw her into the social dusk of that mysterious democracy which Miss Chancel-lor held that the fortunate classes know so little about" (86). Predictably, within a brief span of time Olive finds herself in an untenable position: that of focusing on Verena's loud and shoddy garments as a symbol of her poverty while simultaneously repressing the flirty, vampish qualities of this style of dress. When Olive asserts "Miss Tarrant might wear gilt buttons from head to foot, her soul could not be vulgar," she reveals her anxiety that her own interest in Verena is personal and not the least bit sacramental (87). Like the relationship between Rowland Mallet and Roderick Hudson, Olive's relationship with Verena presents a serious challenge to Olive's psychical defenses, which periodically break down in the course of their friendship: the reactive idea (sexual attraction) is aroused and checked by identical stimuli.

In Olive, James has depicted a classic case of repression, in which the unconscious perception of homosexual inclination has produced a pattern of self-censorship, denial of sexuality, and erasure of self as a "constrained repetition of norms": "In the domain of sexuality these constraints include the radical unthinkability of desiring otherwise, the radical unendurability of desiring otherwise, the absence of certain desires, the repetitive compulsion of others, the abiding repudiation of some sexual possibilities, panic, obsessional pull, and the nexus of sexuality and pain" (Butler, *Bodies That Matter*, 94). We may never entirely understand what motivates Olive's attempt to smother *all* her sexual feelings but we can understand something of the consequences of this unconscious decision. Olive's moral education and breeding ensure that she will repudiate homosexuality and become neurotic. Yet the reader might wonder at her rejection of a heterosexual alternative, for despite her precautions, Olive Chancellor's libido is engaged on many levels. There is something more to her terror of Basil Ransom than meets the eye.

In the opening scenes of *The Bostonians*, Olive and Basil share an intimate moment in Miss Chancellor's parlor. During their chat, Olive experiences a flutter of emotion, which she instantly attempts to suppress: "She could not defend herself against a rich admiration—a kind of tenderness of envy—of any one who had been so happy as to have that opportunity. The most secret, the most sacred hope of her nature was that she might some day have such a chance, that she might be a martyr and die for something. Basil Ransom had lived, but she knew he had lived to see bitter hours" (22). This passage describes Olive's sublimation of her sexual feeling, the redirection of this energy into a more acceptable idea: self-sacrifice. While Olive struggles to regain her poise and to take a firm line with Basil, he has been sizing her up as a mate. Perhaps Olive senses this unspoken aspect of their conversation, perhaps she can respond briefly to his warmth and interest because there is nothing overt or alarming in Basil's manner. Eventually Olive's alarms are set off, and she consciously defends herself against the intruder. It would be a mistake to read Olive's goading of Basil, her testy and outlandish remarks on women's rights, purely as a confirmation of the idea that Olive despises men: "Olive disliked [men] most when they were least unpleasant" (288). On the contrary, her remarks constitute a defensive maneuver: "Miss Chancellor said to her companion, with a concentrated desire to defy him, as a punishment for having thrown her (she couldn't tell why) into such a tremor" (32). Though Olive is disturbed by her attraction to Basil, she is well defended against any male encroachment on her heart: "She thought him very handsome as he said this, but reflected that unfortunately men didn't care for the truth, especially the new kinds, in proportion as they were good-looking" (31).

Olive's "unreasoned terror" of Basil, which appears for the first time right after this passage, is a reversal of affect. Olive relies on this defense to cloak something of a personal nature, which she wishes to keep hidden from others and from herself. She rejects Basil's friendly overtures because any romantic sensation has the power to awaken repressed sexual conflicts. In this sense, Basil functions as more than a heterosexual foil for Olive. He represents the sexual initiate who exudes confidence in his sexual prowess and identity. Olive's attraction to Basil may raise questions for the reader about her sexual orientation, particularly since Olive does not identify herself as a lesbian. This exchange between Olive and Basil illuminates some of the societal conditions that inform both Olive's conscious and subliminal romantic and political choices. Olive recognizes that heterosexual love would allow no scope for her intelligence and her yearning for self-governance. James highlights this aspect of Olive's social critique when he characterizes Basil and Verena's relationship as that between parent and child. To Olive's way of thinking, only same-sex alliances permit reciprocity and equality.

Olive Chancellor's lesbianism is one of the salient points of *The Bostonians*, a fact noted by many twentieth-century critics well before the advent of gay studies: "The psychological motivation for Olive Chancellor's agitation on behalf of her own sex he astutely conceived as hatred or at least fear of the opposite sex—in a word, incipient lesbianism" (Anderson, 310). Lyall Powers claimed that James tried to "persuade his readers of the rightness of Ransom's triumph" by "suggesting (and none too subtly) the streak of perversion in Olive's attraction to the lovely Verena" (58). And F. W. Dupee called Olive "pretty distinctly a case of perverse sexuality; and whether or not James knew what he was doing, he had certainly observed curiously some real instance of Olive's derangement. To William he apologized for including in the novel so much 'descriptive psychology'; and Olive is a rare case in James of a character transfixed in its symptoms" (131). Few contemporary critics would have the nerve to describe lesbianism as pathological. And even those, like Terry Castle, who urge readers to temper their "pious indignation" at James's portrait of Olive are not quite sure what to do with her craziness (152). Olive's critics perpetually describe her symptoms in Freudian terms. And their jejune notations of hysterical stigmata only serve to obscure the historical sources of Olive's illness. They emphasize Olive's peculiarity and suppress the familiar, long-established reality of sexual conflict and Victorian repression. With the exception of Kahane, feminist critics of the novel have left the psychological dimensions of *The Bostonians* to others. And we can see why, when a Freudian approach can so easily collapse into a symptomatology, as Nina Auerbach observes: "It is easy enough to give this image [a ray of moonlight resting on the wall of a prison] a Freudian tinge and to visualize poor crazy Olive as a prisoner of her own unnatural desires and twisted aspirations" (127). Elaine Showalter dodges the question in *Sexual Anarchy*, summarizing Olive's neurosis as a longing for martyrdom (28–29). Judith Fetterley also attempts to downplay Olive's morbidity, calling it "an understandable reaction to the facts of her experience" (136). These explanations oversimplfy Olive's predicament. Certainly episodes in Olive's background, such as dates with young men or competitions with butchers for the attentions of shop girls, have disastrous effects on her, but only because she is a highly strung neurotic: "He wondered why she was agitated, not foreseeing that he was destined to discover, later, that her nature was like a skiff in a stormy sea" (*Boston*, 19). In *The Bostonians*, James does not portray Olive's neurosis as some kind of retribution for sexual deviance, as has been suggested. There is really nothing to be gained from denying the neurotic cast of Olive's personality to avoid the imputation of homophobia, misogyny, or anachronism. *The Bostonians* without its hysterical lesbian feminist is *Huckleberry Finn* without Nigger Jim.

James deliberately gave Olive's psychological conflicts a political cast. This decision underscores the relationship between social ills and mental illness in the novel. Olive relies on her nervous debility as a means of identifying herself with shop girls and washerwomen, though their poverty is clearly a different species of misery from the loneliness and alienation Olive experiences. Olive dwells on the saga of the iniquitous relations between the sexes to redefine herself as a historically constituted entity and to help channel private feelings of guilt and anxiety into the public sphere where she is a victim or where she is at least not accountable for her actions: "But their errors were as nothing to their sufferings; they had expiated, in advance, an eternity, if need be, of misconduct" (187). We might still pause to consider whether this characterization refutes or supports the widely held notion that marriage and motherhood are the only sure means to health and sanity. Does James's revelation of the "incipient lesbianism" informing Olive's political outlook undermine her feminist convictions by overstating the merely personal, psychical necessity prompting her to identify with poor women? Or does this portrayal reinforce Olive's perspective on the rights and wrongs of women by demonstrating that her distress is a function of societal conflict—pervasive inequality, enforced celibacy, and intolerance for sexual difference? We might take a page out of Irving Howe's thoughtful reading of the novel:

> Olive's sexual ambiguity, like her social rootlessness, is in part due to her fastidious incapacity for accepting any of the available modes of life. It would be a gross error to see her feminist ideas simply as a rationalization for her private condition, since part of what she says—it might be remembered—happens to be true. Partly her rebellion is against society, but her mistake is to suppose it entirely against society; she does not see—how can she bear to see?—that it is also against herself. (xxii–iii)

James presents us with a character who is losing her battle against the status quo, who bears the psychological scars of a lifetime spent resisting the pressure to conform to the standards set by the dominant male culture. Olive's problem is not the "streak of perversity in her character," not her "moral incapacity" for heterosexual love and marriage, but the fact that she lives in a society that does not tolerate her proclivities. In most respects, James avoids the crude late-nineteenth-century stereotype of the lesbian as "a viragint who would sit in the public highways and lift up her pseudo-virile voice, proclaiming her sole right to decide questions of war and religion," but Olive's masculine traits and psychology are foregrounded in the novel: "It was a curious incident of her zeal for the regeneration of her sex that manly things were, perhaps on the whole, what she understood best"

(126). James may have been thinking of Katharine Loring, whom Alice James claimed had "all the mere brute superiority which distinguishes man from woman, combined with the most distinctively feminine virtues. There is nothing she cannot do from hewing wood to drawing water to driving runaway horses and educating all the women in North America" (cited in Edel, 3: 68). He may have read about Lucy Ann Slater, alias Reverend Joseph Lobdell, a cross-dressing lesbian whose skill as a marksman earned her the moniker "the Female Hunter of Long Eddy" (Wise, 87–91). Slater was "married" to another woman and supported the household by hunting and trapping before she was arrested for vagrancy and institutionalized for deviancy in 1880.

Olive herself resembles a husband in feminist drag, thinking of original words to the time-honored marriage vow, dreaming of a monogamous relationship: "Olive wished more and more to extract some definite pledge from her; she could hardly say what it had best be as yet; she only felt that it must be something that would have absolute sanctity for Verena and would bind them together for life" (*Boston*, 117–18). Olive's rejection of feminine dress also illustrates her sense of psychological and biological miscasting: "She was habited in a plain dark dress, without any ornaments, and her smooth colourless hair was confined as carefully as that of her sister was encouraged to stray" (19). I do not think that James meant to align himself with conservatives who ridiculed bearded or asexual women, his invocation of these stereotypes of cross-gender identification and androgyny notwithstanding. Rather, his characterization of Olive is meant to reveal the hopelessness of her situation, the triumph of the dominant culture over the opposition of the New Woman. By tacitly accepting established social arrangements, such as the family and class hierarchies, Olive affirms the patriarchal culture in the broadest terms. As Fetterley has observed, Olive loses Verena to Basil because there are no legal, moral, or social sanctions of lesbian unions. Olive cannot negotiate a new world for herself because ultimately her vision of marriage is the same as Basil's: "This is the reality behind the critics' assertion that nature is on the side of Ransom. The force on Ransom's side is not nature; it is the tradition and the power that derives from being able to invoke as one's support 'the way things are'" (126).

It is no accident that Basil Ransom conceives of his relation to Verena in terms similar to Olive's. The many parallels between Basil and Olive, which

Fetterley has painstakingly elaborated in *The Resisting Reader*, tend to detract from James's critique of the special situation of women as a class within the patriarchal culture. The impression conveyed by these reverberations is one of consensus, not difference. However, Olive's masculine or gynecophilic currents of feeling are set off from Basil's lusts in high relief. Basil flatters himself that he is Verena's knight in shining armor, but he doesn't "care a straw, in truth, how he was judged or how he might offend; he had a purpose which swallowed up such inanities as that" (363). Olive is not so fortunate. Olive's evolving self-realization as Verena's devotee and protectress is not a function of vanity but of self-preservation. She is forced to repress the same drives that in Basil's case are reckoned natural and fundamental. Basil's love-making is forthright, uncensored, and unmediated: "My plan is to keep you at home and have a better time with you there than ever" (335).

Though Olive prizes honesty above all else, she is the one character in the novel forced by social conventions and psychical pressures to twist and disguise the reality of her situation: "It was as bad as she could have desired; desired in order to feel that (to take her out of such a milieu as that) she should have the right to draw her altogether to herself" (117). Though James censures Olive's evasion of personal truths and her snobbery, coerciveness, and related deviation from high democratic ideals, he is just as keen to indicate the societal oppression compelling her to take refuge in such delusions and finally in mental illness. Olive appears to have an organic as well as a temperamental predisposition to nervous debility, but the text represents the aggravating pathogenic effects that precipitate her descent into illness as cultural, not just personal, causes. In the world of *The Bostonians*, oppression overdetermines repression, which is why Olive's cousin and mirror image, Basil Ransom, is an oppressor, not a hysteric.

James's characterization of Olive Chancellor opens up interesting avenues for social criticism. Though the patriarchal culture is dominant, it wins through exclusion, confirming Butler's claim that heterosexuality is "an incessant and *panicked* imitation of its own naturalized idealization" (cited in Fuss, 23). Boston, at any rate, cannot accommodate Miss Chancellor's sexuality. The relentless probing of Olive's physiognomy for clues to the secret of her difference and her constant repudiation of that difference lead to one conclusion: "If it were not lesbian, this body would make no sense" (de Lauretis, 29). Olive accomplishes in private life what she fails to do as a public figure advocating social change. It is not her ideology but her personality that challenges the notion that anyone possessed of a certain fortune and social standing—class, education, religion, and skin color—has a place in American life. In James's portrait, what touches the reader most keenly is the revelation of how Olive's marginal status as a woman and a lesbian gives rise to a radical consciousness and a serious mental illness in a woman who, as her surname implies, is a leading citizen deeply committed to her class and country.

FIVE

The Politics of Sexual Dissidence in 'The Princess Casamassima'

In *The Princess Casamassima*, Hyacinth Robinson is torn between the legacy of his dissipated English sire, Lord Frederick Purvis, and that of his murderous French mother, Florentine Vivier, who is the daughter of a revolutionary. This tension leads to the key dilemma of the novel: Will Hyacinth assassinate a scion of English society and set a revolution in motion or will he side with the privileged class against the masses, who would rip to shreds every vestige of cultural achievement? The social critical dimensions of the novel have elicited valuable commentary over the years, most notably from Lionel Trilling, Taylor Stoehr, Mark Seltzer, and John Carlos Rowe. Although I marvel at the ingenuity of their interpretations, I suspect that they do not plumb the novel's depths. What is the raison d'être of *The Princess Casamassima*? Surely it is not an exposition of the novelist's familiarity with international terrorism, derived from a careful study of Bakunin and Nechayev's manual, *The Revolutionary Catechism*, as Trilling and Stoehr suggest (71–72; 122–23). Seltzer's claim that James both upholds and deconstructs his authorial power to police the fictive world he has created in *The Princess Casamassima* and Rowe's claim that the novelist exposes the "social contradictions of a hierarchical society" are far more suggestive (54–55, 156). Several things stand out in these accounts. The novel undeniably expresses a desire to subvert a repressive power of the highest order; in depicting this underlying aim, James participates in the subversion of that authority even as he shores up its appearance of invulnerability. But must we assume that this fierce battle between the internal censors and thwarted impulses rages outside the consciousness of the author or his protagonist?: "With his mixed, divided nature, his conflicting sympathies, his eternal habit of swinging from one view to another, he regarded the prospect in different moods with different intensities" (*Princess* 6: 263).

The protagonist's identificatory dilemma signals the instability of the regulatory norms governing class hierarchy and, as I will argue in this chapter, heterosexual hegemony. By assuming even temporarily the position of abjection, deformity, and femininity occupied by his French mother, Hyacinth embraces the threat of ostracism and the taboo of sexual difference that she represents, and he challenges the Law of the Father, whose surrogate he has sworn to dispatch to the next world. In *The History of Sexuality*, Foucault suggests that the enumeration of unsanctioned activities by church and state had the unintended effect of disseminating the very practices it was designed to constrain. Butler treats this claim as a springboard in *Bodies That Matter*, elaborating on how prohibitions lend cultural intelligibility to heretofore unthinkable practices: "But what happens if the law that deploys the spectral figure of abject homosexuality as a threat becomes itself an inadvertent site of eroticization? If the taboo becomes eroticized precisely for the transgressive sites that it produces?" (97). Hyacinth's eagerness to follow in his mother's footsteps and "put his head in a noose" instantiates the erotic possibilities of self-punishment (*Princess* 6: 51), making him something of a kindred spirit to the late British M. P., Stephen Milligan, who preached family values one day and practiced autoerotic self-strangulation the next ("Sex and the British M. P.," 2). Significantly, Hyacinth's abjection circulates among the denizens of the novel's fraternal underground as an erotic identity sign. Hyacinth is a "rare muff," a queer, an unathletic "pretty lad" who offers himself, albeit unconsciously, to the "big chaps" of his homosocial network: "This rare man he could go on his knees to without a sense of humiliation"

(*Princess* 6: 46; 5: 232; 6: 47; 5: 150). Consequently, the injunction against homosexuality facilitates the formation of a recognizable homosexual identity, which exists in opposition to culturally sanctioned codes of masculine behavior and desire. This identity sign is intelligible to the astonishing variety of people who fancy Hyacinth and "have a go" at him: "Yes, and you nipped him up!" (6: 229).

Though it may seem premature to characterize Hyacinth as a homosexual in 1886, before the Wilde trials had inaugurated the homosexual persona, a variety of forces were already at work legislating norms and defining homosexual behaviors. It is extremely significant that *The Princess Casamassima* was in the early stages of development when the British parliament passed the Labouchère amendment to the Criminal Law Amendment Act on August 7, 1885, criminalizing the full spectrum of homosexual activities between consenting males and setting penalties, ranging from two years to life imprisonment at hard labor.[1] In the wake of this legislation, James had to be less than forthright in his depiction of homosexuality. In fact, it was not until the 1890s that fictional works candidly representing "romantic pederasty" and homosexual relationships were published for distribution among the general public in England (Reade, 51–53). Yet it may also be said that the Labouchère amendment provided James with a sociopolitical context for his treatment of male homosexuality, just as the burgeoning suffragist movement had supplied the social background for his treatment of lesbianism in *The Bostonians*. Recasting the terms in which *The Princess Casamassima* may be read as social commentary, we can see the novel's anarchist melodrama as a screen for the underlying theme of sexual subversion: "He already knew his friend's view of him as mainly ornamental, as adapted only to the softer forms of subversive energy, as constituted in short to show that the revolution was not necessarily brutal and illiterate" (*Princess* 6: 135). However, I do not mean to trivialize the novel's plot as mere pretext. For it is precisely in positing a connection between sexual and political dissidence that James reveals himself fully attuned to the regulatory strain of the emerging discourse on homosexuality. Following Butler, I choose to read James's dissimulation (his recourse to double discourse) as a movement toward the articulation of a homosexual identity, albeit a negative one: the abject victim of a repressive society (*Bodies That Matter*, 145). Therefore, I wish to affirm the cultural legibility of the tropes, tokens, and signs that James employs to tell his tale of forbidden love.

Recognizing the novel's covert sexual thematics permits us to engage with *The Princess Casamassima* on a new plane. James has generally been perceived as an outsider who knew comparatively little of the anarchist circles and shabby neighborhoods recounted in his story. Recognizing the novel's homoerotic subplot accords James insider status, foregrounding his community with the novel's oppressed groups. It also permits us to make sense of the novel's social critique, which, like that of *The Bostonians*, focuses on issues of identity and stigmatization rather than on social injustice per se. The emerging discourse on the nature of the homosexual did not appear in a vacuum; the representation and regulation of the "dangerous classes" factored into this construction because homosexuals amalgamated across class lines and because sexual and political anarchy were equally threatening to the social elites. *The Princess Casamassima* provides a vital connection between allegedly discrete forms of dissidence, which helps us to understand why any breach of the taboo against homosexuality was met with brutal resistance, for it had consequences beyond the challenge posed to dominant modes of sex and gender being, threatening national and class identity, the institution of the family, and the laws of church and state.

The covert issues of *The Princess Casamassima* would have been legible to anyone who cared to read between the lines. While the British were legislating tougher penalties for soliciting and sodomy in the late nineteenth century, the French had placed homosexuality on the same legal ground as heterosexuality in the 1791 constitution (Storzer, 175). Moreover, the English regarded the Code pénal de la révolution Francaise of 1791, which decriminalized sodomy, and the Napoleonic Code of 1810, which backed up this reform, as socially destabilizing corruptions of time-honored civil institutions (Gilbert, 98–113). Thus Hyacinth's French ancestry signifies his blood tie to a revolutionary working-class heritage—and something more. According to George Mosse, during the early nineteenth century the homosexual was "associated with rebellion of all kinds; in England, for example, he was accused of giving aid and comfort to the enemy during the wars of the French Revolution" (25). This is very likely why Hyacinth's socialist coconspirator, Eustache Poupin, is said to draw out the "latent Gallicism" in Hyacinth's character (*Princess* 5: 103). Gerald Storzer has argued that the association of homosexuality with criminal or political subversion persisted into the twentieth century: "In refusing to allow his sexuality—and consequently the very nature of his being—to be structured by social forces, the homosexual figure comes to represent a major revolutionary force both within and without the fictional universe. His disruptive sexuality becomes emblematic of the attempt to safeguard individuality and creativity in the face of stifling exigencies imposed by the social and cultural milieu" (187). Hyacinth's imaginary encounter with his maternal grandfather, the French revolutionary "who had known the ecstasy of the barricade and had paid for it with his life," exemplifies the novel's parallel discourse, in which the political forces proscribing nonreproductive sexuality and the psychic forces repressing homogenic desire mirror each other (*Princess* 6: 121). Just as the anarchist fraternities (the "Subterranean" and "the Sun and Moon") serve a further function in the novel as a homosexual underground, the French Revolution stands for freedom of a dual nature, personal as well as political.

In *Caught in the Act: Theatricality in the Nineteenth-Century English Novel*, Litvak has suggested a useful marriage of social and sexual themes in *The Princess Casamassima*: "For James's own liminal stance, as both in and out of the closet, as both for and against the embarrassment of vulgarity, finds a promising analogue in the double 'vagueness' of Hyacinth's *social* identity— is he the son of his aristocratic father or of his proletarian mother?—and of his *sexual* identity—is he in love with, say, the Princess Casamassima and Millicent Henning or with, say, Captain Sholto and Paul Muniment?" (237). Litvak has rewritten Seltzer's scripting of James's hegemonic strategy in his novel of surveillance in a way that makes room for James's identification with the novel's marginal groups: "What gets elided in Seltzer's account, at any rate, is a sense of James's specificity as an agent of power who, by virtue of his homosexuality, is also one of the most visible and laboriously constructed *objects* of that power" (217). Litvak does not attempt a further treatment of the homosexual themes in this novel, though he offers some excellent hints at such an undertaking. Litvak argues that James signals his marginality through equivocation, "rhetorical caginess," and double discourse, a cycle of "disavowal and reinscription" of homosexual meanings in his texts (216, 218).

If we are to understand James's homosexual thematics, we must place him in perspective, as one of the figures struggling to forge a sexual identity in the early stages of the lay, legal, and professional construction of homosexuality. With the exception of Ambrose Tardieu, J. L. Casper, Valentin Magnan, Westphal, and Ulrichs, few of the experts on sexual inversion had published

182 SEXUAL DISSIDENCE IN 'THE PRINCESS CASAMASSIMA'

by 1885, and their works, because they had not yet been translated, were un-
familiar to most English readers. Crompton points out that English jurists
took pride in the fact that no English equivalents of the French studies in
sexual deviance had been published up to 1897 (4). Dellamora contends that
homosexuality first appeared in English as a word and as a medical and social
category in the 1890s (167). Far from signaling the culmination of psychological and medical forensic studies on homosexuality, the mid-1880s were a
point of origination. The works of Paul Moreau, Benjamin Tarnowsky, Lombroso, Albert Moll, Krafft-Ebing, Freud, Ellis, Charles Féré, and Hirschfeld
appeared after *The Princess Casamassima* was published. In addition, we must
consider what qualities and behaviors constituted male "homosexuality" at
this time. The police characterized homosexuality as a crime, the pathologists treated it as a disease, the homosexual advocates claimed it was an instinct, and the literati extolled it as a platonic ideal. According to Jeffrey
Weeks, late-Victorian homosexuals framed modern conceptions of homosexuality (111–12). Symonds authored two seminal works on the topic, *A
Problem in Greek Ethics* (1883) and *A Problem in Modern Ethics* (1891), while
Carpenter delivered his famous paper, "Homogenic Love," in Manchester,
England, in 1894. Wilde's *The Picture of Dorian Gray* (1891), with its celebration of male beauty and its innuendos about illicit passion, helped shape popular perceptions of homosexuals. Indeed, the Marquis of Queensberry's bar-
rister, Edward Carson, read extensively from the novel at Queensberry's libel
trial, attributing the unsavory proclivities and attitudes of the novel's protagonists to Wilde himself (Cohen, 128). Richard Davenport-Hines notes that
the publicity surrounding the Wilde trials of 1895 enabled many individuals
to label themselves exclusively homosexual for the first time (135).

Moreover, we must be aware of the difficult climate in which the very notion of an alternative sexuality was conceived and expressed. In 1891, four
years before Wilde's famous plea on behalf of himself and other homosexuals, Symonds evoked "the love that dare not speak its name" in his pamphlet
on sexual inversion:

Those who read these lines will hardly doubt what passion it is that I am
hinting at. *Quod semper ubique et ab omnibus*—surely it deserves a name.
Yet I can hardly find a name which will not seem to soil this paper. The
accomplished languages of Europe in the nineteenth century supply no

term for this persistent feature of human psychology, without importing some implication of disgust, disgrace, vituperation. (3)

At the time James was writing, popular perception of homosexuals was shaped by newspaper accounts of the trial of Boulton and Park, which attributed a predilection for certain illegal sex acts (sodomy, fellatio, and mutual masturbation) and a love of frippery, typical of the most conspicuous among them, to homosexuals. Someone like James, who apparently found sexual congress repugnant, who was effeminate but no transvestite, must have wondered at the cultural stereotype that tarred all homosexuals with one brush. Such questions of identity and affinity underlie the novelist's depiction of Hyacinth Robinson, Paul Muniment, and Captain Sholto in *The Princess Casamassima*, which indicates his familiarity with the medico-psychiatric literature on homosexuality. Hyacinth resembles Ulrichs's congenital invert, whose sexual impulses are gaining ground in their battle for recognition. Paul plays the straight man for hire who lends himself to, rather than shares, the passions of others. And Captain Sholto represents the extreme sensualist, the case of acquired inversion.[2] Painting a fairly broad spectrum of homosexualities, all except the most colorful and transparent, James was still taking a chance that his own investment in the portrayal would be discerned. For this reason, the novel's homosexual content lies just below the narrative's surface, rendering the novel a palimpsest of sorts.

If I am reading *The Princess Casamassima* accurately, it seems James felt compelled to join the chorus, really a cacophony, of voices vying to define homosexuality at that time. Foucault has argued that

since the eighteenth century, sex has not ceased to provoke a kind of generalized discursive erethism. And these discourses on sex did not multiply apart from or against power, but in the very space and as the means of its exercise. Incitements to speak were orchestrated from all quarters, apparatuses everywhere for listening and recording, procedures for observing, questioning, and formulating. Sex was driven out of hiding and constrained to lead a discursive existence. (*History*, 1: 32–33)

Because of these multiplying discourses, which defy exact categorization as hegemonic or counterhegemonic, Foucault urged a reevaluation of the widely held conviction that sexual repression dominated Victorian culture—which is not to say that proscribed sexual conduct was not subject to erasure at the precise moment of articulation. Ellis's *Studies in the Psychology of Sex: Volume II, Sexual Inversion* was published and then censored in the same year (1897). What is significant in Foucault's formulation is the ubiquity and novelty of the impulse to render an account of one's sexuality "*ad infinitum*, while exploiting it as *the* secret" within the secular realm (1: 35). The contradictory aims of exposing and concealing sexuality manifest themselves in narrative as double discourse, in which homogenic desire is a liminal, but insistent, presence. Sedgwick's reading of "The Beast in the Jungle" underscores the relation between John Marcher's "secret" and "an embodied male-homosexual thematics" (*Epistemology*, 201). The cabals and trysts between men presented in *The Princess Casamassima* are equally suggestive of same-sex desire: "Secrets? What secrets could you tell her, my pretty lad?"; "Less than ever would an observer have guessed at a good reason why the two young men might have winced as they looked at each other" (*Princess* 5: 232; 6: 203).

Slang and Syllepsis

The Princess Casamassima mirrors the turmoil produced and the introspection encouraged by the new scrutiny of marginal identities in the late nineteenth century. Providing a focus for the study of what Edelman has termed "the historically variable rhetorics, the discursive strategies and tropological formations, in which sexuality is embedded and conceived," *The Princess Casamassima* appears an excellent text for contemporary gay and gender studies (20). Can we attribute this novel's homoerotic content to a conscious strategy on James's part? I would say yes whenever the homosexual meanings of the words and images employed by the novelist can be readily understood in their proper context, the sociolect. If all that stands between a straight and gay interpretation of a term or image is a change of costume or venue, then it is an example of what Miller has called "a form of early Camp" and what Litvak has described as double discourse (Miller, 236). At one point in the novel, Eustache Poupin assures Hyacinth that he is "incapable of drawing aside any veil that you may have preferred to drop over your lacerated personality. Your moral dignity will always be safe with me. But remember at the same time that among the disinherited there's a mystic language which dispenses with proofs—a freemasonry, a reciprocal divination; they understand each other at half a word" (*Princess* 5: 342). James toys with the notion of homosexual visibility in this passage, alluding to the secret signs by which members of the fraternity achieve "reciprocal divination" without proofs. Symonds's *A Problem in Modern Ethics* serves as a guide to the equivocal terminology of *The Princess Casamassima*. Describing a "freemasonry among paederasts," Symonds declares: "In all the great towns of Europe the vice goes creeping around, unobserved by the uninitiated. . . . I said uninitiated advisedly. In antiquity the members of the sect had their own means of mutual recognition. And at the present time, these men know each other at first sight" (28, 27). James casts Hyacinth's insatiable curiosity about life, love, and luxury in the same suggestive language: "It was not so much that he wanted to enjoy as that he wanted to know; his desire was n't to be pampered but to be initiated" (*Princess* 5: 169).

In "The Intertextual Unconscious," Michael Riffaterre explains an important function of these double entendres:

> The concept of syllepsis aptly describes this special case of intertextuality. Syllepsis is a trope consisting in the simultaneous presence of two meanings for one word. I modify this definition thus: the meaning required by the context represses the one incompatible with that context. Repression, however, entails a compensation: it generates a syntagm or even a text in which the repressed meaning reappears in various guises. (375)

Riffaterre's thesis grew out of his study of Proust, whose portrayals of homosexuals (notably in *Cities of the Plain*) are well established. We might also call this process *homographesis*, which is Edelman's term for a text's eventual disclosure of gay meanings, a pattern of clarification that retroactively "produces meaning from phenomena understood initially to be arbitrary and inconsequential" (20). *The Princess Casamassima* is replete with homographs, often highlighted by quotation marks or hyphenation. In his preface to the novel, James describes his protagonist's plight: "Dabbling deeply in a revolutionary politics of a hole-and-corner sort, he would be 'in' up to his neck, and with that precarious part of him particularly involved, so that his tergiversation is the climax of his adventure" (*Princess* 5: xviii).

The *Dictionary of English Phrases* defines "hole and corner" as an expression connoting secret, underhand activities that cannot stand the light of day, "literally done in a hole and corner," but it does not refer to sex (Hyamson, 187). Symonds, however, proves more helpful on this score: "Sometimes [sexual inversion] skulks in holes and corners, hiding an abashed head and shrinking from the light of day, as in the capitals of modern Europe"; "For the present it is enough to remark that a kind of love, however spontaneous and powerful, which is scouted, despised, tabooed, banned, punished, relegated to holes and corners, cannot be expected to show its best side to the world" (*Problem in Modern Ethics*, 1, 111). Where Symonds is objective and dispassionate, James teases an erotic act out of his hero's "dabbling." Although James masks the sexy import of the sentence by substituting upper for lower bodily regions, it does not require much imagination to guess what precarious part of Hyacinth is immersed to the hilt in mire, when the sentence ends with words like *tergiversation* (turning one's back) and *climax*. These expressions seem part of a strategy for encoding homosexual connotations within another related lexicon, which explains why James favors the term *latent* in the novel. He constantly shifts the reader's attention from the phony anarchist drama to the genuinely subversive activities plotted behind the scenes. In the novel's preface, James remarks:

> Should n't I find it in the happy contention that the value I wished most to render and the effect I wished most to produce were precisely those of our not knowing, of society's not knowing, but only guessing and suspecting and trying to ignore, what 'goes on' irreconcilably, subversively, beneath the vast smug surface? I could n't deal with that positive quantity for itself—my subject had another too exacting side; but I might perhaps show the social ear as on occasion applied to the ground, or catch some gust of the hot breath that I had at many an hour seemed to see escape and hover. (*Princess* 5: xxii–iii)

In "Words and Deeds in *The Princess Casamassima*," Stoehr praises James's avoidance of political catchwords and clichés, "the rhetoric of violence" he might have gleaned from newspaper accounts of anarchist activities or from anarchist propaganda (112). Though James has omitted revolutionary catchwords from the novel, it is rife with vulgar epithets and the jargon of thieves.

Given James's accent on the mot juste, it is remarkable that he has provided his conspirators with an inappropriate lexicon. The closest James comes to political speech is an occasional reference to social Darwinism; yet the novelist seems fully versed in the vocabulary of criminals. Many of the slang words in *The Princess Casamassima* pertain to stealing, betting, and counterfeiting. James calls Captain Sholto a "tout," slang for watchman or scout, one who solicits custom; it also connotes one who surreptitiously watches race horses at their paces to make informed bets. Sholto is frequently accused of procuring as well as spying: "He throws his nets and hauls in the little fishes—the pretty little shining, wriggling fishes. They are all for *her*; She swallows 'em down" (*Princess* 5: 259). The characterization of Sholto as a gentleman who loves "rum out of the way nooks" attests to James's familiarity with the double lives many Victorian males led. Sholto's pursuit of Hyacinth is a case in point:

> "Of course he has looked at me," Millicent answered as if she had no interest in denying that. "But you're the one he wants to get hold of."
> "To get hold of!"
> "Yes, you ninny: don't hang back. He may make your fortune." (5: 190)

Though political subversion and criminality are equally destabilizing, the latter is both better suited to disclosing the homosexual intertext and to proclaiming class a valid experiential category rather than a form of false consciousness. When Hyacinth contemplates what his life would have been without the intervention of his foster mother, his reflections on his likely poverty give way to concern over latent criminality: "The workhouse and the gutter, ignorance and cold, filth and tatters, nights of huddling under bridges and in doorways, vermin, starvation and blows, possibly even the vigorous efflorescence of an inherited disposition to crime—these things, which he saw with an unprecedented vividness, suggested themselves as his natural portion" (6: 110). Though James does not specify the crime, it would not be far-fetched to imagine an impoverished Hyacinth prostituting himself to make ends meet, as "nights spent huddling under bridges and in doorways" implies. *Huddling* is such a cozy, intimate word. Clearly ambivalent about the homoerotic transactions implied in these and other passages, Hyacinth significantly associates transgressive sexuality with the threat of punishment, or "blows." And we would not want to overlook the passage's references to dirt, which are indirectly linked to sodomy through their association with fecal matter. Indeed, in *A Problem in Modern Ethics*, Symonds describes casual sex in almost the same language, writing of the "filth and mire of brutal appetite" (120). In *The Princess Casamassima*, homosexuality and criminality are synonymous, linked by their alterity and lawlessness: "They had met three times, he and his fellow-spectator; but they had met in quarters that, to Hyacinth's mind, would have made a furtive wink, a mere tremor of the eyelid, a more judicious reference to the fact than a public salutation" (*Princess* 5: 192).

> "I rather like Englishmen best."
> "Mr. Muniment for example?"
> "I say, what do you know about *him*?" Hyacinth asked. "I've seen him at the Puppins'. I know you and he are as thick as thieves." (5: 183)

The subcultural provenance of these tropes, with their racy import, suggests that James differentiated between the déclassé and the elite worlds of Victorian homosexuals. For the elite group regarded the "rough trade" with mingled feelings of terror and desire: "Ah you *must* be a first-rate man—you're such a brute!" (6: 414). Threatened with physical violence, blackmail, and loss of caste, the elites may well have regarded their working-class lovers as anarchists, in the broadest sense of the term.

Hyacinth Robinson straddles these two worlds. As an east Londoner who plies a trade, he is decidedly working class. Yet Hyacinth's innate refinement marks him as one of nature's aristocrats: "I've blood in my veins that's not the blood of the people" (5: 247). The instability of Hyacinth's class position reflects the shifting relationship of the marginal figure to the dominant group. This tension between states of self is encapsulated in the appellation "cockney," which James affixes to Hyacinth. After Henry Mayhew's *London Labour and the London Poor* was published (1851–61), the cockney was established as a type in the popular imagination. Though Hyacinth outclasses the costermongers, patterers, and proprietors of lodging houses and regards their vices—criminality, drunkenness, lust, and squalor—with horror, his own slanginess, fanciful notions of adornment, theatricality, and above all "roving" ways are highly typical (Herbert, 204–52). Mayhew's four-volume treatise begins with a comparison of London's "wandering hordes" (paupers, beggars, and outcasts) with the "wandering tribes" of the uncivilized portions of the globe (1: 2). Hyacinth is a liminal presence in picturesque London, a passive observer of street life rather than an active participant, and his impressions of cockney culture are intriguingly consistent with Mayhew's, emphasizing the regression and degeneracy of the lower classes and registering a fear of contagion through amalgamation with them:

> Hyacinth used to smile at this pretension in his nightwalks to Paddington or homeward; the populace of London were scattered upon his path, and he asked himself by what wizardry they could ever be raised to high participations. There were nights when every one he met appeared to reek with gin and filth and he found himself elbowed by figures as foul as lepers. Some of the women and girls in particular were appalling—saturated with alcohol and vice, brutal, bedraggled, obscene. (*Princess* 6: 267)

Beyond the purview of the ethnographic literature, the word *cockney* had an altogether different import. A cockney signified a tenderly reared child, a mother's darling, a sissy. Taking the hint, a reader might detect the nuances of what Linda Dowling has called "the late-Victorian 'homosexual code'" in James's description of Hyacinth as effete and wasted (7):

> He was shabby and work-stained, but an observant eye would have caught the hint of an 'arrangement' in his dress (his appearance being plainly not a matter of indifference to himself) while a painter (not of the heroic) would have liked to make a sketch of him. There was something exotic in him, and yet, with his sharp young face, destitute of bloom but not of sweetness, and a certain conscious cockneyism that pervaded him, he was as strikingly as Millicent, in her own degree, a product of the London streets and the London air. He looked both ingenuous and slightly wasted, amused, amusing and indefinably sad. (*Princess* 5: 78–79)

This description of Hyacinth (dapper, "exotic," "slightly wasted") savors of literary decadence. It would be a bit premature to describe the movement as in full flower in 1885, but Ellmann has shown that the Oxford and Cambridge undergraduate's journal took note of the aesthetic movement as early as 1877 (*Oscar Wilde*, 88). James read Pater for the first time between 1873 and 1874, and he was certainly aware of Wilde before writing *The Princess Casamassima*. Artistic "little Hyacinth," as James calls him, is cast in the mold of the fin de siècle aesthete who decked his drawing room and person with exotic flowers to indicate both effeminacy and rarefied taste, a trend Ellmann has marked in his biography of Wilde: "Your poor little pet thinks himself the flower of creation. I don't say there's any harm in that: a fine, blooming, odoriferous conceit is a natural appendage of youth and intelligence" (*Princess* 5: 33–34).

James's rhetoric transparently suggests a connection between aestheticism and the homoerotic subcultures of Oxbridge. As David DeLaura has shown, by the 1870s Pater addressed his criticism to a "new kind of reader" who shared a "homoerotic sensibility" (8). In this small community of likeminded readers, Hellenism circulated as a code for homoerotism (Morgan, 315–32). Of Winckelmann Pater famously observed: "That his affinity with Hellenism was not merely intellectual, that the subtler threads of temperament were interwoven in it, is proved by his romantic, fervent friendships with young men. He has known, he says, many young men more beautiful than Guido's archangel" (122–23). Now we can appreciate the multiple valences of our protagonist's name. Hyacinthus was dear to Apollo (Tyas, 116). Thus Hyacinth's sexual ambivalence is inscribed in the content of the Greek myth from which his floral name is derived.[3] Moreover, in his exposition of Byron's sexual life, Crompton has shown that to Georgian homosexuals, "Hyacinths" signified sexually available youths: "We are surrounded by Hyacinths & other flowers of the most fragrant [n]ature, & I have some intention of culling a handsome Bouquet to compare with the exotics I hope to meet in Asia"; "A word or two about hyacinths. Hyacinth, you may remember was killed by a Coit, but not that 'full and to-be-wished-for Coit'" (127–29).

The hyacinth was a popular symbol of boy love throughout the nineteenth century. Several poems written between 1888 and 1893 and published in the Uranian organ *Artist* bore the title "Hyacinthus," one of which was written by Wilde's lover, Lord Alfred Douglas (Kopelson, 41–43). The novelist's insistence on Hyacinth's immaturity evokes one of the oldest tropes in homoerotic literature: the love of the *senex* for the *puer*: "Then he went on in a different tone: 'M. Hyacinthe is a gifted child, *un enfant très-doué*, in whom I take a tender interest" (*Princess* 5: 112). Hyacinth's pliancy is another reason so many sexually ambiguous men are drawn to the beardless youth: "Paul changed his posture, raising himself, and in a moment was seated Turk-fashion beside his friend. He put his arm over his shoulder and drew him, studying his face" (6: 213). Crompton mentions an 1809 letter of Byron's, in which he penned and then crossed out the line "but you *know boys* are not *safe* amongst the Turks" (132). Turkey, Persia, and Greece were associated with homosexual activity even before Sir Richard Burton's 1885 publication of the *Book of the One Thousand and One Nights*, with its infamous "Terminal Essay," in which Burton outlined his theory that homosexuality was prevalent in warmer climates, regions bordering the Mediterranean, which he called the Sotadic Zone (Karlen, 215). Paul Rycaut's 1668 work, *Present State of the Ottoman Empire*, was very communicative on the topic of homosexuality (Crompton, 112). James derived his representation of Sholto as a well-traveled gentleman who has scoured the world in pursuit of pleasure from this rumor. At one point Sholto invites Hyacinth to his rooms quite literally to look at his etchings: "Half an hour later Hyacinth found himself in Captain Sholto's chambers, seated on a big divan covered with Persian rugs and cushions and smoking the most expensive cigar that had ever touched his lips" (*Princess* 5: 263). By such means *The Princess Casamassima* invites the attention of a new highbrow constituency of readers eager for homoerotic themes in literature and sensitive to their deployment, a strategy that is consistent with the high cultural domain of the novel, even though the other homosexual codes have a low cultural provenance.

Latent or Blatant Homoerotism?

It is initially difficult to gauge James's attitude toward his protagonist's homosexuality. Though Hyacinth is not an active homosexual, he bears all the signs of sexual liminality, from night wandering to impotency with women. James depicts Hyacinth as a self-deceiving character who disdains "mollies" and "fops" and who rankles under the imputation of effeminacy: "Moreover, when old Poupin said 'M. Hyacinthe,' as he had often done before, he did n't altogether enjoy it; he thought it made his name, which he liked well enough in English, sound like the name of a hairdresser. Our young friend was un-

der a cloud and a stigma, but he was not yet prepared to admit he was ridiculous" (*Princess* 5: 113).[4] Note the contrast between the damning French and
the colorless English pronunciations of his name. Apparently, hairdressers
have been the butt of queer jokes for over a century:

> His name was Delancey and he gave himself out as holding a position in
> a manufactory of soda water; but Hyacinth had a secret belief that he
> was really a hairdresser—a belief connected with a high lustrous curl or
> crest which he wore on the summit of his large head, as well as with the
> manner in which he thrust over his ear, as if it were a barber's comb, the
> pencil addressed to his careful note-taking on the discussions conducted
> at the 'Sun and Moon'. His opinions were distinct and frequently ex-
> pressed; he had a watery (Muniment had once called it a soda-watery)
> eye and a personal aversion to a lord. (5: 353)

In "Viraginity and Effemination," Weir supplies further ammunition for interpreting Delancey's sexual proclivities and, more important, he argues for
the cultural currency of the traits associated with homosexuality: "We see
daily on our streets, mild types of effemination in the cigarette smoking,
soda-water-drinking young men whom the caricaturists consider their legitimate prey" (360). Hyacinth's inability to see his resemblance to Delancey
(the other "hairdresser" who has a "personal aversion to a lord," most likely
acquired at a Molly House or at other venues for male prostitution) bears
noting. This blindness demonstrates Hyacinth's repudiation of those signs or
traits that would link him to a newly constituted homosexual identity; as with
Olive Chancellor in *The Bostonians*, Hyacinth's reluctance to occupy the
sexed position of the homosexual reinforces the trope of the abject homosexual as a figure of ridicule, while failing to affirm any heterosexual alternative.

The aforementioned passage would make a good case for anyone seeking
evidence of homophobia and homosexual panic in James's work. For the present, I want to highlight Hyacinth's preference for "straight" men, because
this characterization links Hyacinth to a specific type of homosexual, identified in the new taxonomy as effete, effeminate, and supercivilized and as one
who unconsciously aims to shore up his own masculinity by incorporating
that of a more manly partner: "'Muniment walks straight; the best thing you
can do is to imitate him', Hyacinth said" (*Princess* 6: 372). It is significant that
James associates Paul Muniment with phallic completeness, which Hyacinth

so blatantly lacks. His name is confused with "monument," and he makes Hyacinth think of a battery of guns: "There was something in the face, taken in connexion with the idea that he was concerned in the taking of a stand— it offered our quick youth the image of a rank of bristling bayonets—which made Hyacinth feel the desire to go with him till he dropped" (5: 194, 119). Speculating on the physiological basis for homogenic love, Symonds and Carpenter debated the merits of a theory that the transmission of semen from one male to another increased the virility of the passive partner (*Letters of John Addington Symonds* 3: 797–98). Characterized as an "idle, trifling, luxurious" cosmopolite, the last remnant of a "mouldy 'country family'" run to seed, Captain Sholto also hopes to invigorate himself or, at the very least, to commit a peccadillo in the company of virile working men (*Princess* 6: 82). Describing his forays into the socialist circles of Bloomsbury as "the straw one chews to cheat one's appetite; all the rot one dabbles in because it may lead to something which it never does lead to," Sholto cruises for eligible mates: "He told me he'd give the world to see a really superior working-man's 'interior.' I did n't know at first just where he proposed to cut me open: he wanted a favourable specimen, one of the best; he had seen one or two that he did n't believe to be up to the average" (6: 72; 5: 257).

In contrast to Hyacinth and Sholto, Paul Muniment is an extremely masculine character but one who is equally associated with homosexual signs and indications: "Apparently he cared nothing for women, talked of them rarely and always decently, and had never a sign of a sweetheart save in so far as Lady Aurora Langrish might pass for one" (5: 228). And it should not take a miracle for a peerless beauty to seduce a virile young working man: "It was familiar to Hyacinth that Muniment was n't easily reached or rubbed up by women, but this might perfectly have been the case without detriment to the Princess's ability to work a miracle" (6: 209). "Rubbed up" means sexually aroused; it is not neutral, or even polite, terminology. *The Princess Casamassima* is consistent in presenting Paul as supermasculine in appeal but unreadable as a sexual agent; he tells man and woman alike that his "pleasure's in keeping very cool" (6: 291). Though Hyacinth speculates that Paul will marry and do all the "natural human productive things," there is no textual evidence supporting this view (6: 278). Paul's initial wariness of the beautiful princess suggests that he is in the throes of sexual panic. Though Paul overcomes his embarrassment to "treat the Princess as a woman," to use Trilling's words, he experiences many awkward moments (75). At one point it appears as if Paul means to relieve himself on the princess's rug in panicked response to her solicitations: "Then a strange and, to the Princess, unexpected expression passed over the countenance of her guest; his lips compressed themselves as in the strain of a strong effort, his colour rose and in a moment he stood there blushing like a boy. He dropped his eyes and stared at the carpet while he repeated: 'I don't trust women—I don't trust clever women!'" (*Princess* 6: 231). The princess, of course, is unable to digest this information, unable to imagine the type of man who does not fancy women. In response to Paul's off-putting remark, she coaxes, "But you're the sort of man who ought to know how to use them" (read: sexually) (6: 228).

This characterization of Paul as a bisexual or heterosexual who "dabbles" squares with historians' accounts of late-Victorian casual and long-term relationships among homosexual men, in which class distinctions sometimes took the place of gender divisions: "[Paul] had the complexion of a ploughboy and the glance of a commander-in-chief, and might have been a distinguished young *savant* in the disguise of an artisan. The disguise would have been very complete, for he had several brown stains on his fingers" (5: 114). The mixing of class strata in masculine love was extolled by Symonds as one of its most promising features, which explains why late-Victorian homosexuality was perceived as fostering unnatural alliances and as inimical to class hierarchies: "Where it appears, it abolishes class distinctions, and opens by a single operation the cataract-blinded eye to their futilities. . . . If it could be acknowledged and extended, it would do very much to further the advent of the right sort of Socialism" (*Letters of John Addington Symonds*, 3: 808). Jurists were equally sensitive to this trend. By 1895 it could be insinuated that Wilde's interactions with several working-class men were gross and indecent simply on the grounds that disparities in class, education, breeding, and age rendered these friendships improper (Cohen, 166). This object choice links Hyacinth to Victorian homosexuals known for their dalliances with the queen's guardsman and with sailors and working-class men. A correspondent of Krafft-Ebing's explains the attraction: "As I felt myself drawn exclusively towards powerful, youthful and entirely masculine individuals, that is, to a type that very seldom felt inclined to accede to my wishes, it often happened that I was forced to buy their favours. Since my desires are limited to persons of the lower social order, I could always find someone who could be had for the money" (250). At the same time, Hyacinth is not comfortable with (or even conscious of) a longing for intimacy that goes beyond endearments and chaste embraces. He anticipates Carpenter's ideal of homogenic love, which stands for an ennobling and deep attachment between persons of the same sex, free of the taint of depravity: "It may be explained that 'he' was a reference to Paul Muniment; for Hyacinth had dreamed of the religion of friendship" (*Princess* 6: 141).

Moreover, James seems extremely sensitive to the obstacles Hyacinth would have faced as an effeminate homosexual seeking masculine men as romantic partners: "The sweetness of loafing there in an interval of work with a chum who was a tremendously fine fellow even if he did n't understand the inexpressible" (6: 214). More important than the inference that may be drawn from the term *inexpressible* is the passage's invocation of the chivalrous ideal, the "sweetness" of comrade love. Hyacinth's yearning for the "ethereal comradeship" links him to the idealistic literature on homosexuality emerging in the wake of Whitman's encomiums to male friendship in "Calamus" and *Democratic Vistas* (Symonds, *Problem in Modern Ethics*, 123).[5] In *Notes of a Son and Brother*, James recalled his attempts to minister to the wounded at Portsmouth Grove in 1863 and compared his efforts to those of "dear old Walt" Whitman, whose Civil War poetry James had clearly read and admired (424). In *The Princess Casamassima*, James dwells on the notion of an exalted relation between men, summarized by the reflection that "friendship was a purer feeling than love": "Our hero treated himself to a high unlimited faith in him; he had always dreamed of some grand friendship and this was the best opening he had yet encountered. . . . It disappointed him sometimes that his confidence was not more unreservedly repaid" (6: 219; 5: 228). Krafft-Ebing stressed the same anxieties and frustrations, the same enforced silence, in *Psychopathia Sexualis*: "It is not so with the homosexual. He sees the men that attract him; but he dares not say—nay, not even betray by a look—what his feelings are. He thinks that he alone of all the world has such abnormal feelings. Naturally, he seeks the society of young men; but he does not venture to confide in them" (384).

There is a strong sense in all this that *The Princess Casamassima* was meant as an elaborate sexual fantasy as well as a poignant account of the confusion, denial, and loneliness experienced by homosexuals at the time of James's writing. Though few of the novel's characters experience Hyacinth's homosexual panic, they are well aware of the threat of exposure. A character named Schinkel is so afraid of violating the Criminal Law Amendment Act that he almost misses an assignation with a dapper member of the revolutionists' circle to which he belongs:

> I went down into the street. When he saw me come he walked slowly away, but at the end of a little distance he waited for me. When I came near him I saw him to be a very neat young man indeed—very young and with a very nice friendly face. He was also very clean and he had gloves, and his umbrella was of silk. I liked him very much. He said I should come round the corner, so we went round the corner together. . . . I did n't know what he wanted; perhaps it was some of our business—that's what I first thought—and perhaps it was only a little game. So I was very careful; I did n't ask him to come into the house. Yet I told him that he must excuse me for not understanding more quickly that he wished to speak with me. (*Princess* 6: 378–79)

This passage evokes the "cruisiness" that Sedgwick attributed to the graveyard scene in James's 1903 story, "The Beast in the Jungle" (*Epistemology*, 210). Incidentally, Bolton Street, where James resided at the time he composed *The Princess Casamassima*, was close to Piccadilly Circus, a hot spot for cruising homosexuals at that time. According to Davenport-Hines, "the best-known place for importuning in London was under the County Fire Office arches at Piccadilly Circus, which kept this character until the 1980s. Men were taunted, 'Been up Dilly lately, dear?' even by village bumpkins" (146). Is it inconceivable that Henry James, who dubbed himself "the pedestrian prowler" in his preface to *The Princess Casamassima*, wrote of Schinkel's "little game" from first-hand experience or from an eyewitness account (5: xxii)? More to the point, the passage implies that the legislation enacted against homosexuality eroticized the spectrum of male interactions, since it focused attention and anxiety on the male sexual persona in the public as well as the private domain.

It is unfashionable to consider an author's personal investment in his stories and characters; however, it would be craven to deny my curiosity about what James intended to accomplish in his novel. Reading *The Princess Casamassima* as a *tendenzroman*, a plea for the liberalization of social mores and the decriminalization of homosexuality, seems pointless, both because

James never publicly identified himself as a homosexual and because none of his contemporaries, homosexual activists like Symonds and Carpenter, took any notice of the novel—although they did credit Whitman with expounding their philosophy of Greek love. This is not to deny the novel's documentary power, its depiction of passion driven underground by the fear of persecution combined with guilt and self-loathing: "[Sholto's smile] became intense when it rested on our hero, whom he greeted as he might have done a dear young friend from whom he had been long and painfully separated. He was easy, he was familiar, he was exquisitely benevolent and bland—he was altogether a problem" (*Princess* 5: 255). Krafft-Ebing attributed the higher rate of insanity and nervous disorders among homosexuals to the mental and moral suffering inflicted on them by the legal instruments and social prejudices standing between them and the satisfaction of their natural desires, but in this view he was in the minority (387). Most psychiatrists, physicians, and anthropologists studying sexual inversion ascribed the variation in the genesiac instinct to disease, atavism, or neuropathic heredity. The pathologists generally opposed the decriminalization of sodomy, mutual masturbation, and the like, fearing that congenital inverts might seduce "normal" individuals at a susceptible moment or that this "vicious habit should contaminate our youth" (Ulrichs, cited in Symonds, *Problem in Modern Ethics*, 101). It is interesting that expressions of homophobia in *The Princess Casamassima* occur chiefly in relation to this idea of the contagiousness of antiphysical passion: "Surely: that deep fellow has been the main source of his infection"; "Was it something he had caught in some of those back slums where he went prying about with his mad ideas? It served him right for taking as little good into such places as ever came out of them. Would his fine friends—a precious lot *they* were, that put it off on him to do all the nasty part!—would they find the doctor and the port wine and the money and all the rest when he was laid up?" (*Princess* 6: 251, 332). Hyacinth's heterosexual friends console themselves with the fallacious notion that he has fallen in among reprobates, that he is innocent of any taint himself, while the narrator insists on the congenital basis of Hyacinth's homosexuality.

My aim here is not to pigeonhole James but rather to understand how the novelist's sense of his own unconventional sexual inclinations and the constraint that the doctrines of moral and mental hygiene imposed on those yearnings influenced his depiction of Hyacinth: "There were things in his heart and a torment and a hidden passion in his life which he should be glad enough to lay open to some woman. He believed that perhaps this would be the cure ultimately" (5: 87). The language of cure and infection, of disease and dis-ease, that pervades the novel reveals the fissures in extratextual constructions of sex, gender, and class. Hyacinth's liminality, mirrored by the novel's amazons and bearded women (Madame Poupin has a "bristling moustache"), has a parodic quality that deprives the hegemonic culture of its claim to natural or essential gender categories (5: 96): "In the place of an original identification which serves as a determining cause, gender identity might be reconceived as a personal/cultural history of received meanings subject to a set of imitative practices which refer laterally to other imitations and which, jointly, construct the illusion of a primary and interior gendered self or parody the mechanism of that construction" (Butler, *Gender Trouble*, 138).

In 1888 Krafft-Ebing found that many of his homosexual patients and correspondents engaged in a counteressentializing discourse, describing themselves as actors and referring to their biological gender as a role to which they had been assigned: "Her former period of life spent as a woman seemed strange to her, as if it did not belong to her existence at all; she could play no longer the role of woman"; "What affected her most keenly was the fact that, like an actress, she must move in a strange sphere—i.e., in that of a woman" (215–16). Analogously, Hyacinth's theatricality underscores his alterity and transgressive desire:

> He was on the point of replying that he did n't care for fancy costumes, he wished to go through life in his own character; but he checked himself with the reflexion that this was exactly what he was apparently destined not to do. His own character? He was to cover that up as carefully as possible; he was to go through life in a mask, in a borrowed mantle; he was to be every day and every hour an actor. (*Princess* 5: 86)

Theatrical metaphors abound in *The Princess Casamassima*; the princess is likened to an actress, while the anarchist Hoffendahl is depicted as a master director who actually holds all the wires to the scenery, props, and stage effects of the revolution. These theatrical metaphors also reinforce the novel's performative aspects, emphasizing the highly scripted and discontinuous character of gender identity:

His bones were small, his chest was narrow, his complexion pale, his whole figure almost childishly slight; and Millicent noted afterwards that he had a very delicate hand—the hand, as she said to herself, of a gentleman. What she liked was his face and something jaunty and romantic, almost theatrical, in his whole little person. Miss Henning was not acquainted with any member of the dramatic profession, but she supposed vaguely that that was the way an actor would look in private life. Hyacinth's features were perfect; his eyes, large and much divided, had as their usual expression a kind of witty, almost an impertinent, candour, and a small, soft, fair moustache disposed itself upon his upper lip. (5: 78–79)

Sexuality, Race, and Class

Significantly, the novel's reflections on inversion are not confined to sexuality per se but touch on many aspects of social life. The conflation of sexual and political dissidence in *The Princess Casamassima* serves as a reminder that prohibitions against nonreproductive sexuality (masturbation, homosexuality) legitimize dominant modes of sexuality aimed at reproduction within familial and class confines (Dollimore, 171). Sexuality is but one of many fronts on which the battle for political hegemony is fought. In the novel, a recurring trope handily demonstrates the interplay between the sexual and the political. At the beginning of *The Princess Casamassima*, Hyacinth's childhood sweetheart, the slangy and good-natured Millicent Henning, tells him: "I never thought you'd work with your 'ands," a rather literal and blunt means of denoting Hyacinth's class status as a journeyman printer (5: 90). Though Hyacinth is endowed with a "very delicate" and "gentlemanly" pair of hands, a legacy from his aristocratic sire, he is trapped in the petite bourgeoisie by accident of his birth. On this basis the fraternity of the dispossessed at the "Sun and Moon" concedes that Hyacinth has a large score to settle with civilization, in spite of his smart clothes, posh accent, and possession of "the sort of hand on which there is always a premium—an accident somehow to be guarded against in a thorough-going system of equality" (5: 342).[6] As a conspicuous victim of social infamy and heinous laws, Hyacinth is declared "*ab ovo* a revolutionist," a double entendre signifying both congenital inversion and a first-class grudge against the ruling class (5: 342). By the late nineteenth century, medicoforensic specialists had discovered a family resemblance among the born criminal, his anarchist first cousin, and the homosexual: "Someday—and I greatly fear that day is not very far distant—some professional anarchist . . . will consider that the time is ripe for rebellion, and, raising the fraudulent cry of 'Labor Against Capital', instead of his legitimate cry, which is 'Rapine, Murder, Booty!' will lead this army of degenerates, composed of anarchists, socialists, nihilists, sexual perverts, and congenital criminals, against society" (Weir, "Is It the Beginning of the End?," 804).

Millicent Henning grows impatient with Hyacinth's socialist palaver; swearing that she wouldn't have been a lord's bastard for nothing, she asserts, "Oh the left hand was as good as the right" (*Princess* 6: 343). This phrase derives from the custom of morganatic marriage ("to marry with the left hand"), in which members of the nobility wed their social inferiors without elevating them and without transferring goods, fiefs, or titles to the offspring of the match. In so far as the patrimony does not descend to these "children of the left hand," this idiom is also used to signify illegitimacy. Though Millicent has reinvented herself as a respectable and conservative young lady, her attitude reflects her plebeian origins: "Having the history of the French Revolution at his fingers' ends, Hyacinth could easily see her (if there should ever be barricades in the streets of London) with a red cap of liberty on her head and her white throat bared so that she should be able to shout the louder the Marseillaise of that hour, whatever it might be" (5: 164). As a student of Carlyle, James was undoubtedly aware that the radical wing of the French assembly sat on the left-hand side, prompting the nineteenth-century neologism "left wing."

Furthermore, the postrevolutionary French republic blazed a path to the radical assimilation of illegitimate to legitimate children by extending rights of property and inheritance to natural children in the twelfth brumaire of 1793 (Brinton, 29). The American Weir had no sympathy with constitutional reforms extending privileges to bastards and homosexuals; he blamed the condition of France in 1794, when "Anarchy unfurled its red banner at the head of the most gigantic social revolution the world has ever known," on the sexual libertinism of the aristocracy ("monsters of sensuality and lechery") and on the poverty of the peasantry and the inhabitants of the faubourgs, who "had lapsed into a psychical state closely akin to that of their savage ancestors" ("Is It the Beginning of the End?," 802). The charge of atavism pervades the discourse on both sexual deviancy and socialism at this time; once again, the personal and political spheres blur. In "The Methods of the Rioting Striker an Evidence of Degeneration," Weir asserted that "the anthropologist can detect the physical signs of degeneration in these people at a glance" (953). This claim has resonance for late-nineteenth-century discussions of homosexuality, which also stressed physical stigmata. Shortly after reading Wilde's novel *The Picture of Dorian Gray*, which contains the famous dictum "sin is a thing that writes itself across a man's face" (149), Symonds reproduced this maxim in *A Problem in Modern Ethics*: "It is the common belief that all subjects from inverted instinct carry their lusts written in their faces" (14). One presumes that sin writes itself on the body as well; at least that is the inference to be drawn from James's attribution of the fay *la main parisienne* to Hyacinth (*Princess* 5: 110).

Along with these extratextual reverberations, an intertextual instance of the trope of the left hand merits attention. It occurs when Hyacinth is taken aback by Princess Casamassima's curious greeting; she offers him her left hand instead of her right. Proverbially the gesture signifies a future betrayal, since the left hand of friendship is no promise of fidelity. This gesture also serves as an oblique reference to the princess's illegitimacy, of which only readers of *Roderick Hudson* would have any inkling. Without this background, the princess, a female firebrand, appears insufficiently goaded in her rage against the status quo. In this instance as well, transgressive sexuality is mixed up with revolutionary politics. The princess, "a real profligate female," conspires with revolutionaries for the overthrow of the present elite (5: 230).

As Dollimore has observed, the displacement of social crisis onto sexuality is highly typical in periods of intensified conflict, when the dominant culture requires the sacrifice of a scapegoat to allay its fears (240). The Labouchère amendment must be seen in the broader context of Anglo-American social life as part of a crackdown on lawlessness and nonconformity, which pertains as much to the emergence of a clamorous and sometimes truculent socialist movement in the last quarter of the nineteenth century, Fenian terrorist activity, a crime wave in Britain from 1874 to 1882, and political assassinations on both sides of the Atlantic, as it does to sexual morality (Gurr, 70, 83). Of the contemporary events that might have informed the plot of *The Princess*

202 SEXUAL DISSIDENCE IN 'THE PRINCESS CASAMASSIMA'

Casamassima, Charles Guiteau's attempt on the life of President Garfield on July 2, 1881 surely ranks high on the list.[7] The American newspapers sensationalized the president's dance with death, heralding a recovery, bemoaning a relapse, and inveighing against his assassin for months before Garfield finally succumbed on September 19, 1881 (Rosenberg, 1–12). Henry James was in Washington throughout January 1882 when Guiteau's trial was the hottest ticket in town, a media circus and national attraction that drew crowds from the Library of Congress, the White House, and the Senate. James even had a chat with Garfield's successor, Chester B. Arthur, at a capitol soiree. Home in England on Bolton Street, James missed the opportunity to watch a riot from his bedroom window in February 1886; he returned from his trip to Bournemouth to find his neighbors' mansions boarded up and the street littered with broken glass (Edel 3: 170–71). This is very likely why James summarized the anarchic designs of the "Sun and Moon" men as the impulse to "go out somewhere and smash something on the spot—why not?—smash it that very night" (*Princess* 5: 354).

But it would be oversimplifying James's position to say that he unequivocally sided with the privileged classes against the masses. Beyond his liminal sexual status, his racial identity belied his wealth, breeding, and artistic reputation. Although there is no evidence that any of James's Anglo-Saxon contemporaries tweaked him (or his family members) on his lineage, James would have been exposed to anti-Irish sentiment from other quarters. In 1881 Richard Dugdale, author of a famous treatise on hereditary degeneration (*The Jukes: A Study of Crime, Pauperism, Disease and Heredity* of 1877), published a three-part article called "Origin of Crime in Society" in the *Atlantic Monthly* while James's *The Portrait of a Lady* was in serialization in that same magazine. Dugdale had particularly uncharitable things to say about the people of Ireland, whom he characterized as a lawless and primitive race whose propensity for hooliganism interfered with all civil aspirations: farming, industry, and political and social culture (458). And the Irish, according to Dugdale, are not amenable to civilizing influences. When they emigrate to "countries which have long since outgrown savage life, their proclivities become still more marked; they actually supplant the native offender" (458). William James clearly resented the public opprobrium heaped on the Irish in journalistic accounts of their social and political life. Writing of the senseless violence and havoc instigated by "a lot of pathological Germans &

Poles" during a recent Chicago riot, William commented, "I'm amused at the anti gladstonian capital which the english papers are telegraphed to be making of it. All the irish names are among the killed and wounded police-man. Almost every anarchist name is continental" (*CWJ* 2: 40).

Henry's attitude was more complex. On the one hand, he celebrated his sister's passionate advocacy of Home Rule for Ireland; on the other, he appears to have absorbed contemporary notions of Irish inferiority: "She was really an Irishwoman!—transplanted, transfigured—but none the less fundamentally national—in spite of her so much larger and finer than Irish intelligence" (*HJL* 3: 482). As the question of Home Rule for Ireland came to a head from 1885 to 1886, Henry expressed dissatisfaction with pettifogging Tories and Liberals alike ("Party-politics, ferocious, dishonest and vulgar, are the only thing that exists. I hate 'em—that I do"), but he was no proponent of franchise for the people of Ireland (3: 106): "I see no greatness, nor any kind of superiority in them, and they seem to me an inferior and third rate race, whose virtues are of the cheapest and commonest and shallowest order, while their vices are peculiarly cowardly and ferocious" (Edel 3: 170). Such sentiments reek of ethnic self-hatred, of a desire to distance himself from the "Celtic genius" of his forbears (3: 170). Henry went to great lengths to ingratiate himself to the cream of English society, eventually seeking naturalization as a British citizen, and it is this deliberate move away from the margins of ethnic and class identity that also informs Hyacinth's journey from dingy Lomax Place to the sunny grandeur of Medley.

In his 1907 preface to the novel, James paradoxically both confirmed and denied his confraternity with Hyacinth by comparing his own London life with that of his protagonist: "This difference would be that so far as all the swarming facts should speak of freedom and ease, knowledge and power, money, opportunity and satiety, he should be able to revolve round them but at the most respectful of distances and with every door of approach shut in his face. For one's self, all conveniently, there had been doors that opened" (*Princess* 5: vi). This claim strikes me as disingenuous. Far from reveling in a self-satisfied mood of acceptance and belonging, James was plagued by loneliness throughout his life, a sense of isolation typical of the exile and outsider. In a memorial essay, James's intimate friend Gosse characterized James as a "homeless man in a peculiar sense," one who had broken all ties to America while forging only superficial bonds in London, where he was

looked upon as a foreigner (1: 680). Maxwell Geismar described James's of-
ficial literary personality, exemplified by the prefaces to the New York Edition, as a "massive, portentous, ponderous social facade of 'omnipotence,'"
which hid from view a man terrified by "visions of failure, impotence and rejection" (217–18). The duality in James's subjective position as both patrician and pariah reverberates in his depiction of Hyacinth, whose "mixed, divided nature" and "conflicting sympathies" signify a range of (dis)identifica-
tions and contradictions within the normative framework of class hierarchy
and compulsory heterosexuality. For, like Olive Chancellor's radical posture,
Hyacinth's oppositional stance has been foisted upon him by a system intol-
erant of nonconformity on any level: "Fancy the strange, the bitter fate: to
be constituted as you're constituted, to be conscious of the capacity you
must feel, and yet to look at the good things of life only through the glass of
the pastry-cook's window!" (*Princess* 6: 61). In this respect, the social critique
that emerges from *The Princess Casamassima* goes a step further than that of
The Bostonians, in that it bemoans the social elite's exclusion of a votary of
high culture on the grounds of class snobbery as well as sexual difference and
bigotry.

The Princess Casamassima underscores the connection between allegedly
discrete forms of difference. Through its own covert depiction of homosexuality, the text exemplifies the convergence of late-nineteenth-century discourses on sexuality, race, and class, illustrating the means by which new categories of difference are pieced together from preexisting ideologies. The
nineteenth-century human sciences constructed representational systems to
mark the boundary between civilized and primitive, normal and pathological. Wilde's quip "sin is a thing that writes itself across a man's face" might
have served the fin de siècle anthropologist, sexologist, jurist, and social re-
former as a dictum for all occasions. In his 1891 article, "Immigration and
Degradation," Francis Walker bemoaned the "indiscriminate hospitality" of
the United States and summarized the "varying liabilities" of the swarming
foreigners in terms "of disease, of physical infirmity, or of criminal impulse"
(644, 634). It is hard to tell from Walker's diatribe whether he attributes the
immigrants' plight to innate inferiority or to a vastly lower standard of living, but his language affirms Gilman's observation that "the Other is 'impaired,' 'sick,' 'diseased'" (*Difference*, 25). Walker blamed the infusion of foreigners for declining birthrates among the better class of Americans, argu-

ing that the foreigners' dilapidated housing, lack of culture, and "neglected, dirty, unkempt" and "half-naked" children had administered a "shock to the principle of population among the native element" (641, 640). Fearing contagion and demoralization, Americans shrank from both social companionship and industrial competition with the barbarians.

The process of "racialization" serves as another example of how representation factors into the regulation and consolidation of social groups (Omi, 51). In the antebellum period, the Irish were classified as "nonwhite" and, after the Civil War, they were stigmatized as savage and childlike, a characterization deriving from their earlier association with Blacks. (Takaki, 115; Ignatiev, 34–59). And for Dugdale, the Irish were a striking example of the force of hereditary degeneracy in the formation of the criminal character (458). Weir's vilification of labor organizers as degenerates, anarchists, socialists, nihilists, congenital criminals, and sexual perverts is perhaps the best example of the scientific pursuit of racial, sexual, and class homogeneity through the categorization and regulation of difference. Similarly, physicians, social reformers, and literary critics waged war against the pernicious influence of fin de siècle literary movements, decadence, and certain types of realism, decrying their preoccupation with the déclassé as well as their morbidity: "There are among them art and poetry, but it is the stuff that comes from nature's slums; it is the stenching secretion of the diseased growth; it is nature, to be sure, for death and disease are natural; but it has nothing in common with the healthful life and the effectiveness of the race" (Dana, "Are We Degenerating?" 462–63). James is implicated in this critique on several levels. *The Princess Casamassima* is one of two novels that he wrote in the naturalist vein, sketching life among London's poor, and it is riddled with grotesque descriptions of prisons, ports, and slums. As a contributor to the *Yellow Book* and the author of a variety of works laden with the trappings of literary aestheticism, James was closely associated with the decadents. Charles Dana's invective concerning the "essential disease and depravity" underlying these art forms is a veiled attack on the homosexual literary subculture. Though Dana's June 1895 article makes no mention of Wilde's recent debacle or his homosexuality, Wilde figures for Dana as the supreme example of a "pseudo-genius" and a "degenerate" (463).

The theoretical implications of the convergence of late-nineteenth-century discourses on sexuality, race, and class are manifold, suggesting that any attempt to privilege sexual difference as more fundamental than other forms of difference is both reductive and anachronistic. This convergence also raises questions about recent trends in the theorization of homosexuality, such as the attempt by some gay scholars and activists to characterize homosexuality as a form of "ethnic" identification. Less rigidly essentialist than other theories articulating the fundamental differences between homosexuals and heterosexuals, this ethnic analogy, though positioning gays to take advantage of the groundwork established by the civil rights movement, poses certain risks as well. As Steven Epstein argues in "Gay Politics, Ethnic Identity: The Limits of Social Constructionism," such arguments "can lend support to eugenicist arguments and are also disturbingly compatible with the contemporary understanding of AIDS as a 'gay disease'" (22). In marking boundaries and categorizing people along these lines, do we not risk duplicating the errors and bigotries of the nineteenth-century human sciences or subjecting ourselves to a revamped critique of the degenerate Other? *The Princess Casamassima* exemplifies the misery incurred by individuals who internalize society's proscriptions against "abnormal" and "untoward" behavior. Though the novelist succeeds in eroticizing the threat of punishment, rendering the abject homosexual as a kind of nineteenth-century poster child for same-sex love, he cannot avoid equating homosexuality with deviance, criminality, and disease. Is it any wonder that Hyacinth takes his own life at the end of the novel? If critical theory is to serve the aims of gay liberation and multiculturalism, we would do well to scrutinize and then reject the paradigms through which we have always schematized race, class, and sexuality; they do not appear to lend themselves to rehabilitation and cooption.

SIX

Signing Plenitude from the Abyss in 'The Wings of the Dove'

In this final chapter, I will shift from the more coercive mechanisms of the disciplinary society on display in Chapters 4 and 5 to high cultural forms of social regulation, which are logically continuous with the former. James's atomization of the cultural logic of museums in *The Wings of the Dove* (1902) provides an institutional correlative to the internal censors that wreaked havoc with Rowland Mallet, Olive Chancellor, and Hyacinth Robinson. It is not the artist per se who falls in line with the self-regulatory imperative of the state but the metropolitan bourgeois who assimilates norms of comportment and civility on display in the urban theaters of the real: the park, the museum, and the salon: Admiring the frumpy and industrious lady copyists at the National Gallery, with whom she imaginatively trades place, the American heiress Milly Theale wishes away her wealth and the possibilities of pleasure that come with it: "She should have been a lady-copyist—it met so the case. The case was the case of escape, of living under water, of being at once impersonal and firm. There it was before one—one had only to stick and stick" (*Wings* 19: 288). As if seeking an object lesson in the management of emotion, Milly withdraws her attention from the Titians and Turners with their vibrant colors and overpowering affect. Though her voyeurism represents a contraction of her field of vision in one sense, "her shrinkage of curiosity" as far as masterpieces are concerned, her contemplation of the plodding copyists is not untroubled (19: 289). Schooled to accept the museum as "one of the highest aids to culture," Milly grows "ashamed" of her fascination with the copyists, "wondering what would be thought by others of a young woman, of adequate aspect, who should appear to regard them as the pride of the place" (19: 287, 288). Milly recognizes that both people and pictures are on display in the magnificent galleries, with their multiple vistas and approaches, and she attempts to divert attention from herself by feigning interest in the art. Sedgwick might infer the teleology of Milly's attitude from her urgency not to be "flagrantly caught" in the act of looking at women (19: 289); for Sedgwick, this caution would signify a "foreclosure of her lesbian desire" (*Tendencies*, 86). Though much taken with Sedgwick's "queering" of *The Wings of the Dove*, I want to argue that James's concretion of the notion that the repression of homosexuality stands at the gateway to culture, symbolized by Milly's predicament in the National Gallery, has broader significance, compassing the full range of affective and sexual self-censorship.

Just as nineteenth-century natural history museums deployed prehistoric artifacts and ethnographic objects as props for an evolutionary narrative culminating in the Victorian Homo economicus, "the history of the progress of painting," in the words of one nineteenth-century informant, "is connected with the history of manners, morals, and government," which can be "exemplified visibly by a collection of specimens in painting" (Bennett, 167). Organized by historical period and national style, the salons of the National Gallery readily disclose the principles of classification governing the visitor's itinerary. For the deracinated millionairess of *The Wings of the Dove*, who begins her tour of the royal galleries botanizing the local and imported fauna on display, "they were cut out as by scissors, coloured, labelled, mounted," classifying people by national characteristics is both an amusing pastime and a defense against self-knowledge (*Wings* 19: 290). She falls back on her "native wood-note," incongruously rendered as "the tone of New York agitation," when she requires an impersonal cover for her ravaged consciousness of the intimacies implied by Merton Densher and Kate Croy's outing (19: 295–96).

Milly registers what Pierre Bourdieu calls "the hidden persuasion of an implicit pedagogy" (*Outline of a Theory*, 94) when she elaborates on the connection between her restrained social performance and the exhibition space itself: "The way they let all phrasing pass was presently to recur to our young woman as a characteristic triumph of the civilised state" (*Wings* 19: 294). It is not clear whether Milly squelches her rage and despair because she is in love with Mr. Densher, with Miss Croy, or with both of them, but it is impossible to mistake the imprimatur of decorousness justifying for her their collective behavior: "Whatever the facts, their perfect manners, all round, saw them through" (19: 295). The metonymic remainder of pain expressed by Milly's nervousness is the only evidence of the "symbolic taxes" she has paid in tribute to this ideal (Bourdieu, *Outline of a Theory*, 95). Milly's homage to "sublimely civilised" behavior, which takes on the quality of a ritual obeisance through repetition, is no ringing endorsement of cultural sublimation, for the payoff, in terms of pleasure, is negligible (*Wings* 19: 295). The National Gallery's arrangement of its exemplary collection exposed the visitor to constant supervision to economize on attendants and to maximize the opportunities for self-surveillance. In *The Wings of the Dove*, the publicity of the gaze within the exhibition space ensures a face-saving resolution to an embarrassing encounter, since the museum functions as a repository of gestures, postures, and looks assembled for the express purpose of teaching people how to behave themselves.

In *Henry James and the Art of Power*, Seltzer claims that "far from escaping from the mechanisms of power, James's techniques of representation discreetly reproduce social modes of policing and regulation and reproduce them the more powerfully in their very discretion, in the very gesture of disowning the shame of power" (139). This is a crucial observation, but one that mistakes James's relation to power and even his contribution to the cultural hegemony of the bourgeoisie, which is complicated by his identification with a persecuted group and by the passional sacrifice he himself made in the name of mental hygiene and social viability. In *The Wings of the Dove*, James schematizes the "violent conformity" forced upon private individuals in society in terms of the mechanisms of panopticism, institutional and domestic modes of surveillance and coercion, precisely because he would expose the techniques of the disciplinary society (19: 60).[1] The novel as wrought object, flexuous and ornamental, patterns itself after the rarefied techniques of power exerted under the aegis of the bourgeois social order. Calling his material "one of those chances for *good taste*, possibly even for the play of the very best in the world, that are not only always to be invoked and cultivated, but that are absolutely to be jumped at from the moment they make a sign," in his preface, James affirms the intercalation of art within the scheme of social production without any sort of demur (19: vi).

Yet James's insistence on the complications and embarrassments involved in working up his material, especially his tip that a dying heroine was not "what one thought of as a 'frank' subject," jeopardizes James's prefatorial posture of stolid conventionality (19: v). Though the public account is evasive, in his *Notebooks* James admits to expunging the "nastiness" of a sexual consummation from his heroine's dance card: "It has bothered me in thinking of the little picture—this idea of the physical possession, the brief physical, passional rapture which at first appeared essential to it; bothered me on account of the ugliness, the incongruity, the nastiness, *en somme*, of the man's 'having' a sick girl" (103). James's excessive fastidiousness is responsible for the sexual stalemate that confronts Milly Theale in her intimate contacts; she becomes quarantined within a moral cordon sanitaire. It is no coincidence that her medical advisor qualifies his admonishment to live the remainder of life to the fullest: "He clearly desired to deny her no decent source of interest" (*Wings* 19: 251). However, by arguing that "civilization at its highest" entails the regulation of every spontaneous feeling and the repression of any emotion that falls outside the pale of decency, James privileges sexuality as the measure of individuation (19: 219). Moreover, James seems to enjoy rubbing up against the boundaries of sexual expression; as Foucault might say, the pattern of "attractions, evasions, these circular incitements traced around bodies and sexes" in James's writing are devices of "sexual saturation" (*History*, 45).

In *The Birth of the Museum*, Tony Bennett elaborates on Foucault's explication of the juridicodiscursive functions of high cultural practices, from curbing vice and lawlessness to civilizing the masses (22–23). Though I will go on to remark on the distinctions Foucault draws between sovereign and executive brands of authority, I am more interested here in the modern instance: the conversion of cultural institutions in the nineteenth century into "spaces of emulation" in which civilized behavior might be learned, internalized, and perpetuated as a legacy passed from parent to child, teacher to student, actor to audience, and guide to tourist (Bennett, 24). Reviewing innovations in exhibitionary architecture, Bennett highlights the principle of self-surveillance incorporated into the design of museum galleries, which provided elongated transits and elevated vantage points. I am indebted to Bennett for helping me to make sense of the novel's own "exhibitionary complex," which serves as a comment on the bourgeois organization of the relations between space and vision in order to maximize the power of the "controlling look" (101): "He had been looked at so, in blighted moments of presumptuous youth, by big cold public men, but never, so far as he could recall, by any private lady" (*Wings* 19: 82–83). Representing panopticism as a strategy for maintaining or acquiring power and as a goad to self-discipline, omnipresent in the lives of the characters, the novel recovers the links between the penal facility and its generalized functions manifest in bourgeois decorum: "No doubt she had been seen. Of course she had been seen. [Kate] had taken no trouble not to be seen, and it was a thing she was clearly incapable of taking. But she had been seen how?—and what *was* there to see?" (19: 60).

In *The Wings of the Dove*, James elects a two-tiered approach to disclosing the machinery of the disciplinary society. He maps the residual and emerging technologies of control—manners, taste, and custom—that ordinarily pass without comment by plotting the ascent of Kate Croy up the social ladder, representing her course as a series of stations traversed from middle-class Bayswater to tony Lancaster Gate to the "great historic house," Matcham (19: 208). This hierarchical scheme, rendered knowingly by the author as a social "geography," hypostatizes the caste distinctions "locally disciplined" by convention, such as the breach between Kate and her dowdy sister, Mrs. Condrip (19: 191). At the same time, James represents the arbitrary nature of these fixed points on the "social map" by semanticizing social divisions as "the difference, the bridge, the interval, the skipped leaves of the social atlas" and by appealing to literature for an explanation of this side of English life rather than to the historic social register or to genealogical tables (19: 191–92). Kate's lucky escape from the "hole" her sister occupies and from the social ignominy that "washed" her father, Lionel Croy, off the map completely into the wastes of Chirk Street has been staged by Maud

Lowder (19: 43, 68). A defector from the petite bourgeoisie herself, Mrs. Lowder's desire to see her niece "high up—high up and in the light" is mixed up with her acquired class chauvinism (19: 82). In so far as the bourgeoisie "poses itself as an organism in continuous movement, capable of absorbing the entire society, assimilating it to its own cultural and moral level," it requires exemplary stories of "organic passage" to higher states in confirmation of this posture (Gramsci, cited in Bennett, 98). But this democratization of access to the finer things is invidious, imposing conditions on Kate and restricting free intercourse between the plebeians and their wealthy neighbors.

Textually and historically, the "migration of the display of power" from court festivals and public hangings to the cultural sector has made the museum into a disciplinary institution that regulates conduct, discriminates between populations—the elites and the masses—and fosters social cohesion through its nationalization of artifacts (Bennett, 98, 144). In the earliest days of the British Museum, exclusivity rather than inclusiveness was the rule. Museum curators were so wary of the harm that might result from unrestricted access to collections that various conditions for entry such as clean shoes, sobriety, and letters of admission were strictly enforced. Failure to illuminate museum halls effectively restricted attendance to the leisure and professional classes. It was not until 1883 that the British Museum undertook a program of electrification to facilitate evening hours. In 1857 the South Kensington Museum (later known as the Victoria and Albert Museum) lay the groundwork for the modern museum, with an open admissions policy and Sunday and evening hours, which proved attractive to the general public. As Bennett notes, the South Kensington Museum "marked a significant turning-point in the development of British museum policy in clearly enunciating the principles of the modern museum conceived as an instrument of public education" (71). Coincidentally, Maud Lowder's residence, "the tall rich heavy house," is close to the South Kensington Museum (*Wings* 19: 26). Approached by a gridlike pattern of "long, straight, discouraging vistas, perfect telescopes of streets, and which kept lengthening and straightening," the mansion at Lancaster Gate looms in Kate Croy's memory as a remote and imposing structure, infrequently visited, just now liberally opening its doors to a poor relation (19: 26). Lancaster Gate is a "guardhouse" or "toll-gate" (19: 30) to a world of privilege even as the public museum facilitates the mixing of elites and plebeians who had "hitherto tended towards separate forms of assembly" (Bennett, 93).

Significantly, Maud's patterns of acquisition and display reproduce the exhibitionary apparatuses of institutions like the Victoria and Albert Museum, designed to promote the "general acceptance of ruling-class cultural authority" through its demonstration of the superiority of British technology and its hoard of colonial treasures (109). Dubbed "Britannia of the Market Place" by her niece (*Wings* 19: 30), who is evidently familiar with Ruskin's precis on the national obsession with "The Goddess of Getting-on" (293), Maud Lowder arranges her rooms to maximum effect so that the details that lend a mid-Victorian aura to her home also underwrite the "display of her power" (*Wings* 19: 80). Leaving Kate's suitor, Merton Densher, to his own devices in her drawing room, Maud evidently wants Densher to take a "hint" from the "huge heavy objects that syllabled his hostess's story" and that lay bare her ambition (19: 78, 80). Reflecting on the "message of her massive florid furniture, the immense expression of her signs and symbols," Densher proves a laconic semiotician (19: 76). What makes the collection "conclusively British" is not the profusion of fringes, spangles, scallops, and tucks per se but the appropriation of third-world resources as raw material for Victorian extravagance: "They constituted an order and abounded in rare material—precious woods, metals, stuffs, stones" (19: 78). Maud's prodigality and unscrupulousness are consubstantial with the brutalities of colonialism, which explains why the "language of the house" strikes Densher as "ominously so cruel" (19: 78). If Maud's "things" represent a "portentous negation of his own world of thought" as Densher supposes, it is not because Maud herself is powerful (19: 79). The authority she wields is depersonalized; she is a figurehead for the "great public mind" that Densher, as journalist, "must keep setting up 'codes' with" (19: 91). The novel is not concerned with the working out of a conscious plan of domination so much as it is with defining the rules that govern a specific set of discursive practices associated with Maud's ordering of objects. The "strange idols, the mystic excrescences" that decorate Maud's drawing room, trophies from the far reaches of the empire that are said to belong to "the car of the Juggernaut," trumpet the cultural and political ascendancy of the bourgeoisie, which rides roughshod over the peoples of the world like Vishnu and his fabled car (19: 90).

Like the novel's furniture, the protagonists of *The Wings of the Dove* are

not "unamenable, on certain sides, to classification" (19: 48). The novel performs the work of a comparative ethnography, sorting out the typical features of "the London girl" and the American heiress in an effort to disclose
the distinct "mark of race" deemed responsible for disparities in the characters' outlooks and conduct (19: 171, 169). In its recourse to the terminology
of the natural and social sciences, the invocation of "instinct" and "taboo" as
familiar terms of reference, the novel is positioned as a fictional counterpart
to ethnography (19: 169, 277, 195). Contained within the temporal and re-
gional taxonomies are all manner of minutely detailed class attributes, which
are surveyed and treated as *artifacts*. Though Merton Densher may lack the
hallmarks of a purebred Briton as far as Aunt Maud, a connoisseur, is concerned, the American tourist ladies classify him as handsome in "the English
style" when they come upon him in the Dutch salon of the National Gallery
(19: 90, 291). The confusion between paintings and people—Milly Theale
thinks at first that the ladies are debating the merits of a picture—underscores the representational conventions informing the collection, a catalog
of exemplary works associated with national characteristics. Though ethnographic collections purporting to recreate a vanished or remote culture are
essentially salvage operations, collections of fragments standing in "contigu-
ous relation to an absent whole," as Barbara Kirshenblatt-Gimblett explains,
the exhibitionary practices of art and natural history museums are more alike
than not (in Karp, 388). Whether detaching objects from their original context and displaying them in a fabricated "life" environment or grouping
them according to origin, material, age, use, or artistry, the museum is engaged in the art of metonymy.[2]

Analogously, the technique of rhetorical condensation contributes an air
of reality to the fictional representation by dissimulating the laborious construction of textual reality. In so far as metonymy relies on a privileged relationship between signifier and referent to achieve legibility, textual semiotics
must be in dialog with external social *reality* in some sense as well. The
metonyms of *The Wings of the Dove* behave like those of social science. In
one brilliant illustration, James signals woman's reproductive function in a
capitalist system (the reproduction of social mores and domestic arrangements as well as future generations of laborers) by identifying Densher's
mother as a "lady-copyist" whose "distinguished industry" and aptitude for
knocking off famous pictures enabled her to provide Merton, the clergy-

man's son, with the education and bearing of a "gentleman" (*Wings* 19: 93, 48). Though Densher deprecates the public's taste, doubtless in imitation of his ambitious mother, he is proud enough of the refined "tone," neither gossipy nor vulgar, that earns him the job of correspondent at large on Fleet Street (19: 87). It little matters that women transmit the values of the dominant group or that they embody power, as in Mrs. Lowder's case, for the techniques of the disciplinary society are detachable from the individuals who employ them.

Furnished with manly effects, such as "brawny Victorian bronzes" and photographs of eminent men, which signify the vaunted objectivity of the scientific mind through the "clean truths, unfringed, unfingered" of a Spartan simplicity, Sir Luke Strett's waiting room offers a study in contrasts to Maud Lowder's house (19: 237). The juxtaposition of personal effects, the objective correlatives of Victorianism available to the medical professional and to the doyenne of the marketplace, attest to differences of degree, not kind. Enumerating the gradations of social importance attached to the possession of certain objects in *Collectors and Curiosities*, Krzysztof Pomian invokes the testimony of a Chinese author: "To avoid any confusion between the different ranks, everyone must treasure the values suited to his rank. The social hierarchy is inseparable from the hierarchy of values" (33). Although this maxim dates from the first century B.C. and, taken in its entirety, sanctions the caste distinctions it atomizes, this quotation speaks volumes about the exhibitionary complex. For it recognizes the performative aspect of privilege maintained through the acquisition and ordering of objects in pedagogical and ceremonial display. Although James locates the discursive techniques of bourgeoisification in private life, these techniques are of a piece with the exhibitionary practices of Victorian natural history museums, which arrange objects in hierarchical sequences (from primitive to complex or civilized) and which form a "totalizing order of things and people" (Bennett, 96). The biological and ethnological guidelines informing the exposition of the global story of human progress are coextensive with panopticism, substituting a body of knowledge for the visible signs of authority: "Such a power has to qualify, measure, appraise, and hierarchize, rather than display itself in its murderous splendor; it does not have to draw the line that separates the enemies of the sovereign from his obedient subjects; it effects distributions around the norm" (Foucault, *History*, 144). Along with clinical medicine, the new branches of science help establish what Foucault has called a "society of normalisation," locally disciplined by taxonomies of human achievement, conduct, and desire (*Power/Knowledge*, 107).

In *The Wings of the Dove*, Milly Theale surrenders "with a supreme pointless quaver" to the magisterial gaze of her physician, impressed by his casual resemblance to both a bishop and a general of his monopoly on knowledge and power: "'He asked me scarcely anything—he does n't need to do anything so stupid,' Milly said. 'He can tell. He knows,' she repeated" (19: 231, 232). The novel supports Foucault's thesis that the disciplines, the panopticisms of daily life, micromanage individuals more efficiently and cost effectively than carceral systems because they nip deviant behavior in the bud through self-actuating prohibitions reinforced by the subject's conviction in the eye of power's vigilance. (*Discipline and Punish*, 222). Though panopticism disrupts the "see/being seen dyad" by automating power, by placing it in institutional and discursive frameworks rather than in individual hands, the mechanisms of power circulate among individuals: "They are not only its inert or consenting target; they are always also the elements of its articulation" (Foucault, *Discipline and Punish*, 202; *Power/Knowledge*, 98). This is an important distinction, for it reinstates the "see/being seen dyad" in terms of the shifting positions an individual occupies while engaged in making discourse. Through its recourse to hyphenated categories of experience, patently authorized by the new empirical sciences and by cultural technologies serving bourgeois hegemony, *The Wings of the Dove* splits the human subject into a victim and an agent of the disciplinary society: "There was no such misfortune, or at any rate no such discomfort, she further reasoned, as to be formed at once for being and for seeing" (19: 33).

Sexing the Subject

This partitioning of the subject has the effect of disengaging the novel's discursive systems from the intentions of a "thinking, knowing, speaking subject," such that the apodictic discourse of medicine or museology rises above the polyphony of human voices caught within the disciplinary web (Foucault, *Archaeology of Knowledge*, 55). Sir Luke Strett may personify "the highest type of scientific mind," but his conversation betrays none of the signs of

his stock and trade (*Wings* 19: 240). Instead, medicoscientific discourse functions like a free radical in the text. When Mrs. Susan Stringham schemes to
learn what is "the matter" with Milly Theale, her inquiries shade impercep-
tibly into diagnostic procedures: "She felt her attention secretive, all the
same, and her observation scientific. She struck herself as hovering like a spy,
applying tests, laying traps, concealing signs" (19: 117). Divorced from the
intentions of the practitioner, the mechanisms of panopticism inhere within
the methodological and conceptual frameworks of the sciences themselves.
The above quotation rhetorically instantiates the annexation of scientific
methodology by a generalized policing power. Forensic medicine is not Mrs.
Stringham's forte, but her uneasiness with techniques of surveillance and evidence gathering goes beyond her inexperience. Under the cover of professional curiosity, Susan finds herself in a new privileged relation to Milly, as
one who sees without being seen: "To watch was after all, meanwhile, a way
of clinging to the girl, not less than an occupation, a satisfaction in itself.
The pleasure of watching moreover, if a reason were needed, came from a
sense of her beauty" (19: 117).

The homographic pleasure chronicled in this passage is an unexpected
dividend accruing to the observer. By definition, the panopticon employs a
system of checks and balances designed to sanitize relations within the penal
institution and to prevent abuses of power; the perfect optical machine must
not degenerate into a peep show and betray its origin in popular spectacles.
As a generalized function within society, the panoptic schema divides and
conquers the citizenry, imposing a self-regulatory onus on the private individual to secure improvements in public morality and productivity (Foucault, *Discipline and Punish*, 207). No sooner has Susan admitted to the surplus of pleasure she feels upon her scrutiny of Milly than she begins to cast
about for a decent cover. As with Milly's foreclosure of desire in the National
Gallery, Susan snaps out of her reverie when she realizes that her infatuation
might strike others as odd: "It would take a great deal of explaining" (*Wings*
19: 117). Without overstating the case for homosexual panic, since Mrs.
Stringham conceals rather than repudiates her pleasure, Sedgwick illustrates
the disciplinary force of the interdiction against homosexuality through
Stringham's "mendacious, intensely performative silence whose history is
that of the closet" (*Tendencies*, 79). Susie herself states that she will reveal her
"passion—the rare passion of friendship, the sole passion of her little life"

only when "driven to her last entrenchments and well cornered" (*Wings* 20: 45). In claiming for Stringham both the vantage point of the closet and an "obsolescent but legitimated proto-lesbian identity," Sedgwick locates this character at the crossroads in the social construction of female homosexuality (*Tendencies*, 79). The mid-Victorian tolerance for romantic female friendships or for Boston marriages had eroded by the turn of the century.[3]

In light of this history, Susan Stringham's tortuous calculations regarding the terms to use when discussing Mildred Theale's charm, with both less and particularly with more discerning individuals, betrays her paranoia even about mutual recognition: "Then she both warmed to the perception that met her own perception, and disputed it, suspiciously, as to special items" (*Wings* 19: 117). By "concealing signs" and withholding confidences, Susan resists categorization and rejects the consolations of lesbian solidarity. Paradoxically, the imposed discursive isolation and social invisibility that symbolize Lionel Croy's "unspeakable" act and punish his wickedness prove to be a kind of monastic refuge for Susan Stringham: "That has been a part of the silence, the silence that surrounds him, the silence that, for the world, has washed him out. He does n't exist for people" (19: 16, 68). Social ostracism is the most basic technique for enforcing the interdiction of sexuality, and *The Wings of the Dove* is manifestly concerned with elaborating the mechanisms of community censure, from the disapproval of immediate family members to the jurist's criminalization of sodomy and the doctor's pathologization of homosexuality. Allying herself with this social entourage, Mrs. Stringham unconsciously patterns herself after the homophobic oppressor, extracting furtive pleasure from "the power that questions, monitors, watches, spies, searches out, palpates, brings to light" rather than from any direct challenge to heterosexual hegemony (Foucault, *History*, 45).

In foregrounding the "technology of sex" deployed in relation to Milly Theale and the investigation of her illness, James's novel substantiates Foucault's claim that in the nineteenth century "the mechanisms of power are addressed to the body, to life, to what causes it to proliferate, to what reinforces the species, its stamina, its ability to dominate, or its capacity for being used. Through the themes of health, progeny, race, the future of the species, the vitality of the social body, power spoke *of* sexuality and *to* sexuality; the latter was not a mark or a symbol, it was an object and a target" (146–47). Regulation and discipline of the body politic, not the suppression of homosexuality per se, are the impetuses behind the clinical, statistical, and juridical focus on sex. In *The Wings of the Dove*, the legal and social proscription of certain sexual acts inflames curiosity. Revolving around the axis of eroticized taboo and constrained licentiousness, the disciplinary machinery of the novel, like the repressive mechanisms of the psyche and the state, is saturated with sexuality.

Following Butler, Sedgwick employs the trope of "queer stigmatization" to forge a legible homosexual identity for Lionel Croy in lieu of explicit same-sex desires (*Tendencies*, 79). Sedgwick's intricate explanation of the process of sexing and gendering that operates under the sign of Croy's "homosexual disgrace" in *The Wings of the Dove* functions as a versatile alternative to the oedipal scenario driven by its categorical imperative: parental figures of opposite sexes (78). Indeed, Sedgwick's rapprochement with psychoanalysis depends on her ability to restructure the dynamic of the primal scene to escape heterosexist presumption. But does she escape? Tracing the psychogenesis of Kate Croy's sexual anesthesia back to her father's indifference, Sedgwick paves the way for a conclusion that is quite the reverse of the one she herself draws; the deflection in favor of homoerotic attachment may signal the melancholy foreclosure of heterosexual possibility. Thwarted at every turn in her effort to enlist her "disengaged" father's vanity, self-interest, and sympathy so that she might be permitted to live with him, Kate eventually confesses the selfish aim actuating her display of filial piety: "I should *have* you, and it would be for my benefit. Do you see?" (*Wings* 19: 10, 22). Indeed, Lionel is quick to discern the state of affairs implicit in Kate's words and to disabuse her of the notion that he would sanction a marriage deemed unsuitable by Aunt Maud. Psychologically, the daughter's need to revisit her childhood and to renegotiate the incest barrier is predicated on her intuition that something was missing from the primary run through of the oedipal script, which stood in the way of heterosexualization: reciprocated desire, perhaps?

Lionel Croy's tutelary function in the novel is deficient as well as destabilizing. He organizes Kate's desire around the scopic drive and calls her attention to the body imago but he forsakes her at this point without marshaling her desires toward any definite object: "He judged meanwhile her own appearance, as she knew she could always trust him to do; recognising, estimating, sometimes disapproving, what she wore, showing her the interest he continued to take in her. He might really take none at all, yet she virtually knew herself the creature in the world to whom he was least indifferent" (*Wings* 19: 9). Sexual intimacy is out of the question for one who has neither resolved nor, for that matter, experienced an oedipal crisis. As a case of "arrested" development, Kate manages to enjoy Merton Densher's attentions—"his long looks were the thing in the world she could never have enough of"—without feeling that she need compensate him in any way: "As if she might work them in with other and alien things, privately cherish them and yet, as regards the rigour of it, pay no price" (19: 61). Kate's ability to maintain even this marginal attachment to Densher is conditioned by her formative relationship with an emotionally unavailable father. Among the terms James employs to characterize Lionel Croy, denoting his social ignominy as well as his status in the family, is the word *impossible*: "Something or other happened that made him impossible. I mean impossible for the world at large first, and then, little by little, for mother" (19: 66). Reflecting on the patronizing airs Croy put on during his visits-what amounted to a criminal's furlough—to Lexham Gardens, Kate focuses on his feigned gentility. There is little resemblance between Lionel Croy and Merton Densher, except from Kate's perspective; Densher's good manners, foreign education, and ineligibility as a suitor prove all the material she requires to bring him into a nearer relation with her father: "She was making him out as all abnormal in order that she might eventually find him impossible" (19: 94).

The sexual stalemate tersely summarized in this sentence does not tell the whole story, since Densher would not excite the least interest in Miss Croy if certain associations did not cluster around him. Shiftless in spite of his employment at the newspaper, unambitious, and blasé, Densher is an anomaly who cannot be squeezed into the gray suits, priest's collars, and uniforms sported by typical Englishmen: "Yet, though to that degree neither extraordinary nor abnormal, he would have failed to play straight into an observer's hands" (19: 48). It would be a bit premature to include the word *straight* in the homosexual lexicon of 1902, but as Litvak has shown, "rhetorical caginess" is often a textual marker of sexual waywardness (216). Habituated to her father's double dealing, Kate shrugs off the latest evidence of his duplicity: "He might be ill and it might suit you to know it, but no contact with him, for this, could ever be straight enough" (*Wings* 19: 7). Kate's urgency to establish a relationship with a *straight* man is not an allusion to heterosexual intercourse but a metonymy of her desire never again to be "hustled" by Lionel Croy (*Wings* 19: 23). Kate is not in love with Merton; she has formed a transference to him, which enables her to sustain the imposture of love. Musing on their sexless romance, Densher spells out the conditions of his relationship with Kate: "It had come to be definite between them at a primary stage that, if they could have no other straight way, the realm of thought at least was open to them" (19: 65). Frankly sexual in his feelings for Kate, Densher views their conversations as a poor substitute for physical intimacy, and he is vaguely discomfited by the realization that she gets more out of their verbal foreplay than he: "Our young man, it must be added, was conscious enough that it was Kate who profited most by this particular play of the fact of intimacy" (19: 66).

Quite naturally, Densher lacks the theoretical framework for making sense of the benefit Kate extracts from their intercourse, which might be described as symbolic realization. By cathecting with Kate, Densher allows her to hallucinate the healing presence and engagement of her absent father even as the child symbolizes the return of the absent mother in "fort! da!" (Freud, 11: 284–85). The couple's little game of "floating island," an imaginary realm in the psychoanalytic sense of that word, approximates narcissistic symbiosis for Kate, a reunion with the preoedipal phallic mother. In this game, they pretend that everything outside their idyllic relationship is unreal, they are "only making believe everywhere else," but Densher maintains this pretense only to humor Kate; he is conscious of the Real impinging on their imaginary dyad (*Wings* 19: 66). Similarly, Densher's "long looks" simulate the visual gestalt through which Kate is constituted as a separate person in her own right and as an object available to others from their own point of view: "It was n't, in a word, simply that their eyes had met; other conscious organs, faculties, feelers had met as well, and when Kate afterwards imaged to herself the sharp deep fact she saw it, in the oddest way, as a particular performance" (19: 53). From the cross-referencing of visual and corporeal sensations experienced as uncanny, Kate's free associations link this meeting with an early event in her personal history: her emergence from the mirror stage in infancy.

According to Lacan, the subject is constituted in language, the symbolic order, by virtue of the ego's splitting during the mirror phase: "The deflection of the specular *I* into the social *I*" locates the subject in interpersonal relations in which her outlook is now mediated by the desire of the other (*Écrits*, 5). The subject speaks, first of all, to evoke a response, that of the mother, "because the first object of desire is to be recognized by the Other" (58). This formula roughs out the mechanisms of alienation that originate with the advent of the subject into personhood and relationality, encompassing both the specular image and the speaking subject. Sedgwick's deft transcription of the opening scene of *The Wings of the Dove*, in which Kate stares fixedly at her own image in her father's parlor mirror, elides crucial elements of Kate's psychological portrait in its eagerness to install Lionel's disgrace as the tutelary model from which Kate derives her sexuality and gender identity. Lacan's formulation could only enhance Sedgwick's effort to reconcile Kate's frigidity with her role as the textual embodiment of sexuality. In Lacanian terms, the pleasure gleaned from Kate's self-objectifying display before the mirror is alienated; it is "the *jouissance* of the Other," as the novel confirms (42): "Slender and simple, frequently soundless, she was somehow always in the line of the eye—she counted singularly for its pleasure" (*Wings* 19: 5). By this I do not mean to discount the thrust of Sedgwick's argument that Lionel Croy's affront to social custom has forced his daughter "the more grindingly to articulate and embody" the constraints of normative gender categories (*Tendencies*, 84). My complaint is that Sedgwick misrepresents the power of the hermeneutic method she grudgingly employs to decipher sexual meanings in the text. In her groundbreaking article, "Visual Pleasure and Narrative Cinema," Laura Mulvey is quite serious about finding a political use for psychoanalysis. Convinced by her reading of Lacan that misogyny and, she might as well say, homophobia are imprinted in humankind from the moment language is acquired, Mulvey positions herself to take advantage of the analytic tools at her disposal within patriarchy. Mulvey purposes to demystify the gaze, to destroy the erotic pleasure and reassurance that men derive from scotomizing women as passive and silent objects of fantasy (16). If the gender conventions of narrative cinema—the "active/passive heterosexual division of labor"—uphold patriarchy and disavow the castration threat as Mulvey argues, the scheme of gender representation employed in *The Wings of the Dove* would seem to offer a precocious challenge to the canons of the late-Victorian ruling order (20).

With women usurping male prerogatives by treating one another as sexual objects ("when I want to reach my niece I know how to do it straight") and undermining the myth of female passivity by impersonating men of action ("she had something in common, even in repose, with a projectile, of great size, loaded and ready for use"), the female protagonists in the novel frustrate desire and throw the male protagonist back on his fears of social and sexual inadequacy: "It had n't yet been so distinct to him that he made no show—literally not the smallest; so complete a show seemed made there all about him; so almost abnormally affirmative, so aggressively erect, were the huge heavy objects that syllabled his hostess's story" (*Wings* 19: 81, 169, 76). The power assumed by Maud Manningham Lowder in this guise is plainly "a mode of masquerade, in imitation of the masculine, phallic subject" (Grosz, 72). Through its heaped congeries of masculine fetishes, the novel insists that privilege is a social convention maintained through instrumental display mounted in the theater of the Real. When Lionel Croy declares, "I trust her with my eyes shut," he calls attention to the collateral that Maud is able to post in the phallic economy, as if to say "I can't see it, but I know it's there" (*Wings* 19: 22). By encoding Densher's emasculation in terms of an economic ineffectuality, a "very small quantity," that can be measured against Mrs. Lowder's "complete" show, the novel schematizes gender difference within a capitalist framework and not simply in accordance with received notions (19: 83, 76). At the same time, it represents the ascendancy of the patriciate and its minions as something immutable, assured by the configuration of the nuclear family operating in accordance with the "Order of Law," which has been "lying in wait for each infant born since before his birth, and seizes him before his first cry, assigning him his place and role, and hence his fixed destination" (Althusser, 211). Though the novel offers no method for evading the toils of patriarchy, it reproduces the self-alienation experienced by the protagonists, male and female, as they struggle to define themselves in relation to the dominant paradigm: "always-already a subject" who will have to attain the sexual identity, "which it already is in advance" (176). In so doing, it enumerates the benefits and penalties accruing to the male heterosexual subject, that lucky stiff, under the regime of the phallus. Louis Althusser's summary of Lacan's notion of the preexisting guidelines organizing human experience sheds further light on Densher's abjection before Mrs. Lowder's display of prowess. From the moment the subject becomes conscious of the gaze, he attempts to adapt to it, to seduce it, for it is in the visual field of the other that the ideal self is realized. Failing to elicit the desire of the (m)other, the subject experiences a double privation as he emerges from the mirror stage an autonomous individual; the combined effects of ego fragmentation (splitting) and narcissistic injury constitute a castration threat presaging the subject's castration within the order of signification (Lacan, *Four Fundamental Concepts*, 104).

Hypothesized from this point of view, in which the castration threat predates the oedipal stage or any foreknowledge of woman's anatomical difference, castration anxiety is symptomatic of a primary loss or lack occasioned by the perceived indifference of the caretaker. Through the gift of love, the (m)other creates a "specular mirage" for her infant son, allowing him to share in the gratifying illusion of plenitude associated with the phallic mother, or she prostrates herself before the male demigod she has created, vesting the infant with phallic potential through her adoring gaze (Lacan, *Four Fundamental Concepts*, 268). Revisiting Mulvey's thesis in a critical humor, "the castrated woman" seems an afterthought, a means of deflecting the female gaze that constitutes the male subject's first mirror and assuring him of his monopoly on power and potency (14). In line with Kaja Silverman's view, female castration could be seen as "the product of an externalizing displacement of masculine insufficiency, which is then biologically naturalized, the castration against which the male subject protects himself through disavowal and fetishism must be primarily his own" (46). *The Wings of the Dove* certainly schematizes the seeing/being seen dyad in terms of phallic presence and absence. Aunt Maud's desire to see her niece "high up and in the light," the cynosure of all eyes, places her in the feminine position of *being* rather than *having* the phallus (*Wings* 19: 82). However, in its very theatricality, this staging of gender difference through anatomical props (fetishes) and role-playing demonstrates that men and women are "positioned in sexual difference" (Tagg, in Bryson, 85). Anatomy is not destiny; it is simply the point of departure for a representational regime that has chosen the phallus as its heraldic emblem, as Griselda Pollock has suggested: "Subjectivity is invented by means of a sexual differentiation that represents itself by a figuration of the body (indicated by the symptomatic insistence on the phallus, or on penis envy, in Lacan and Freud respectively). This figuration is written onto our bodies, which are then disciplined to perform historically, culturally, and socially specific regimes of sexual difference" (in Bryson, 7).

The Space of the Look

In this topography, the sexing of the subject is an ongoing process mediated by fluctuations in social life, such as urbanization, and facilitated by new discursive formations, such as the bourgeoisie's ethos of possessive individualism. The ascendancy of the bourgeoisie imposed new restrictions on middle-class women, whose access to the pleasures of the city (salons, theaters, shops, and parks) was circumscribed by their exposure to insult and loss of caste in the crowded thoroughfares. In spite of her confidence that a "contemporary London female, highly modern, inevitably battered, honourably free" is proof against the indignities and promiscuities of urban life, Kate Croy bridles at the reflection that she might be mistaken for a dallying servant, "the housemaid giggling to the baker" (*Wings* 19: 56). Ever conscious of what Pollock has called the "space of the look" (*Vision and Difference*, 66), Kate uneasily negotiates the discipline of the streets, masking her eagerness to converse with Merton Densher, whom she met by chance on the underground, from "one of the persons opposite, a youngish man with a single eye-glass which he kept constantly in position, [who] had made her out from the first as visibly, strangely affected" (*Wings* 19: 55). In contrast to the male flâneur, who enjoys the full privileges of the gaze, Kate exists as a spectacle, a woman imprisoned within a sexual economy that cancels out female desire through self-regulating prescriptions—modesty, decency, gentility.

The female gaze is not erotic, mobile, impersonal, arrogant; it *shows* more than it is permitted to *see*. In spite of Kate's confidence that she exists to see as well as to be, James's dozen textual references to Kate's "looks" metaleptically render them as the "peculiar property of somebody else's vision" (19: 225, 257). Summoning up a mental image of the lovers' tryst as seen by a third party—what a "long engagement!"—Kate conveys the highly disciplined character of a life carried on within the space of the look, "the presumed diagnosis of the stranger" (19: 59). James's schematization of the social organization of the gaze foregrounds gender difference, contrasting the privileges men and women are assigned within the field of vision. Milly's trick of filtering her own desire for Kate through the lens of an interested third party facilitates and regulates desire, culminating in a kind of homosexual panic. "All she had meant to do was to insist that this face was fine; but what she had in fact done was to renew again her effect of showing herself to its possessor as conjoined with Lord Mark for some interested view of it" (19: 163–64). In this scene, the gaze is an "object lost and suddenly refound in the conflagration of shame, by the introduction of the other" (Lacan, *Four Fundamental Concepts* 182). In his novel, James always figures desire as an erotic triangle in which one person is abject, a mere onlooker in the scene of pleasure because of a "boundary-constituting taboo" (Butler, *Gender Trouble*, 133).[4] Textually, Mildred's psychical alignment with the "historic patriciate" is determined by the social organization of the gaze, which secures woman's objectification within the space of the look. As Lord Mark explains to Milly, "To be seen, you must recognise, *is*, for you, to be jumped at; and, if it's a question of being shown, here you are again" (*Wings* 19: 152, 155).

The taboo on vulgarity that disciplines Kate Croy's speech, demeanor, and behavior with the force of law is the ideational counterpart to a "technique of the body," Marcel Mauss's term for actions and habits shaped by tradition and education (104). Transmission may seem implausible in this dynamic, that of a maternal figure tagged with the sobriquet "colossally vulgar," but Aunt Maud understands exactly which qualities to promote in her niece in order to land a politician or an aristocrat: "Did n't it by this time sufficiently shine out that it was precisely *as* the very luxury she was proving that [Kate] had, from far back, been appraised and waited for?" (*Wings* 19: 213). If Kate is not Maud's revenge on aristocrats for real or perceived slights, a missile aimed at the heart of the bloods, then she is a tool of power and access: "She was made for great social uses" (19: 212). The mechanisms of social mobility are mimicked by the text's deviation from a presentist temporal scheme; Kate belongs to the future perfect: "She became thus, intermittently, a figure conditioned only by the great facts of aspect, a figure to be waited for, named and fitted" (19: 212). Mrs. Lowder's views on Kate exceed her own personal aspirations and capabilities; James is quite clear about this, as if underscoring Foucault's notion "the power of the bourgeoisie is self-amplifying, in a mode not of conservation but of successive transformations" (*Power/Knowledge*, 160). Kate's sense of the obligation she has incurred in exchange for her aunt's protection and favor bespeaks her conditioning within the cultural milieu of capitalism: "If I were to sign my aunt's agreement I should carry it out, in honour, to the letter" (*Wings* 19: 19). Explicitly modeled on a contractual exchange of services for goods, the domestic arrangement between Kate and the scheming burgess illustrates the "economic functionality of power," which fosters bourgeois class dominance through the actions of private citizens committed to the juridical ideal (Foucault, *Power/Knowledge*, 88).

Without challenging Sedgwick's reading of the sexual dynamics of the momentous scene in which Merton Densher watches Mrs. Lowder put Kate Croy through her paces at a dinner party (92–93), which focuses on Densher's abjection before the drama of female entanglement, I would like to urge another interpretation of this multifaceted social performance, emphasizing "the older woman's technical challenge" to the younger (*Wings* 20: 35). Kate's "raked" and "disciplined face" registers Maud's management style: "Aunt Maud's appreciation of that to-night was indeed managerial, and the performer's own contribution fairly that of the faultless soldier on parade" (20: 34). This performance is the short course in the bodily disciplines aimed at optimizing capability, channeling energy, and fostering servility to ensure social success: "That was the story—that she was always, for her beneficent dragon, under arms; living up, every hour, but especially at festal hours, to the 'value' Mrs. Lowder had attached to her" (20: 34).

In *The Wings of the Dove*, class as much as gender regulates populations and hedges personal inclination. As if to correct the impression that wealth insulates people from the constraints under which Kate operates, the narrative directly contradicts her assertion that with "so deep a pocket," Milly Theale's "range was thus immense" (19: 175). Miss Theale has been in the hands of one or another of her retainers since infancy: "It was the first time in her life that this had happened; somebody, everybody appeared to have known before, at every instant of it, where she was; so that she was now suddenly able to put it to herself that that had n't been a life" (19: 250–51). Having taken to the streets in a blind impulse to embrace "the human race at large," she soon discovers that her maid's absence does not automatically put her on an intimate footing with the costermongers, scrub women, and their "grimy children" (19: 247, 249). The city's business districts, wealthy residential neighborhoods, monuments, museums, palaces, and parks, are the material record of the concentration in a few hands of economic and political power, and social and cultural cachet, a message brought home by the imposing facades and sentry boxes of public buildings and private mansions and by the bridle paths and "hired chairs" symbolizing the distinguishing marks of "superiority" in the wide open spaces (19: 250). The signs of wealth and power are part of a visual regime aimed at segregating rich and poor; they have their complement in the forbidding aspect of the gloomy, seamy bystreets. The heiress's brisk tour of what "she hoped were slums" excites the curiosity of the locals, who turn the tables on the lady ethnographer and force her to weigh her difference against the norm they represent: "She found herself moving at times in regions visibly not haunted by odd-looking girls from New York, duskily draped, sable-plumed, all but incongruously shod and gazing about them with extravagance" (19: 249). Assuming a defensive posture to battle for her life, mixed up in Milly's imagination with a responsible career of "experiment or struggle" apparently connected with the subjugation or reform of the poor, Milly braces herself for contact with the "unwashed" masses by shedding the psychic vestiges of femininity, figured as "some friendly ornament, a familiar flower, a little old jewel," and taking up "some queer defensive weapon, a musket, a spear, a battle-axe" in their stead (19: 248).

Milly's fear of "overdoing the character" of a soldier or adventurer is another instance of a female character flaunting the incongruity between the socially constructed body and fantasmatic masculinity (19: 249). Milly is not as adept as Maud Manningham, or Kate Croy for that matter, at circumnavigating the social geography of London through this type of imposture. Milly lacks the mobile consciousness of a successful improvvisatrice, for she is committed to the idea that "the real thing" can be discovered behind the mask of social prestige that she herself will drop in the company of ordinary persons, "just in the same box," who share her anxiety about the "practical question of life" (19: 250). The pathos of Milly's situation inheres in the mental divestiture of the trappings of wealth and position as she contemplates her own mortality. In the company of Luke Strett, whose consideration for her plight has the effect of "directly divesting, denuding, exposing," Milly imagines herself "a poor girl—with her rent to pay for example—staring before her in a great city. Milly had her rent to pay, her rent for her future, everything else but how to meet it fell away from in her pieces, in tatters" (19: 253–54). This elegant rendition of the poor-little-rich-girl theme, a reprise of Kate Croy's reflection that "Mildred Theale was not, after all, a person to change places, to change even chances with," puts the heroine in conflict with the general outlook of the dramatis personae (19: 176). Squalor and early death are not commensurate fates from any point of view but

Milly's. The only plausible resemblance between the heiress and the gamine is a shared lookout—"staring before her in a great city"; any other sign of resemblance is fanciful, even disingenuous. When Milly stumbles upon Regent's Park, an apt reminder of her station in life, she makes rather a poor show of bonding with the underclass, whom she perceives, from the vantage of a public bench, "down on their stomachs in the grass, turned away, ignoring, burrowing" like rodents (19: 254).

Milly is trapped within the space of the look. Framed and boxed in by the novelist's knack of visualizing her as a work of art or a precious jewel, Milly occupies space, but not the temporal dimension. Though every character in the novel is obviously a rhetorical construct, Milly has been denied the illusion of momentum or development, the narrative equivalent of "living": "She slipped in the observation that her Milly was incapable of change" (20: 45). The reader wonders what Kate is *up to* but wonders *about* Milly. As an object of textual epistemophilia, Milly lends herself to the metonymic substitution of the fragment for the whole: "All her little pieces had now then fallen together for him like the morsels of coloured glass that used to make combinations, under the hand, in the depths of one of the polygonal peepshows of childhood" (19: 243). But this holds true only for general and material facts, such as her "New York mourning" and "New York hair" (19: 105). As a personality, she "escapes measure" (19: 117). For Susan Stringham, she is "the real thing, the romantic life itself," an epithet very much at odds with Milly's use of the term (*Wings* 19: 107). The belatedness of Milly's opportunities at self-definition authorizes earlier conceptions, such as the artfully constructed image of Milly as the "pale sister" of Bronzino's "very great personage" (19: 222, 221), perhaps *Lucrezia Panciatichi* (Tintner, 98). Bronzino, an artist known for his formidable technical skills, spent hours with his sitters and months with their raiments and jewelry, as one may infer from the tendency of articles of dress to crowd his portraits and to dominate the physiognomies of their subjects.[5] James's distillation of Milly's portrait brings the human elements to the fore, with "recorded jewels," "brocaded and wasted reds" receding into the background of the picture but divests them of individuality. *Lucrezia*, with her "Michael-angelesque squareness, her eyes of other days," is a priceless objet d'art with a distinguished history; she belongs to no human community (*Wings* 19: 221).

The misconstructions that devolve from Milly's identification with the portrait, which reduces her to tears, annihilate the sitter: "Milly recognised her exactly in words that had nothing to do with her. 'I shall never be better than this'" (19: 221). If ever there was an occasion for elaboration of a character's point of view, this is it. But the matter at stake in the resemblance, which Milly denies on the face of it, has less to do with character psychology and more to do with her position within the narrative's scopic regime, which ratifies its social and symbolic hierarchies. Lord Mark's failure to understand that Milly is experiencing "as good a moment as she should have with anyone, or have in any connexion whatever" negatively reinforces her affinity with Bronzino's dutchess "unaccompanied by a joy" (19: 221). Within a knot of admirers, suppliants, and handlers, Milly is set apart through aesthetic objectification: "Lady Aldershaw meanwhile looked at Milly quite as if Milly had been the Bronzino and the Bronzino only Milly" (19: 223). *Lucrezia Panciatichi* is an allegorical representation of Milly's impending doom, "she was dead, dead, dead," which instantiates the chronic psychological disjunction between the princess and even her peers: "I think I could die without its being noticed" (19: 221, 228). At the same time, illness and health are employed as temporal tropes, textual markers of the migration of power from the sovereign to the citizen: "When pity held up its telltale face like a head on a pike, in a French revolution, bobbing before a window, what was the inference but that the patient was bad?" (19: 240). Squeezed by the historical frame, Milly is hard pressed to break out of her musty cell, where she paces like "a caged Byzantine," and embrace life (19: 256). The vitality Mildred perceives in Kate Croy, "*she* would never in her life be ill," is the effect of forward momentum and relentless class striving (19: 258). Patently out of step with contemporary mores and modes of self-presentation, Milly is at a practical disadvantage in the face of the combined tactical forces of Matcham and Lancaster Gate, themselves merely way stations in the transmission and exercise of national technologies of power: "The worker in one connexion was the worked in another; it was as broad as it was long—with the wheels of the system, as might be seen, wonderfully oiled" (19: 179). Textually and historically, this concatenation of agents-cum-victims of the disciplinary society focuses on the cultural technologies enlisted to bring body and soul into harmony with the goals of the polity: bourgeoisification, normalization, and modernization.

In *The Ethnography of Manners*, Nancy Bentley portrays Henry James as "ambiguously partaking" of the "interlocking energies of cultural mastery and anxiety" through a clinical scrutiny of bourgeois social life (8–9). Certainly this statement applies to *The Wings of the Dove*, in which the pleasure of surveillance and the wariness of social discipline are interimplicated. If James makes less of Milly's "unused margin as an American girl" and rather more of her storybook attributes, he still treats his "princess" like an informant throughout the first volume. He has not given up the strategy of producing a comparative ethnography of manners; rather, he has refined his plan to include the symbolic register. Beyond the patented formula for talking about rich young ladies, James has a reason for staging the contrast between a leisure-class American and "a mere middle-class nobody in Bayswater" in such terms as these: "Milly was the wandering princess: so what could be more in harmony now than to see the princess waited upon at the city gate by the worthiest maiden, the chosen daughter of the burgesses? It was the real again, evidently, the amusement of the meeting for the princess too; princesses living for the most part, in such an appeased way, on the plane of mere elegant representation" (19: 174, 171). The passage trails off in the direction I am headed, introducing one panel of the diptych that comprises James's vision of Mildred Theale as "the potential heiress of all the ages" and the doomed princess "dragged shrieking to the guillotine—to the shambles" (19: 109; *Notebooks*, 103).

Semiophore People

We have no idea what is wrong with Milly Theale in *The Wings of the Dove*. She seems to suffer only mental anguish and to deny wholly her relation to her physical being. Discussing Milly's demise in the preface to the New York Edition, James begged off responsibility for the minutiae: "Heaven forbid we should 'know' anything more of our ravaged sister than what Densher darkly pieces together" (*Wings* 19: xviii). In the novel, this reverence for privacy takes on a ceremonial dimension, hiding the heroine's illness and death from view behind a silver curtain of elegant formalities: "He had n't only never been near the facts of her condition—which counted so as a blessing for him; he had n't only, with all the world, hovered outside an impenetrable ring fence, within which there reigned a kind of expensive vagueness made up of smiles and silences and beautiful fictions and priceless arrangements, all strained to breaking" (20: 298). Even her doctor respects the inviolability of the regent, declining to examine the sick princess or to describe her physical complaint. What else does one expect from a knight of the realm? At the same time, as a mere modern girl and a private individual, Milly cedes authority to the new disciplinarians, men of "genius" such as Sir Luke Strett: "The great ladies of that race—it would be somewhere in Gibbon—were apparently not questioned about their mysteries. But oh poor Milly and hers! Susan at all events proved scarce more inquisitive than if she had been a mosaic at Ravenna" (19: 236, 256).

In *Discipline and Punish*, Foucault outlines the juridicotheological mechanisms of the iconography used to elaborate the relationship between the mortal body of the king and the enduring institution of monarchy, including rituals that bind the king to the crown, such as coronation ceremonies and funeral rites (28–29). Of the diverse spectacles associated with Mildred Theale's royal mandate, one stands out: her introduction to court life at Matcham, where she runs the "gauntlet" of curious assembled Londoners, "the lingering eyes that took somehow pardonable liberties," and perfects the "bland stare that" marks "civilisation at its highest," followed by her figurative coronation: "The beauty and the history and the facility and the splendid midsummer glow: it was a sort of magnificent maximum, the pink dawn of an apotheosis coming so curiously soon" (*Wings* 19: 218–20). Just as an "ideal and ordered world unfolds before and emanates from the privileged and controlling perspective of the prince" at court festivals, James's assorted pageants draw their majesty and unity from his princess's rapt appreciation, even if she performs this function as a figurehead (Bennett, 97): "When Milly smiled it was a public event—when she did n't it was a chapter in history" (*Wings* 19: 118). Describing the "semio-technique" of princely power associated with the Renaissance *studiolo*, a miniature universe comprised of cupboards and cabinets decorated with symbolic images to whose hidden contents the prince alone was privy, Bennett contends that, as royal collections began to enter the public domain in the eighteenth century, they retained this strategy of making the prince's power visible and performable (36).[6] In *The Wings of the Dove*, consideration of the omniscient perspective of the mistress of all she surveys is laced with irony: "She was looking down on the kingdoms of the earth, and though indeed that of itself might well go to the brain, it would n't be with a view of renouncing them. Was she choosing among them or did she want them all?" (19: 124). The great good fortune of her position is compromised, from the first, by the qualification of Milly's belatedness as "the last fine flower—blooming alone, for the fullest attestation of her freedom—of an 'old' New York stem" and as a princess condemned to mount the scaffold rather than to ascend to the throne (19: viii; 20: 342).

Whatever Mrs. Stringham's motive for glamorizing Miss Theale, "to treat her as a princess was a positive need of her companion's mind," the particular elisions and exaggerations required for this transfiguration bear noting (19: 255). Milly possesses innate refinement as a trapping of her class, a characterization wholly in keeping with Bourdieu's observation that elites throughout history have regarded culture as innate, as divine manna reserved for them (*Love of Art*, 4). Equipped with monographs on royalty and visions of aristocratic patronage of the arts, Mrs. Stringham takes it on faith that Miss Theale of New York represents an advanced stage of culture: "Susan had read history, had read Gibbon and Froude and Saint-Simon; she had high lights as to the special allowances made for the class, and, since she saw them, when young, as effete and overtutored, inevitably ironic and infinitely refined, one must take it for amusing if she inclined to an indulgence verily Byzantine" (*Wings* 19: 255). According to Bourdieu, the invidious gradations of refinement associated with artistic culture depend on a sliding scale of effort, in which the pedant and autodidact are equally remote from the ideal of unconscious acquisition: "In the final analysis, the tiny and infinite nuances of an authentically cultivated disposition where nothing is allowed to betray the effort of acquisition reflect a particular mode of acquisition" (*Love of Art*, 65). Having grown up amid old masterworks and chiseled busts, Milly embodies this ideal explicitly without effort or training: "The key of knowledge was felt to click in the lock from the moment it flashed upon Mrs. Stringham that her friend had been starved for culture" (*Wings* 19: 109). From the admittedly banal perspective of Susan Stringham, fiction writer at large, whose single claim to the attention of the reading public is the "art of showing New England without showing it wholly in the kitchen," Mildred Theale represents a truly "literary" subject, "a girl with a background" (19: 107, 108–9). Having, at first, no greater ambition than to translate the heiress's "romantic life" into a story for the *Transcript*, Susan eventually loses perspective on her material altogether, recalling "herself to manners, to the law of court-etiquette" as if she stepped out of the picture papers herself or, perhaps, an asylum (19: 107, 255). At least, this gentle delusion inoculates her against the moral blight rampant among her peers. Rather than bilking Milly for whatever goods are to be had at her expense, Susan pays tribute as if to the person of the sovereign:

> "She's, you know, my princess, and to one's princess—"
> "One makes the whole sacrifice?" (20: 209)

Pomian has pointed out that the higher a representative is placed in the social hierarchy, the more she surrounds herself with "semiophores," objects whose value resides in their ability to signal relations between the visible and invisible, whose function derives from meaningfulness rather than from practical utility (30–32). James shielded the reader from any concrete picture of Milly's purchasing habits. She is ensconced in the historic Palazzo Leporelli, where the possibilities of finer aesthetic vibrations appear infinite. Milly's largesse and extravagant mode of living are conditioned by the symbolism of sovereignty itself, which, as Foucault explains, "permits the foundation of an absolute power in the absolute expenditure of power. It does not allow for a calculation of power in terms of the minimum expenditure for the maximum return" (*Power/Knowledge*, 105). Of course the sovereign's cultural authority is connected with the display of wealth, but even more so with the symbolism of rank. In *The Wings of the Dove*, the New York princess is a goddess to whom her subjects burn incense: "Her freedom, her fortune and her fancy were her law; an obsequious world surrounded her, she could sniff up at every step its fumes" (*Wings* 19: 175). However, Milly Theale's apotheosis in the palazzo, under the sign of Veronese, is not deployed as a corrective to Maud Lowder's vulgarity but as an elaboration of the social, psychological, and economic forces informing the collecting impulse (20: 213). The notion of the semiophore helps us to understand Lowder and Theale as points on a continuum rather than as contrasting figures. As Pomian writes, "the division into the useful and the meaningful, into things and semiophores, where the former are subordinated to the latter, because these have links with the invisible," underwrites a social hierarchy in which Milly is on top by virtue of her ability to surround herself with rare, beautiful, and costly objects of no utility and with retainers who enable her to abstain from utilitarian activity

(32). In the course of the novel, Milly becomes a semiophore person, representing her ties to the invisible order of significance through her apparent transcendence of practical affairs, morbidity, and allegorization: "With which she felt herself ever so delicately, so considerately, embraced; not with familiarity or as a liberty taken, but almost ceremonially and in the manner of an *accolade*; partly as if, though a dove who could perch on a finger, one were also a princess with whom forms were to be observed" (*Wings* 19: 283).

Milly in her way and James in his endeavor to make Milly's body disappear behind a cloud of tulle, painterly allusions, or delicate phrases. A "striking apparition" of ghostly pallor, Milly is a wraithlike creature who possesses "too much forehead, too much nose and too much mouth," as if she has succeeded in starving herself to a fashionable thinness, anticipating Wallis Simpson's dictum "One can never be too rich or too thin" (19: 118). In the novel's most famous scene, she leaves off her inveterate mourning costume for a couturier shroud (20: 213–14). Milly's illness, whatever it may be, is implicitly tied to her status as a leisure-class American; she is a social type as well as a romantic concoction: "Little Miss Theale's individual history was not stuff for his newspaper; besides which, moreover, he was seeing but too many little Miss Theales (20: 10). Milly and her family are suffering from the degenerative effects of overcivilization and overwork: "Her visitor's American references, with their bewildering immensities, their confounding money-eyed New York, their excitements of high pressure, their opportunities of wild freedom, their record of used-up relatives" (19: 174). Milly's fatigue and decline are resonant of nineteenth-century medical characterizations of consumptives and nervous invalids as having exhausted their "limited capital" of energy, of having "overdrafted" and "overtaxed" their store of health and vitality. Economic metaphors proliferate in the medical discourse of the period, especially with respect to the "female economy of life," or reproductive system. As Mitchell put it, "if the mothers of a people are sickly and weak, the sad inheritance falls upon their offspring" (30). This is precisely what accounts for Milly's debility. Along with a great deal of money, Milly has inherited an organic predisposition to illness: "'When I was ten years old there were, with my father and my mother, six of us. I'm all that's left. But they died,' she went on, to be fair all round, 'of different things'" (*Wings* 19: 242).

Here the specter of racial degeneration rears its head in one of James's aesthetic triumphs. But that is not all. Milly's anorexia, her refusal to inhabit

a fleshy feminine body, defies biological and social reproduction.[7] Unlike
Maud Lowder, who "sat somehow in the midst of her money, founded on it
and surrounded by it" with every appearance of pleasure, Milly resists being
conflated with her property: "She was at any rate far away on the edge of it,
and you hadn't as might be said, in order to get at her nature, to traverse, by
whatever avenue, any piece of her property" (19: 196). Milly's uneasiness
with the burden of wealth—"she could n't dress it away, nor walk it away,
nor read it away, nor think it away" (19: 121)—reflects the reification of the
person into a "thing of two parts," a social and a private self, a mind and a
body (Bennett, 189). Milly doubts the value of a social success founded on
wealth; she has an internal conviction, based on experience, that status pre-
empts selfhood: "She could n't have lost it if she had tried—that was what it
was to be really rich. It had to be *the* thing you were" (*Wings* 19: 121). Her
consciousness is that of a mind scarred and seared by coercions and induce-
ments to an approved type of being.

   In *The Political Unconscious*, Fredric Jameson calls subjectivity effects of this
kind a protest against reification that backfires, serving instead as "part of the
more general containment strategy of a late nineteenth-century bourgeoisie
suffering from the aftereffects of reification" (221). There is no question that
Mrs. Lowder and Kate Croy exemplify the ethos of possessive individualism,
believing as they do in "the 'freedom' and equality of sheer market equiva-
lence" (221). For them, Milly's wealth is the outstanding fact—"the mere
money of her, the darling, if it is n't too disgusting at such a time to mention
that!"—affording her scope for any plan of life, lived on her terms, anywhere
in the civilized world she should choose to call home: "This impression was
a tribute, a tribute positively to power, power the source of which was the last
thing Kate treated as a mystery," if only "*she* had had so deep a pocket—!"
(*Wings* 20: 341; 19: 175). This atomized view of Milly is correct from a certain standpoint, but James's "successive centres" of consciousness cannot, by
definition, hold the key to her character (19: xii). The very tensions between
the novel's discursive systems, the secular and symbolic, appear to confirm
Jameson's claim that "more desperate myths of the self" are generated as
confidence in the "old 'autonomy' of the bourgeois self" collapses in the
course of human affairs (221). What I resist in Jameson's compelling presentation of the aesthetic dilemmas that arise for Henry James in response to
capitalism is his overemphasis on reaction and inadvertence (222).

James's monadic subjects revolve like planets around a central star about whom each entertains a theory, and the novelist encourages the reader to flip from one perspective to the next indifferently. If the general atmosphere of sublimity leaves the strongest impression, it is nevertheless the case that every refinement of motive and play of consciousness is textually anchored to something base, unspeakable, and repressed. Describing Densher's absolution, "the essence was that something had happened to him too beautiful and too sacred to describe. He had been, to his recovered sense, forgiven, dedicated, blessed," James instantly grounds this miraculous reparation of self-respect in Merton's duplicity with Mildred, textually echoed by the deception he practices on the mistress of Lancaster Gate: "But this he could n't coherently express. It would have required an explanation—fatal to Mrs. Lowder's faith in him—of the nature of Milly's wrong" (*Wings* 20: 343). With its crowded picture of mercenary intrigues and gross betrayals, *The Wings of the Dove* fulfills a condition of all "Symbolic texts," Jameson's term for fictional works that set out "systematically to satisfy the objections of the nascent 'reality principle' of capitalist society and of the bourgeois superego or censorship" to a cherished outcome by surmounting obstacles the author himself has invented (183). The difference between James and Balzac, of whom Jameson has written "his incorrigible fantasy demands ultimately raise History itself over against him, as absent cause, as that on which desire must come to grief," is that James recognizes "the fallen world of capitalism" as his domain (183–84). *The Wings of the Dove* appears to qualify as an "allegory of irony" in Paul de Man's terms, treating the past as "pure mystification" and the future as "harassed forever by a relapse within the inauthentic" (228, 222) through the figuration of Milly and Kate respectively: "Her memory's your love"; "We shall never be again as we were!" (*Wings* 20: 405). For James, the process of demystification, the "breakup of hope," is complete (Jameson, 184). Only his characters struggle feebly to escape the toils of capitalism in a world where the pace of private life is set to the rhythms of the marketplace: "'We've succeeded.' She spoke with her eyes deep in his own. 'She won't have loved you for nothing.' It made him wince, but she insisted. 'And you won't have loved *me*'" (*Wings* 20: 333).

In making Milly a semiophore person, James seems to extricate his heroine from the tawdry American "drama of nerves" and the "mere mercenary" motives of Lancaster Gate and place her on a higher plane (19: 116, 282).

But James subverts his own discursive practice of beatifying Milly's person and creating touching subjectivity effects for her by demonstrating the dependence of such tropes on an impossible otherworldliness. Within the fictional construct, Milly's "imaginary transposition of [the] real conditions of existence" entails a repression of *her* real conditions of existence ad infinitum (Althusser, 162). The renunciation of fortune and flesh initiates a phase of nonexistence that presages death. However, in making Milly's aura a textual fetish even before her death, James signals the reinvestment of displaced desire, now diffused throughout the novel as a perfume. Milly is "a Christian maiden in the arena, mildly, caressingly, martyred" (*Wings* 20: 42). Continuous with abjection, the "transvaluation of something originally part of the identity into a defiling otherness," Milly's hystericized rejection of economic and sexual intercourse invests these pursuits with a hyperbolical profanity (Butler, *Gender Trouble*, 133): "I give and give and give—there you are; stick to me as close as you like and see if I don't. Only I can't listen or receive or accept—I can't *agree*. I can't make a bargain" (*Wings* 20: 161).

Doting over Milly's last will and testament, marvelously transcribed as a "maimed child" wrapped in innumerable layers of swaddling and stashed in a "sacred corner," Merton thinks of the letter "as a priceless pearl cast before his eyes—his pledge given not to save it" (20: 396). This allusion to *Othello*, "Like the base Indian, threw a pearl away Richer than all his tribe," plays upon the resemblance between the duped male protagonists, who agonize over the imputed sexual misconduct of wife and mistress respectively (v.ii.338). The double entendre—pearl is a synonym for the clitoris—functions like an anamorphic device in painting, a concealed or aberrant meaning that shadows the referential function of textual language.[8] Milly's ascension is both assured and arrested by the intrication of codes (cultural, proairetic, symbolic, and hermeneutic) strung together like a lengthy, heavy, priceless double chain of pearls: "Yet he knew in a moment that Kate was just now, for reasons hidden from him, exceptionally under the impression of that element of wealth in her which was a power, which was a great power, and which was dove-like only so far as one remembered that doves have wings and wondrous flights" (*Wings* 20: 218). Having fallen in love with Milly's purity, the antidote to Kate's ruthless materialism, Densher requires that she never speak her desire. Perhaps James meant to signal this tragic stalemate by endowing Milly with that extraordinary red hair, blazing against her pallid face, signifying an unconscious aversion to the sepulchral cool imposed upon her body and desires, which Densher himself discommends as "a not altogether lucky challenge to attention" (20: 214).

Contemplating the immense show mounted to screen Milly off from inquiring minds and solicitous friends, Densher resorts to a pictorial conceit to express his sense of the impending disaster, "the great smudge of mortality across the picture" (20: 207). Sheila Teahan groups this image with the Bronzino portrait, but a prior association exists that clarifies the trope (207). Imagining Milly as the subject of a study for one of the better magazines, Susan Stringham worries that any incidental refinement or alteration of her ideal would be an "ugly smutch on perfection" (*Wings* 19: 112). What James, in another place, styled the "painter's tenderness of imagination" about Milly bristles with innuendo (19: xxii). When an impossible purity is called for, as is the case in *Othello*, the least suspicion sullies the image and clouds the mind. To return to the Bronzino portrait, Lord Mark's banter concerning Lady Lucrezia's virtue, "one doubts if she was good," sets the stage for Milly's initiation into the traffic in sex (19: 221). At a time when Milly is said to be "impossibly without sin," the proleptic epithet "painted sister" aligns Milly with a prostitute-duchess alter ego (19: 228). Milly may be as unconscious of sex as a baby, which is not to say that she is asexual; the "smudge" or "smutch" soiling her portrait perversely reinscribes her earthly desires.

It turns out that a virgin dove is as improbable as a virgin mother. In the famous scene in which Milly dons white for the first time, inspiring awe and adulation among her fellows, James introduces an incongruous effect, an image of inadvertent masturbation. "The long, priceless chain [of pearls], wound twice round the neck, hung, heavy and pure, down the front of the wearer's breast—so far down that Milly's trick, evidently unconscious, of holding and vaguely fingering and entwining a part of it, conduced presumably to convenience" (20: 217–18). This image recurs at the end of the novel just in time to complicate James's sanctification of Milly's relics. She is sick with desire and longing, a diagnosis suggested by Densher's reflections on his love affair with Kate: "Their mistake was to have believed that they *could* hold out—hold out, that is . . . against an impatience that, prolonged and exasperated, made a man ill. He had known more than ever, on their separating in the court of the station, how ill a man, and even a woman, could feel from such a cause" (20: 6–7). We might object that at this point Milly is wholly out of the picture, but elsewhere James obliquely acknowledges a bond of suffering among his "reflectors," or centers of consciousness, by refusing knowledge of "what Kate pays, heroically" on her visit alone to Merton's lodging in the same breath that he abridges the harrowing details of Milly's illness (19: xviii). Noting that the rhetorical gesture of disavowal, which raises the specter of Lionel Croy's disgrace through the trope of "unspeakability," invites speculation about Milly's secret complaint, Sedgwick hits on a wonderful formulation: "the pornography of illness" generated around the heroine (*Tendencies*, 89). However, as Sedgwick is the first to allow, this prurient atmosphere is so diffuse as to escape notice.

Authorial Evasions

What prevented James from elucidating Milly's sexual neurasthenia, "how ill . . . *even a woman*" (emphasis added) could feel when deprived of a physical outlet for her desires? In his *Notebooks*, James explains the "greater prettiness" of making Milly "already too ill" to be taken by Densher. "On account of something rather pitifully obvious and vulgar in the presentation of such a remedy for her despair—and such a remedy only. 'Oh, she's dying without having had it? Give it to her and let her die'—that strikes me as sufficiently second-rate" (103). In this passage, vulgarity, which has served as a textual synonym for pecuniary ostentation, poverty, and homosexual liminality, becomes a logical copula explaining the prohibition against sexual frankness: "It had a vulgar sound—as throughout, in love, the names of things, the verbal terms of intercourse, were, compared with love itself, horribly vulgar" (*Wings* 20: 7). It is hard to say with assurance that James violated the spirit of this taboo, while preserving outward decorum, as a gesture of defiance against "the bourgeois superego" rather than unwittingly, as if by failing to comply with the demands of censorship. James's coy insistence on the disciplinary mechanisms constraining the author's "free hand" in the development of his story, in which market share is an aim of production, is noteworthy in this regard: "The free hand, in this connexion, was above all agreeable—the hand the freedom of which I owed to the fact that the work had ignominiously failed, in advance, of all power to see itself 'serialised'" (19: xi).

Within the space of this anecdote, feelings of hyperbolical shame and heady freedom ("sour grapes may at moments fairly intoxicate") vie for dominance before the chastened storyteller shifts into gear and practices the accommodations required of him: "Still, when not too blighting, they often operate as a tax on ingenuity—the ingenuity of the expert craftsman which likes to be taxed very much to the same tune to which a well-bred horse likes to be saddled" (19: xii). James eroticizes the punishment meted out to him by the editorial syndic, as if to say that he has outwitted popular canons of taste and made the best of a bad bargain. Discussing the impact of bourgeois aesthetics and the culture industry on artists, Bourdieu describes an emergent process of differentiation in which creators of "art-as-pure-signification, produced according to a purely symbolic intent for purely symbolic appropriation, that is, for disinterested delectation" look down their noses at hack writers, illustrators, and makers of bibelots (*Field of Cultural Production*, 113–14). From this vantage point, James's tactic of refining Milly's passion out of existence has less to do with censorship and more to do with the invidious distinction between semiophores and commodities. Of course this very distinction rhetorically instantiates the relationship between bourgeois canons of taste and cultural sublimation.

Describing the narrative strategy of indirection and evasion as a complement to the personal "arts and idiosyncrasies" that enable Mildred to supplant Kate as the object of Merton's affections (*Wings* 19: 115), Sheila Teahan has styled *The Wings of the Dove* an allegory for "the capacity of language to turn against itself" to revoke its premises and revise its goals (213). By Teahan's lights, this "troping or reversal on which the entire novel turns" is an "abysmal trap" (the term is James's) for the author and reader who lose faith in the illusion of mastery (205, 212). She does not see the advantages of this ironic and destabilizing modality, that of a mind unwilling "to accept any stage in its progression as definitive" (de Man, 220). Freedom and "infinite agility" are the boons accruing from the endless process of "self-destruction and self-invention" (220). Both in terms of the play of consciousness and of the thematic substance of the novel itself, James aligns himself with the character who best exemplifies this detachment from the human plight, Lionel Croy: "He gave you absurd feelings, he had indescribable arts, that quite turned the tables" (*Wings* 19: 8). Recognizing social reality as a "game" played with words, Lionel dismantles the edifice of bourgeois respectability simply by rephrasing its tenets: "Of the deplorably superficial morality of the age. The family sentiment, in our vulgarised brutalised life, has gone utterly to pot. There was a day when a man like me—by which I mean a parent like me—would have been for a daughter like you quite a distinct value; what's called in the business world, I believe, an 'asset'" (19: 17, 19).

Croy's speech disfigures the scheme of good repute by amplifying the mercenary motives governing social arrangements and by revealing their collusion, echoing Merton Densher's appraisal of "the general attestation of morality and money, a good conscience and a big balance" (19: 79). The worst thing Croy says about this system is that he agrees with it: "But I'm not, after all, quite the old ruin not to get something *for* giving up" (19: 17). Lionel Croy's exclusion may be a function of homophobic asepsis, a reaction against his queer locution or campiness ("old ruin"), but it certainly underscores the threat such a person poses to bourgeois hegemony when he has assimilated knowledge without sacrificing his attitude of ironical detachment, as when Croy advocates marriage to the right sort of "booby" as a hedge against poverty (19: 22). Concluding that Merton Densher *"must* be an ass!" for wanting to be "kind" to a reprobate like him, Lionel Croy effortlessly adopts a self-canceling conservative outlook, without the phony patina of moral conviction to be sure (19: 23). In short, Lionel is for beating the system, not for joining up. In this sense, "speech-act performativity" is a generalized strategy for unmasking the arbitrariness of all codes for interpreting, rendering, and structuring reality in the novel (Sedgwick, "Shame and Performativity," 220). In failing to revoke Croy's banishment and to bring him from the margins to center stage as he had planned, "he but 'looks in', poor beautiful dazzling, damning apparition that he was to have been," James addresses his social critique to a select coterie of readers; his gorgeous narrative tapestry turns out to be a kind of filibuster on the subject of homosexuality (*Wings* 19: xiv).

Coda

In closing, I would like to say a word about the appropriation of Henry James by the culture industry, what sort of man critical reevaluation and recent adaptations of his work have made him out to be. Reviewing Iain Softley's adaptation of *The Wings of the Dove* in the *New Yorker*, Daphne Merkin speculates that James was a lifelong virgin who "would have loved the vicarious embrace of the movies" (73 (11/10/97): 122). This comment is striking for a number of reasons. First, it evidences the trickle-down effect of literary scholarship on popular conceptions of authorship. James's celibacy is treated as fact, even by a journalist. It is no exaggeration to say that James's virginity is universally imputed and generally bemoaned. Second, film is seen as an outlet for sexual desires that found expression neither in James's personal life nor in his fictional world, not frankly, at any rate. Merkin implies that Jane Campion and Softley have read aright James's thwarted desires and have projected those desires onto his characters with exhilarating results. This formulation perpetuates the old-guard version of James as an anchorite without doing justice to more recent speculation that James's alleged passionlessness was intricately bound up with homoerotism and homosexual panic. We have witnessed a spate of movies heralded for "outing" the erotic tensions buried in James's novels; yet none of the complacent critics seem to realize that the films's scenes of nudity and groping are poor substitutes for the erotic complexity of the literary texts themselves, very likely, because they neither miss nor mind the filmmakers' erasure of homoerotic themes and entanglements.

Softley's decision, in his film version of *The Wings of the Dove*, to explain Lionel Croy's misbehavior as an opium addiction rather than to explore the textual trope of Croy's "unspeakable" crime against Victorian sexual reputability is but one facet of the film's erasure of same-sex desire, and not just for the reasons already given by Sedgwick and me, Susan Stringham's attachment to Milly Theale, Maud Lowder and Kate Croy's impersonation of the "butch-femme" relationship, Milly and Kate's mutual attraction, but because the template of sexual repression is so badly mishandled in the film. What is repression but a synonym for forbidden love? Softley clearly believes his audience requires confirmation that Kate Croy did want Merton Densher 'that way' badly enough to seduce him in a public street, a surprising turn of events recalling the film *Henry and June*, in which Anaïs Nin has sexual intercourse with her husband (or is it Henry Miller?) in a back alley during carnival. Nothing is more jarring to the reader's conception of James's novel than Softley's insistence on Merton's prominence, which is engineered in the film at the expense of Maud Lowder's textual preeminence and Susan Stringham's hovering presence, another gesture toward silencing the homoerotic register. Finally, in Softley's version, Milly herself resolves James's issue with the crudity, from a literary as well as social vantage point, of "the man's 'having' a sick girl" by propositioning Merton and being turned down. These revisions lessen rather than heighten the sexual tensions in the story by demystifying them, as when Alison Elliott and Helena Bonham Carter jostle a group of embarrassed gentleman in the foreign-language section of a bookstore where they giggle conspiratorially over a pornographic illustration. One wonders why Softley feels, in this the era of AIDS and abortion clinic bombings, that contemporary audiences would fail to respond to a film about thwarted love or a repressive society.

Which brings me to Softley's decision to push the story ahead eight years, from 1902 to 1910. Certainly with its exquisite decor and costumes, the film makes a case for abandoning Milly's inveterate black, the mourning attire of the late-Victorian heroine, in favor of turquoise and gold dresses by Fortuny, Poiret, and Paquin. But with the introduction of color and the loosely draped empire silhouette, the film loses touch with the socially informed Victorian body. The drab and corseted figure of the lady bespoke wealth and social position without pretension to the luxury of personal freedom. Similarly, Softley's rejection of the symbolism of the Bronzino portrait in favor of that of Gustav Klimt's "The Kiss" (1907/8) and "Danae" (1907/8), which proclaims its redheaded subject's sexuality with all the subtlety of Jerry Lee Lewis crooning "big-legged women, why don't you keep your dresses down?" sidesteps the novelist's thematic conflation of sex and death. The intrication of these two instinctual forces, also found in Densher's formulation for frustrated desire, "how ill a man, and even a woman, could feel from such a cause," cuts two ways in the novel. Sexual repression is treated as a source of psychological distress and even as a physical illness. Society enforces the constraint against nonreproductive sexuality through the threat of punishment, even unto death.

Unfortunately, society is missing from Softley's canvas. Milly and Kate are Lord Mark's sole guests at Matcham. Milly never undergoes an apotheosis before the thronging masses and ruling classes at the great historic house. She is called a princess only once in the film. The imposing vistas of the National Gallery, with its structural and decorous restraints against impulsive behavior, are discarded in favor of the cramped quarters and indifferent publicity of an anonymous gallery. By interiorizing the dramas played out in the name of sexual expression by confining them to the agonized relations of a handful of characters, the movie obscures the social critique of the book. I take a salutary lesson from such missteps as Softley's, which sacrifice fidelity to James's experience and vision while striving for a Henry James "our contemporary" effect. For this reason, I have avoided detaching the biographical material discussed in *Henry James's Thwarted Love* from its literary exegeses or work of historical contextualization, because to do so would be to reduce the scope of the book to a study of James's sexual preferences. It is all important that James's life and work are both emblematic of Victorian sexuality and conditioned by an emerging set of modernisms, discourses that continue to frame debates about race, gender, sexuality, health, and culture.

Reference Matter

Notes

INTRODUCTION

1. The English psychologists Herbert Spencer, Henry Maudsley, and Alexander Bain posited that mental illness had a physiological component. These diseases might be hereditary and they might be brought on by immoral and unhealthful behavior. The mental-hygiene ethos preached that clean living, will power, and healthy habits could offset or slow down the degenerative process.

I. HENRY JAMES'S THWARTED LOVE

1. As an example of scholars' timid forays into this area, see Rosenzweig's 1944 article in which he raises "the possible role of constitutional bisexuality" only to drop the subject (454). See also *Henry James and the Jacobites*, in which Geismar merely touches on the issue of homoerotism, suggesting in a footnote that James's "idealized portraits of youth, masculinity and virility reflect probably some kind of recessive homosexual yearning" (277). It was not until the publication of Sarotte in 1978 that James's own homosexuality was considered.

2. See Fletcher, "The law of the Oedipal polarity in effect states: 'you cannot *be* what you desire; you cannot *desire* what you wish to be,'" 101.

3. Krafft-Ebing, paraphrased in Symonds, *Problem*, 59. According to Foucault, Westphal's 1870 article on "contrary sexual sensations" inaugurated the discourse on homosexuality as a psychical phenomenon characterized by gender inversion (*History of Sexuality*, vol. 1, 43).

4. See Weeks, "Inverts," 195–211. The anonymously authored *The Sins of the Cities of the Plain, or the Recollections of a Mary-Anne*, a work detailing the experiences of a male homosexual prostitute in London, was published in 1881. The book included many anecdotes about the notorious Boulton and Park.

5. See Cohen, who remarks that the effeminacy popularly attributed to the male aesthete in the 1880s "had not yet produced an immediate corollary association with

sexual relations between men" (136). Cohen argues that this connotation emerged from newspaper accounts of the Wilde trials of 1895.

6. See Robert Martin, 171. Martin argues that frank expressions of affection and even passion between men were conventionally accepted throughout the 1850s. He suggests that the prohibition on genital contact may have allowed these essentially homoerotic relationships to flourish. In the 1880s, the tide began to shift and such friendships raised suspicion.

7. Dana argues that masturbation rarely causes serious health problems in normal individuals, although he acknowledges that quacks, advertisers, and medical circulars claim it causes epileptic insanity. Dana himself says masturbation occasionally causes epilepsy ("Clinical Lecture," 243).

2. WILLIAM JAMES ON ENERGY AND ENTROPY

1. Henry Senior gave William a microscope on Christmas Day in 1857. William's son Henry reported that William discovered the bill of sale shortly before Christmas and could hardly contain his excitement. It was a gift prized above all others (*LWJ* 1: 21).

2. Habegger has made much of Henry Senior's attachment to the physicist Henry Joseph, an associate from the Albany Academy. Habegger draws an invidious comparison between the intellectual giant Henry Joseph and his former pupil. In 1843 James wrote to the professor, asking whether "all the phenomena of physics [might not be] explained and grouped under laws *exclusively spiritual*—that they are in fact only the material expression of spiritual truth—or as Paul says the visible forms of invisible substance" (*The Father*, 204–5). Habegger finds Henry Senior's notion of a "*fundamental unity* of the different sciences" laughable, but by the 1870s physicists were, in fact, trying to discover "a unified theory of gravitation, heat, electricity, and so forth" (204). Habegger discounts as a "grand mania" Henry Senior's attempt to reconcile theology and science, but he does not realize that Henry Senior's aspiration was far from eccentric even among Victorian scientists (205). What distinguished Henry Senior's outlook from creationism was his confidence that laws *will be* discovered; the spiritual truth he sought was not set down in the Bible.

3. Lyell's uniformitarianism had taken hold in the geological sciences in the 1830s and was appropriated by the biological sciences, where it would lead to the theory of evolution in spite of Lyell's dissent. For a succinct definition, see William James: "The Philosophy of Evolution tries to show how the world at any given time may be conceived as absolutely identical, except in appearance, with itself at all past times" (*WWJ* 5: 37).

4. Bjork's biography is richly detailed and well worth reading for the case it pleads: that William relied on his aesthetic sensibility to learn to paint with words. Reacting against Feinstein's psychobiography, Bjork takes no notice of William's neurasthenia until his subject is in his midtwenties.

5. Apart from its technical applications (intelligence testing and the like), functional psychology in James's day may be known by its tenets: the notion that human behavior is elicited by the environment, that emotional experience is determined by physical reactions, and that the full range of mental activity can be reduced to laws of energy and motion.

6. James addressed the perils and advantages of a college education in "The True Harvard" (1903), "The Ph.D. Octopus" (1903), and "The Social Value of the College-Bred" (1907) in *WWJ* 17: 74–77; 67–74; 106–12. For other contemporaneous discussion of the changing goals of American universities, see Veblen, also Dewey. Bledstein provides an excellent overview.

7. This letter was written shortly after William recovered from a case of varioloid. William was explaining his resolve to abandon the expedition and return home; as it happens, William remained for some months in Brazil, complaining all the while that he was losing his eyesight. The letter's disparaging tone suggests that William was grieved by his unfitness for exploration and, more generally, by his failure to take part in the Civil War. On their way south, Agassiz's party spotted the smoke and flames rising from the conflagration at Richmond, the coup de grâce of the Civil War (Bjork, 59). William's South American dispatches were laden with martial terminology and references to his brothers and peers' war service.

8. This fear of failure, coupled with anxiety over disappointing the expectations of others, pervades *Roderick Hudson*: "He was talking passionately, desperately, sincerely, from an irresistible need to throw off the oppressive burden of his mother's confidence" (*RH*, 272). Nearing his debacle, Roderick echoes William's lamentation, declaring to his doting mother and fiancée: "I'm a dead failure, that's all; I'm not a first-rate man. I'm second-rate, tenth-rate, anything you please. After that, it's all one!" (*RH*, 273)

9. See "Dread of the Jew" for a sample calumny: "In Germany it is much the same story, and there the Jews are believed, unless stopped in time, to be about to monopolise the Universities" (338).

10. See Cranefield, "Organic Physics" and "Philosophical and Cultural Interests," for an account of the aims and accomplishments of the biophysics program.

11. Bain's notions of organic determinism were commonplaces among psychologists by the 1860s; Maudsley and Spencer's treatises superseded Bain's work in the 1870s. For a discussion of William James's forays into scientific psychology, see Mackenzie, 175–85. For a summary of Spencer's appropriation and generalization of Darwin's laws, see Ronald Martin, 32–58. Spencer explained the higher mental functions as evidence of the mobile mental energy required for adaptation to the environment.

12. In *A Pluralistic Universe*, William James celebrated the genius of the theoretical physicist Gustav Fechner in terms strikingly similar to those he employed to describe his father in a memorial tribute. Describing Fechner as a scientific pluralist who was stricken at age thirty-eight by an attack of nervous prostration from which his theological and cosmological faith rescued him after a prolonged struggle,

William endeavored to reconcile Fechner's religious monism with his broad intellectual sympathies (*WWJ* 4: 63–82).

13. Writing to his father from Berlin in 1867, William remarked: "I have read your article which I got in Teplitz several times carefully. I must confess that the darkness wh. to me has allways hung over what you have written on these subjects is hardly at all cleared up. Every sentence seems written from a point of view wh. I nowhere get within range of, and on the other hand ig[n]ores all sorts of questions wh. are visible from my point of view" (*CWJ* 4: 195).

14. Cotkin contends that James's pragmatism was strongly inflected with religious idealism, citing *The Will to Believe* as one example of the marriage of existential and utilitarian philosophy in James's canon (103). Cotkin also describes William's emergence from his debilitating depression in 1873 as a time of intellectual and professional caution, noting that the works for which James is famous were written in the last two decades of his life.

15. *The Wild Ass's Skin* invokes the principles of conservation and dissipation, weighs the costs and benefits of sublimation and celibacy, and concludes that it is better to burn than to save. The most telling anecdote in the novel concerns not Valentin but the consumptive he takes for his model: "This man had not spoken one word for ten years, and had trained himself to breathe only six times a minute in the dense atmosphere of a cow-house while following an extremely light system of dieting. 'I model myself on that man!' thought Raphael, who was determined to live at any price" (201).

16. Robert Palter, Professor Emeritus at Trinity College, where he taught philosophy and the history of science, very graciously read this chapter and offered some suggestions from his disciplinary standpoint. Noting that Henry Adams was mistaken in his assumption of a necessary decline in the physical and mental capacities of individuals (or civilizations) as they age, Dr. Palter pointed out that the second law of thermodynamics does not preclude the development and enhancement of individual bodies and faculties, so long as there are corresponding changes (exchanges of matter and energy) between the individual and his environment. In the case of the human mind, entropy *decreases* as the brain acquires new skills and notions throughout life. This line of reasoning is particularly suggestive for *Roderick Hudson*, which plumbs the mechanics of artistic creativity and maintains that an artist who is cut off from the sources of his inspiration, who has no opportunity to replenish his imagination, will rot like a tomato in a neglected garden.

17. William James framed the dilemma in similar terms in "Spencer's Definition of Mind": "One man may say that the law of mental development is dominated solely by the principle of conservation; another, that richness is the criteria of mental evolution; a third, that pure cognition of the actual is the essence of worthy thinking—but who shall pretend to decide which is right?" (*WWJ* 5: 15)

18. For a statement of this law as a nineteenth-century physicist understood it,

see Helmholtz, 359: "Heat can perform work; it is destroyed in the operation. Chemical forces can perform work, but they exhaust themselves in the effort. Electrical currents can perform work, but to keep them up we must consume either chemical or mechanical forces, or heat."

19. Henry James had a rudimentary grasp of mathematics and physics. He was enrolled for some months between October 1859 and September 1860 at the Institution Rochette, a Swiss scientific polytechnic, an experience he abhorred. Henry eventually joined William at the Geneva Academy, where he elected a course in literature (*Autobiography*, 239–47).

20. There are also literary sources for this juxtaposition of inanition and willpower. Balzac's Raphael Valentin is said to have devoted his youth to the production of a treatise called the *Theory of the Will* before frittering his time and energy away at orgies and gambling salons (*Wild Ass's Skin*, 111). In 1873 James wrote "The Madonna of the Future," another work of descriptive psychology, in which abulia prevents a painter from realizing his brilliant vision: "'The elements of it are all *here*'. And he tapped his forehead with that mystic confidence which had marked the gesture before. 'If I could only transpose them into some brain that had the hand, the will!'" (*Tales* 2: 229).

21. Writing to his fiancée, William begged off a promised visit, explaining that he needed time alone to recover good habits disrupted by work and courtship: "But for your sake quite as well as mine now it behooves me to be *hygienic* before everything. I am still used up with wakefulness, and I must at any cost get gradually back to good habits in that respect by fleeing every disturbance" (*CWJ* 4: 564–65).

22. For an opposing viewpoint see Garrison and Madden, 207–21. They take James to task for being scant in terms of his understanding of social problems and with regard to his political activism.

23. G. Gunn discusses C. B. MacPherson's formula, 33. Like Lentricchia, Gunn suggests that possessive individualism may be seen as an attempt to reconcile personal freedom with the needs of the community. Certainly a spirit of civic-mindedness pervades much of William James's public discourse, but it is in tension with his concept of the self as spiritual monad.

24. Curious as to how a practicing physicist would regard this claim, I enlisted the aid of Dr. Andrew Sessler, director emeritus of Lawrence Berkeley Laboratory at the University of California at Berkeley and member of the Academy of Sciences. Dr. Sessler objected to several formulations of William James's concerning energy conservation; he was particularly struck by the fact that a trained scientist would treat the human body as a closed system, subject to the same laws as the steam engine.

25. James borrowed the title "Gospel of Relaxation" from a phrase Herbert Spencer used during his celebrated American lecture tour of 1882: "In brief, I may say that we have had somewhat too much of the 'gospel of work'. It is time to preach the gospel of relaxation" (cited in Youmans, 34–35).

3. DISSIPATION AND DECORATION IN 'RODERICK HUDSON'

1. Sam Singleton is chiefly responsible for the reader's perception of Roderick himself as a work of art. Apprised of the news that Roderick has gone to the dogs, he comments: "In my memories of this Roman artist life he will be the central figure. He will stand there in extraordinary high relief, as beautiful and clear and complete as one of his own statues!" (*RH*, 268). Although I draw parallels between Friedrich Nietzsche's *The Birth of Tragedy* (1872) and *Roderick Hudson*, it is unlikely that James read Nietzsche much before July 1875, when Thomas Sergeant Perry, a friend of the James family, reviewed *Untimely Meditations* for the *North American Review* (Donadio, 17). A French translation of *Untimely Meditations*, published in 1907, was found in the library of Lamb House after James's death.

2. Contemplating Roderick's statuette of a naked boy, Rowland observes, "The figure might have been some beautiful youth of ancient fable—Hylas or Narcissus, Paris or Endymion" (*RH*, 31). Hylas was the page and lover of Herakles, and, as Dover has argued, even Narcissus, Paris, and Endymion may be taken for eromenoi, not simply for their beauty but because the goddesses who loved them assumed the role of the older male in courtship (172). Rowland falls in love with this statuette of a boy draining the cup of life to the dregs before he meets, and becomes infatuated with, Roderick, the figure made flesh.

3. Henry Senior had to sue his father's estate for a full share of three million dollars, and he lived off the income generated by inherited real estate holdings and stocks. Of particular interest is a rider attached to William of Albany's testament, which empowered the trustees to disinherit any heir who led a "grossly immoral, idle or dishonorable life" (Lewis, 28). Originally dealt a third of his father's estate, Rowland repels the claims of a charitable institution to a still larger share by due process of law, but he gives the contested sum to another charity at the conclusion of the lawsuit to underscore his indifference to money (*RH*, 29).

4. Leavenworth's iteration of phrases such as "false to itself" calls attention to his hypocrisy; he has dispensed with any sentiment that might assert his individuality in the interest of conforming to the leisure class. The author of *Degeneration*, Max Nordau, who became a Zionist in his later years in the wake of the Dreyfus affair, was convinced that Jewish attempts at assimilation had been a failure. Mosse paraphrases Nordau in his introduction to *Degeneration*, xxv: "Moreover, the assimilated Jew was unstable and, inwardly sick, acted the part of a hypocrite. As with everything not genuine, this kind of Jew was offensive to anyone with true aesthetic feeling."

5. Gerber surveys stereotypical perceptions of Jews among the financial elites (creditors, tradesman, and bankers) in Buffalo, New York, 1830 to 1860 (201–32). The account is instructive because the focus group is contemporaneous and regionally consistent with the James clan, whose patriarch, William of Albany, made a fortune in real estate, dry goods, and liquor on the banks of the Hudson river (Habegger, *The Father*, 9–29).

6. Haviland proposes a startling redefinition of James's race thinking, emphasizing James's concern for the construction and preservation of ethnic identity rather than his xenophobia. Similarly, Blair portrays James as both partaking of and resisting contemporary definitions of self and other while engaged in his own cultural project: forging the American race.

7. Opera is indelibly marked by gender incongruities, such as the long history of castrated men playing female parts. Koestenbaum comments: "I have always feared the falsetto: voice of the bogeyman, voice of the unregenerate fag; voice of horror and loss and castration; floating voice, vanishing voice" (165).

8. Max Nordau's Zionist tracts urged Jews to become "men of muscle instead of remaining slaves to their nerves" (xxviii). Nordau's efforts to place the blame for modern malaise and neurasthenia on technology and decadent cultural movements is a defensive maneuver against antisemitic invectives decrying the pernicious influence of Jewish immigrants.

9. See Du Maurier's *Trilby* for a masterpiece of antisemitic characterization. The Jew Svengali hypnotizes a beautiful urchin, giving her the gift of song at the expense of her health, happiness, and freedom. Svengali is a spider who traps his prey in a web of intrigue and drains her life force at his leisure, for profit, pleasure, and revenge against the Jew-hating world.

10. See Djikstra, 366–71, for a discussion of works, most notably Eduard von Hartmann's *The Sexes Compared* and Frank Norris's *McTeague*, that equate woman's hunger for gold with sexual desire and consequently blame the nineteenth-century woman in her twin capacities as spendthrift and vamp for the physiological and psychological overstrain experienced by her partner.

11. All of the women in *Roderick Hudson* are dangerous. Informed that his mother is coming to Rome to rescue him from his dissipations, Roderick exclaims, "my mother can't hurt me now!" (*RH*, 210). Mary Garland of West Nazareth, Massachusetts, is a perverse Madonna: "She likes me as if I were good to eat. She's saving me up, cannibal-fashion, as if I were a big feast" (*RH*, 232). For further discussion of James's antipathy to women, see my essay "Henry James and the Mother Complex."

12. This debate is partly a response to Henry James Senior's definition of the aesthetic man or artist who defies popular mores in his pursuit of self-realization. Henry Junior's reference to the postman and cook playfully evokes the elder James's notion that "the humblest theatre of action," a hostelry even, may furnish the individual with an opportunity to realize the highest spiritual aims, so long as his attention to beauty and his conception of his task are entirely "*sui generis*" (*HJSr*, 131).

13. See Freud's "Civilization and Its Discontents," *Penguin Freud Library* 12: 268 n. 1: "No other technique for the conduct of life attaches the individual so firmly to reality as laying emphasis on work; for his work at least gives him a secure place in a portion of reality, the human community. The possibility it offers of displacing a large amount of libidinal components, whether narcissistic, aggressive or even erotic, on to professional work and on to the human relations connected with it lends it a

value by no means second to what it enjoys as something indispensable to the preservation and justification of the existence of society."

14. Bersani's "Sexuality and Aesthetics" contains an outstanding critique of Freud's various attempts to theorize sublimation. Bersani argues that Freud scuttled the evidence linking creativity and perversion. Posnock touts the one Freudian formulation of artistic sublimation that does not entail repression, the study of Leonardo da Vinci, as representative, which it is not (45–50).

15. It has been suggested that Pater lost a university proctorship in 1874 when certain love letters he had written to an undergraduate, William Money Hardinge, came to light (Inman, 1–20). In spite of the clerical party's dominance in matters of college appointments and educational policy, Pater could count among his colleagues many who shared his tastes. Dellamora discusses Pater's romantic friendship with his former student and literary executor, Charles Shadwell. Where there is no evidence of sexual intimacy, Dellamora considers this attachment to have exceeded the bounds of acceptable homosociality (59).

16. Murtaugh argues that James's increasing acceptance of his own homosexuality in the years 1875 to 1907 can be gauged by his revisions to the novel. Certainly James became more communicative about such matters in his personal correspondence and more inclined to pursue a physical relationship (with Hendrick Anderson), as Murtaugh demonstrates; however, it is a mistake to underplay James's discomfort with the heightened public scrutiny of the homosexual persona, which Murtaugh suggests put James more at ease.

17. Milliman glosses the novel's critique of Roderick's "ineffectual romanticism," reducing the novel to a prosaic contest between the advocates of work and play (232). Milliman's emphasis on James's use of romantic stereotypes derived from popular fiction precludes a serious consideration of Roderick's affinity with romanticism. In his essay on the novel, Engelberg argues that Roderick fails because he is deprived of fresh sources of inspiration and guiltless enjoyment of his experiences, a demise fully in keeping with romantic conceptions of the special requirements of artistic genius but in no wise reducible to moral formulas (95).

18. Roderick's objections to the ugly physiognomy of the Jew are noteworthy. In 1878 Roderick explains that he will attempt few Old Testament figures because "I don't like the Jews; I don't like pendulous noses" (RH2, 93). In the later edition, Roderick's contempt is modulated, yet the fascination with the Jewish nose, a staple of antisemitic discourse, remains prominent: "I don't like the Jews; I like the big nose, as any sculptor must, but only the Christian, or still better the pagan, form" (RH, 87).

19. This statement anticipates Nietzsche's celebration of Greek tragedy for unifying the full spectrum of human experience. Henry Senior's challenge to Christian ethics does not rise to the level of Nietzsche's inversion of conventional ethics in *Beyond Good and Evil* and *The Genealogy of Morals*. Henry Senior's willingness to countenance self-interest and aggression as a stage of human development passing away under the influence of the social instinct and the progress toward divine equality is a

far cry from Nietzsche's endorsement of the will to power. Like Charles Fourier, Henry Senior awaited the dissolution of society in the service of new ideals, whereas Nietzsche hoped to see the triumph of the autonomous individual.

20. My own thinking about the "masochistic economy" of *Roderick Hudson* has been informed by Stevens's use of this concept (80).

21. Along with a host of minor characters who beat or bullied their spouses, all of the novel's chief figures are romantically attached to people who spurn them (*RH*, 45, 86, 91, 115, 181). See McWhirter for a consideration of the author's investment in the thematics of masochism.

22. This notion was to become a convention of literary decadence. See Huysmans: "Their liaison continued, but before long Des Esseintes's sexual fiascos became more frequent; the effervescence of his mind could no longer melt the ice in his body, his nerves would no longer heed the commands of his will, and he was obsessed by the lecherous vagaries common in old men" (115).

23. Kristeva explains that two contrary influences bring about the narcissistic crisis. One is the excessive stringency of the Other, and the second is the "lapse of the Other, which shows through the breakdown of objects of desire" (15). Advertising the many tourist attractions of Rome to his "mammy," Hudson makes what will shortly be called a Freudian slip, indicating the Circus Maximus by the term *Cloaca Maxima*, or Rome's big womb, site of carnage (*RH*, 216).

4. DEGENERATION AND FEMINISM IN 'THE BOSTONIANS'

1. Critics of *The Bostonians* have generally agreed with Daughtery that James's command of the goals, grievances, and methods of nineteenth-century feminists was poor; however, Davis defends James's credibility as an informant on nineteenth-century feminism.

2. Among the earliest and best discussions of the interplay between gender roles and the etiology and treatment of nervous illness, see Douglas; Haller and Haller; Rosenberg, "Sexuality"; Smith-Rosenberg; and Sicherman.

3. Neurasthenia and hysteria were considered distinct illnesses in the nineteenth century, but similar psychological, familial, and social stresses are evident in the recorded case histories. Whether a patient suffered from an excess of nervous energy (hysteria) or a lack of nerve force (neurasthenia), she was still a nerve case. Although diagnosed as a physiological problem, neurasthenia also served as a euphemism for psychosomatic complaints. The majority of physicians diagnosed neurasthenia when the patient was wealthy, educated, male, and sedate.

4. According to William James, all of Boston read Miss Birdseye as a thinly veiled portrait of Elizabeth Peabody (*HJL* 3: 68). Henry disclaimed any such intention, remarking that he had not seen or thought of Miss Peabody for twenty years. This is patently untrue. In 1878 Henry visited the Isle of Wight expressly to spend a few

days with Miss Peabody (*HJL* 2: 170). The association between historical personages is strengthened by James's decision to place Dr. Prance in Miss Birdseye's rooming house.

5. As the leading woman physician of her day, Dr. Jacobi was impatient with the slack preparation in disease etiology, dissection, and surgery that female medical colleges provided. She resigned her teaching position in 1888 over a pedagogical dispute (Morantz-Sanchez, 184–202).

6. The report of Runnels is typical of the medical arguments mounted to combat women's pursuit of higher education: "A writer says that out of 705 female college graduates recently communicated with, only 196 are married. Of the 196 married, 66 have had no children and the remaining 130 have had 263 children, 232 of which are living. Thus it seems that 'higher education' in women, desirable though it may be, so far has not conduced to connubiality and fecundity" (297).

5. THE POLITICS OF SEXUAL DISSIDENCE IN 'THE PRINCESS CASAMASSIMA'

1. Symonds recaps the main points of the legislation in *Problem in Modern Ethics*: "(1) Sodomy is a felony, defined as the carnal knowledge (per anum) of any man or of any woman by a male person; punishable with penal servitude for life as a maximum, for ten years as a minimum. (2) the attempt to commit sodomy is punishable with ten year's penal servitude as a maximum. (3) The commission, in public or private, by any male person with another male person, of 'any act of gross indecency,' is punishable with two years' imprisonment and hard labour" (135 n. 1).

2. Edward Carpenter summarized contemporary views of sexual inversion in "Homogenic Love":

> The leaning of sexual desire to one of the same sex—is in a vast number of cases quite instinctive and congenital, mentally and physically, and therefore twined in the very roots of individual life and practically ineradicable. To Men and Women thus affected with an innate homosexual bias, Ulrichs gave the name Urning, since pretty widely accepted by scientists. Too much emphasis cannot be laid on the distinction between these born lovers of their own sex, and that class of persons, with whom they are so often confused, who out of mere carnal curiosity or extravagance of desire, or from the dearth of opportunities for more normal satisfaction (as in schools, barracks, etc.) adopt some homosexual practices. (in Reade, 332)

3. James was familiar with the Victorian tradition of floral emblems. In *The Bostonians*, James named his two warring principals: Basil and Olive. Today the name Olive is associated with the olive branch of peace, but in James's day the olive plant called to mind Athena, the virgin goddess of wisdom, crafts, and war (Tyas, 145).

Basil is aptly named; Tyas says the name means "hatred" and that "Poverty has been represented as a female form covered with rags, seated near a Basil plant" (23). In *The Princess Casamassima*, Rose Muniment tells Hyacinth: "Your name, like mine, represents a flower" (5: 126). Rose also uses the language of flowers to describe two of the novel's aristocrats, Lady Aurora and the princess: "And wasn't it a rare picture to think of them moving hand in hand, like great twin lilies, through the bright upper air?" (*Princess* 6: 206). According to Tyas, the lily symbolizes majesty and purity (127). Of the two women, Lady Aurora is a genuine lily and the princess only a gilded one.

4. For a discussion of gay nomenclature, see Trumbach, who indicates that some transvestites referred to themselves as "princess" at this time (138–39).

5. Though Whitman was at pains to deny homoerotic undercurrents in his life and works, Symonds argued that Whitman's "chivalry of adhesiveness" between men represented a purity of attachment closely allied with the gospel of comradeship (*Problem*, 115–25). See also Charles Kains-Jackson, "The New Chivalry," in Reade, 313–19.

6. In her treatment of *Dr. Jekyll and Mr. Hyde*, Showalter argues for "a Victorian homosexual trope of the left hand of illicit sexuality" (115). She overstates the case, misconstruing Jekyll's insistence that he would go to any lengths for his beloved Lanyon ("I would not have sacrificed my left hand to help you") as an offer to part with the inferior member, when Jekyll clearly signifies his willingness to sacrifice the more indispensable (right) hand (Stevenson, 94). She also intimates that Symonds's famous figure of a useless hand "clenched in the grip of an unconquerable love" refers to the left hand, but the text of Symonds's *Memoirs* reads: "I knew that my right hand was useless—firmly clenched in the grip of an unconquerable love" (119–20).

7. In his essay on *The Princess Casamassima*, Trilling compiles his own list of precipitating events, such as the assassination of Alexander II of Russia in 1881, attempts on the lives of the kings of Spain and Italy, the murders of Lord Frederick Cavendish, secretary for Ireland, and Undersecretary Thomas Burke by Irish extremists in 1882, and an explosion in the House of Commons in 1885 (73).

6. SIGNING PLENITUDE FROM THE ABYSS IN
'THE WINGS OF THE DOVE'

1. Foucault discusses Jeremy Bentham's Panopticon, a model of prison reform that organized cells around a central observation tower to ensure the total visibility of the incarcerated to the inspector's gaze, in *Discipline and Punish*. See 216–17 especially.

2. For a discussion of the "life group" and its status in the evolving museology of the late nineteenth century as well as for background on evolutionary and typological schema, see Jacknis, 75–111.

3. In a footnote, Sedgwick links Susan Stringham's tentative pathologization of Milly Theale as a case of "American intensity" to the medicalization of homosexual-

ity and the abrogation of the Boston marriage as an acceptable alternative to hetero-sexual coupling at the turn of the century (*Tendencies*, 91). It seems to me that James was at pains to show that same-sex friendships between women were suspect much earlier. In *The Bostonians*, Olive Chancellor's nervous intensity is stoked by others' scrutiny of her highly charged relationship with Verena Tarrant.

4. Butler's meaning is somewhat more specific than my own. However, I see no reason why vision cannot be disciplined by the taboos associated with eating, drink-ing, and sex, which establish "boundaries of the body which are also the first contours of the subject," because shame and defilement are closely allied.

5. Peter Stallybrass made this observation after a lecture at Vassar College, De-cember 10, 1997.

6. Bennett points out that the practice of organizing paintings and sculpture by national schools and historical periods, an innovation of the royal art exhibition, was adopted wholesale after the French Revolution. Following the revolution, the Louvre administrators kept up the statist principles informing its inception, simply recodifying images of royalty to celebrate the power of the state and the sovereignty of the citizen. The main differences in the exhibitionary strategy of monarchs and bureaucrats were that the former group collected rare, curious, and precious objects to symbolize their own power, whereas the demotic approach emphasized typicality. Public museums were a civics lesson disguised as recreation (36–37).

7. To the best of my knowledge, Rhodes was the first to propose anorexia as Milly's mysterious complaint and to try to place Milly's wasting disease within the context of leisure-class patterns of consumption.

8. *The Pearl*, a "Journal of Facetiae and Voluptuous Reading," was published from July 1879 to December 1880 (Kendrick, 75).

Works Cited

Abelove, Henry. "Freud, Male Homosexuality, and the Americans." In *The Lesbian and Gay Studies Reader*, ed. Henry Abelove, Michele Barale, and David Halperin, pp. 381–93. New York: Routledge, 1993.

Abrams, M. H. *The Mirror and the Lamp: Romantic Theory and the Critical Tradition*. London: Oxford University Press, 1979.

Adams, Henry. *The Degradation of the Democratic Dogma*. New York: Peter Smith, 1949.

———. *The Education of Henry Adams*. New York: Random House, 1931.

Adams, James Eli. *Dandies and Desert Saints: Styles of Victorian Masculinity*. Ithaca: Cornell University Press, 1995.

Allen, Gay Wilson. *William James: A Biography*. New York: Viking, 1967.

Althusser, Louis. *Lenin and Philosophy and Other Essays*. Trans. Ben Brewster. New York: Monthly Review, 1971.

Anderson, Charles. "James's Portrait of the Southerner." *American Literature* 27 (1955–56): 309–31.

Arnold, Matthew. *Culture and Anarchy*. Cambridge, Eng.: Cambridge University Press, 1978.

Arreat, Lucien. "Pathology of Artists." *The Alienist and Neurologist* 14 (1893): 79–93.

Auchard, John. *Silence in Henry James: The Heritage of Symbolism and Decadence*. University Park: Pennsylvania State University Press, 1986.

Auerbach, Nina. *Communities of Women: An Idea in Fiction*. Cambridge, Mass.: Harvard University Press, 1978.

Babcock, Warren. "On the Morbid Heredity and Predisposition to Insanity of the Man of Genius." *Journal of Nervous and Mental Disease* 22 (Dec. 1895): 749–69.

Balzac, Honoré de. *The Wild Ass's Skin*. Trans. Herbert Hunt. New York: Penguin, 1977.

Banta, Martha. *Taylored Lives: Narrative Productions in the Age of Taylor, Veblen, and Ford*. Chicago: University of Chicago Press, 1993.

Barker-Benfield, G. J. *The Horrors of the Half-Known Life: Male Attitudes Toward Women and Sexuality in Nineteenth-Century America*. New York: Harper and Row, 1976.

Barnes, Barry, and Steven Shapin, eds. *Natural Order: Historical Studies of Scientific Culture*. Beverly Hills: Sage, 1979.

Beard, George Miller. *American Nervousness: Its Causes and Consequences, A Supplement to Nervous Exhaustion* (Neurasthenia). New York: Arno, 1972.

———. *A Practical Treatise on Nervous Exhaustion (Neurasthenia): Its Symptoms, Nature, Sequences, Treatment*. New York: William Wood, 1880.

Bennett, Tony. *The Birth of the Museum: History, Theory, Politics*. London: Routledge, 1995.

Bentley, Nancy. *The Ethnography of Manners: Hawthorne, James, Wharton*. Cambridge, Eng.: Cambridge University Press, 1995.

Bersani, Leo, and Ulysse Dutoit. *Arts of Impoverishment: Beckett, Rothko, Resnais*. Cambridge, Mass.: Harvard University Press, 1993.

———. *A Future for Astyanax: Character and Desire in Literature*. New York: Columbia University Press, 1984.

———. "Is the Rectum a Grave?" In *Aids: Cultural Analysis, Cultural Activism*, ed. Douglas Crimp, pp. 197–222. Cambridge, Mass.: MIT Press, 1988.

———. "Sexuality and Aesthetics." October 28 (Spring 1984): 27–42.

Bjork, Daniel. *William James: The Center of His Vision*. New York: Columbia University Press, 1988.

Blair, Sara. *Henry James and the Writing of Race and Nation*. Cambridge, Eng.: Cambridge University Press, 1997.

Bledstein, Burton. *The Culture of Professionalism: The Middle Class and the Development of Higher Education in America*. New York: Norton, 1978.

Bloom, Harold. *The Anxiety of Influence: A Theory of Poetry*. London: Oxford University Press, 1973.

Bourdieu, Pierre. *The Field of Cultural Production: Essays on Art and Literature*. Trans. Randal Johnson. New York: Columbia University Press, 1993.

Bourdieu, Pierre, and Alain Darbel. *The Love of Art: European Art Museums and their Public*. Trans. Caroline Beattie and Nick Merriman. Stanford: Stanford University Press, 1990.

———. *Outline of a Theory of Practice*. Trans. Richard Nice. Cambridge, Eng.: Cambridge University Press, 1977.

Brantlinger, Patrick, ed. *Energy & Entropy: Science and Culture in Victorian Britain*. Bloomington: Indiana University Press, 1989.

Brinton, Crane. *French Revolutionary Legislation on Illegitimacy 1789–1804*. Cambridge, Eng.: Cambridge University Press, 1936.

Brush, Stephen. *The Temperature of History: Phases of Science and Culture in the Nineteenth Century*. New York: Burt Franklin, 1978.

Bryson, Norman, Michael Ann Holly, Keith Moxey, eds. *Visual Culture: Images and Interpretations.* Hanover: Wesleyan University Press, 1994.

Busst, A. J. L. "The Image of the Androgyne in the Nineteenth Century." In *Romantic Mythologies*, ed. Ian Fletcher, pp. 1–95. London: Routledge and Kegan Paul, 1967.

Butler, Judith. *Bodies That Matter: On the Discursive Limits of "Sex."* New York: Routledge, 1993.

———. *Gender Trouble: Feminism and the Subversion of Identity.* New York: Routledge, 1990.

———. "Imitation and Gender Insubordination." In *Inside/Out: Lesbian Theories, Gay Theories*, ed. Diana Fuss, pp. 13–31. New York: Routledge, 1991.

Calder, Jenni. *Robert Louis Stevenson: A Life Study.* New York: Oxford University Press, 1980.

Castle, Terry. *The Apparitional Lesbian: Female Homosexuality and Modern Culture.* New York: Columbia University Press, 1993.

Chauncey, George, Jr. "From Sexual Inversion to Homosexuality: Medicine and the Changing Conceptualization of Female Deviance." *Salmagundi* 58–59 (Fall/Winter 1982–83): 114–46.

Cohen, Ed. *Talk on the Wilde Side: Toward a Genealogy of a Discourse on Male Sexualities.* London: Routledge, 1993.

Collins, Joseph. *The Doctor Looks at Biography: Psychological Studies of Life and Letters.* New York: Doran, 1925.

Colvin, Sidney. "Robert Louis Stevenson and Henry James." *Scribner's Magazine* 75 (Jan.–June 1924): 315–26.

Cominos, Peter. "Late-Victorian Sexual Respectability and the Social System." *International Review of Social History* 8 (1963): 18–48, 216–50.

Cooter, Roger. "The Power of the Body: The Early Nineteenth Century." In *Natural Order: Historical Studies of Scientific Culture*, ed. Barry Barnes and Steven Shapin, pp. 73–90. Beverly Hills: Sage, 1979.

Cotkin, George. *William James, Public Philosopher.* Baltimore: Johns Hopkins University Press, 1990.

Cott, Nancy. *The Bonds of Womanhood: "Woman's Sphere" in New England, 1780–1835.* New Haven: Yale University Press, 1977.

Cowles, Edward. "Insistent and Fixed Ideas." *American Journal of Psychology* 1 (Nov. 1887): 222–70.

Cranefield, Paul. "The Organic Physics of 1847 and the Biophysics of Today." *Journal of the History of Medicine and Allied Sciences* 12 (1957): 407–23.

———. "The Philosophical and Cultural Interests of the Biophysics Movement of 1847." *Journal of the History of Medicine and Allied Sciences* 21 (1966): 1–7.

Crompton, Louis. *Byron and Greek Love: Homophobia in 19th-Century England.* Berkeley and Los Angeles: University of California Press, 1988.

Dana, Charles. "Are We Degenerating?" *Forum* 19 (June 1895): 458–65.

———. "Clinical Lecture: On Certain Sexual Neuroses." *Medical and Surgical Reporter* 65 (Aug. 15, 1891): 241–45.

Daughtery, Sarah. "Henry James, George Sand, and *The Bostonians*: Another Curious Chapter in the Literary History of Feminism." *Henry James Review* 10 (Winter 1989): 42–49.

Davenport-Hines, Richard. *Sex, Death and Punishment: Attitudes to Sex and Sexuality in Britain Since the Renaissance*. London: Collins, 1990.

Davis, Susan de Saussure. "Feminist Sources in The Bostonians." *American Literature* 50 (1979): 570–89.

DeLaura, David. "Reading Inman Reading Pater Reading: A Review Essay." *Pater Newsletter* 26 (1991): 2–9.

de Lauretis, Teresa. "Sexual Indifference and Lesbian Representation." In *Performing Feminisms: Feminist Critical Theory and Theatre*, ed. Sue-Ellen Case, pp. 17–39. Baltimore: Johns Hopkins University Press, 1992.

Dellamora, Richard. *Masculine Desire: The Sexual Politics of Victorian Aestheticism*. Chapel Hill: University of North Carolina Press, 1990.

de Man, Paul. *Blindness and Insight: Essays in the Rhetoric of Contemporary Criticism*. Minneapolis: University of Minnesota Press, 1983.

Dewey, John. *Democracy and Education: An Introduction to the Philosophy of Education*. New York, 1916.

Djikstra, Bram. *Idols of Perversity: Fantasies of Feminine Evil in Fin-de-Siècle Culture*. New York: Oxford University Press, 1986.

Dollimore, Jonathan. *Sexual Dissidence: Augustine to Wilde, Freud to Foucault*. Oxford: Clarendon Press, 1991.

Donadio, Stephen. *Nietzsche, Henry James, and the Artistic Will*. New York: Oxford University Press, 1978.

Douglas Wood, Ann. "'Fashionable Diseases': Women's Complaints and Their Treatment in Nineteenth-Century America." *Journal of Interdisciplinary History* 4 (Summer 1973): 25–52.

Dover, K. J. *Greek Homosexuality*. Cambridge, Mass.: Harvard University Press, 1989.

Dowling, Linda. *Language and Decadence in the Victorian Fin de Siècle*. Princeton: Princeton University Press, 1986.

———. "Ruskin's Pied Beauty and the Constitution of a 'Homosexual Code.'" *Victorian Newsletter* 75 (1989): 1–8.

"The Dread of the Jew." *Spectator* 83 (Sept. 9, 1899): 338–39.

Drennan, Jennie. "Sexual Intemperance." *New York Medical Journal* 73 (Jan. 5, 1901): 19–20.

Duberman, Martin, ed. *Hidden from History: Reclaiming the Gay and Lesbian Past*. New York: Meridian, 1989.

DuBois, Ellen. "The Radicalism of the Women's Suffrage Movement: Notes

Toward the Reconstruction of Nineteenth-Century Feminism." *Feminist Studies* 3 (Fall 1975): 63–71.

Dugdale, Richard. "Origin of Crime in Society." *Atlantic Monthly* 48 (Oct. 1881): 452–62; 48 (Dec. 1881): 735–46.

Du Maurier, George. *Trilby.* New York: Oxford University Press, 1995.

Dupee, F. W. *Henry James.* New York: William and Morrow, 1974.

Eakin, Paul John. "Henry James's 'Obscure Hurt': Can Autobiography Serve Biography?" *New Literary History* 19 (Spring 1988): 675–92.

Edel, Leon. *Henry James.* 5 vols. New York: Avon Books, 1953–72.

Edelman, Lee. *Homographesis: Essays in Gay Literary and Cultural Theory.* New York: Routledge, 1994.

Edes, Robert. "The New England Invalid." *Boston Medical and Surgical Journal* 133 (July 18, 1895): 53–57; 133 (July 25, 1895): 77–81; 133 (Aug. 1, 1895): 101–7.

Edson, Cyrus. "American Life and Physical Deterioration." *North American Review* 157 (Oct. 1893): 440–51.

———. "Do We Live Too Fast?" *North American Review* 154 (Mar. 1892): 281–86.

Ellmann, Richard. "Henry James Among the Aesthetes." *Proceedings of the British Academy* 69 (1983): 209–28.

———. *Oscar Wilde.* New York: Knopf, 1988.

Engelberg, Edward. "James and Arnold: Conscience and Consciousness in a Victorian 'Kunstlerroman.'" *Criticism* 10 (1968): 93–114.

Epstein, Steven. "Gay Politics, Ethnic Identity: The Limits of Social Constructionism." *Socialist Review* 93–94 (May–Aug. 1987): 9–54.

Erikson, Erik. *Identity: Youth and Crisis.* New York: Norton, 1968.

Esquirol, J. E. D. *Mental Maladies: A Treatise on Insanity.* New York: Hafner, 1965.

Faderman, Lillian. *Surpassing the Love of Men: Romantic Friendship and Love Between Women from the Renaissance to the Present.* New York: William and Morrow, 1981.

Feinstein, Howard. *Becoming William James.* Ithaca: Cornell University Press, 1984.

Fetterley, Judith. *The Resisting Reader: A Feminist Approach to American Fiction.* Bloomington: Indiana University Press, 1977.

Fletcher, John. "Freud and His Uses: Psychoanalysis and Gay Theory." In *Coming on Strong: Gay Politics and Culture,* ed. Simon Shepherd and Mick Wallis, pp. 90–118. London: Unwin Hyman, 1989.

Foucault, Michel. *The Archaeology of Knowledge.* Trans. A. M. Sheridan Smith. New York: Harper and Row, 1972.

———. *Discipline and Punish: The Birth of the Prison.* Trans. Alan Sheridan. New York: Vintage, 1979.

———. *The History of Sexuality.* 3 vols. Trans. Robert Hurley. New York: Vintage, 1980–1986.

———. *Power/Knowledge: Selected Interviews and Other Writings, 1972–1977.* Ed. Colin Gordon. New York: Pantheon, 1980.

Fredrickson, George. *The Inner Civil War: Northern Intellectuals and the Crisis of the Union.* New York: Harper and Row, 1965.

Freedman, Jonathan. *Professions of Taste: Henry James, British Aestheticism, and Commodity Culture.* Stanford: Stanford University Press, 1990.

Freud, Sigmund. *The Penguin Freud Library.* 15 vols. Trans. James Strachey. London: Penguin Books, 1991–93.

Furnas, J. C. *Voyage to Windward: The Life of Robert Louis Stevenson.* New York: Sloane, 1951.

Fuss, Diana, ed. *Inside/Out: Lesbian Theories, Gay Theories.* New York: Routledge, 1991.

Gagnon, John H. And William Simon. "Sexual Scripts." *Society* 22 (Nov.–Dec. 1984): 53–60.

Gallop, Jane. *The Daughter's Seduction: Feminism and Psychoanalysis.* Ithaca: Cornell University Press, 1982.

Gard, Roger, ed. *Henry James and the Critical Heritage.* London: Routledge and Kegan Paul, 1968.

Garrison, George, and Edward Madden. "William James—Warts and All." *American Quarterly* 29 (Summer 1977): 207–21.

Geismar, Maxwell. *Henry James and the Jacobites.* Boston: Houghton Mifflin, 1963.

Gerber, David. "Cutting Out Shylock: Elite Anti-Semitism and the Quest for Moral Order in the Mid-Nineteenth-Century American Marketplace." In *Anti-Semitism in American History*, ed. David Gerber, pp. 201–32. Urbana: University of Illinois Press, 1986.

Gilbert, Arthur. "Sexual Deviance and Disaster During the Napoleonic Wars." *Albion* 9 (Spring 1977): 98–113.

Gilbert, James. *Work Without Salvation: America's Intellectuals and Industrial Alienation, 1880–1910.* Baltimore: Johns Hopkins University Press, 1977.

Gilman, Sander. *Difference and Pathology: Stereotypes of Sexuality, Race, and Madness.* Ithaca: Cornell University Press, 1985.

———. *Disease and Representation: Images of Illness from Madness to AIDS.* Ithaca: Cornell University Press, 1988.

———. *Freud, Race, and Gender.* Princeton: Princeton University Press, 1993.

———. *The Jew's Body.* New York: Routledge, 1991.

Godkin, E. L. "American Overwork." Nation 35 (Nov. 16, 1882): 417.

Goldstein, Jan. "The Wandering Jew and the Problem of Psychiatric Anti-Semitism in Fin-de-Siècle France." *Journal of Contemporary History* 20 (Oct. 1985): 521–51.

Gosse, Edmund. "Henry James." *London Mercury* 1 (Apr. 1920): 673–84.

———. "Henry James." *London Mercury* 2 (May 1920): 29–40.

Graham, Wendy. "Henry James and the Mother-Complex." *Arizona Quarterly* 54, no.1 (Spring 1998): 27–64.

Grant, Madison. *The Passing of the Great Race: Or the Racial Basis of European History.* New York: Scribners, 1916.

Grosz, Elizabeth. *Jacques Lacan: A Feminist Introduction.* London: Routledge, 1990.

Gunn, Giles. *Thinking Across the American Grain: Ideology, Intellect, and the New Pragmatism.* Chicago: University of Chicago Press, 1992.

Gunn, Peter. *Vernon Lee: Violet Paget, 1856–1935.* New York: Arno Press, 1965.

Gurr, Ted Robert. *Rogues, Rebels, and Reformers: A Political History of Urban Crime and Conflict.* London: Sage, 1976.

Habegger, Alfred. *The Father: A Life of Henry James, Sr.* New York: Farrar, Straus, and Giroux, 1994.

———. *Henry James and the "Woman Business."* Cambridge, Eng.: Cambridge University Press, 1989.

Hale, Nathan, Jr., ed. *James Jackson Putnam and Psychoanalysis: Letters Between Putnam and Sigmund Freud, Ernest Jones, William James, Sandor Ferenczi, and Morton Prince, 1877–1917.* Cambridge, Mass.: Harvard University Press, 1971.

Hall, Richard. "An Obscure Hurt: The Sexuality of Henry James: Part I." *New Republic* (Apr. 28, 1979): 25–31.

———. "An Obscure Hurt: The Sexuality of Henry James: Part II." *New Republic* (May 5, 1979): 25–29.

———. "Henry James: Interpreting an Obsessive Memory." *Journal of Homosexuality* 8 (1983): 83–97.

———. "Leon Edel Discusses Richard Hall's Theory of Henry James and the Incest Taboo." *Advocate* (Sept. 20, 1979): 49–53.

Haller, John, and Robin Haller. *The Physician and Sexuality in Victorian America.* Urbana: University of Illinois Press, 1974.

Hamilton, Allan M'Lane. "The Civil Responsibility of Sexual Perverts." *American Journal of Insanity* 53 (Apr. 1896): 503–11.

Harrington, Anne. *Medicine, Mind, and the Double Brain: A Study of Nineteenth-Century Thought.* Princeton: Princeton University Press, 1987.

Haviland, Beverly. *Henry James's Last Romance: Making Sense of the Past and the American Scene.* New York: Cambridge University Press, 1997.

Hawthorne, Nathaniel. *The Marble Faun: or The Romance of Monte Beni.* New York: New American Library, 1987.

Haydon, Benjamin Robert. *The Autobiography and Memoirs of Benjamin Robert Haydon.* 2 vols. New York, Harcourt Brace and Company, n.d.

Hellman, George S. "Stevenson and Henry James: The Rare Friendship Between Two Famous Stylists." *Century Monthly Magazine* 89 (Nov. 1925–Apr. 1926): 336–45.

Helmholtz, Hermann von. *Popular Lectures on Scientific Subjects.* Trans. E. Atkinson. New York: Appleton, 1873.

Herbert, Christopher. *Culture and Anomie: Ethnographic Imagination in the Nineteenth Century.* Chicago: University of Chicago Press, 1991.

Hillman, James. "Senex and Puer." In *Puer Papers,* ed. James Hillman, pp. 3–53. Dallas: Spring, 1979.

Hirschman, Albert O. *The Passions and the Interests: Political Arguments for Capitalism Before Its Triumph.* Princeton: Princeton University Press, 1977.

Holly, Carol. *Intensely Family: The Inheritance of Family Shame and the Autobiographies of Henry James.* Madison: University of Wisconsin Press, 1995.

Howard, William Lee. "Effeminate Men and Masculine Women." *New York Medical Journal* 71 (May 5, 1900): 686–87.

———. "Psychical Hermaphroditism." *Alienist and Neurologist* 18 (Apr. 1897): 111–18.

———. "Sexual Perversion." *Alienist and Neurologist* 17 (Jan. 1896): 1–6.

Howe, Irving. *Introduction to The Bostonians.* New York: Modern Library, 1956.

Hughes, C. H. "Brain Bankruptcy of Business Men." *Alienist and Neurologist* 20 (1899): 463–68.

———. "The Brain and Nerve Destroying Policy of Railways." *Alienist and Neurologist* 21 (1900): 689–90.

Huysmans, J. K. *Against Nature.* Trans. Robert Baldick. London: Penguin, 1959.

Hyamson, Albert, ed. *Dictionary of English Phrases.* London, 1922.

Hyde, H. Montgomery. *The Cleveland Street Scandal.* London: Weidenfeld and Nicolson, 1977.

Ignatiev, Noel. *How the Irish Became White.* New York: Routledge, 1995.

Inman, Billie Andre. "Estrangement and Connection: Walter Pater, Benjamin Jowett, and William M. Hardinge." In *Pater in the 1990s,* ed. Laurel Brake and Ian Small, pp. 1–20. Greensboro: ELT Press, 1990.

Jacknis, Ira. "Franz Boas and Exhibits: On the Limitations of the Museum Method of Anthropology." In *Objects and Others: Essays on Museums and Material Culture,* ed. George Stocking, Jr., pp. 75–111. Madison: University of Wisconsin Press, 1985.

Jacobi, Mary Putnam. *Essays on Hysteria, Brain-Tumor and Some Other Cases of Nervous Disease.* New York: Putnam, 1888.

———. *Mary Putnam Jacobi, M.D., a Pathfinder in Medicine.* Ed. The Woman's Medical Association of New York City. New York, 1925.

———. "Modern Female Invalidism." *Boston Medical and Surgical Journal* 133 (Aug. 15, 1895): 174–75.

———. "The Question of Rest for Women During Menstruation." The Boylston Prize Essay of Harvard University for 1876. New York: Putnam, 1886.

———. "Shall Women Practice Medicine?" *North American Review* 134 (Jan.–June 1882): 52–75.

James, Henry, Sr. "Mr. Henry James on Marriage." *Nation* 10 (June 9, 1870): 366–68.

James, William. *Essays, Comments, and Reviews*. Vol. 17 of *The Works of William James*. Cambridge, Mass.: Harvard University Press, 1987.

——. *Essays in Philosophy*. Vol. 5 of *The Works of William James*. Cambridge, Mass.: Harvard University Press, 1978.

——. *Essays in Psychology*. Vol. 13 of *The Works of William James*. Cambridge, Mass.: Harvard University Press, 1983.

——. *Essays in Religion and Morality*. Vol. 11 of *The Works of William James*. Cambridge, Mass.: Harvard University Press, 1982.

——. *The Meaning of Truth*. Vol. 2 of *The Works of William James*. Cambridge, Mass.: Harvard University Press, 1975.

——. *A Pluralistic Universe*. Vol. 4 of *The Works of William James*. Cambridge, Mass.: Harvard University Press, 1977.

——. *Pragmatism*. Vol. 1 of *The Works of William James*. Cambridge, Mass.: Harvard University Press, 1975.

——. *The Principles of Psychology*. Vols. 8–10 of *The Works of William James*. Cambridge, Mass.: Harvard University Press, 1981.

——. *Talks to Teachers on Psychology and to Students on Some of Life's Ideals*. Vol. 12 of *The Works of William James*. Cambridge, Mass.: Harvard University Press, 1983.

——. *The Varieties of Religious Experience*. Vol. 15 of *The Works of William James*. Cambridge, Mass.: Harvard University Press, 1985.

——. *The Will to Believe*. Vol. 6 of *The Works of William James*. Cambridge, Mass.: Harvard University Press, 1979.

Jameson, Fredric. *The Political Unconscious: Narrative as a Socially Symbolic Act*. Ithaca: Cornell University Press, 1981.

Kahane, Claire. "Hysteria, Feminism, and the Case of The Bostonians." In *Feminism and Psychoanalysis*, ed. Richard Feldstein and Judith Roof, pp. 280–97. Ithaca: Cornell University Press, 1989.

Kaplan, Fred. *Henry James: The Imagination of Genius, A Biography*. New York: William and Morrow, 1992.

Karlen, Arno. *Sexuality and Homosexuality: A New View*. New York: Norton, 1971.

Karp, Ivan, and Steven Lavine, eds. *Exhibiting Cultures: The Poetics and Politics of Museum Display*. Washington: Smithsonian, 1991.

Kendrick, Walter. *The Secret Museum: Pornography in Modern Culture*. New York: Penguin, 1987.

Kipling, Rudyard. *Life's Handicap: Being Stories of Mine Own People*. Garden City: Doubleday, 1913.

Kirshenblatt-Gimblett, Barbara. "Objects of Ethnography." In *Exhibiting Cultures: The Poetics and Politics of Museum Display*, ed. Ivan Karp and Steven Lavine., pp. 386–443. Washington: Smithsonian, 1991.

Koestenbaum, Wayne. *The Queen's Throat: Opera, Homosexuality, and the Mystery of Desire*. New York: Vintage, 1993.

Kopelson, Kevin. "Wilde's Love-Deaths." *Yale Journal of Criticism* 5 (Fall 1992): 31–60.

Krafft-Ebing, Richard von. *Psychopathia Sexualis: With Especial Reference to the Antipathic Sexual Instinct.* Trans. Franklin Klaf. New York: Stein and Day, 1978.

Kristeva, Julia. *Powers of Horror: An Essay on Abjection.* Trans. Leon Roudiez. New York: Columbia University Press, 1982.

Kuhns, Richard. "The Beautiful and the Sublime." *New Literary History* 13 (Winter 1982): 287–307.

Lacan, Jacques. *Écrits: A Selection.* Trans. Alan Sheridan. New York: Norton, 1977.

———. *The Four Fundamental Concepts of Psycho-Analysis.* Trans. Alan Sheridan. New York: Norton, 1981.

———. *Speech and Language in Psychoanalysis.* Trans. Anthony Wilden. Baltimore: Johns Hopkins University Press, 1968.

Lang, Andrew. *Adventures Among Books.* London: Longman, 1905.

Lee, Gerald Stanley. *The Voice of the Machines: An Introduction to the Twentieth Century.* Northampton: Mount Tom, 1906.

Lee, Vernon. *Miss Brown.* 3 vols. Ed. Ian Fletcher and John Stokes. Hamden: Garland, 1978.

———. *Vanitas: Polite Stories.* New York, 1892.

Lentricchia, Frank. "On the Ideologies of Poetic Modernism." In *Reconstructing American Literary History*, ed. Sacvan Bercovitch, pp. 220–49. Cambridge, Mass.: Harvard University Press, 1986.

Lewes, Kenneth. *The Psychoanalytic Theory of Male Homosexuality.* New York: New American Library, 1988.

Lewis, R. W. B. *The Jameses: A Family Narrative.* New York: Farrar, Straus and Giroux, 1991.

Litvak, Joseph. *Caught in the Act: Theatricality in the Nineteenth-Century English Novel.* Berkeley and Los Angeles: University of California Press, 1992.

Lombroso, Cesare. *The Man of Genius.* New York: Scribners, 1910.

Lutz, Tom. *American Nervousness, 1903.* Ithaca: Cornell University Press, 1991.

Lydston, G. Frank. "Sexual Perversion, Satyriasis and Nymphomania." *Medical and Surgical Reporter* 61 (Sept. 7, 1889): 253–85.

Mackenzie, Lynne. "William James and the Problem of Interests." *Journal of the History of the Behavioral Sciences* 26 (Apr. 1980): 175–85.

Maher, Jane. *Biography of Broken Fortunes: Wilkie and Bob, Brothers of William, Henry and Alice James.* Hamden: Archon Books, 1986.

Martin, Ronald. *American Literature and the Universe of Force.* Durham: Duke University Press, 1981.

Martin, Robert K. "Knights-Errant and Gothic Seducers: The Representation of Male Friendship in Mid-Nineteenth-Century America." In *Hidden from History: Reclaiming the Gay and Lesbian Past*, ed. Martin Duberman, pp. 169–82. New York: Meridian, 1989.

Maudsley, Henry. *Responsibility in Mental Disease*. New York: Appleton, 1900.

Mauss, Marcel. *Sociology and Psychology: Essays*. Trans. Ben Brewster. London: Routledge, 1979.

Mayhew, Henry. *London Labour and the London Poor*. 4 vols. New York: Dover, 1968.

McChesney, G. G. "The Psychology of Efficiency." *Journal of Applied Psychology* 1 (1917): 176–79.

McDonald, Henry. "Nietzsche, Wittgenstein, and James." *Texas Studies in Literature and Language* 34 (Fall 1992): 403–49.

McWhirter, David. "Restaging the Hurt: Henry James and the Artist as Masochist." *Texas Studies in Literature and Language* 33 (Winter 1991): 464–91.

Meyers, Gerald. *William James: His Life and Thought*. New Haven: Yale University Press, 1986.

Meyers, Greg. "Nineteenth-Century Popularizations of Thermodynamics and the Rhetoric of Social Prophecy." In *Energy & Entropy: Science and Culture in Victorian Britain*, ed. Patrick Brantlinger, pp. 307–38. Bloomington: Indiana University Press, 1989.

Miller, D. A. *The Novel and the Police*. Berkeley and Los Angeles: University of California Press, 1988.

Miller, Karl. *Doubles: Studies in Literary History*. New York: Oxford University Press, 1985.

Milliman, Craig. "The Fiction of Art: Roderick Hudson's Pursuit of the Ideal." *Henry James Review* 15 (Fall 1994): 231–41.

Mitchell, S. Weir. *Wear and Tear, or Hints for the Over-worked*. Philadelphia: Lippincott, 1887.

Morais, Nina. "Jewish Ostracism in America." *North American Review* 133 (1881): 265–75.

Morantz-Sanchez, Regina Markell. *Sympathy and Science: Women Physicians in American Medicine*. New York: Oxford University Press, 1985.

Morgan, Thais. "Reimagining Masculinity in Victorian Criticism: Swinburne and Pater." *Victorian Studies* 36 (Spring 1993): 315–32.

Moss, Donald. "Introductory Thoughts: Hating in the First Person Plural: The Example of Homophobia." *American Imago* 49 (Fall 1992): 277–91.

Mosse, George L. *Nationalism and Sexuality: Respectability and Abnormal Sexuality in Modern Europe*. New York: Howard Fertig, 1985.

Mosso, Angelo. *Fatigue*. Trans. Margaret Drummond and W. B. Drummond. London: George Allen, 1915.

Mulvey, Laura. *Visual and Other Pleasures*. Bloomington: Indiana University Press, 1989.

Murtaugh, Daniel. "An Emotional Reflection: Sexual Realization in Henry James's Revisions to Roderick Hudson." *Henry James Review* 17 (Spring 1996): 183–203.

Nietzsche, Friedrich. *Beyond Good and Evil*. Chicago: Henry Regnery, 1949.

———. *The Birth of Tragedy and The Genealogy of Morals*. Trans. Francis Golffing. New York: Doubleday, 1956.

———. *Philosophy and Truth: Selections from Nietzsche's Notebooks of the Early 1870's*. Trans. Daniel Breazeale. New Jersey: HPI, 1990.

———. *Twilight of the Idols and The Anti-Christ*. Trans. R. J. Hollingdale. London: Penguin, 1990.

———. *Untimely Meditations*. Trans. R. J. Hollingdale. Cambridge, Eng.: Cambridge University Press, 1983.

Nordau, Max. *Degeneration*. Lincoln: University of Nebraska Press, 1993.

Norris, Frank. *Novels and Essays: Vandover and the Brute, McTeague, The Octopus, Essays*. New York: Library of America, 1986.

Omi, Michael, and Howard Winant. "By the Rivers of Babylon: Race in the United States, Part 1." *Socialist Review* 71 (Sept.–Oct. 1983): 31–65.

Parton, James. "Our Israelitish Brethren." *Atlantic Monthly* 26 (Oct. 1870): 385–403.

Pater, Walter. *The Renaissance: Studies in Art and Poetry*. Oxford: Oxford University Press, 1986.

Pearsall, Ronald. *The Worm in the Bud: The World of Victorian Sexuality*. New York: Macmillan, 1969.

Perry, Ralph Barton. *The Thought and Character of William James*. 2 vols. Boston: Little, Brown, 1935.

Person, Leland. "Henry James, George Sand, and the Suspense of Masculinity." *PMLA* 106 (May 1991): 515–28.

Pollock, Griselda. "Feminism/Foucault—Surveillance/Sexuality." In *Visual Culture: Images and Interpretations*, ed. Norman Bryson, Michael Ann Holly, Keith Moxey, pp. 1–41. Hanover: Wesleyan University Press, 1994.

———. *Vision and Difference: Femininity, Feminism, and the Histories of Art*. London: Routledge, 1988.

Pomian, Krzysztof. *Collectors and Curiosities, Paris and Venice, 1500–1800*. Trans. Elizabeth Wiles-Potter. Cambridge, Eng.: Polity, 1990.

Posnock, Ross. *The Trial of Curiosity: Henry James, William James, and the Challenge of Modernity*. New York: Oxford University Press, 1991.

Powers, Lyall. *Henry James and the Naturalist Movement*. East Lansing: Michigan State University Press, 1971.

Praz, Mario. *The Romantic Agony*. Trans. Angus Davidson. Cleveland: Meridian, 1956.

Putnam, James Jackson. "Sketch for a Study of New England Character." *Journal of Abnormal Psychology* 12 (1917–18): 73–99.

Rabinbach, Anson. *The Human Motor: Energy, Fatigue, and the Origins of Modernity*. Berkeley and Los Angeles: University of California Press, 1992.

Reade, Brian, ed. *Sexual Heretics: Male Homosexuality in English Literature from 1850 to 1900*. New York: Coward-McCann, 1970.

Rhodes, Karen. "Capitalism, Consumption, and Capacity: Milly Theale's Mysterious Dis-ease." Paper presented at the Interdisciplinary Nineteenth-Century Studies Conference, Portland State University, Portland, Oregon, 1989.

Ribot, Théodule. *The Diseases of the Will.* Trans. Merwin-Marie Snell. Chicago: Open Court, 1896.

Riffaterre, Michael. "The Intertextual Unconscious." *Critical Inquiry* 13 (Winter 1987): 371–85.

Rose, Jacqueline. *Sexuality in the Field of Vision.* London: Verso, 1986.

Rosenberg, Charles. "Sexuality, Class and Role in 19th-Century America." *American Quarterly* 25 (May 1973): 131–53.

———. *The Trial of the Assassin Guiteau: Psychiatry and the Law of the Gilded Age.* Chicago: University of Chicago Press, 1968.

Rosenzweig, Saul. "The Ghost of Henry James." *Partisan Review* 11 (Fall 1944): 436–55.

Rowe, John Carlos. *The Theoretical Dimensions of Henry James.* Madison: University of Wisconsin Press, 1984.

Runnels, Moses T. "Physical Degeneracy of American Women." *Medical Era* 3 (Apr. 1886): 297–302.

Ruskin, John. "Traffic." In *Selections from the Works of John Ruskin,* ed. Chauncey Tinker, pp. 277–304. Boston: Houghton Mifflin, 1908.

Sahli, Nancy. "Smashing: Women's Relationships Before the Fall." *Chrysalis* 8 (Summer 1979): 18–27.

Sarna, Jonathan. "The 'Mythical Jew' and the Jew Next Door." In *Anti-Semitism in American History,* ed. David Gerber, pp. 57–78. Urbana: University of Illinois Press, 1986.

Sarotte, Georges-Michel. *Like a Brother, Like a Lover: Male Homosexuality in the American Novel and Theater from Herman Melville to James Baldwin.* New York: Anchor/Doubleday, 1978

Sedgwick, Eve Kosofsky. *Between Men: English Literature and Male Homosocial Desire.* New York: Columbia University Press, 1985.

———. *The Epistemology of the Closet.* Berkeley and Los Angeles: University of California Press, 1990.

———. "Paranoid Reading and Reparative Reading; or, You're So Paranoid, You Probably Think This Introduction Is About You." In *Novel Gazing: Queer Readings in Fiction,* ed. Eve Kosofsky Sedgwick, pp. 1–37. Durham: Duke University Press, 1997.

———. "Shame and Performativity: Henry James's New York Edition Prefaces." In *Henry James's New York Edition: The Construction of Authorship,* ed. David McWhirter, pp. 206–39. Stanford: Stanford University Press, 1995.

———. *Tendencies.* Durham: Duke University Press, 1993.

Seltzer, Mark. *Bodies and Machines.* New York: Routledge, 1992.

————. *Henry James and the Art of Power*. Ithaca: Cornell University Press, 1984.

Serres, Michel. *Hermes: Literature, Science, Philosophy*. Ed. Josu Harari and David Bell. Baltimore: Johns Hopkins University Press, 1982.

"Sex and the British M. P." *New York Times*, Feb. 13, 1994, p. 2.

Shaw, J. C., and G. N. Ferris. "Perverted Sexual Instinct." *Journal of Nervous and Mental Disease* 10 (Apr. 1883): 185–204.

Shell, Marc. *Money, Language, and Thought*. Baltimore: Johns Hopkins University Press, 1982.

Shepherd, Simon, and Mick Wallis, eds. *Coming on Strong: Gay Politics and Culture*. London: Unwin Hyman, 1989.

Showalter, Elaine. *Sexual Anarchy: Gender and Culture at the Fin de Siècle*. New York: Viking, 1990.

Shrady, George. "Perverted Sexual Instinct." *Medical Record* 26 (July 19, 1884): 70–71.

Sicherman, Barbara. "The Uses of a Diagnosis: Doctors, Patients and Neurasthenia." *Journal of the History of Medicine and Allied Sciences* 32 (Jan. 1977): 33–54.

Silverman, Kaja. *Male Subjectivity at the Margins*. New York: Routledge, 1992.

Smith, F. B. "Labouchère's Amendment to the Criminal Law Amendment Bill." *Historical Studies* 17 (Oct. 1976): 165–75.

Smith-Rosenberg, Carroll. *Disorderly Conduct: Visions of Gender in Victorian America*. New York: Oxford University Press, 1985.

Sontag, Susan. "Notes on 'Camp.'" *Against Interpretation and Other Essays*. New York: Delta, 1967.

Stanton, Elizabeth Cady. "The Other Side of the Woman Question." *North American Review* 129 (Nov. 1879): 413–39.

Stearns, Henry Putnam. *Insanity: Its Causes and Prevention*. New York: Putnam, 1883.

Stehle, Philip. *Order, Chaos, Order: The Transition from Classical to Quantum Physics*. New York: Oxford University Press, 1994.

Steiner, George. *In Bluebeard's Castle: Some Notes Towards the Redefinition of Culture*. New Haven: Yale University Press. 1971.

Stevens, Hugh. *Henry James and Sexuality*. Cambridge, Eng.: Cambridge University Press, 1998.

Stevenson, Robert Louis. *Dr. Jekyll and Mr. Hyde*. New York: Signet, 1987.

Stocking, George, Jr., ed. *Objects and Others: Essays on Museums and Material Culture*. Madison: University of Wisconsin Press, 1985.

Stoehr, Taylor. "Words and Deeds in The Princess Casamassima." *English Literary History* 37 (1970): 95–135.

Storzer, Gerald. "The Homosexual Paradigm in Balzac, Gide, and Genet." In *Homosexualities and French Literature*, ed. George Stambolian and Elaine Marks, pp. 186–209. Ithaca: Cornell University Press, 1979.

Sulloway, Frank. *Freud, Biologist of the Mind: Beyond the Psychoanalytic Legend.* Cambridge, Mass.: Harvard University Press, 1992.

Symonds, John Addington. *The Letters of John Addington Symonds,* Volume III, 1885–1893. Ed. Herbert Schueller and Robert Peters. Detroit: Wayne State University, 1969.

———. *The Memoirs of John Addington Symonds.* Ed. Phyllis Grosskurth. New York: Random House, 1984.

———. *A Problem in Modern Ethics: An Inquiry into the Phenomenon of Sexual Inversion.* New York: Benjamin Blom, 1971.

Tagg, John. "The Discontinuous City: Picturing and the Discursive Field." In *Visual Culture: Images and Interpretations,* ed. Norman Bryson, Michael Ann Holly, Keith Moxey, pp. 83–103. Hanover: Wesleyan University Press, 1994.

Takaki, Ronald. *Iron Cages: Race and Culture in 19th-Century America.* New York: Oxford University Press, 1979.

Teahan, Sheila. "The Abyss of Language in The Wings of the Dove." *Henry James Review* 14 (Spring 1993): 204–14.

Temkin, Owsei. "Materialism in French and German Physiology of the Early Nineteenth Century." *Bulletin of the History of Medicine* 20 (1946): 322–27.

Thwaite, Ann. *Edmund Gosse: A Literary Landscape, 1849–1928.* Chicago: University of Chicago Press, 1984.

Tintner, Adeline. *Henry James and the Lust of the Eyes: Thirteen Artists in His Work.* Baton Rouge: Louisiana State University Press, 1993.

Townsend, Kim. *Manhood at Harvard: William James and Others.* New York: W. W. Norton, 1996.

Trachtenberg, Alan. *The Incorporation of America: Culture and Society in the Gilded Age.* New York: Hill and Wang, 1982.

Trilling, Lionel. *The Liberal Imagination: Essays on Literature and Society.* New York: Viking Press, 1951.

Trumbach, Randolf. "The Birth of the Queen: Sodomy and the Emergence of Gender Equality in Modern Culture, 1660–1750." In *Hidden from History: Reclaiming the Gay and Lesbian Past,* ed. Martin Duberman, pp. 129–40. New York: Meridian, 1989.

Tyas, Robert. *The Language of Flowers; or Floral Emblems of Thoughts, Feelings, and Sentiments.* London: Routledge, 1875.

Tyler, Carole-Anne. "Boys Will Be Girls: The Politics of Gay Drag." In *Inside/Out: Lesbian Theories, Gay Theories,* ed. Diana Fuss, pp. 32–70. New York: Routledge, 1991.

Veblen, Thorstein. *The Higher Learning in America.* New Brunswick: Transaction, 1993.

Veeder, William. "The Portrait of a Lack." In *New Essays on "The Portrait of a Lady,"* ed. Joel Porte, pp. 95–121. Cambridge, Eng.: Cambridge University Press, 1985.

Walker, Francis. "Immigration and Degradation." *Forum* 11 (Aug. 1891): 634–44.

Wardley, Lynn. "Woman's Voice, Democracy's Body, and *The Bostonians*." *English Literary History* 56 (Fall 1989): 639–65.

Weber, Max. *The Protestant Ethic and the Spirit of Capitalism*. Trans. Talcott Parsons. New York: Scribners, 1958.

Weeks, Jeffrey. "Inverts, Perverts, and Mary-Annes: Male Prostitution and the Regulation of Homosexuality in England in the Nineteenth and Early Twentieth Centuries." In *Hidden from History: Reclaiming the Gay and Lesbian Past*, ed. Martin Duberman, pp. 195–211. New York: Meridian, 1989.

———. *Sex, Politics, and Society: The Regulation of Sexuality Since 1800*. London: Longmans, 1981.

Weir, James. "Genius and Degeneration." *Medical Record* 46 (Aug. 4, 1894): 131–33.

———. "Is It the Beginning of the End?" *Medical Record* 46 (Dec. 29, 1894): 801–4.

———. "The Methods of the Rioting Striker an Evidence of Degeneration." *Century* 48 (Oct. 1894): 952–54.

———. "Viraginity and Effemination." Medical Record 45 (Sept. 16, 1893): 359–60.

Wells, Kate Gannett. "The Transitional American Woman." *Atlantic Monthly* 66 (Dec. 1880): 817–23.

White, Hayden. *Metahistory: The Historical Imagination in Nineteenth-Century Europe*. Baltimore: Johns Hopkins University Press, 1973.

Wilde, Oscar. *The Picture of Dorian Gray*. Oxford: Oxford University Press, 1981.

Wilkins, W. H. "Immigration Troubles of the United States." *Nineteenth Century* 30 (Oct. 1891): 583–95.

Wing, Edwin. "An Analysis of A Treatise on the Degenerations: Physical, Intellectual, and Moral, of the Human Race, and the Causes Which Produce Their Unhealthy Varieties by Dr. B. A. Morel with Notes and Remarks by the Translator." *Medical Circular* 10–12 (Mar. 18, 1857–Mar. 17, 1858).

Wise, P. M. "Case of Sexual Perversion." *Alienist and Neurologist* 4 (Jan. 1883): 87–91.

Woods, Gregory. "High Culture and High Camp: The Case of Marcel Proust." In *Camp Grounds: Style and Homosexuality*, ed. David Bergman, pp. 121–33. Amherst: University of Massachusetts Press, 1993.

Wynne, Brian. "Physics and Psychics: Science, Symbolic Action, and Social Control in Late Victorian England." In *Natural Order: Historical Studies of Scientific Culture*, ed. Barry Barnes and Steven Shapin, pp. 167–86. Beverly Hills: Sage, 1979.

Yeazell, Ruth Bernard. *The Death and Letters of Alice James*. Berkeley and Los Angeles: University of California Press, 1981.

Youmans, Edward, ed. *Herbert Spencer on the Americans and the Americans on Herbert Spencer*. New York: Appleton, 1883.

Young, Robert. "Man's Place in Nature." In *Changing Perspectives in the History of Science*, ed. Mikuls Teich and Robert Young, pp. 344–438. Dordrecht: Reidel, 1973.

Zola, Émile. *La Bête Humaine*. Trans. Leonard Tancock. London: Penguin Books, 1986.

———. "The Experimental Novel." In *Documents of Modern Literary Realism*, ed. George Becker, pp. 162–96. Princeton: Princeton University Press, 1963.

Index

In this index an "f" after a number indicates a separate reference on the next page, and an "ff" indicates separate references on the next two pages. A continuous discussion over two or more pages is indicated by a span of page numbers, e.g., "57–59." *Passim* is used for a cluster of references in close but not consecutive sequence.

Library of Congress Cataloging-in-Publication Data

Graham, Wendy
   Henry James's thwarted love / Wendy Graham.
     p.   cm.
   ISBN 0-8047-3539-5 (cloth : alk. paper).—ISBN 0-8047-3847-5 (pb. : alk. paper)
   1. James, Henry, 1843–1916—Criticism and interpretation. 2. Sex in literature.
3. Psychological fiction, American—History and criticism. 4. Androgyny (Psychology) in literature. 5. Sexual abstinence in literature. 6. Psychoanalysis and litera-
ture. 7. Homosexuality and literature. 8. Sublimation (Psychology) in litera-
ture. 9. Gay men in literature. 10. Love in literature.
I. Title.
PS2127.S48G72   1999
813'.4—dc21   99-21521

Original printing 1999
Last figure below indicates year of this printing:
07 06 05 04 03 02 01 00 99

Typeset by Robert C. Ehle in 10/14 Janson